PACKET TRACER FOR YOUNG INTERMEDIATE ADMINS

iTst@rt

Authors: Damian Strojek, Jerzy Kluczewski
English translation: Julia Skutela

The book **PACKET TRACER FOR YOUNG, INTERMEDIATE ADMINS** includes advice for those who want to improve their skills and knowledge in terms of managing LAN and WLAN and configuring with Cisco devices.

As a reader, you will find descriptions and examples concerning protocols: **RIP, EIGRP, OSPF, BGP**, creating statistic routes, **ACL**, the basics of **VoIP technology**, **STP, RSTP, Frame Relay** and **PPP** protocols. You will learn how to design, develop, and manage **VLAN** networks using **VTP** protocol. The book also contains exercises in configuration of protocols: **RADIUS, NETFLOW, VPN, NAT** and in configuration of switches working in the third layer in the ISO/OSI model. The authors use many examples and exercises while describing the administration of networks.

Cover design by ***Daniel Pliszka***

Editorial and composition: ***Marek Smyczek and Marcin Kaim***

English translation: ***Julia Skutela***

IT publishing house:

http://www.itstart.pl

email: itstart@itstart.pl

This publication was designed to help the acquisition of practical content related to computer networks.

ISBN 978-83-65645-80-7

First edition – Piekary Śląskie 2023

TABLE OF CONTENTS

CHAPTER 1

INTRODUCTION

1 Introduction

The book **PACKET TRACER FOR YOUNG, INTERMEDIATE ADMINS** is designed for those who want to increase their knowledge and abilities in areas of management of LAN and WLAN networks. As a reader, you will find descriptions and examples concerning configuring Cisco devices. It is a continuation of the book, published under the title **PACKET TRACER FOR YOUNG BEGINNERS ADMINS**.

Authors of the book went by the rule **minimum theory – maximum practical examples** which will allow reader to learn to administrate ICT networks and many complex device configurations with no need to buy expensive Cisco equipment.

The first part of the book contains many practical examples, that includes basics of configuring protocols, network services and techniques such as: **dynamic RIP routing, EIGRP, OSPF, eBGP, static routing, access control list, VoIP, STP, RSTP, VTP, FRAME RELAY, PPP, PAP and CHAP authentication, RADIUS, NETFLOW, NAT, L2NAT, VPN, tunneling.** This part covers also configuration of **3560-24PS and 3650-24PS multilayer switches.**

The next part of the book contains 59 practical exercises and solution tips for the following issues: **RIP** protocol, **EIGRP** protocol, **OSPF** protocol, **static routes**, basic and extended **ACL lists**, **STP** protocol, **VTP** protocol, **Frame Relay** protocol, **PPP** protocol, **RADIUS** protocol, **NETFLOW** protocol, static and dynamic **NAT** and **L2NAT** translation, virtual private networks **VPN**, configuration of networks that contain **3560-24PS and 3650-24PS multilayer switches**.

The final section provides: **a glossary of key terms, a table of abbreviated IOS commands, a list of file names with examples and exercises**.

To make it convenient to perform practical exercises, authors prepared numerous examples and exercises that are listed on our publishing house's dedicated website at **http://ptfyia.itstart.pl**. To have full access to the files you must log in using login: **ptfyia** and password: **ptfyia@INT**.

The files have been divided into two categories: **Examples** and **Exercises** are available in subfolders with the same names (**examples and exercises**).

To be able to open and use it, you will need to have installed Packet Tracer software in 8.2.0 version at least. Neither the publisher nor the authors are responsible for the malfunction of files in lower versions of the software. The current latest version of the program is 8.2.0.

We wish you good luck and persistence in learning.

The Authors

CHAPTER 2

DYNAMIC ROUTING PROTOCOLS

2 DYNAMIC ROUTING PROTOCOLS

This chapter describes basic terms relating to routing and basic classification of dynamic routing protocols.

2.1 Broadcast Domains, an Introduction to the Routing

Routers divide the bigger network into smaller logical subnets (network segments), called broadcast domains. **A broadcast domain** is what we call a group of network devices in which each device can transmit packets to other devices in the domain without having to go through routing devices.

An example of splitting the network into multiple subnets is shown in the figure below.

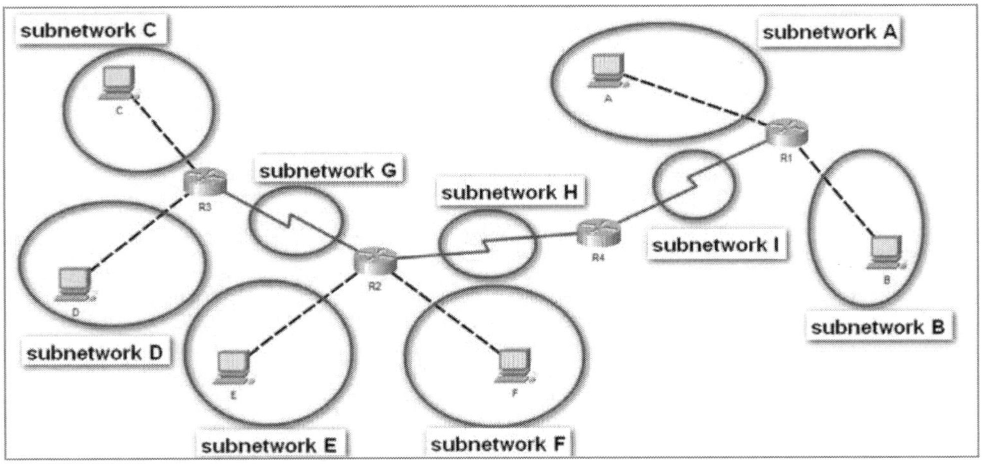

Figure 2.1 First example of network topology with broadcast domains.

The figure shows nine **broadcast domains** (logical subnets) marked with consecutive letters of the alphabet: A, B, C, D, E, F, G, H, I.

Suppose that the network with address 192.168.0.0 has been divided and addressed according to the following table:

Name of the subnet	Address of the subnet
A	192.168.1.0/24
B	192.168.2.0/24
C	192.168.3.0/24
D	192.168.4.0/24
E	192.168.5.0/24

F	192.168.6.0/24
G	192.168.7.0/24
H	192.168.8.0/24
I	192.168.9.0/24

Table 2.1 Subnet addressing scheme.

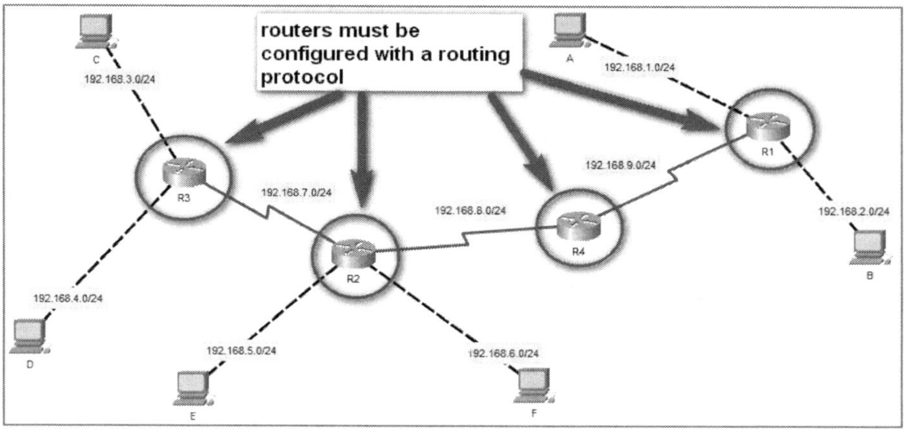

Figure 2.2 First example of network topology with marked routers and subnet addressing.

In order to transmit packets between subnets: A, B, C, D, E, F, G, H and I, we need to configure the appropriate routing protocol on routers: R1, R2, R3, R4. Second example of broadcast domains is shown in the figure below.

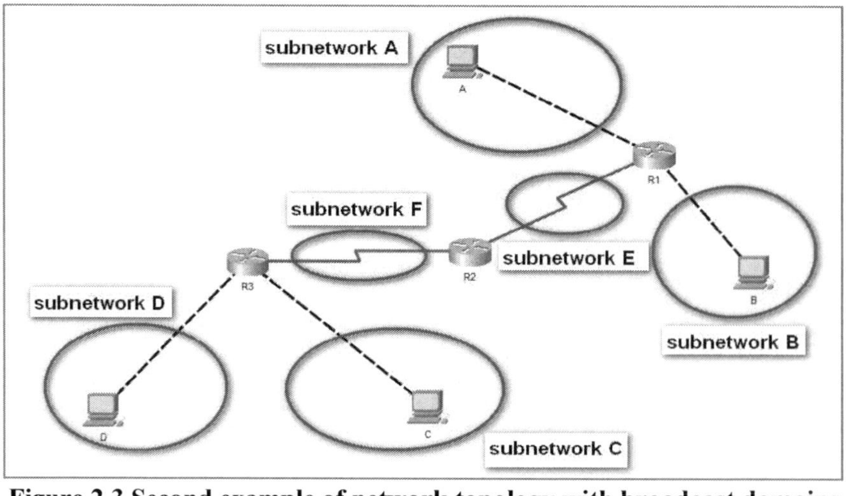

Figure 2.3 Second example of network topology with broadcast domains

The figure shows six **broadcast domains** (logical subnets) marked with consecutive letters of the alphabet: A, B, C, D, E, F.

Suppose that the network with address 10.10.0.0 was addressed according to the following table:

Name of the subnet	Address of the subnet
A	10.10.1.0/28
B	10.10.2.0/28
C	10.10.3.0/28
D	10.10.4.0/28
E	10.10.5.0/28
F	10.10.6.0/28

Table 2.2 Subnet addressing scheme with mask /28.

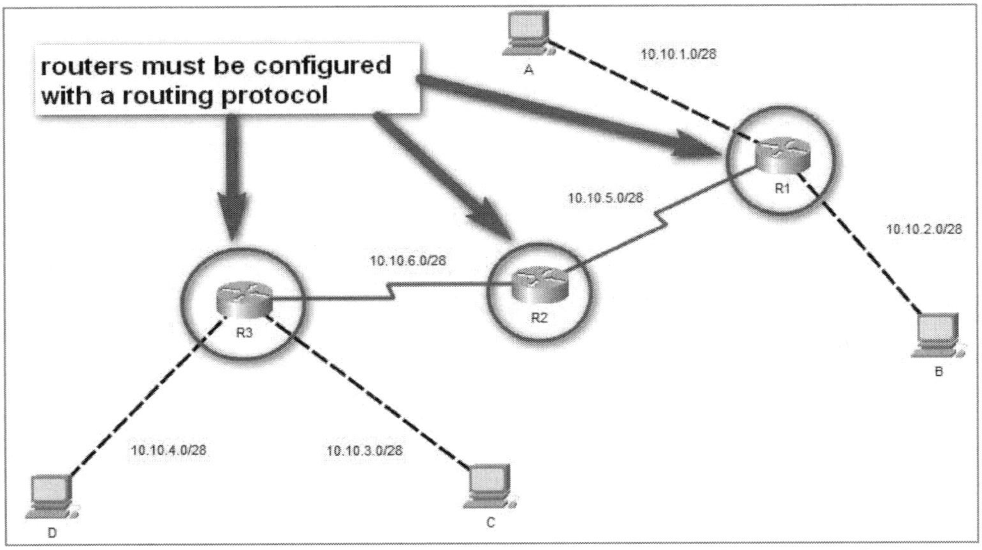

Figure 2.4 Second example of network topology with marked routers and subnet addressing.

To transmit packets between subnets: A, B, C, D, E, F we need to configure the appropriate routing protocol on the routers: R1, R2, R3. The following section of this chapter will introduce the basic concepts of routing and configuration if the basic types of dynamic and static routing.

2.2 Basic Concepts of Routing

2.2.1 Neighbor Routers

Neighbor routers are routers connected directly to a particular router. They can exchange information with given router directly, without the need to use routing protocol. In the figure shown, the neighbor (adjacent) routers with router **R2** are routers: **R1, R3, R4**.

A special Cisco CDP protocol automatically detects neighbor routers and is active by default when the Cisco router is turned on.

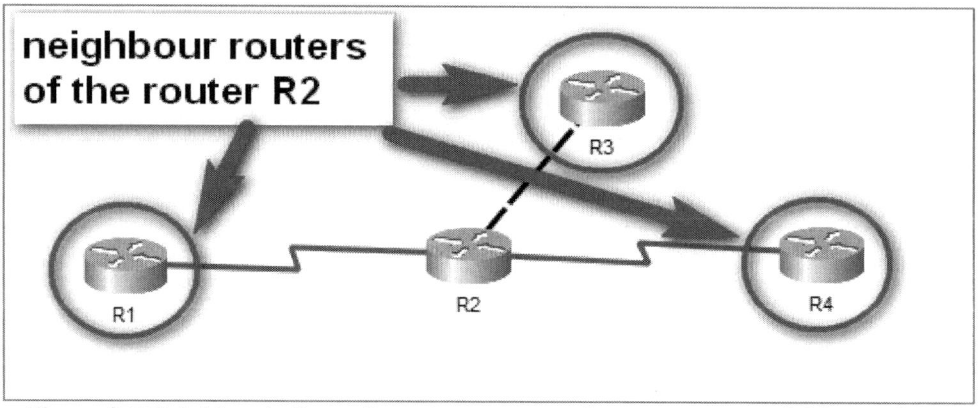

Figure 2.5 Neighbor (adjacent) routers, routers that are router-neighbors of the router R2.

2.2.2 Directly Connected Network

Directly connected network - it is a subnet directly connected to the router interface. The figure shows three networks connected directly to central router called **MAIN**.

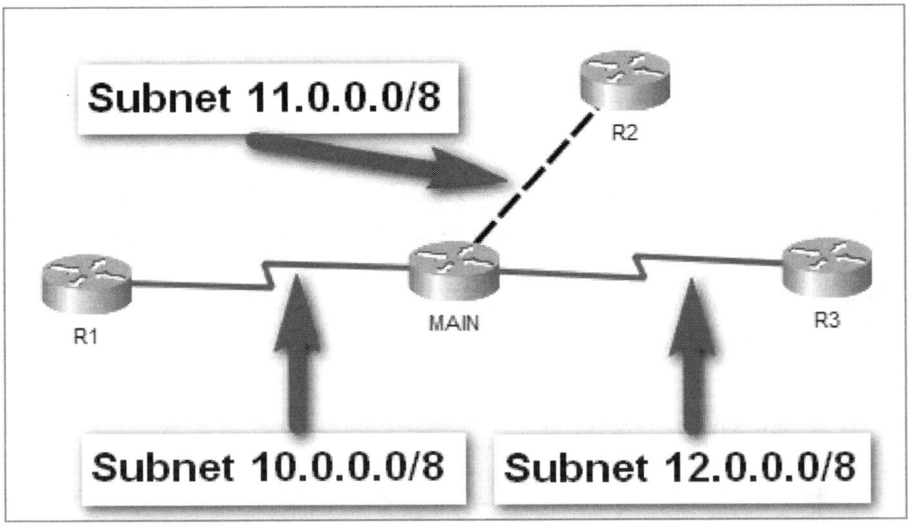

Figure 2.6 Networks connected directly to the MAIN router.

It is possible to check where (meaning to which interface of the router) and which subnet is the adjoining network (connected directly) to the MAIN router. To do this in the most simple way, we will execute the command: **`show ip route connected`**.

```
MAIN#show ip route connected
 C    10.0.0.0/8  is directly connected, Serial1/0
 C    11.0.0.0/8  is directly connected, FastEthernet2/0
 C    12.0.0.0/8  is directly connected, Serial0/0
```

Figure 2.7 Display of a list of subnets directly connected to the MAIN router.

2.2.3 The Code of Source of the Routing Information

The code of source of the routing information is a one - or two - character symbol which gives information about which routing process created the route in question. The most common codes for dynamic protocols are:

- **C** – directly connected network,
- **I** – IGRP protocol,
- **R** – RIP protocol,
- **B** – BGP protocol,
- **D** – EIGRP protocol,
- **O** – OSPF protocol.

The code is displayed in the first column after execution of the "show" command **`show ip route`**. A full codes list will be obtained after execution if the command **`show ip route`**, displayed above the routing table.

```
MAIN#show ip route
Codes: C - connected, S - static, I - IGRP, R - RIP, M - mobile, B - BGP
       D - EIGRP, EX - EIGRP external, O - OSPF, IA - OSPF inter area
       N1 - OSPF NSSA external type 1, N2 - OSPF NSSA external type 2
       E1 - OSPF external type 1, E2 - OSPF external type 2, E - EGP
       i - IS-IS, L1 - IS-IS level-1, L2 - IS-IS level-2, ia - IS-IS inter area
       * - candidate default, U - per-user static route, o - ODR
       P - periodic downloaded static route
```

Figure 2.8 A full list of routing types.

2.2.4 Administrative Distance

Administrative distance (AD) is a numerical value associated with given dynamic or static route (**depends** on the protocol type). For the route to the network connected directly is 0. If there are multiple possible routes to the same destination subnet, the router will choose the one with **the lowest administrative distance**.

The rule of the route destination can be summarized in a short sentence: **"The lower the AD value, the higher the route priority"**.

Imagine that two different routing protocols were configured on the **R2** router: **RIP v2** and **OSPF**. Both routing protocols propose their routes to the target subnetwork **192.168.2.0/24**:

```
R 192.168.2.0/24 [120/1] via 12.0.0.2, 00:00:06,
FastEthernet3/0
O 192.168.2.0/24 [110/65] via 11.0.0.2, 00:02:30,
Serial1/0
```

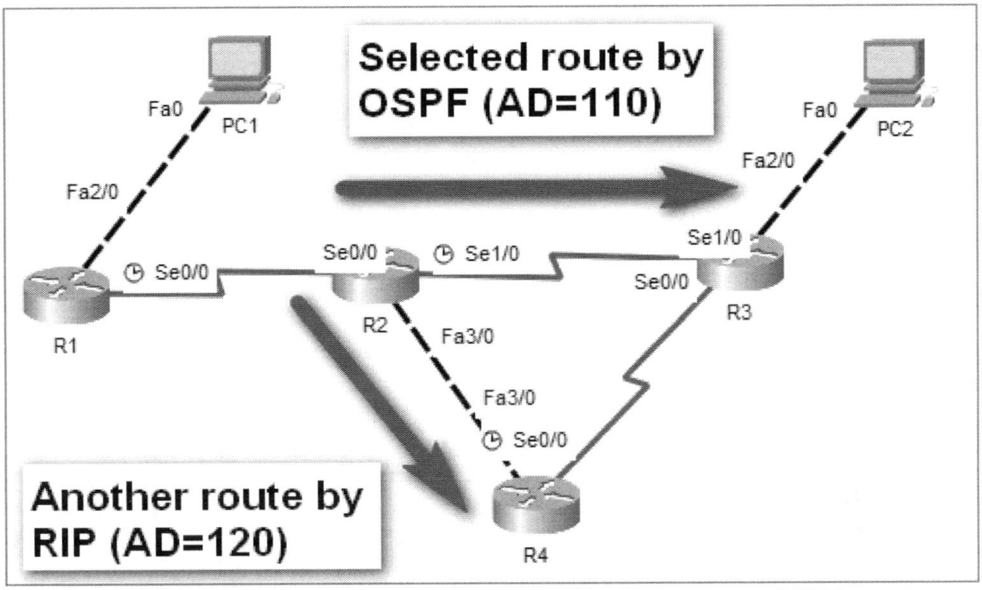

Figure 2.9 Selection of a higher priority route (R2 selected an OSPF route).

Router **R2** selected a route according to **OSPF** protocol and placed it in the routing table because its AD value is **less** than the AD value for the **RIP v2** protocol.

Standard administrative distances **(AD)** are presented in the table below.

Routing type (route or protocol)	AD default value
Route to the directly connected subnet	**0**
Static route	**1**
EIGRP summed route	**5**
BGP external route	**20**
EIGRP internal route	**90**
IGRP route	**100**
OSPF route	**110**
RIP route	**120**
EIGRP external route	**170**
BGP internal route	**200**
Unknown route	**255**

Table 2.3 Standard administrative distances.

2.2.5 Routing Metric

Metric is an information that allows to make decisions while viewing the routing table within a given routing type, in order to select the most advantageous route. Each protocol uses different metric. For example, RIP protocol uses **the number of hops**.

RIP protocol always chooses the route with the smallest metric (with the smallest number of hops between routers).

To send an information from router **R1** to subnet 192.168.8.0/24, it chose the best route, which led through address 172.16.0.2 of the **R5** router (two hops) instead of address of the **R2** router (four hops).

Route to the subnet 192.168.8.0/24 through router **R2** includes **four hops** and therefore is suboptimal.

Compare the number of hops from router R1 to router R6 through R3 (4 hops) and from router R1 to R6 through R5 (2 hops).

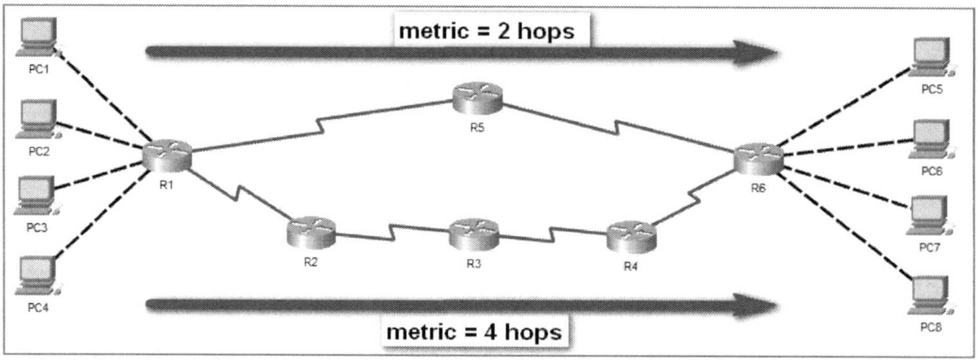

Figure 2. 10 Selecting route with the smallest metric (for RIP protocol).

2.2.6 Routing Table

Routers use a routing table to route packets to appropriate subnets. Routing table includes information about neighbor routers and routes to **remote** networks. Remote networks are networks located outside the given router.

Routing table is used to search for the optimal path to send packet to the destination address on the network.

```
R    172.18.0.0/16 [120/1] via 172.16.0.1, 00:00:04, Serial0/0
R    172.19.0.0/16 [120/2] via 172.16.0.1, 00:00:04, Serial0/0
R    172.20.0.0/16 [120/2] via 172.17.0.2, 00:00:04, Serial1/0
R    172.21.0.0/16 [120/1] via 172.17.0.2, 00:00:04, Serial1/0
R    192.168.1.0/24 [120/1] via 172.16.0.1, 00:00:04, Serial0/0
R    192.168.2.0/24 [120/1] via 172.16.0.1, 00:00:04, Serial0/0
R    192.168.3.0/24 [120/1] via 172.16.0.1, 00:00:04, Serial0/0
R    192.168.4.0/24 [120/1] via 172.16.0.1, 00:00:04, Serial0/0
R    192.168.5.0/24 [120/1] via 172.17.0.2, 00:00:04, Serial1/0
R    192.168.6.0/24 [120/1] via 172.17.0.2, 00:00:04, Serial1/0
R    192.168.7.0/24 [120/1] via 172.17.0.2, 00:00:04, Serial1/0
R    192.168.8.0/24 [120/1] via 172.17.0.2, 00:00:04, Serial1/0
```

Figure 2.11 Sample RIP routing table.

2.2.7 Routing Updates

Routing updates are messages sent between routers to update the routing table and/or other tables e.g. tables storing a database of network topologies (periodically or caused by the topology).

Protocol type	Update time period
RIPv1	30 seconds
RIPv2	30 seconds
EIGRP	15 seconds
OSPF	10 seconds in Point-to-Point networks or 30 seconds in broadcast networks
BGP	10 seconds

Table 2.4 Standard update times for basic routing types.

2.2.8 Routes Summarization

Routing routes summarization involves representing involves representing by a single route in the routing table a larger set of subnetworks and is performed at the border of the main network. Use of routes summarization to subnets enables saving space in the router's memory.

Instead of saving information on all of the networks you can save only one route on the router. When subnets are available via the same router, then we can configure one route for all subnets.

This technique is very convenient for big networks, especially in remote networks. When using multiple networks within the internal network of an organization or company, we can use the technique of "gluing" together multiple addresses into one shortened address.

For example, for routes to subnetworks:

Address of the subnet	Subnet mask	Next hop
192.168.5.0	255.255.255.0	172.16.0.2
192.168.6.0	255.255.255.0	172.16.0.2
192.168.7.0	255.255.255.0	172.16.0.2
192.168.8.0	255.255.255.0	172.16.0.2

Table 2.5 Sample addressing

we can configure a single summarized route with a **255.255.240.0** shortened mask:

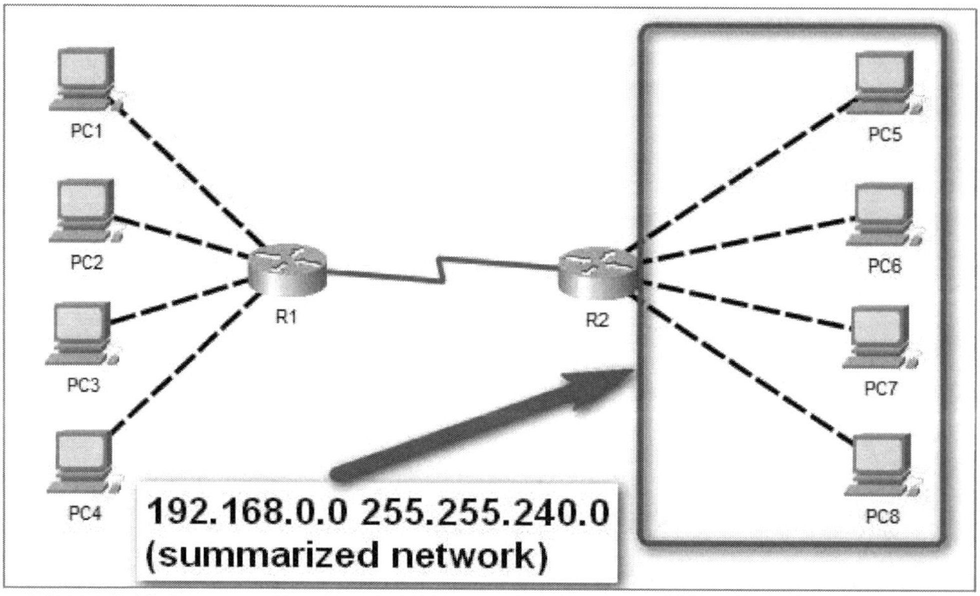

Figure 2.12 An example of summarized 192.168.0.0 network with 255.255.240.0 mask.

2.2.9 Split Horizon

Split Horizon technique is used in routing protocols to eliminate layer 3 network loop. Because of this technique protocol updates will not be sent over the router interface on which they were received, what prevents loops between two neighbors. This technique allows only local network information to be sent in routing updates.

Example below presents situation in which **Split Horizon** technique is **disabled** on all router interfaces.

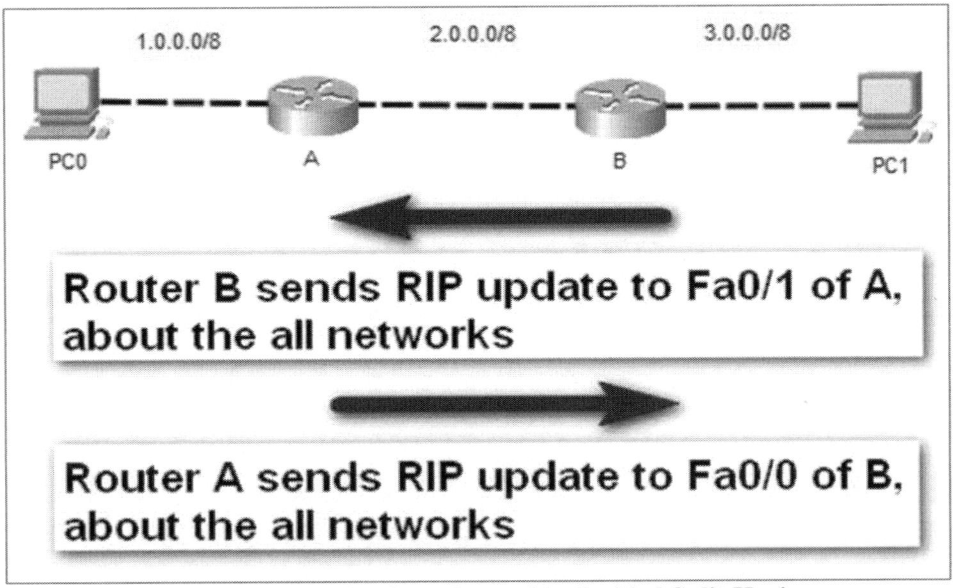

Figure 2.13 Example of topology with disabled Split Horizon.

Assumptions:

A command **`no ip split-horizon`** was executed on each interface and in order to observe the exchange of the information between routers, the command **`debug ip rip`** was executed in privileged mode. On the consoles of both routers we can observe the following messages:

Router B is sending an update to A and router A is receives an update from B.

```
RIP: build update entries
      network 1.0.0.0 metric 2
      network 2.0.0.0 metric 1
      network 3.0.0.0 metric 1
RIP: sending  v1 update to 255.255.255.255 via FastEthernet0/0 (2.0.0.2)
```

Figure 2.14 Sending a RIP routing update from router B.

```
A#RIP: received v1 update from 2.0.0.2 on FastEthernet0/1
      1.0.0.0 in 2 hops
      2.0.0.0 in 1 hops
      3.0.0.0 in 1 hops
```

Figure 2.15 Receiving a RIP routing update on router A.

Router A is sending received update back to router B.

```
RIP: build update entries
      network 1.0.0.0 metric 1
      network 2.0.0.0 metric 1
      network 3.0.0.0 metric 2
RIP: sending  v1 update to 255.255.255.255 via FastEthernet0/1 (2.0.0.1)
```

Figure 2.16 Sending a RIP routing update from router A.

Conclusion: Router A sends tentative, unnecessary information to router B (about networks 2.0.0.0/8 and 3.0.0.0/8) The only important information for router B is information about network 1.0.0.0/8.

Example below presents situation in which Split Horizon technique is **enabled** on all router interfaces.

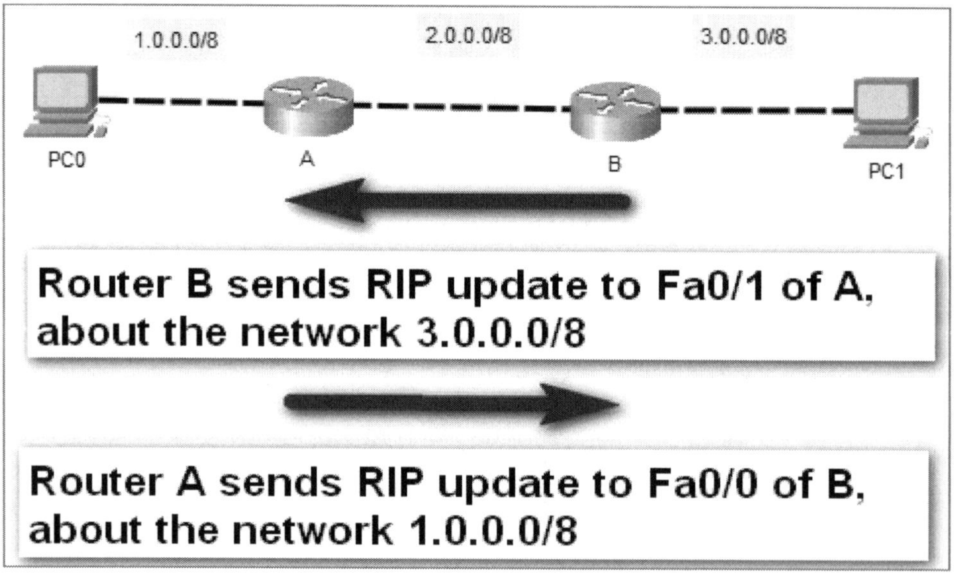

Figure 2.17 Example of topology with enabled Split Horizon.

Assumptions:

A command **`ip split-horizon`** was executed on each interface and in order to observe the exchange of the information between routers, the command **`debug ip rip`** was executed in privileged mode. On the consoles of both routers we can observe the following messages:

```
RIP: build update entries
      network 3.0.0.0 metric 1
RIP: sending  v1 update to 255.255.255.255 via FastEthernet0/1 (3.0.0.1)
```

Figure 2.18 Sending a RIP routing update from router B.

```
RIP: received v1 update from 2.0.0.2 on FastEthernet0/1
      3.0.0.0 in 1 hops
```

Figure 2.19 Receiving a RIP routing update on router A.

```
RIP: sending  v1 update to 255.255.255.255 via FastEthernet0/1 (2.0.0.1)
```

Figure 2.20 Sending a RIP routing update from router A.

Conclusion: Router B sends information to router A (informing about network 3.0.0.0/8) and router A sends information to router B (informing about network 1.0.0.0/8). There is no need to send information about other (adjacent) networks because the routes to these networks are already known to the routers.

2.3 RIPv1 Protocol

The manual discusses two versions of the protocol: **RIPv1**, **RIPv2**. Today, production networks no longer use RIP protocol (main reasons: long time to obtain network convergence, link parameters are not taken into account). The provided examples are for educational purposes only, as they have such advantages as **easy way to understand the basics of dynamic routing and simple configuration.**

2.3.1 Basic Features of the RIPv1 Protocol

RIP protocol comes in three versions: RIPv1, RIPv2 and RIPng. The **RIPv1** is characterized by the following features:

- it's a dynamic protocol, meaning it's a process that automatically recognizes routing routes,
- supports only class networks (continuous networks)
- has an automatic summation enabled,
- routing updates are broadcasted only to neighboring routers,
- the standard value of the administrative distance is 120,
- uses the number of hops between routers as metric,
- can handle a maximum of 15 hops.

The main advantage of the RIP protocol is the simplicity of configuration, while its main disadvantage is the long time to achieve network convergence. **RIPv1** protocol isn't currently used practically but can be used for educational purposes. The given examples are posted for educational purposes only. The common features and differences of the RIPv1 and RIPv2 versions are described later in the manual.

2.3.2 Configuring IP Addresses for Interfaces

In order to perform the IP address configuration for the interfaces on each network device, we'll use the following topology and a table containing the interface addressing scheme.

Device	Interface	IP Address	Subnet mask	Default gateway's address
A	Fa0	172.16.0.2	255.255.224.0	172.16.0.1
B	Fa0	172.16.32.2	255.255.224.0	172.16.32.1
C	Fa0	172.16.64.2	255.255.224.0	172.16.64.1
R1	Fa2/0	172.16.0.1	255.255.224.0	Does not apply
R1	Fa3/0	172.16.32.1	255.255.224.0	Does not apply
R1	Fa4/0	172.16.64.1	255.255.224.0	Does not apply
R1	Se0/0	192.168.1.1	255.255.255.0	Does not apply
R2	Se1/0	192.168.1.2	255.255.255.0	Does not apply
R2	Fa2/0	172.17.0.1	255.255.224.0	Does not apply
D	Fa0	172.17.0.2	255.255.224.0	172.17.0.1

Table 2.6 An example of an interface addressing scheme.

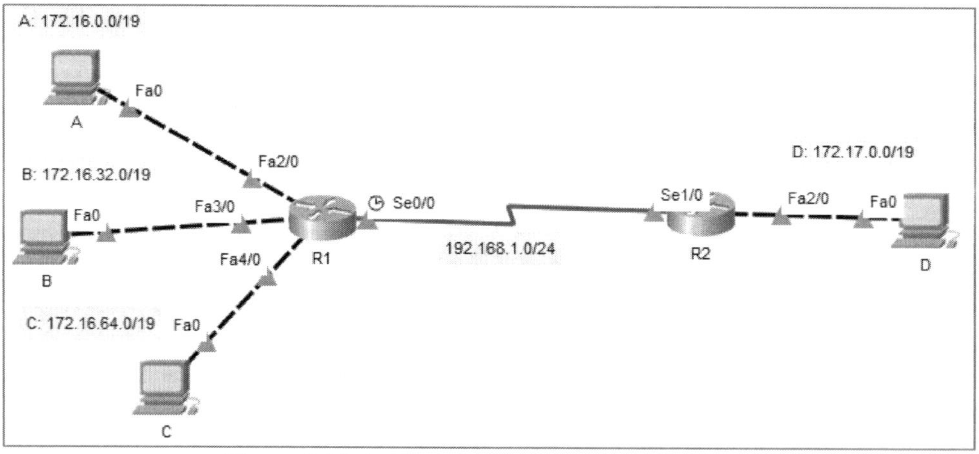

Figure 2.21 An example of topology diagram.

In the Packet Tracer program, RIPv1 protocol can be configured in two ways:

- graphically, using a **Config** tab,
- or via IOS system commands (recommended).

2.3.3 RIP Protocol Configuration via Config Tab

To configure the RIP v1 protocol for a router named **R1**, we need to click on the router, select the **Config** tab and then, in the vertical list on the left, click on the **RIP** button (see figure).

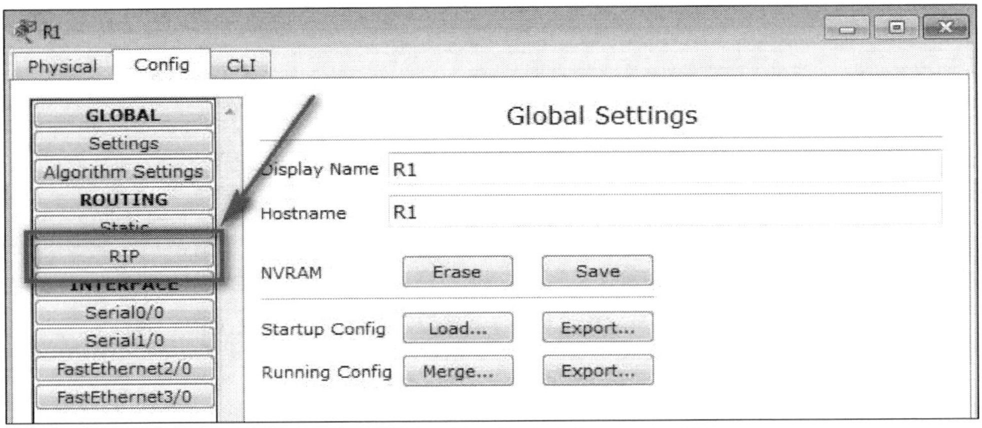

Figure 2.22 The Config tab in router R1.

In the **RIP** configuration dialog box, enter the address of the adjacent subnet in the **Network** field and then click **Add** (see figure).

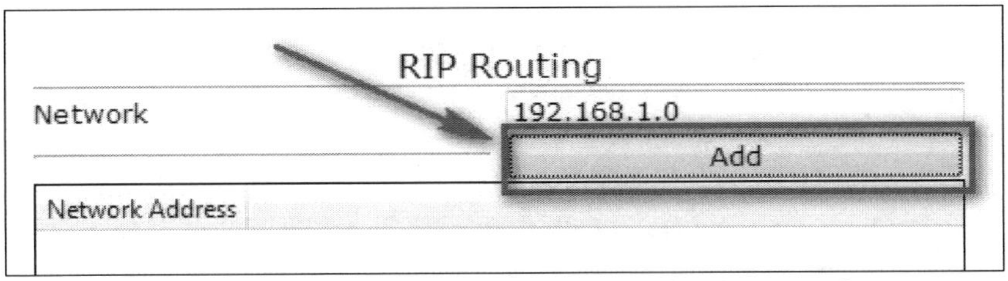

Figure 2.23 RIPv1 protocol – addition of adjacent subnet

This operation is repeated for each adjacent (neighbor) network.

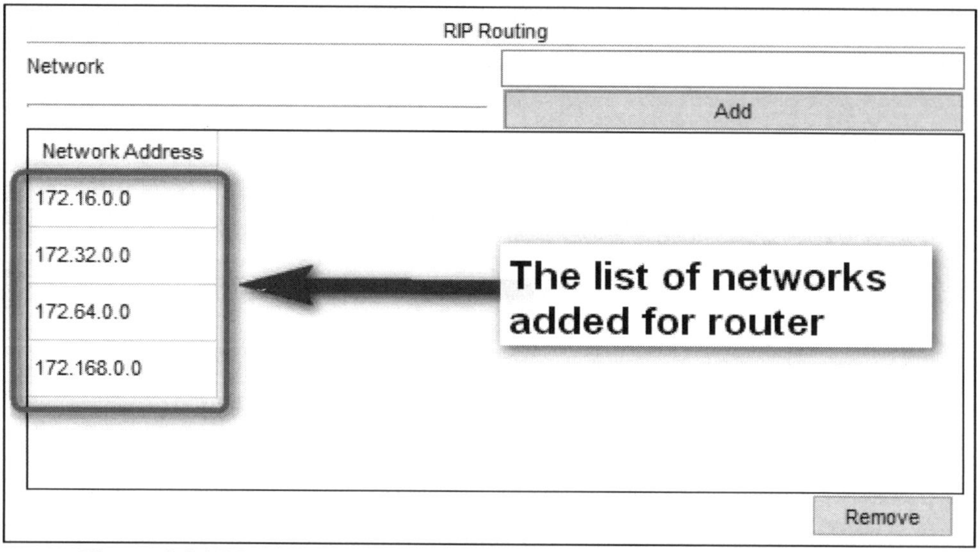

Figure 2.24 RIPv1 protocol – the list of networks added for router R1.

2.3.4 RIP Protocol Configuration via IOS Commands

Configuring the RIPv1 protocol using IOS commands is very simple and requires only two commands: **`router`** and **`network`**. To do so, we need to click on router **R1**, select the **CLI** tab (IOS command line entry) and then enter **RIP** configuration mode (see figure).

Switch to global configuration mode and execute the command

`rip router`

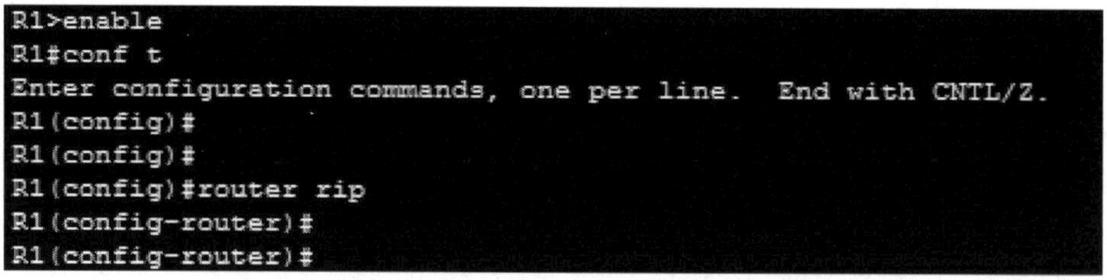

Figure 2.25 RIPv1 routing configuration mode.

Because we are in RIP routing configuration mode, we can now add the addresses of the subnets adjacent to router **R1**. We execute the following commands in sequence:

```
network 172.16.0.0
network 172.16.32.0
network 172.16.64.0
```

```
network 192.168.1.0
```

```
R1(config-router)#network 172.16.0.0
R1(config-router)#network 172.16.32.0
R1(config-router)#network 172.16.64.0
R1(config-router)#network 192.168.1.0
```

Figure 2.26 Adding adjacent subnets in RIPv1 routing configuration mode.

Repeat the above configuration scheme for each router.

NOTE: To enter (RIPv2 configuration) and adjust (RIPv2 version) you need to execute the command:

```
version 2
```

in configuring RIP routing mode:

```
R1>
R1>en
R1#
R1#conf t
Enter configuration commands, one per line.  End with CNTL/Z.
R1(config)#router rip
R1(config-router)#version 2
R1(config-router)#
```

Figure 2.27 Mode of RIPv2 routing configuration.

2.3.5 Automatic Network Summarization

Automatic network summarization consists of representing a single network matching a number of sub-networks.

For example, the three subnets: 172.16.0.0/19, 172.16.32.0/19, 172.16.64.0/19, can be represented by a **network** with the address **172.16.0.0/16. RIPv1** protocol always executes automatic network summarization.

```
R1#show ip route rip
     172.16.0.0/19 is subnetted, 3 subnets
R    172.17.0.0/16 [120/1] via 192.168.1.2, 00:00:12, Serial0/0
```

Figure 2.28 Automatic network summarization in RIPv1 routing.

2.3.6 RIP Protocol Configuration Check

To check current RIPv1 configuration we'll use command displaying the current configuration of the router: `show running-config`.

```
!
router rip
 network 172.16.0.0
 network 172.32.0.0
 network 172.64.0.0
 network 192.168.1.0
!
```

Figure 2.29 A fragment of the current configuration of router R1, concerning RIP v1.

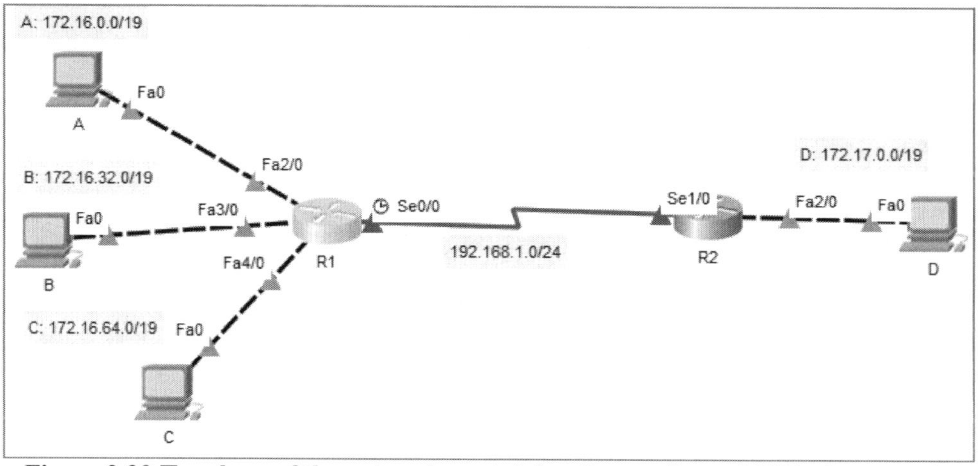

Figure 2.30 Topology of the network containing the configured RIP v1 protocol.

2.3.7 Display of Existing Routes in the Routing Table

To display current routes in the table obtained through RIP routing, we will execute the **`show ip route rip`** command. Routes resulting from RIP routing are denoted by the **R** symbol.

```
R1#show ip route rip
     172.16.0.0/19 is subnetted, 3 subnets
R    172.17.0.0/16 [120/1] via 192.168.1.2, 00:00:07, Serial0/0
```

Figure 2.31 Current R routes in R1 router.

```
R2#show ip route rip
R    172.16.0.0/16 [120/1] via 192.168.1.1, 00:00:09, Serial1/0
```

Figure 2.32 Current R routes in R2 router.

2.3.8 Display of Current RIP Protocol Settings

To view the current RIP protocol settings, we will use the router command: **`show ip protocol`**.

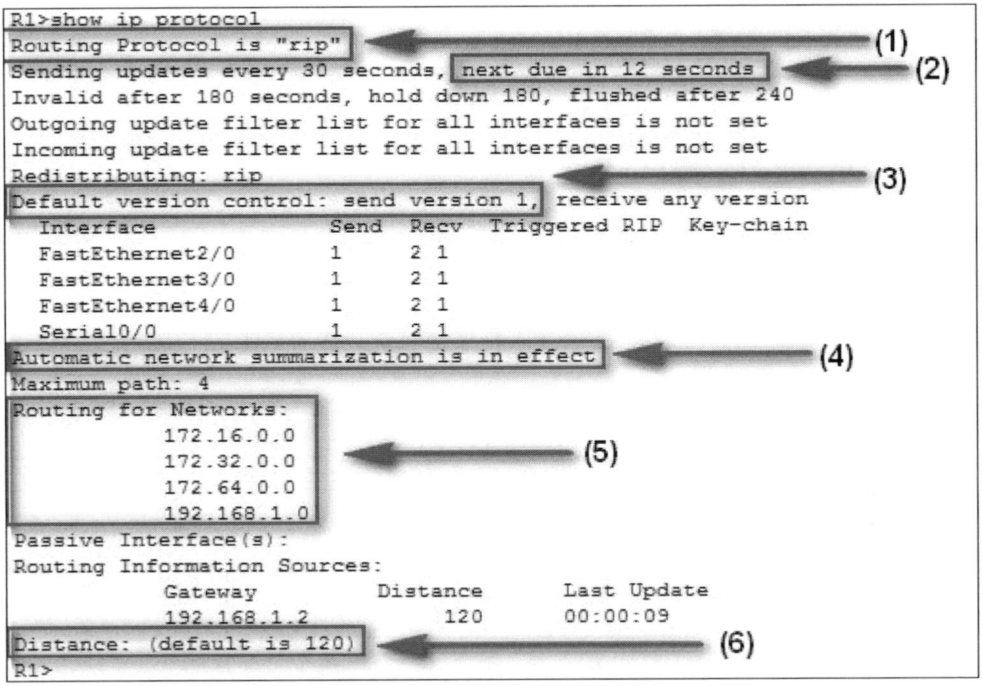

```
R1>show ip protocol
Routing Protocol is "rip"
Sending updates every 30 seconds, next due in 12 seconds
Invalid after 180 seconds, hold down 180, flushed after 240
Outgoing update filter list for all interfaces is not set
Incoming update filter list for all interfaces is not set
Redistributing: rip
Default version control: send version 1, receive any version
  Interface             Send  Recv  Triggered RIP  Key-chain
  FastEthernet2/0       1     2 1
  FastEthernet3/0       1     2 1
  FastEthernet4/0       1     2 1
  Serial0/0             1     2 1
Automatic network summarization is in effect
Maximum path: 4
Routing for Networks:
          172.16.0.0
          172.32.0.0
          172.64.0.0
          192.168.1.0
Passive Interface(s):
Routing Information Sources:
          Gateway         Distance      Last Update
          192.168.1.2          120      00:00:09
Distance: (default is 120)
R1>
```


Figure 2.33 Current RIP protocol settings on router R1.

Executing the **show ip protocol** command will display detailed information on the routing protocol used, among other things (see figure):

- **(1)** the currently used routing protocol on the router,
- **(2)** time value specifying how many seconds the next routing update will be sent in (in this case, the time is 12 seconds),
- **(3)** RIP protocol version (RIP v1 updates sent),
- **(4)** the router performs automatic route summarization at class network boundaries,
- **(5)** list of networks that the router includes in routing updates,
- **(6)** the current administrative distance for the RIP (in this case 120).

2.3.9 Configuring the Timers for the RIP Protocol

The counters (so-called timers) of the RIP protocol can be set for the RIP protocol. These are the following parameters that determine the detailed behavior of the protocol:

- Update timer,
- Invalid timer,
- Hold down timer,

- Flash timer.

The **timers basic** router command in RIP configuration mode **(config-router)#** is used to configure the counters. Counter values are given in seconds.

Command formulation:

```
timers basic <update>  <invalid> <hold-down> <flush>
```

The table below shows the names of the meters and their purpose.

Name of the counter	Purpose of the counter	Default value (seconds)
<update>	Time between sending continuous RIP updates (to a broadcast address).	30
<invalid>	The time after which the router has not received an update and marks the route as unreachable. The route isn't removed from the routing table (the router still uses this route for routing).	180
<hold-down>	Holding time for an unreachable route (router is still using this route for routing).	180
<flush>	Time that passed since the last RIP update. **(60 sec. higher than update-timer by default)** If this time is exceeded, the route is removed from the routing table.	240

Table 2.7 RIP meters and their purpose.

You can use router command **show ip protocols** in privileged mode # to display the current counter values.

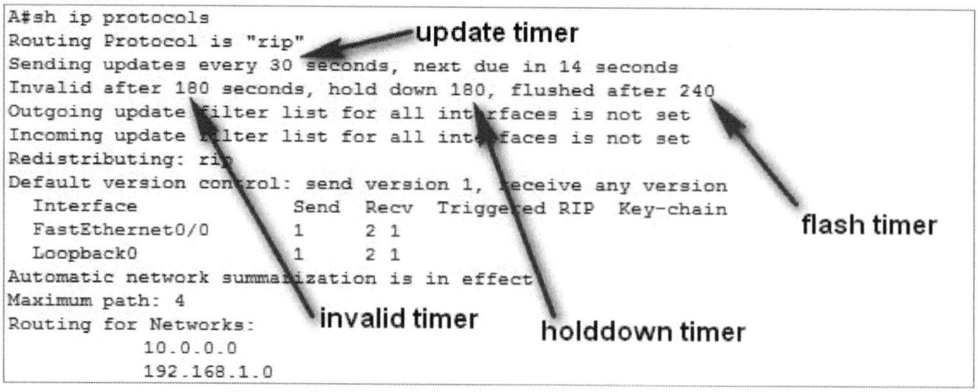

```
A#sh ip protocols
Routing Protocol is "rip"
Sending updates every 30 seconds, next due in 14 seconds
Invalid after 180 seconds, hold down 180, flushed after 240
Outgoing update filter list for all interfaces is not set
Incoming update filter list for all interfaces is not set
Redistributing: rip
Default version control: send version 1, receive any version
  Interface             Send  Recv  Triggered RIP  Key-chain
  FastEthernet0/0       1     2 1
  Loopback0             1     2 1
Automatic network summarization is in effect
Maximum path: 4
Routing for Networks:
          10.0.0.0
          192.168.1.0
```


Figure 2.34 Display of current RIP counters.

An example of how to configure counters for the RIP protocol on router B is shown in the following figure.

```
B#enable
B#config terminal
Enter configuration commands, one per line.  End with CNTL/Z.
B(config)#router rip
B(config-router)#timers basic 10 60 60 60
```

Figure 2.35 Configuring RIP counters.

2.4 RIPv2 Protocol

The **RIPv2** protocol uses classless **CIDR** routing. Examples presented in this chapter are for educational purposes only

The RIPv2 protocol, like RIPv1, is characterized by a limited metric value **(the maximum number of hops is 15)**. That's why its use is limited to small and medium-sized networks.

The main advantage of the **RIPv2** protocol is the ability to support classless networks. It's implemented in wireless devices such as ISRs (known commercially as Wi-Fi routers). Currently, it's mainly used in small networks, such as home networks.

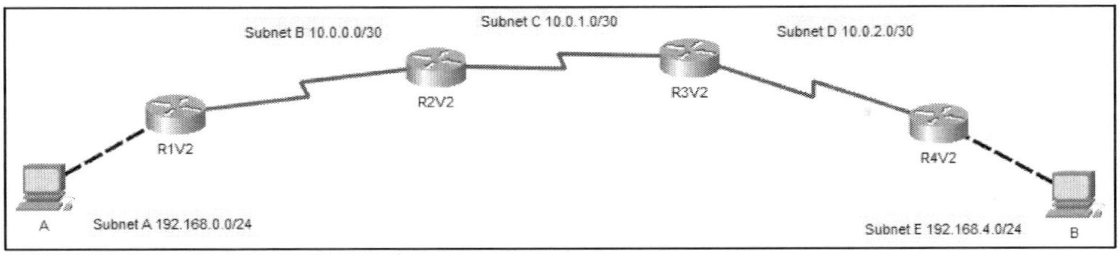

Figure 2.36 An example of topology with RIPv2 protocol.

2.4.1 Common Features of RIP Protocol Version 1 and 2

The **RIPv1** and **RIPv2** versions are characterized by the following common features:

RIP v1	RIP v2
The default administration distance is 120.	
Uses the number of hops between routers as metric,	
The maximum number of hops is 15.	
Long time to achieve network convergence.	
Updates are sent by default every 30 seconds.	
Simplicity of configurating.	

Table 2.8 Common features of RIPv1 and RIPv2.

2.4.2 Differences between Protocols RIP v1 and RIP v2

There are following differences between the RIPv1 and RIPv2 versions:

RIPv1	RIPv2
Does not support classless CIDR routing.	Supports classless CIDR routing.
Uses 255.255.255.255 broadcasting address for updates.	Uses multicast address type 224.0.0.9 for automatic distribution of updates.
Always performs automatic summation of routes at the border of the main networks.	By default, automatic route summarization at the border of main networks, but can be switched off.
It is not possible to switch off the automatic summation of routes.	It is possible to switch off the automatic summation of routes.
Does not support MD5 authentication.	Supports MD5 authentication.

Table 2.9 Differences between RIPv1 and RIPv2.

2.5 EIGRP Protocol

2.5.1 Introduction to EIGRP

Enhanced Interior Gateway Routing Protocol (EIGRP) is a routing protocol used for routing within the autonomous system. Designed by Cisco Systems. The protocol uses metrics based on distance vector and links state, i.e. minimum bandwidth and total delay on the path to the target network. The default administrative distance for this protocol is 90. It uses the Diffused Update Algorithm (DUAL) to calculate routes.

Main features of EIGRP protocol:

- supports variable mask addressing techniques (VLSM),
- has complicated metric,
- works only with Cisco Systems' products,
- has a shorter convergence time compared to the IGRP protocol.
- the protocol has a low utilization of network resources during normal operating (changes in the network only result in changes to parts of the routing table).

2.5.2 Basic Concepts on EIGRP

Autonomous System is what we call a collection of networks under common administration and using the same internal routing rules (for example a collection of networks located in a company or an institution).

On each router with running EIGRP protocol are stored three tables:

- neighbor table,

- topology table,
- routing table.

Neighbor Table is a table in which the router stores information about the adjacent routers (neighbors). Routers that are indirectly connected to this router via another router are not registered in this table, i.e. they are not considered neighbors.

Topology table stores routes determined from routing table information obtained from neighbors. Doesn't store all of the routes, just the ones that were determined by EIGRP.

Routing table stores information about best routes to the destination in question. This information is obtained from the topology table.

The primary cost-effective route in EIGRP is the route chosen as the main route leading to a given destination network. The DUAL algorithm determines it based on the information contained in the neighbor and topology tables and then stores it in the routing table. There can be up to four main routes for each destination.

Feasible Successor Route in EIGRP is a route which will be used in case of emergency of the primary route. It is established at the same time as the primary route, but is only stored in the topology table. The router can store several alternate routes in the topology table.

2.5.3 Basic Configuration and Verification Commands

To perform a basic configuration of the EIGRP protocol on the router, we will use the following IOS commands:

- activation of EIGRP configuration mode on a stand-alone system:

```
router eigrp <autonomous_system_no.>
```

where: **<autonomous-system-no.>** is a 16-bit number between 1 and 65535,

- the inclusion of networks (or subnets) in EIGRP routing updates is performed using the command:

```
network <network-address>
```

- the inclusion of classless networks (or classless subnets) in EIGRP routing updates is performed by using the command:

```
network <network-address> <wildcard-mask>
```

- deactivation of the mechanism for automatic summation of routes at class boundaries. In order not to use automatic route summarization on class boundaries in EIGRP routing updates, we execute the command:

```
no auto-summary
```

- to display the EIGRP neighbors table (in order to check whether the EIGRP router has created adjacencies with its neighbors), we execute the command:

```
show ip eigrp neighbors
```

- to display the EIGRP topology table we use the command:

```
show ip eigrp topology
```

- to display the EIGRP routing table we use the command:

```
show ip route eigrp
```

2.5.4 Example of Configurating and Checking the EIGRP Protocol

In order to configure the EIGRP protocol on autonomous system number 1, we will create the following topology:

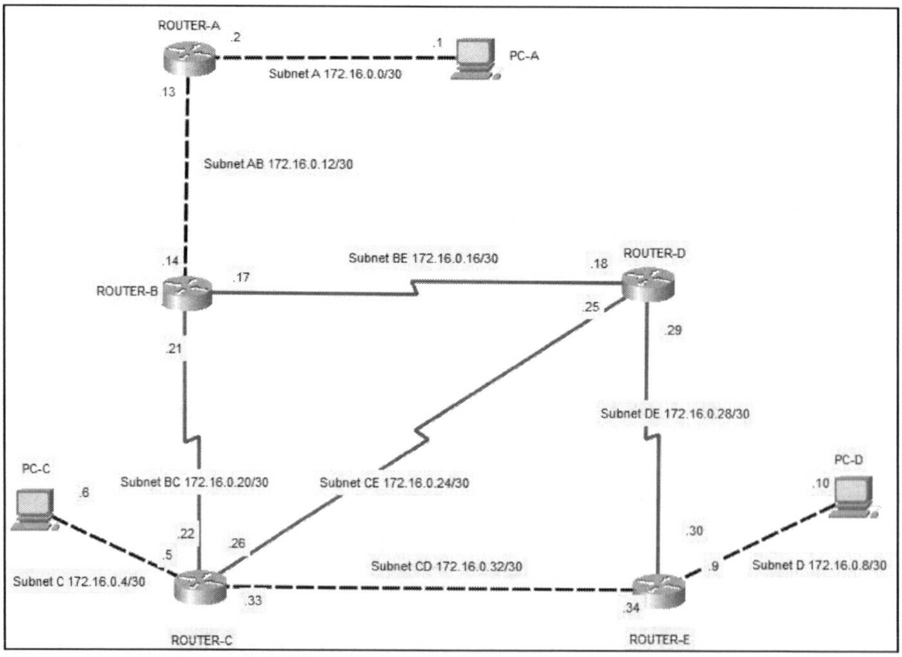

Figure 2.37 Topology of autonomous system AS 1.

The autonomous system is a network with address 172.16.0.0/24 divided into nine subnets:

- 172.16.0.0/30,
- 172.16.0.4/30,
- 172.16.0.8/30,
- 172.16.0.12/30,
- 172.16.0.16/30,
- 172.16.0.20/30,
- 172.16.0.24/30,
- 172.16.0.28/30,
- 172.16.0.32/30,

and five router (called: **ROUTER-A, ROUTER-B, ROUTER-C, ROUTER-D, ROUTER-E**).

To configure the above standalone system, we need to configure all network interfaces correctly according to the topology. We then proceed to configure the EIGRP protocol.

We will perform the same steps on each router, following the example for the **ROUTER-C** router, changing the subnet addresses accordingly. Example of configurating for router **ROUTER-C** – step-by-step.

Step 1. We define the subnets directly adjacent to the router

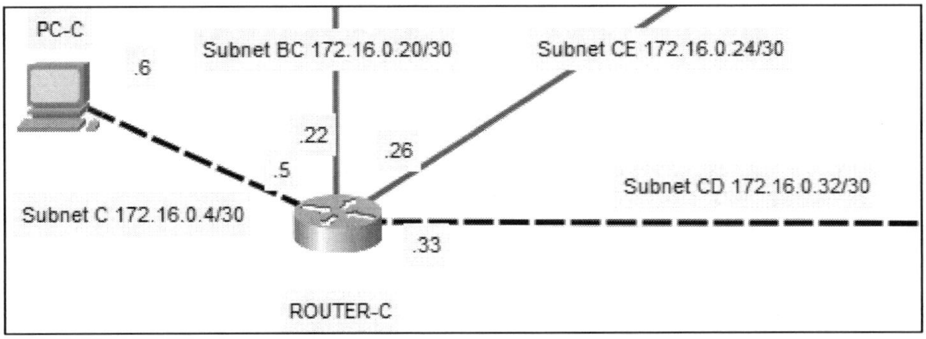

Figure 2.38 Subnets adjacent to the ROUTER-C router.

In our case, we have four subnets directly adjacent to the router:

- 172.16.0.4/30,
- 172.16.0.20/30,
- 172.16.0.24/30,
- 172.16.0.32/30.

Step 2. We calculate the wildcard mask according to the formula:

$$\begin{array}{r} 255.255.255.255 \\ - \quad subnet\ mask \\ \hline wildcard\ mask \end{array}$$

Figure 2.39 Formula for calculating the wildcard mask.

For the subnet mask prefix (**/30**), we determine the subnet mask (**255.255.255.252**) and then calculate the wildcard mask according to the formula (we must subtract the binary subnet mask from the binary form of the number 255.255.255.255).

Results of binary subtraction for prefix **/30**:

$$\begin{array}{r} 11111111.11111111.11111111.11111111 \\ - \, 11111111.11111111.11111111.11111100 \\ \hline 00000000.00000000.00000000.00000011 \end{array}$$

Figure 2.40 Results of binary subtraction

After converting the binary numbers to decimal, we obtain the following form of wildcard mask **0.0.0.3**.

Step 3. We configure EIGRP on the router according to the given syntax:

```
router eigrp <sutonomous_system_no>
network <subnetwork_address>
<blanket_mask_network_address>
network <subnetwork_address>
<blanket_mask_network_address>
network <subnetwork_address>
<blanket_mask_network_address>
```

```
ROUTER-C(config)#router eigrp 1
ROUTER-C(config-router)#network 172.16.0.4 0.0.0.3
ROUTER-C(config-router)#network 172.16.0.20 0.0.0.3
ROUTER-C(config-router)#network 172.16.0.24 0.0.0.3
ROUTER-C(config-router)#network 172.16.0.32 0.0.0.3
ROUTER-C(config-router)#
```

Figure 2.41 EIGRP configuration commands for the ROUTER-C router.

Repeat the above configuration scheme for each router.

Step 4. Checking the operation of the EIGRP protocol on a router

To check the performance of the EIGRP protocol on a given router, we will use the following IOS commands:

`show running-config,`
`show ip eigrp neighbors,`
`show ip eigrp topology,`
`show ip route eigrp.`

```
!
router eigrp 1
 network 172.16.0.4 0.0.0.3
 network 172.16.0.20 0.0.0.3
 network 172.16.0.24 0.0.0.3
 network 172.16.0.32 0.0.0.3
 auto-summary
!
```

Figure 2.42 A piece from the result of the show running-config command for ROUTER-C.

```
ROUTER-C#show ip eigrp neighbors
IP-EIGRP neighbors for process 1
H   Address         Interface       Hold Uptime    SRTT   RTO   Q   Seq
                                    (sec)          (ms)         Cnt Num
0   172.16.0.34     Gig0/1          10   00:10:23  40     1000  0   19
1   172.16.0.25     Se0/0/1         10   00:10:18  40     1000  0   24
2   172.16.0.21     Se0/0/0         10   00:10:16  40     1000  0   20
```

Figure 2.43 The result of the show ip eigrp neighbors command for ROUTER-C.

The column description for the result of the **`show ip eigrp neighbors`** command is as follows:

- **H** – neighbors in the order in which they were found
- **Address** – IP address of a neighbor (neighboring router),
- **Interface** – the local interface of the router on which the HELLO packet was received,
- **Hold** – current hold time (in seconds),
- **Uptime** – the elapsed time since the neighbor was added to the array of neighbors,
- **SRTT (Smooth Round Trip Timer)** i **RTO (Retransmit Interval)** – This parameter will not be discussed in this book (advanced option),
- **Q Cnt** – parameter should always be 0. If the value is higher, EIGRP packets are waiting to be sent. Won't be discussed in this book (advanced option),
- **Seq Num** – a parameter used to track update, query and response packets. Won't be discussed in this book (advanced option).

The frequency with which the EIGRP interface sends HELLO packets is the period (**interval**) occurring between consecutive HELLO packets. The default is 5 seconds.

Routers detect neighbors and form so-called adjacencies with neighboring routers using HELLO packets. In most networks, HELLO packets are sent every 5 seconds by default. The router assumes that as long as it receives HELLO packets from a neighbor, that neighbor and its routes are usable. When a new device is detected, its address and interface information is stored.

- **Hold** – current hold time.
- **Hold time** gives the router the maximum time the router should wait to receive the next HELLO packet before it considers its neighbor unreachable. The default hold time is equal to **three times** the HELLO interval, or **15 seconds**. If the hold time runs out, EIGRP considers the route to be out of service and the DUAL algorithm either looks for a new route in the topology table or sends out queries.

```
ROUTER-C#show ip eigrp topology
IP-EIGRP Topology Table for AS 1/ID(172.16.0.33)

Codes: P - Passive, A - Active, U - Update, Q - Query, R - Reply
       r - Reply status

P 172.16.0.0/30, 1 successors, FD is 3014656
         via 172.16.0.21 (3014656/2502656), Serial0/0/0
P 172.16.0.4/30, 1 successors, FD is 5120
         via Connected, GigabitEthernet0/0
P 172.16.0.8/30, 1 successors, FD is 5376
         via 172.16.0.34 (5376/5120), GigabitEthernet0/1
P 172.16.0.12/30, 1 successors, FD is 3012096
         via 172.16.0.21 (3012096/2500096), Serial0/0/0
P 172.16.0.16/30, 2 successors, FD is 2681856
         via 172.16.0.21 (2681856/2169856), Serial0/0/0
         via 172.16.0.25 (2681856/2169856), Serial0/0/1
P 172.16.0.20/30, 1 successors, FD is 2169856
         via Connected, Serial0/0/0
P 172.16.0.24/30, 1 successors, FD is 2169856
         via Connected, Serial0/0/1
P 172.16.0.28/30, 1 successors, FD is 2170112
         via 172.16.0.34 (2170112/2169856), GigabitEthernet0/1
         via 172.16.0.25 (2681856/2169856), Serial0/0/1
P 172.16.0.32/30, 1 successors, FD is 2816
         via Connected, GigabitEthernet0/1
ROUTER-C#
```

Figure 2.44 The result of the show ip eigrp topology command for ROUTER-C.

Description of the result of command **`show ip eigrp topology`** is as follow:

- **P** – passive route, i.e. ready to use,
- **A** – active route, i.e. route being calculated by the DUAL algorithm,

- Destination network address in the format A.B.C.D/p (p - prefix),
- **FD** (viable distance) - the lowest calculated metric to each destination of a given subnetwork.
- **Interface** – the interface through which the destination of a given subnetwork can be reached.

The topology table is formed by all EIGRP protocol routing tables in the autonomous system. Based on the information contained in the neighbor table and the topology table, the DUAL algorithm calculates the lowest cost routes to each destination network.

The EIGRP protocol keeps track of this information so that EIGRP routers can quickly find alternative routes and be switched to them. The information obtained by the router using the DUAL algorithm is used to determine the primary cost-effective route. This is used to determine the primary (best) route. This information is obtained from the topology table.

The router stores a separate topology table for each configured network protocol. The table contains information about all routes to the destination network obtained by the router.

```
ROUTER-C#show ip route eigrp
     172.16.0.0/16 is variably subnetted, 13 subnets, 2 masks
D       172.16.0.0/30 [90/3014656] via 172.16.0.21, 00:17:15, Serial0/0/0
D       172.16.0.8/30 [90/5376] via 172.16.0.34, 00:17:20, GigabitEthernet0/1
D       172.16.0.12/30 [90/3012096] via 172.16.0.21, 00:17:15, Serial0/0/0
D       172.16.0.16/30 [90/2681856] via 172.16.0.21, 00:17:15, Serial0/0/0
                       [90/2681856] via 172.16.0.25, 00:17:14, Serial0/0/1
D       172.16.0.28/30 [90/2170112] via 172.16.0.34, 00:17:13, GigabitEthernet0/1
```

Figure 2.45 The result of the show ip route eigrp command **for ROUTER-C.**

The EIGRP routing table stores information about the best routes to a given destination, obtained by running the DUAL algorithm. Itis used to forward IP packets between logical subnets.

2.5.5 Selecting the Best Route in the EIGRP Protocol

The best route selected by the EIGRP protocol is the route with the smallest value of the calculated metric. The metric in the EIGRP protocol is calculated according to the following general formula:

$$Metric = 256 * \left[K1 * Throughput + \frac{K2 * Throughput}{(256 - Load)} + K3 * Delay\right] * \frac{K5}{(Reliability + K4)}$$

Equation 2.1 Full formula for calculating the metric.

where:

K1, K2, K3, K4, K5 are factors. The default values of the coefficients are respectively: K1 = 1, K2 = 0, K3 = 1, K4 = 0, K5 = 0

General formula for metrics for EIGRP:

$$Metric = 256 * \left[\mathbf{1} * Throughput + \frac{\mathbf{0} * Throughput}{(256 - Load)} + \mathbf{1} * Delay\right] * \frac{\mathbf{0}}{(Reliability + \mathbf{0})}$$

Equation 2.2 General formula

and the link parameters are:

- **Throughput** is calculated from the formula:

$$Throughput = \frac{10\,000\,000}{Bandwidth}$$

Equation 2.3 Throughput calculation

- **Bandwidth** - the smallest bandwidth for all output interfaces en route to the destination network given in kilobits,
- **Bandwidth selection** (for ROUTER-C, the smallest possible value is selected: 1000 kb/s, 2000000 kb/s, 2000000 kb/s), i.e. **1000 kb/s**.
- **Delay** - sum of delays on the interfaces belonging to the route (note: value given in 1/10 microsecond).
- **Reliability** will be taken as equal to 1 (explanation of this parameter is beyond the scope of the manual)

With default values for K1 = 1, K2 = 0, K3 = 1, K4 = 0, K5 = 0, the formula takes the following simplified form:

$$Metric = 256 * (Throughput + Delay)$$

Equation 2.4 Simplified formula

Throughput is the throughput in kbps of the slowest interface present on the route.

Delay is the sum of the delays [given in 1/10th of a microsecond] on the interfaces belonging to the route, i.e. divided by 10.

Note that in the example topology on the route from PC-1 to router B, it makes no sense to analyze the optimal route (no branches). Therefore, we will start the analysis from router B.

For the topology shown in the figure, we will analyze the selection of the optimal route from B to PC-2. In general, we have a choice of the following routes that can be used to transmit packets:

B → D → E → PC-2
B → D → C → E → PC-2
B → C → E → PC-2
B → C → D → E → PC-2

Figure 2.46 Packet transmission routes

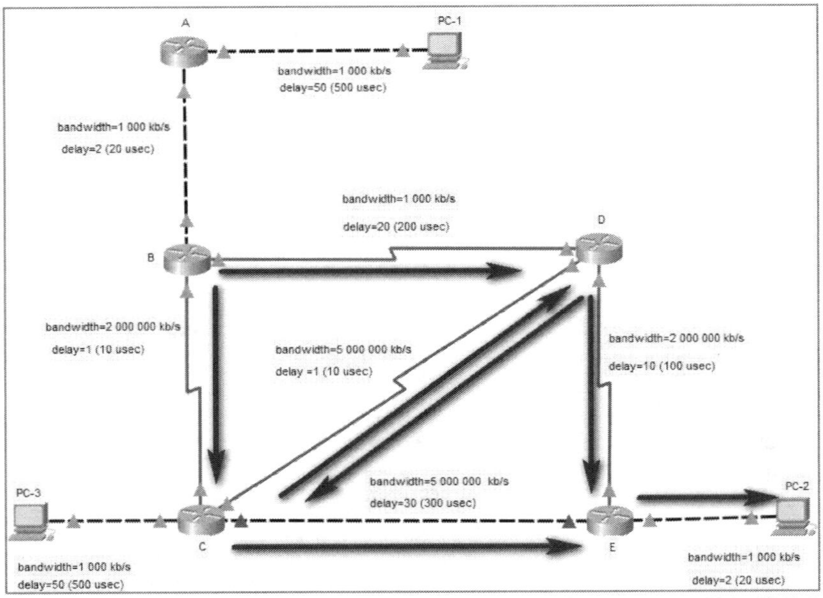

Figure 2.47 Possible routes for sending a packet from router B to PC-2.

The parameters of the output interfaces involved in the selection of the optimal route between the devices are shown in the table.

Router Output interface	Bandwidth [kbps] (bandwidth)	Delay [μsec]
B Gi0/0	1 000	20
B Se0/0/0	1 000	200
B Se0/0/1	2 000 000	10
C Se0/0/0	2 000 000	10

C Se0/0/1	5 000 000	10
C Gi0/1	5 000 000	300
D Se0/1/0	2 000 000	100
D Se0/0/0	5 000 000	10
E Se0/0/0	2 000 000	100
E Gi0/1	5 000 000	300

Table 2.10 Parameters of output interfaces.

We now calculate the metrics for each of the possible routes from router **B** to **PC-2**. The results of the calculation are presented in the table below.

No	Route	The smallest bandwidth on route	Throughput	delay 1 (10 µs)	delay 2 (10 µs)	delay 3 (10 µs)	delay 4 (10 µs)	Sum of delays	Metric value
1	B->D->E	1000	10000	20	0	10	2	32	2568192
2	B->D->C->E	1000	10000	20	1	30	2	53	2573568
3	B->C->E	1000	10000	1	30	0	2	33	2568448
4	B->C->D->E	1000	10000	1	1	10	2	14	2563584
								Minimum of metric	2563584

Table 2.11 Results of the metrics calculation for the different routes.

Conclusion:

The EIGRP protocol selects route 4, i.e. **B→C→D→E** because it has the metric with the smallest value.

Verification:

To check whether the selection of the optimal route has been performed by the EIGRP protocol, we execute the **show ip route** command on router **B**.

After executing the command, the router's console will display the current routing table. PC-2 is on the 172.16.0.8/30 subnet, so we are looking for an entry with this subnet. From the third column in square brackets, we can read the value of the administrative distance (**90**) and the value of the metric (**2563072**).

```
     172.16.0.0/16 is variably subnetted, 12 subnets, 2 masks
D       172.16.0.0/30 [90/2562816] via 172.16.0.13, 00:01:17, GigabitEthernet0/0
D       172.16.0.4/30 [90/2562816] via 172.16.0.22, 00:01:10, Serial0/0/1
D       172.16.0.8/30 [90/2563072] via 172.16.0.22, 00:01:10, Serial0/0/1
C       172.16.0.12/30 is directly connected, GigabitEthernet0/0
L       172.16.0.14/32 is directly connected, GigabitEthernet0/0
C       172.16.0.16/30 is directly connected, Serial0/0/0
L       172.16.0.17/32 is directly connected, Serial0/0/0
C       172.16.0.20/30 is directly connected,
L       172.16.0.21/32 is directly connected,
D       172.16.0.24/30 [90/1792] via 172.16.0.                    /1
D       172.16.0.28/30 [90/4352] via 172.16.0.22, 00:01:10, Serial0/0/1
D       172.16.0.32/30 [90/1792] via 172.16.0.22, 00:01:10, Serial0/0/1
```

optimal metric

Figure 2.48 Checking the metrics in the routing table of router B.

```
B#show ip route eigrp
     172.16.0.0/16 is variably subnetted, 12 subnets, 2 masks
D       172.16.0.0/30 [90/2562816] via 172.16.0.13, 00:14:37, GigabitEthernet0/0
D       172.16.0.4/30 [90/2562816] via 172.16.0.22, 00:14:31, Serial0/0/1
D       172.16.0.8/30 [90/2563072] via 172.16.0.22, 00:14:31, Serial0/0/1
D       172.16.0.24/30 [90/1792] via 172.16.0.22, 00:14:31, Serial0/0/1
D       172.16.0.28/30 [90/4352] via 172.16.0.22, 00:14:31, Serial0/0/1
D       172.16.0.32/30 [90/1792] via 172.16.0.22, 00:14:31, Serial0/0/1
```

Figure 2.49 Result of the command: `show ip route eigrp` on router B.

2.5.6 Configuration of Parameters for Interfaces in the EIGRP Protocol

For each router interface, we can set the values of the following parameters:

- **bandwidth** - the smallest bandwidth for all output interfaces on the route to the destination network given in kilobits,
- **delay** - sum of delays on the interfaces belonging to the route (note: value given in 1/10 microsecond).

To change the above parameters, we use the **bandwidth** and **delay** commands, in the configuration mode of the respective interface. The syntax of these commands is simple:

`bandwidth`

the **bandwidth** option is an integer between 1 and 10 000 000 specifying the bandwidth of the interface in kilobits per second,

`delay`

the **delay** option is an integer between 1 and 16 777 215 specifying the delay occurring on the link connected to the interface.

Note:

However, we must remember to first divide the actual delay value in microseconds by 10, and then enter the result of the division in the **delay** command. Example of setting a bandwidth of **1,000** kbps and a delay of **200** microseconds, on interface **Se0/0/0**:

```
enable
configure terminal
interface Se0/0/0
Router(config-if)# bandwidth 1000
Router(config-if)# delay 20
```

```
B#enable
B#configure terminal
Enter configuration commands, one per line.  End with CNTL/Z.
B(config)#interface Se0/0/0
B(config-if)#bandwidth 1000
B(config-if)#delay 20
B(config-if)#exit
B(config)#
```

Figure 2.50 Example of setting Se0/0/0 parameters on router B.

2.6 OSPFv2 Protocol

2.6.1 Introduction to OSPFv2

Open Shortest Path First (OSPFv2) *is a classless dynamic link-state routing protocol for determining the best route to an IPv4 destination network.* It is used inside large autonomous systems, e.g. corporate systems, because it has a relatively short network convergence time.

The main task of the protocol is to create a database reflecting the current network topology. Topology information is only created for routers located in the same administrative areas (called areas). The OSPFv2 protocol is defined in the documents: RFC 1247, RFC 1583, RFC 2328 as an open public standard. The default administrative distance for this protocol is 110. The protocol uses a metric based on link state i.e. a cost that is inversely proportional to the **bandwidth** of the link. The OSPF protocol uses Dijkstra's Shortest Path First (**SPF**) algorithm to calculate routes.

Main features of OSPF protocol:

- uses the SPF algorithm, invented by the Dutch theoretical computer scientist as an algorithm for finding the shortest paths in a graph.
- open (support for devices from different manufacturers),

- supports variable mask addressing techniques (VLSM),
- short convergence time in a stand-alone network,
- metrics using bandwidth-based cost,
- complete and synchronized topology view,
- low probability of routing loops,
- high levels of memory and processing power usage,
- requires the design of a hierarchical network,
- configuration requires appropriate administrator knowledge.

2.6.2 Basic Concepts of OSPFv2

Cost is the basic metric of OSPF. The formula for calculating the metric (OSPF cost) is

$$Cost = \frac{100\,000\,000}{Bandwidth}$$

Equation 2.5 Formula for calculating the cost

The bandwidth is given in kbps. The higher the bandwidth value, the better the metric.

DR - Designated Router is the primary OSPF router that generates the LSA packets. This router has **the highest priority**.

Note: In a situation where two or more routers are assigned the same priority, the router with the highest ID number will be selected. The ID number is the highest number (IP address) that is assigned to the router on any interface.

BDR - Backup Designated Router is the backup OSPF router, if defined. This is the router that is selected as the **Designated Router** when the **DR** fails.

The **HELLO packet** is a packet used to create OSPF neighbor information.

A **DBD packet** is a packet used to create information in the local OSPF link-state database.

A **link-state advertisement (LSA) packet** is a broadcast packet used to broadcast information about neighbors and link states.

A **link-state request (LSR) packet** is a packet used to request additional information about neighbors and link states.

A **link-state advertisement (LSU) packet** is a packet used to broadcast information about neighbors and link states.

A **link-state acknowledgement (LSAck) packet** is a packet used to acknowledge receipt of an LSU packet.

2.6.3 SPF Algorithm

SPF algorithm (*Shortest Path First*) is used to find the shortest paths in networks.

The algorithm was developed by Edsger Dijkstra and is used to find the shortest path from a single source in a graph.

In the case of computer networks, the term **graph** should be understood as a collection of routers connected by **point-to-point** links. The following assumptions apply:

Each link has a corresponding cost assigned to it, OSPF uses so-called costs, assigned to each link (i.e. interface) with a maximum value in the range: **1 - 65535**. The cost is by default inversely proportional to the bandwidth on the link - it is calculated based on the formula:

$$Cost = \frac{100\ 000\ 000}{Bandwidth}$$

Equation 2.6 Formula for calculating cost

The cost of a link can be set administratively using the command: `ip ospf cost`

Bandwidth is given in kbps.

- each node on the network, i.e. the router, has a name.
- each router stores a topology database,
- all databases of link states are identical.

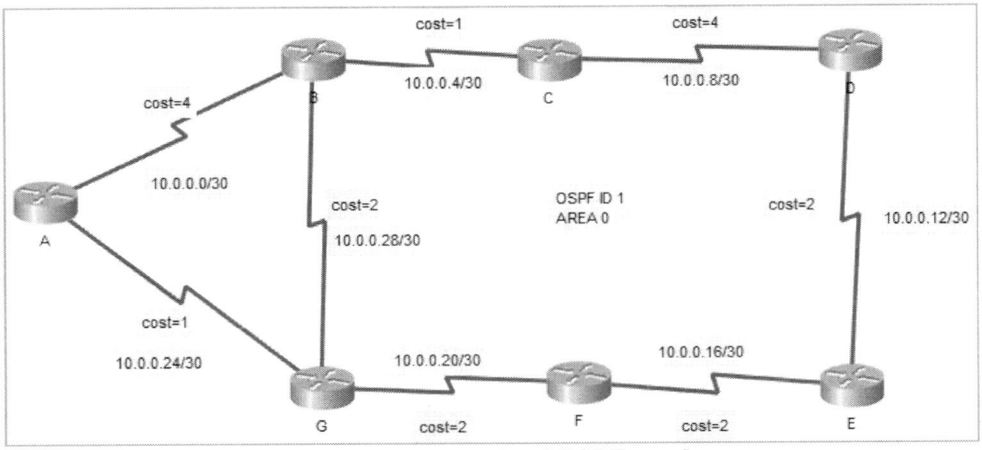

Figure 2.51 An example of OSPF topology.

The following table shows the base of neighbor topologies that router A obtained from the entire OSPF network informing about the cost of data transmission from source routers to individual neighboring (adjacent) routers. The values of the cost of point-to-point links between routers are placed in round brackets (see the drawing of an example OSPF topology).

Source router	A	B	C	D	E	F	G
Router (cost)	**B (4)**	A (4)	B (1)	C (4)	D (2)	E (2)	A (1)
Router (cost)	**G (1)**	C (1)	D (4)	E (2)	F (2)	G (2)	B (2)
Router (cost)	-	G (2)	-	-	-	-	F (2)

Table 2.12 Example of neighbor topology base for router A for OSPF.

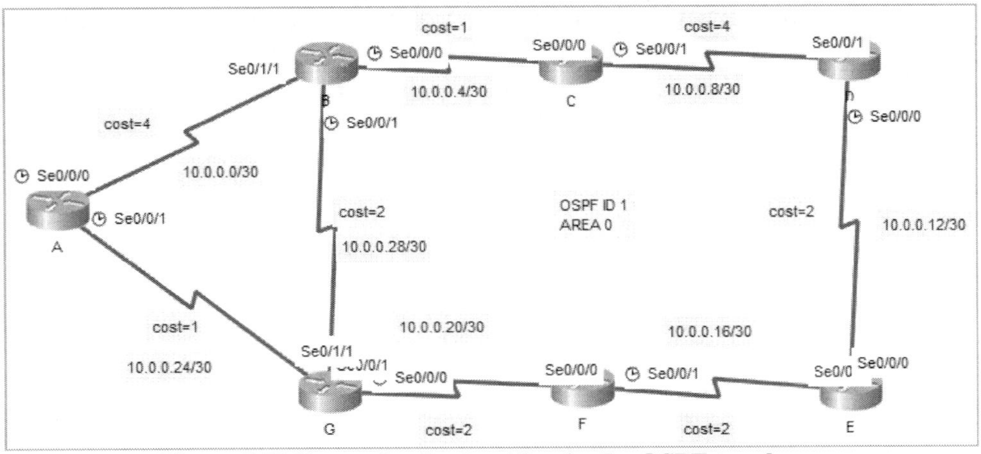

Figure 2.52 Example of subnetting in the OSPF topology.

In order to select the optimal route **from router A to router E**, router A will analyze the above table and determine routes to networks adjacent to router E:

- 10.0.0/30,
- 10.0.24/30.

The **SPF** algorithm will select the route with the lowest total cost:

- Optimal route for network 10.0.12/30: A → G → F → E (***sum of costs:*** *5*)
- Optimal route for network 10.0.16/30: A → G → F → E (***sum of costs:*** *5*)

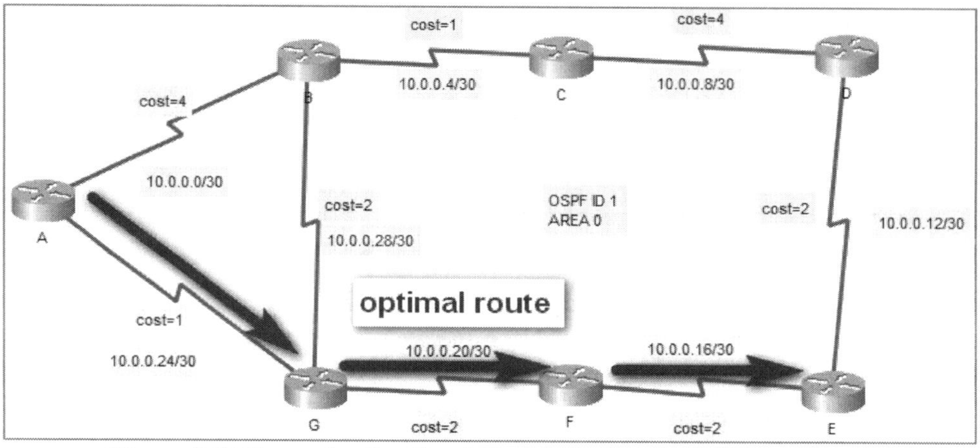

Figure 2.53 Example of optimal route selection in OSPF topology

```
A#show ip route ospf
     10.0.0.0/8 is variably subnetted, 10 subnets, 2 masks
O       10.0.0.4 [110/4] via 10.0.0.25, 00:15:51, Serial0/0/1
O       10.0.0.8 [110/8] via 10.0.0.25, 00:15:51, Serial0/0/1
O       10.0.0.12 [110/7] via 10.0.0.25, 00:15:51, Serial0/0/1
O       10.0.0.16 [110/5] via 10.0.0.25, 00:15:51, Serial0/0/1
O       10.0.0.20 [110/3] via 10.0.0.25, 00:16:01, Serial0/0/1
O       10.0.0.28 [110/3] via 10.0.0.25, 00:16:01, Serial0/0/1
```

Figure 2.54 An example OSPF routing table for router A

The operation of the **SPF** algorithm can be presented in the form of several steps;

- Stage 1 – Recognizing adjacent networks and selecting a DR router.
- Stage 2 – Database synchronization.
- Stage 3 – Creating a topology base.
- Stage 4 – Creating a routing table.

Stage 1 – Recognizing adjacent networks and selecting a DR router.

The router sends HELLO packets to establish communications with directly adjacent routers. These packets are sent by default every **10 seconds** to the multicast address **224.0.0.5** (all OSPF routers), which is specially reserved for this purpose.

Before routers can establish OSPF adjacency, both interfaces on the two routers must be part of the same network and must have the same subnet mask. Routers referred to as:

- Designated Router (DR),
- Backup Designated Router (BDR).

The designated (**root**) router (**DR**) is chosen the one with the higher ID. The ID is assigned based on the highest IP address on the interface.

The HELLO packet contains the following fields, among others:

- **DR router** - the ID of the designated router, if any,
- **BDR router** - the ID of the backup designated router, if any,
- **neighbor list** - a list of identifiers of neighboring OSPF routers..

Stage 2 – Database synchronization

Once a neighbor is established, the router that has been selected as the **DR** starts synchronizing databases. The neighboring routers send data from their database to each other, after which synchronization begins until the two databases are identical. **Link-state request (LSR)** and **link-state update (LSU)** and **link-state acknowledgement (LSack)** packets are used to synchronize the databases.

When a router receives an **LSU** packet, it sends an **LSack** acknowledgment back. When a router receives an LSA packet from a neighboring router, it immediately sends it from all its interfaces except the one on which it received the packet.

Stage 3 – Creating a topology base

The creation of a topology base is done at each router to construct a complete map of the network topology. The SPF algorithm sums the cost of each path from source to destination. The algorithm also creates an SPF tree representing the network topology.

Using the SPF tree, each router can independently determine the shortest path to each network.

Cost of sending a packet :

The cost of sending a packet in OSPF is calculated using the formula:

$$Cost = \frac{100\ 000\ 000}{Bandwidth}$$

Equation 2.7 Formula for calculating the cost

where:

Bandwidth is expressed in kbps. This value applies to the output side of each router interface. The lower the cost for a given interface, the more likely it is that the interface will be used to send data.

The cost can be configured by the system administrator with command:

```
ip ospf cost <value>
```

where:

<value> in an integer in range from 1 to 65535.

Example:

```
(config)# interface s0/0/0
(config-if)# ip ospf cost 7
```

The **cost** parameter can be set statically by the network administrator, or it can be calculated dynamically based on incoming updates on a given OSPF router interface (in this example, we are concerned with setting the cost parameter by the administrator).

Stage 4 – Creating a routing table

The SPF algorithm creates the shortest routes, which are added to the routing table. The example routing table for router A was created by the OSPF protocol. On router A, routes for subnets adjacent to router E:

- 10.0.12.0/30,
- 10.0.16.0/30.

you can see it after command: `show ip route`.

```
A#show ip route ospf
     10.0.0.0/8 is variably subnetted, 10 subnets, 2 masks
O       10.0.0.4 [110/4] via 10.0.0.25, 00:15:51, Serial0/0/1
O       10.0.0.8 [110/8] via 10.0.0.25, 00:15:51, Serial0/0/1
O       10.0.0.12 [110/7] via 10.0.0.25, 00:15:51, Serial0/0/1
O       10.0.0.16 [110/5] via 10.0.0.25, 00:15:51, Serial0/0/1
O       10.0.0.20 [110/3] via 10.0.0.25, 00:16:01, Serial0/0/1
O       10.0.0.28 [110/3] via 10.0.0.25, 00:16:01, Serial0/0/1
```

Figure 2.55 Routing table created by OSPF on router A.

2.6.4 Selection of Routers DR and BDR in OSPFV2

To reduce the amount of traffic in the OSPF protocol area, the protocol specifies a master router, the so-called designated router **DR** (designated router), and a backup designated router **BDR** (backup designated router).

The designated router is responsible for updating all other OSPF routers (called **DROthers**).

DROthers form full adjacencies with **DR** and **BDR** routers. This means that instead of sending out updates via LSA packets to all routers on the network, ***DROthers*** only sends its LSA packets to **DR** and **BDR** routers at the group address **224.0.0.6** (all **DR** routers).

General rules for selecting a Designated Router (**DR**):

- OSPF chooses router with highest priority
- if priorities are equal, OSPF selects router (in the following steps) :
- with highest router's ID (if it was configured)
- or with highest IP address of router's Loopback interforce (if configured)
- or with highest router's interface IP address

2.6.5 Configuring Protocol OSPFV2

Configuring the OSPF v2 protocol using IOS commands is very simple. It requires the use of only two commands: **router** and **network**. We assume that we are configuring an OSPF process with the number 1 (**OSPF ID = 1**) in area 0 (**area = 0**).

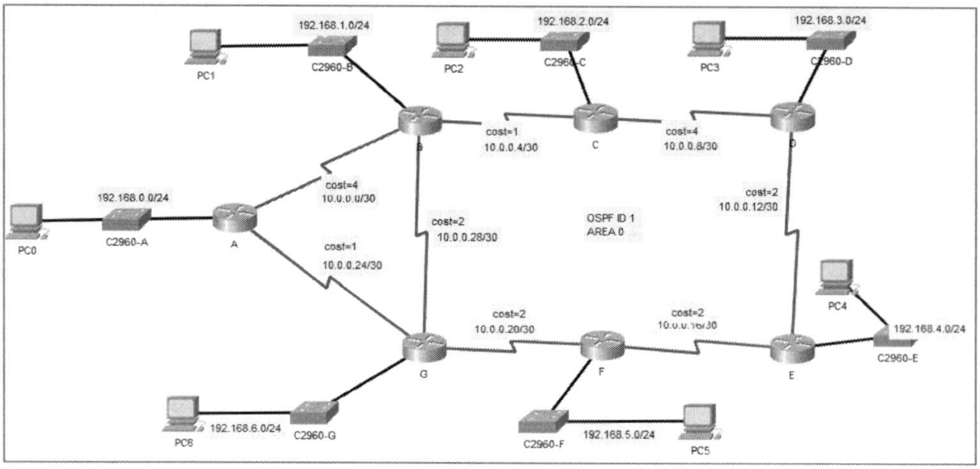

Figure 2.56 OSPF network topology

Step 1. Display of a list of subnets directly connected to the MAIN router.

Router **A** has three adjacent subnets:

- 192.168.0.0/24,
- 10.0.0.0/30,
- 10.0.0.24/30

For which blanket masks must be calculated.

Step 2. Calculating blanket masks for directly adjacent subnets

Reminder:

Wildcard mask is a string of binary zeros and ones, used to filter individual IP addresses or groups of them. The zeros indicate the bits of the IP address to be matched, and the ones indicate the bits to be ignored. For example, a blank mask of 0.0.0.3 means matching the first 30 bits of an IP address.

We calculate wildcard mask with formula:

$$\begin{array}{r} 255.255.255.255 \\ - \quad subnet\ mask \\ \hline wildcard\ mask \end{array}$$

Figure 2.57 Formula for calculating a wildcard mask.

Area	Subnet	Subnet mask	Wildcard mask
0	192.168.0.0	255.255.255.0	**0.0.0.255**
0	10.0.0.0	255.255.255.252	**0.0.0.3**
0	10.0.0.24	255.255.255.252	**0.0.0.3**

Table 2.13 Wildcard masks for subnets adjacent to router A.

Accordingly, for all other routers, we apply the above formula.

Step 3. Add subnets directly adjacent to the OSPF protocol

We move to the global configuration mode of the router and execute the command (for ***OSPF process ID** = **1***)

```
router ospf 1
```

```
A>
A>en
A#conf t
Enter configuration commands, one per line.  End with CNTL/Z.
A(config)#router ospf 1
A(config-router)#
```

Figure 2.58 Configuration mode of routing OSPF.

We are in OSPF routing configuration mode: **`(config-router)#`** .

We can now add the addresses of subnets adjacent to router A. We execute the following commands:

```
network 192.168.0.0 0.0.0.255 area 0
network 10.0.0.0 0.0.0.3 area 0
network 10.0.0.24 0.0.0.3 area 0
```

```
A(config-router)#network 192.168.0.0 0.0.0.255 area 0
A(config-router)#network 10.0.0.0 0.0.0.3 area 0
A(config-router)#network 10.0.0.24 0.0.0.3 area 0
A(config-router)#
```

Figure 2.59 Adding adjacent subnets in OSPF routing configuration mode.

OSPF configuration command syntax:

```
router ospf < process_id_OSPF>
network <adjacent_network_address> <blanket_mask >
<area_no.>
network <adjacent_network_address> <blanket_mask >
<area_no.>
```

network <adjacent_network_address> <blanket_mask > <area_no.>

Repeat the above configuration scheme for each router.

2.6.6 Display Existing OSPF Routes in the Routing Table

To display the current routes in the table obtained using OSPF routing, we will run the command **show ip route ospf** . Routes resulting from OSPF routing are denoted by the symbol **O**.

```
A#show ip route ospf
     10.0.0.0/8 is variably subnetted, 10 subnets, 2 masks
O       10.0.0.4 [110/4] via 10.0.0.25, 00:09:39, Serial0/0/1
O       10.0.0.8 [110/8] via 10.0.0.25, 00:09:39, Serial0/0/1
O       10.0.0.12 [110/7] via 10.0.0.25, 00:09:29, Serial0/0/1
O       10.0.0.16 [110/5] via 10.0.0.25, 00:09:29, Serial0/0/1
O       10.0.0.20 [110/3] via 10.0.0.25, 00:09:39, Serial0/0/1
O       10.0.0.28 [110/3] via 10.0.0.25, 00:09:39, Serial0/0/1
O    192.168.1.0 [110/4] via 10.0.0.25, 00:09:39, Serial0/0/1
O    192.168.2.0 [110/104] via 10.0.0.25, 00:09:39, Serial0/0/1
O    192.168.3.0 [110/8] via 10.0.0.25, 00:09:29, Serial0/0/1
O    192.168.4.0 [110/105] via 10.0.0.25, 00:09:29, Serial0/0/1
O    192.168.5.0 [110/103] via 10.0.0.25, 00:09:29, Serial0/0/1
O    192.168.6.0 [110/101] via 10.0.0.25, 00:09:39, Serial0/0/1
```

Figure 2.60 Updated O routes in router A.

2.6.7 Route Distributions between Different Protocols

Why are we using routing routes distributions?

Causes:

- we use different routing protocols in our networks,
- different routing protocols are not designed to work with each other,
- each protocol collects different types of information and reacts differently to topology changes.

The exchange of route information between different routing protocols is called **route redistribution.**

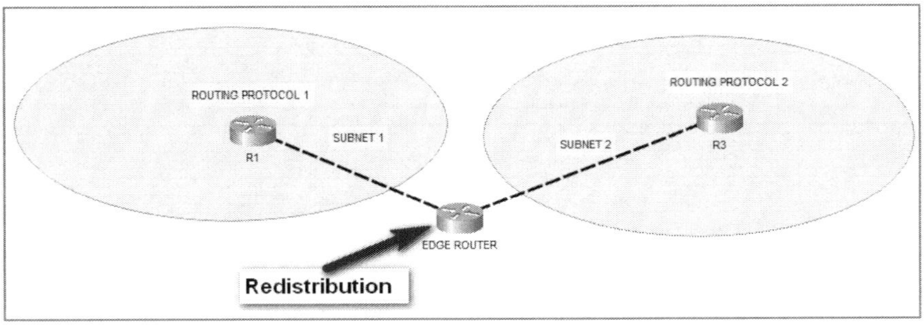

Figure 2.61 Route redistribution between different routing protocols

- PROTOCOL 1 – routing protocol in network on the left (R1)
- SUBNET 1 – subnet adjacent to the edge router
- SUBNET 2 – subnet adjacent to the edge router
- PROTOCOL 2 – routing protocol in network on the right (R3)
- EDGE ROUTER – router, it acts redistribution

To ensure communication between different routing protocols (so-called two-way redistribution):

- we specify which edge router will act as a proxy router,
- in EDGE ROUTER we need to configure both PROTOCOL1 and PROTOCOL2 protocols:
- i.e. in PROTOCOL1 we add the SUBNET1 subnet,
- i.e. in PROTOCOL2 we add the SUBNET2 subnet.
- to the PROTOCOL1 protocol configuration we add a command to redistribute (propagate routes) obtained via the PROTOCOL2 protocol
- to the PROTOCOL2 protocol configuration you add a command to redistribute (unbundle) the routes obtained via PROTOCOL1

2.6.8 Route Distributions between RIPV2 and OSPF Protocols

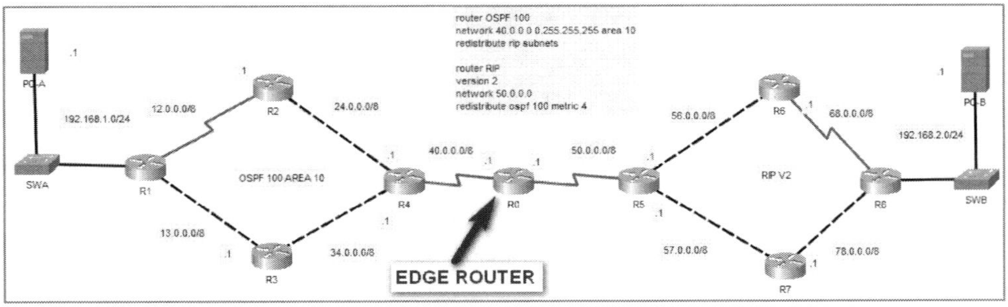

Figure 2.62 Route redistribution between OSPF and RIPv2 protocols

Command for OSPF protocol

`redistribute rip subnets` – broadcasting (also known as route injection) of routes derived from the RIP protocol (classless mask)

Command for RIP protocol

`redistribute ospf ID_PROCESS metric N` – broadcast (also referred to as route injection) of routes derived from the OSPF protocol with process number PROCESS_ID

If you have a maximum of N skips in the RIP network, then use the metric N-1.

For example:

```
router OSPF 100
network 40.0.0.0 0.255.255.255 area 10
redistribute rip subnets

router RIP
version 2
network 50.0.0.0
redistribute ospf 100 metric 4
```

2.6.9 Route Distributions between OSPF protocols with different process ID

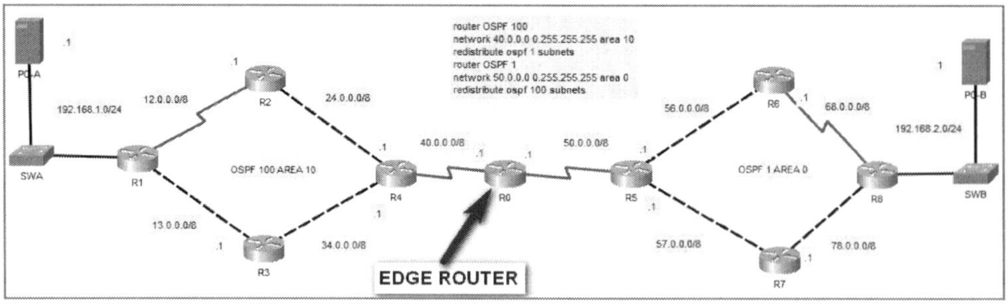

Figure 2.63 Route redistribution between OSPF protocols with different process ID

Command for OSPF protocol:

`redistribute ospf PROCESS_ID subnets` – broadcast (also referred to as route injection) of routes obtained from the OSPF protocol with a process number: PROCESS_ID

For example:

```
router OSPF 100
network 40.0.0.0 0.255.255.255 area 10
redistribute ospf 1 subnets

router OSPF 1
network 50.0.0.0 0.255.255.255 area 0
redistribute ospf 100 subnets
```

2.7 BGPV4 Protocol

2.7.1 Introduction to BGPv4

BGP v4 (*Border Gateway Protocol*) is a protocol belonging to the EGP (Exterior Gateway Protocols) class of protocols. The main task of the BGP protocol is the exchange of network information between autonomous systems (the creation of routes between autonomous systems that will not contain loops and the exchange of information about network topology changes between the edge routers of autonomous systems).

An Autonomous System (AS) is a collection of networks under common administration and using the same routing rules.

BGP v4 is a path-vector protocol. It implements dynamic routing between multiple autonomous systems (domains). Routers create so-called BGP sessions that allow them to exchange routing information, which in turn allows them to determine the optimal route to the destination networks.

There are two types of BGP session in BGP protocol:

- **iBGP** (*Internal BGP*) – creates and operates internal routes in the AS autonomous system (intra-domain routing),
- **eBGP** (*External BGP*) – creates and operates external routes between autonomous systems (domain-to-domain routing).

The BGP protocol is defined in documents: RFC 1771, RFC 4271 as an open standard. The default administrative distance for **eBGP** external routes is **20**, while for **iBGP** internal routes it is **200**.

To select the best route, the BGP v4 protocol uses advanced algorithms that make use of various attributes and properties of the available routes. The algorithms for the BGP protocol will not be described in this book. The main features of the GBP v4 protocol are:

- supports variable mask addressing techniques (VLSM),
- path-vector type protocol,
- the protocol works over TCP on port 179,
- any change in the network causes an update message to be sent,
- the full routing table is only exchanged between routers during the initial BGP session.

2.7.2 Basic IOS Commands Configuring eBGPv4

This chapter introduces the basic commands that configure the **eBGP** protocol on routers in Packet Tracer.

Note: Packet Tracer program supports eBGP protocol only.

`interface Loopback<no.>`

`ip address <loopback_address> <loopback_mask>` – configuring the loopback interface of the BGP router specifying the BGP router ID.

`router bgp <autonomic_system_no.>` – move to the configuration of the stand-alone system.

`bgp router-id <IP_address>` – manually configuring the BGP router ID in IP address format (four octets separated by a dot).

`network <adjacent_network> mask <network_mask>` –configuring the adjacent network.

`Neighbor <neighbor_router_address> remote-as <neighbor_system_address>` – configuring a router-neighbor belonging to another autonomous system.

`show ip bgp summary` – display of status and information about the BGP protocol.

2.7.3 Configuring protocol eBGPv4

Step 1. Configuring IP addresses for devices

We configure the devices based on the **eBGP** topology, which contains four autonomous systems: **AS 4, AS 5, AS 6, AS 7**. We will first set the addresses of the devices according to the data shown in the addressing table.

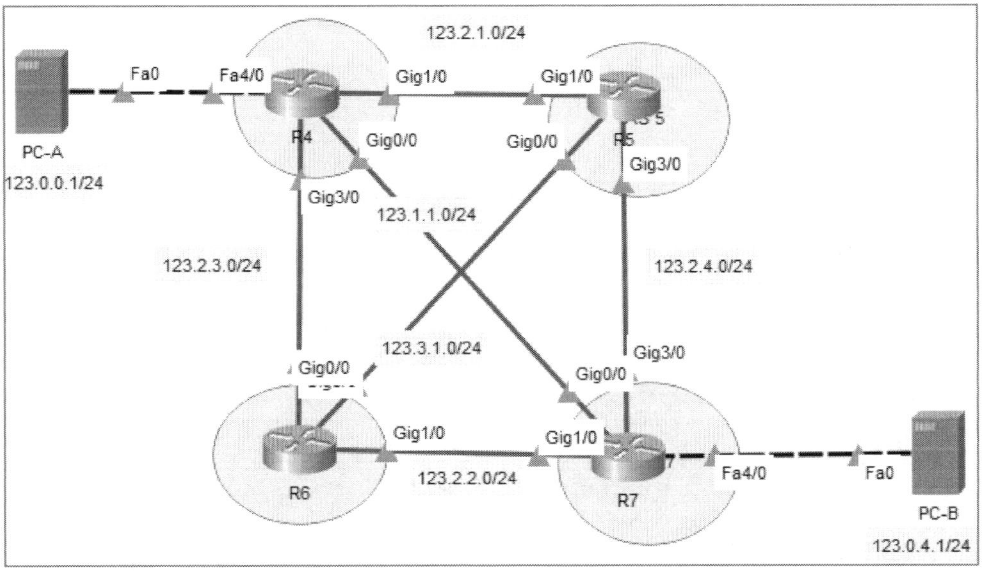

Figure 2.64 eBGP network topology consisting of four autonomous networks.

AS – autonomous system number.

Device Interface	Subnet	Subnet mask	Default gateway	AS
PC-A Fa0	123.0.0.1	255.255.255.0	123.0.0.2	4
PC-B Fa0	123.0.4.1	255.255.255.0	123.0.4.2	7
R4 Loopback4	4.4.4.4	255.255.255.0	Does not apply	4
R4 Fa4/0	123.0.0.2	255.255.255.0	Does not apply	4
R4 Gi0/0	123.1.1.1	255.255.255.0	Does not apply	4
R4 Gi1/0	123.2.1.1	255.255.255.0	Does not apply	4
R4 Gi3/0	123.2.3.1	255.255.255.0	Does not apply	4
R5 Loopback5	5.5.5.5	255.255.255.0	Does not apply	5
R5 Gi0/0	123.3.1.1	255.255.255.0	Does not apply	5
R5 Gi1/0	123.2.1.2	255.255.255.0	Does not apply	5
R5 Gi3/0	123.2.4.1	255.255.255.0	Does not apply	5
R6 Loopback6	6.6.6.6	255.255.255.0	Does not apply	6
R6 Gi0/0	123.3.1.2	255.255.255.0	Does not apply	6

R6 Gi1/0	123.2.2.1	255.255.255.0	Does not apply	6
R6 Gi3/0	123.2.3.2	255.255.255.0	Does not apply	6
R7 Loopback7	7.7.7.7	255.255.255.0	Does not apply	7
R7 Fa4/0	123.0.4.2	255.255.255.0	Does not apply	7
R7 Gi0/0	123.1.1.2	255.255.255.0	Does not apply	7
R7 Gi1/0	123.2.2.2	255.255.255.0	Does not apply	7
R7 Gi3/0	123.2.4.2	255.255.255.0	Does not apply	7

Table 2.14 Addressing devices scheme.

Step 2. Configuring autonomous systems.

To configure autonomous systems in **eBGP** topology we execute command:

for system AS 4:

```
enable
configure terminal
interface Loopback4
ip address 4.4.4.4 255.255.255.0
router bgp 4
neighbor 123.2.1.2 remote-as 5
neighbor 123.2.3.2 remote-as 6
neighbor 123.1.1.2 remote-as 7
network 4.4.4.0 mask 255.255.255.0
network 123.0.0.0 mask 255.255.255.0
network 123.1.1.0 mask 255.255.255.0
network 123.2.1.0 mask 255.255.255.0
network 123.2.3.0 mask 255.255.255.0
```

for system AS 5:

```
enable
configure terminal
interface Loopback5
ip address 5.5.5.5 255.255.255.0
router bgp 5
neighbor 123.2.1.1 remote-as 4
neighbor 123.3.1.2 remote-as 6
neighbor 123.2.4.2 remote-as 7
```

```
network 5.5.5.0 mask 255.255.255.0
network 123.2.1.0 mask 255.255.255.0
network 123.2.4.0 mask 255.255.255.0
network 123.3.1.0 mask 255.255.255.0
```

for system AS 6:

```
enable
configure terminal
interface Loopback6
ip address 6.6.6.6 255.255.255.0
router bgp 6
neighbor 123.2.3.1 remote-as 4
neighbor 123.3.1.1 remote-as 5
neighbor 123.2.2.2 remote-as 7
network 6.6.6.0 mask 255.255.255.0
network 123.2.2.0 mask 255.255.255.0
network 123.2.3.0 mask 255.255.255.0
network 123.3.1.0 mask 255.255.255.0
```

for system AS 7:

```
enable
configure terminal
interface Loopback7
ip address 7.7.7.7 255.255.255.0
router bgp 7
neighbor 123.1.1.1 remote-as 4
neighbor 123.2.4.1 remote-as 5
neighbor 123.2.2.1 remote-as 6
network 7.7.7.0 mask 255.255.255.0
network 123.0.4.0 mask 255.255.255.0
network 123.1.1.0 mask 255.255.255.0
network 123.2.2.0 mask 255.255.255.0
network 123.2.4.0 mask 255.255.255.0
```

Step 3. Checking routing tables.

To check the routes obtained in the **eBGP** topology, we can display the routing tables located in the individual routers - to do this, we execute the command

```
show ip route bgp
```

on each router:

```
R4#show ip route bgp
B     5.5.5.0 [20/0] via 123.2.1.2, 00:00:00
B     6.6.6.0 [20/0] via 123.2.3.2, 00:00:00
B     7.7.7.0 [20/0] via 123.1.1.2, 00:00:00
B     123.0.4.0 [20/0] via 123.1.1.2, 00:00:00
B     123.2.2.0 [20/0] via 123.2.3.2, 00:00:00
B     123.2.4.0 [20/0] via 123.1.1.2, 00:00:00
B     123.3.1.0 [20/0] via 123.2.3.2, 00:00:00
```

Figure 2.65 Result of command `show ip route bgp` on router R4.

```
R5#show ip route bgp
B     4.4.4.0 [20/0] via 123.2.1.1, 00:00:00
B     6.6.6.0 [20/0] via 123.3.1.2, 00:00:00
B     7.7.7.0 [20/0] via 123.2.4.2, 00:00:00
B     123.0.0.0 [20/0] via 123.2.1.1, 00:00:00
B     123.0.4.0 [20/0] via 123.2.4.2, 00:00:00
B     123.1.1.0 [20/0] via 123.2.4.2, 00:00:00
B     123.2.2.0 [20/0] via 123.3.1.2, 00:00:00
B     123.2.3.0 [20/0] via 123.3.1.2, 00:00:00
```

Figure 2.66 Result of command `show ip route bgp` on router R5.

```
R6#show ip route bgp
B     4.4.4.0 [20/0] via 123.2.3.1, 00:00:00
B     5.5.5.0 [20/0] via 123.3.1.1, 00:00:00
B     7.7.7.0 [20/0] via 123.2.2.2, 00:00:00
B     123.0.0.0 [20/0] via 123.2.3.1, 00:00:00
B     123.0.4.0 [20/0] via 123.2.2.2, 00:00:00
B     123.1.1.0 [20/0] via 123.2.2.2, 00:00:00
B     123.2.1.0 [20/0] via 123.2.3.1, 00:00:00
B     123.2.4.0 [20/0] via 123.2.2.2, 00:00:00
```

Figure 2.67 Result of command `show ip route bgp` on router R6.

```
R7#show ip route bgp
B     4.4.4.0 [20/0] via 123.2.4.1, 00:00:00
B     5.5.5.0 [20/0] via 123.2.4.1, 00:00:00
B     6.6.6.0 [20/0] via 123.2.2.1, 00:00:00
B     123.0.0.0 [20/0] via 123.2.4.1, 00:00:00
B     123.2.1.0 [20/0] via 123.2.4.1, 00:00:00
B     123.2.3.0 [20/0] via 123.2.2.1, 00:00:00
B     123.3.1.0 [20/0] via 123.2.2.1, 00:00:00
```

Figure 2.68 Result of command `show ip route bgp`.

CHAPTER 3

STATIC ROUTING

3 STATIC ROUTING

This chapter describes the basic concepts for creating static routes.

3.1 Introduction to Static Routing

Static routing is used to introduce fixed routes, i.e. routes that do not change over a longer period of time. Most often, the static protocol creates a default route to the ISP's router (to the so-called residual network).

Advantages of static routes:

- all routes are well known,
- low use of router memory and processing power,
- fastest convergence time in the network,
- low administrative distance value is used (1),
- higher security - greater resistance to attacks,
- no advanced administrator knowledge is required for configuration.

Disadvantages of static routes:

- static routing is not scalable,
- for a large network requires a lot of operations from the administrator,
- very prone to administrators' errors,
- does not support networks with redundant topology,
- for large networks is inefficient and complex,
- not adaptable to changing networks.

3.2 Basic Concepts of Static Routing

Destination network – the subnet to which packets are routed based on information in the routing table.

Stub network – a subnetwork that has only one path to the external network, reachable via an intermediary device such as an edge router.

Stub router – an edge router through which there is only one route to the external (backbone) network adjacent to it.

Default route is the route the router will choose if it doesn't find a route in the routing table that matches the destination network address.

3.3 Static Routes Configuration Types

To manually configure a static route, we need to use the command: `ip route`. The parameters of this command are: **the address of the network**, including **the mask**, and information about **where the router should send packets** destined for this network.

This information can have one of the forms:

- the specific IP address of the next router along the route, i.e. the address of the next hop to the gateway to which the packets should be forwarded.

or

- directly connected output interface in the router

We can distinguish between two types of static route configuration:

- configuration via next hop address,
- configuration via output interface.

The syntax of the command configuring the static route (**for the next hop address**) is as follows:

```
ip route <destination_network> <network_mask>
<next_hop_address>
```

The syntax of the command configuring the static route (**for the output interface**) is as follows:

```
ip route <destination_network> <network_mask>
<output_interface_name>
```

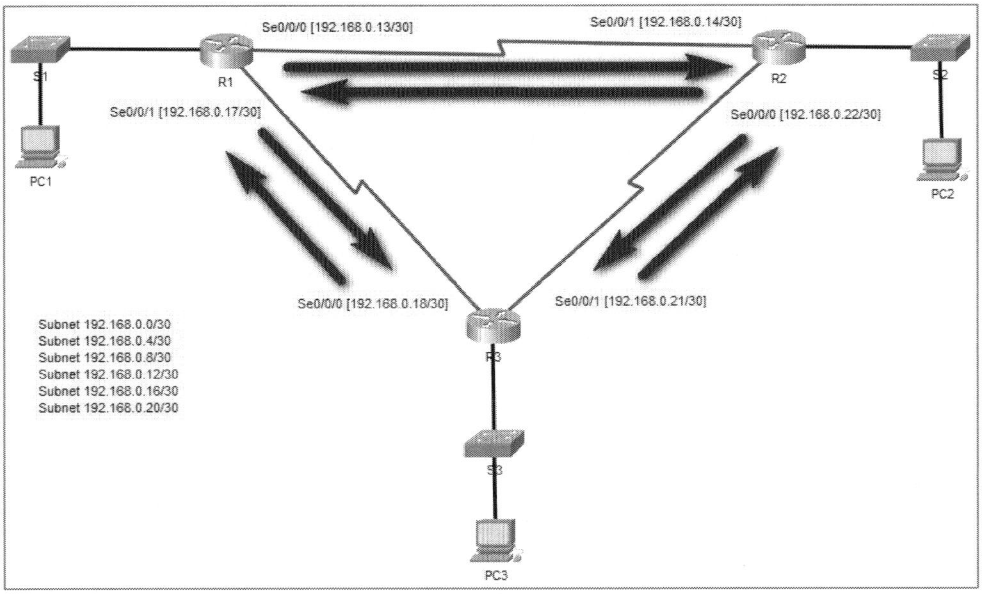

Figure 3.1 Network topology for static routing.

3.4 Configuring Routes Using Next Hop Address

Step 1. We configure device interfaces.

We configure the devices according to the data given in the addressing table.

Device Interface	Subnet	Subnet mask	Default gateway
PC1 Fa0	192.168.0.1	255.255.255.252	192.168.0.2
PC2 Fa0	192.168.0.9	255.255.255.252	192.168.0.10
PC3 Fa0	192.168.0.5	255.255.255.252	192.168.0.6
R1 Fa0/0	192.168.0.2	255.255.255.252	Does not apply
R1 Se0/0/0	192.168.0.13	255.255.255.252	Does not apply
R1 Se0/0/1	192.168.0.17	255.255.255.252	Does not apply
R2 Fa0/0	192.168.0.10	255.255.255.252	Does not apply
R2 Se0/0/0	192.168.0.22	255.255.255.252	Does not apply

R2 Se0/0/1	192.168.0.14	255.255.255.252	Does not apply
R3 Fa0/0	192.168.0.6	255.255.255.252	Does not apply
R3 Se0/0/0	192.168.0.18	255.255.255.252	Does not apply
R3 Se0/0/1	192.168.0.21	255.255.255.252	Does not apply

Table 3.1 Addressing devices table.

Step 2. We configure static routes using the next hop address.

We configure routes on each router for all remote LAN subnets.

Router R1:

Target network	Subnet mask	Next hop address
192.168.0.4	255.255.255.252	192.168.0.18 in router R3
192.168.0.8	255.255.255.252	192.168.0.14 in router R2

Table 3.2 Static routes in R1.

On router R1 we execute the following commands:

```
enable
configure terminal
ip route 192.168.0.4 255.255.255.252 192.168.0.18
ip route 192.168.0.8 255.255.255.252 192.168.0.14
```

Router R2:

Target network	Subnet mask	Next hop address
192.168.0.0	255.255.255.252	192.168.0.13 in router R1
192.168.0.4	255.255.255.252	192.168.0.21 in router R3

Table 3.3 State routes in R2.

On router R2 we execute the following commands:

```
enable
```

```
configure terminal
ip route 192.168.0.0 255.255.255.252 192.168.0.13
ip route 192.168.0.4 255.255.255.252 192.168.0.21
```

Router R3:

Target network	**Subnet mask**	**Next hop address**
192.168.0.0	255.255.255.252	192.168.0.17 in router R1
192.168.0.8	255.255.255.252	192.168.0.22 in router R2

Table3.4 Static routes in R3.

On router R3 we execute the following commands:

```
enable
configure terminal
ip route 192.168.0.0 255.255.255.252 192.168.0.17
ip route 192.168.0.8 255.255.255.252 192.168.0.22
```

Step 3. Checking communication between LAN sub-networks

We use the ping command to check communication between computers located on remote LAN subnets.

```
PC>
PC>ping 192.168.0.9

Pinging 192.168.0.9 with 32 bytes of data:

Reply from 192.168.0.9: bytes=32 time=1ms TTL=126
Reply from 192.168.0.9: bytes=32 time=1ms TTL=126
Reply from 192.168.0.9: bytes=32 time=1ms TTL=126
Reply from 192.168.0.9: bytes=32 time=1ms TTL=126

Ping statistics for 192.168.0.9:
    Packets: Sent = 4, Received = 4, Lost = 0 (0% loss),
Approximate round trip times in milli-seconds:
    Minimum = 1ms, Maximum = 1ms, Average = 1ms
```

Figure 3.2 Example of the result of a ping command from PC1 to PC2.

Step 4. We check the routing tables in the routers for correctness

Using command **`show ip route`** we check the state of the routing tables in the routers and compare them with the configuration data found in step 2.

```
C       192.168.0.0 is directly connected, FastEthernet0/0
S       192.168.0.4 [1/0] via 192.168.0.18
S       192.168.0.8 [1/0] via 192.168.0.14
C       192.168.0.12 is directly connected, Serial0/0/0
C       192.168.0.16 is directly connected, Serial0/0/1
```

Figure 3.3 Example of routing table in R1.

```
S       192.168.0.0 [1/0] via 192.168.0.13
S       192.168.0.4 [1/0] via 192.168.0.21
C       192.168.0.8 is directly connected, FastEthernet0/0
C       192.168.0.12 is directly connected, Serial0/0/1
C       192.168.0.20 is directly connected, Serial0/0/0
```

Figure 3.4 Example of routing table in R2 .

```
S       192.168.0.0 [1/0] via 192.168.0.17
C       192.168.0.4 is directly connected, FastEthernet0/0
S       192.168.0.8 [1/0] via 192.168.0.22
C       192.168.0.16 is directly connected, Serial0/0/0
C       192.168.0.20 is directly connected, Serial0/0/1
```

Figure 3.5 Example of routing table in R3.

3.5 Configuring Routes Using the Output Interface

Step 1. We configure device interfaces:

We configure the devices according to the data given in the addressing table in the previous section.

Stop 2. We configure the static routes using output interface.

We configure routes on each router for all remote LAN subnets.

Router R1:

Target network	Subnet mask	Output interface
192.168.0.4	255.255.255.252	Se0/0/0
192.168.0.8	255.255.255.252	Se0/0/1

Table 3.5 Static routes in R1.

On router Rl we execute the following commands:

```
enable
configure terminal
ip route 192.168.0.4 255.255.255.252 Se0/0/0
ip route 192.168.0.8 255.255.255.252 Se0/0/1
```

Router R2:

Target network	Subnet mask	Output interface
192.168.0.0	255.255.255.252	Se0/0/1
192.168.0.4	255.255.255.252	Se0/0/0

Table 3.6 Static routes in R2.

On router R2 we execute the following commands:

```
enable
configure terminal
ip route 192.168.0.0 255.255.255.252 Se0/0/1
ip route 192.168.0.4 255.255.255.252 Se0/0/0
```

Router R3:

Target network	Subnet mask	Output interface
192.168.0.0	255.255.255.252	Se0/0/0
192.168.0.8	255.255.255.252	Se0/0/1

Table 3.7 Static routes in R3.

On router R3 we execute the following commands:

```
enable
configure terminal
ip route 192.168.0.0 255.255.255.252 Se0/0/0
ip route 192.168.0.8 255.255.255.252 Se0/0/1
```

Step 3. We check the communication between LAN subnets:

Using the ping command to check communication between computers located on remote LAN subnets.

```
PC>
PC>ping 192.168.0.9

Pinging 192.168.0.9 with 32 bytes of data:

Reply from 192.168.0.9: bytes=32 time=2ms TTL=126
Reply from 192.168.0.9: bytes=32 time=1ms TTL=126
Reply from 192.168.0.9: bytes=32 time=1ms TTL=126
Reply from 192.168.0.9: bytes=32 time=1ms TTL=126

Ping statistics for 192.168.0.9:
    Packets: Sent = 4, Received = 4, Lost = 0 (0% loss),
Approximate round trip times in milli-seconds:
    Minimum = 1ms, Maximum = 2ms, Average = 1ms
```

Figure3.6 Example result of ping command from PC3 to PC2.

Stop 4. We check the correctness of routing tables in routers:

Using command **`show ip route`** we check the state of the routing tables in the routers and compare them with the configuration data found in step 2.

```
C        192.168.0.0 is directly connected, FastEthernet0/0
S        192.168.0.4 is directly connected, Serial0/0/0
S        192.168.0.8 is directly connected, Serial0/0/1
C        192.168.0.12 is directly connected, Serial0/0/0
C        192.168.0.16 is directly connected, Serial0/0/1
```

Figure 3.7 Example of routing table in R1.

```
S        192.168.0.0 is directly connected, Serial0/0/1
S        192.168.0.4 is directly connected, Serial0/0/0
C        192.168.0.8 is directly connected, FastEthernet0/0
C        192.168.0.12 is directly connected, Serial0/0/1
C        192.168.0.20 is directly connected, Serial0/0/0
```

Figure 3.8 Example of routing table in R2.

```
S        192.168.0.0 is directly connected, Serial0/0/0
C        192.168.0.4 is directly connected, FastEthernet0/0
S        192.168.0.8 is directly connected, Serial0/0/1
C        192.168.0.16 is directly connected, Serial0/0/0
C        192.168.0.20 is directly connected, Serial0/0/1
```

Figure 3.9 Example of routing table in R3.

3.6 Configuring Multiple Static Routes

Step 1. We create a network topology for static routing

We create the network topology according to the figure.

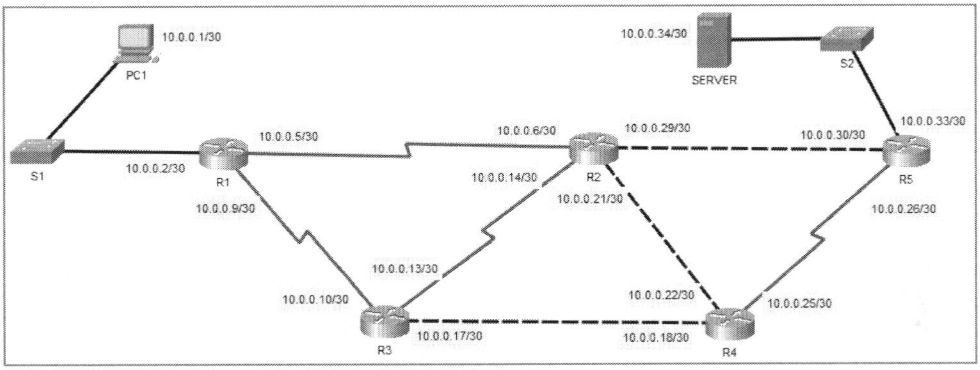

Figure 3.10 Network topology for static routing.

Step 2. We configure device interfaces.

We configure the devices according to the data given in the addressing table.

Device Interface	Subnet	Subnet mask	Default gateway
PC1 Fa0	10.0.0.1	255.255.255.252	10.0.0.2
SERWER Fa0	10.0.0.34	255.255.255.252	10.0.0.33
R1 Fa0/0	10.0.0.2	255.255.255.252	Does not apply
R1 Se0/0/0	10.0.0.5	255.255.255.252	Does not apply
R1 Se0/0/1	10.0.0.9	255.255.255.252	Does not apply
R2 Fa0/0	10.0.0.21	255.255.255.252	Does not apply
R2 Fa0/1	10.0.0.29	255.255.255.252	Does not apply
R2 Se0/0/0	10.0.0.14	255.255.255.252	Does not apply
R2 Se0/0/1	10.0.0.6	255.255.255.252	Does not apply
R3 Fa0/0	10.0.0.17	255.255.255.252	Does not apply

R3 Se0/0/0	10.0.0.10	255.255.255.252	Does not apply
R3 Se0/0/1	10.0.0.13	255.255.255.252	Does not apply
R4 Fa0/0	10.0.0.18	255.255.255.252	Does not apply
R4 Fa0/1	10.0.0.22	255.255.255.252	Does not apply
R4 Se0/0/0	10.0.0.25	255.255.255.252	Does not apply
R5 Fa0/0	10.0.0.33	255.255.255.252	Does not apply
R5 Fa0/1	10.0.0.30	255.255.255.252	Does not apply
R5 Se0/0/0	10.0.0.26	255.255.255.252	Does not apply

Table 3.8 Devices addressing table.

Step 3. We configure static routes to all subnets

We configure static routes on router R1 (**in global configuration mode**) to all remote LAN subnets and inter-router subnets. We select routes that lead to the destination network using the least number of hops:

```
R1(config)#
R1(config)#ip route    10.0.0.12    255.255.255.252    10.0.0.10
R1(config)#ip route    10.0.0.16    255.255.255.252    10.0.0.10
R1(config)#ip route    10.0.0.20    255.255.255.252    10.0.0.6
R1(config)#ip route    10.0.0.24    255.255.255.252    10.0.0.6
R1(config)#ip route    10.0.0.28    255.255.255.252    10.0.0.6
R1(config)#ip route    10.0.0.32    255.255.255.252    10.0.0.6
R1(config)#
```

Figure 3.11 Configuring static routes on router R1.

We configure static routes on the R2 router (**in global configuration mode**) to all remote LAN subnets and inter-router subnets. We select routes that lead to the destination network using the least number of hops:

```
R2(config)#
R2(config)#ip route    10.0.0.0    255.255.255.252    10.0.0.5
R2(config)#ip route    10.0.0.8    255.255.255.252    10.0.0.13
R2(config)#ip route    10.0.0.16   255.255.255.252    10.0.0.13
R2(config)#ip route    10.0.0.24   255.255.255.252    10.0.0.22
R2(config)#ip route    10.0.0.32   255.255.255.252    10.0.0.30
R2(config)#
```

Figure 3.12 Configuring static routes on routerR2.

We configure static routes on the R3 router (**in global configuration mode**) to all remote LAN subnets and inter-router subnets. We select routes that lead to the destination network using the least number of hops:

```
R3(config)#
R3(config)#ip route   10.0.0.0    255.255.255.252    10.0.0.9
R3(config)#ip route   10.0.0.4    255.255.255.252    10.0.0.9
R3(config)#ip route   10.0.0.20   255.255.255.252    10.0.0.18
R3(config)#ip route   10.0.0.24   255.255.255.252    10.0.0.18
R3(config)#ip route   10.0.0.28   255.255.255.252    10.0.0.14
R3(config)#ip route   10.0.0.32   255.255.255.252    10.0.0.14
R3(config)#
```

Figure 3.13 Configuring static routes on router R3.

We configure static routes on router R4 (**in global configuration mode**) to all remote LAN subnets and inter-router subnets. We select routes that lead to the destination network using the least number of hops:

```
R4(config)#
R4(config)#ip route   10.0.0.0    255.255.255.252    10.0.0.17
R4(config)#ip route   10.0.0.4    255.255.255.252    10.0.0.21
R4(config)#ip route   10.0.0.8    255.255.255.252    10.0.0.17
R4(config)#ip route   10.0.0.12   255.255.255.252    10.0.0.17
R4(config)#ip route   10.0.0.28   255.255.255.252    10.0.0.21
R4(config)#ip route   10.0.0.32   255.255.255.252    10.0.0.26
R4(config)#
```

Figure 3.14 Configuring static routes on router R4.

We configure static routes on the R5 router (**in global configuration mode**) to all remote LAN subnets and inter-router subnets. We select routes that lead to the destination network using the least number of hops:

```
R5(config)#
R5(config)#ip route   10.0.0.0    255.255.255.252    10.0.0.29
R5(config)#ip route   10.0.0.4    255.255.255.252    10.0.0.29
R5(config)#ip route   10.0.0.8    255.255.255.252    10.0.0.29
R5(config)#ip route   10.0.0.12   255.255.255.252    10.0.0.29
R5(config)#ip route   10.0.0.16   255.255.255.252    10.0.0.25
R5(config)#ip route   10.0.0.20   255.255.255.252    10.0.0.25
R5(config)#
```

Figure 3.15 Configuring static routes on router R5.

Step 4. Checking routing tables in routers for correctness (static routes)

Using command **`show ip route static`** we check the state of the static routing tables.

```
R1#show ip route static
     10.0.0.0/30 is subnetted, 9 subnets
S       10.0.0.12 [1/0] via 10.0.0.10
S       10.0.0.16 [1/0] via 10.0.0.10
S       10.0.0.20 [1/0] via 10.0.0.6
S       10.0.0.24 [1/0] via 10.0.0.6
S       10.0.0.28 [1/0] via 10.0.0.6
S       10.0.0.32 [1/0] via 10.0.0.6
```

Figure 3.16 Static routes in routing table on router R1.

```
R2#show ip route static
     10.0.0.0/30 is subnetted, 9 subnets
S       10.0.0.0 [1/0] via 10.0.0.5
S       10.0.0.8 [1/0] via 10.0.0.13
S       10.0.0.16 [1/0] via 10.0.0.13
S       10.0.0.24 [1/0] via 10.0.0.22
S       10.0.0.32 [1/0] via 10.0.0.30
```

Figure 3.17 Static routes in routing table on router R2.

```
R3#show ip route static
     10.0.0.0/30 is subnetted, 9 subnets
S       10.0.0.0 [1/0] via 10.0.0.9
S       10.0.0.4 [1/0] via 10.0.0.9
S       10.0.0.20 [1/0] via 10.0.0.18
S       10.0.0.24 [1/0] via 10.0.0.18
S       10.0.0.28 [1/0] via 10.0.0.14
S       10.0.0.32 [1/0] via 10.0.0.14
```

Figure 3.18 Static routes in routing table on router R3.

```
R4#show ip route static
     10.0.0.0/30 is subnetted, 9 subnets
S       10.0.0.0 [1/0] via 10.0.0.17
S       10.0.0.4 [1/0] via 10.0.0.21
S       10.0.0.8 [1/0] via 10.0.0.17
S       10.0.0.12 [1/0] via 10.0.0.17
S       10.0.0.28 [1/0] via 10.0.0.21
S       10.0.0.32 [1/0] via 10.0.0.26
```

Figure 3.19 Static routes in routing table on router R4.

```
R5#show ip route static
     10.0.0.0/30 is subnetted, 9 subnets
S       10.0.0.0 [1/0] via 10.0.0.29
S       10.0.0.4 [1/0] via 10.0.0.29
S       10.0.0.8 [1/0] via 10.0.0.29
S       10.0.0.12 [1/0] via 10.0.0.29
S       10.0.0.16 [1/0] via 10.0.0.25
S       10.0.0.20 [1/0] via 10.0.0.25
```

Figure 3.20 Static routes in routing table on router R5.

Step 5. Checking static from co computer to server

Using command **`tracert`** we check the path of the packets from **PC1** to the **SERVER** computer.

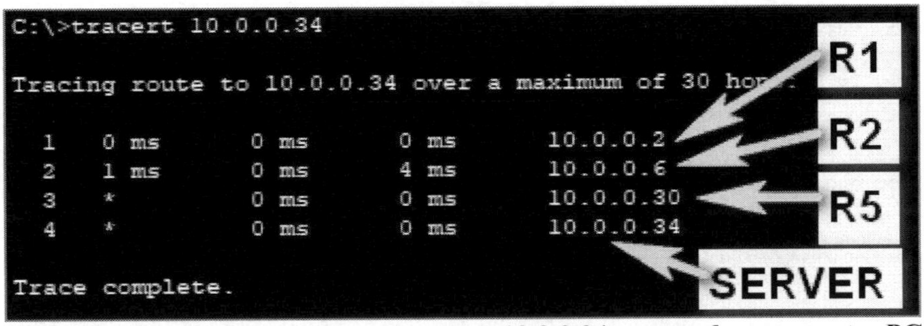

Figure 3.21 Result of the command tracert 10.0.0.34 executed on computer PC1.

The route by which the packet is transmitted from **PC1** to **SERVER** is via routers:

- R1,
- R2,
- R5.

3.7 Configuring Backup Routes

Suppose there is a link failure between router R1 and router R2 on the route from **PC1** to **SERVER**.

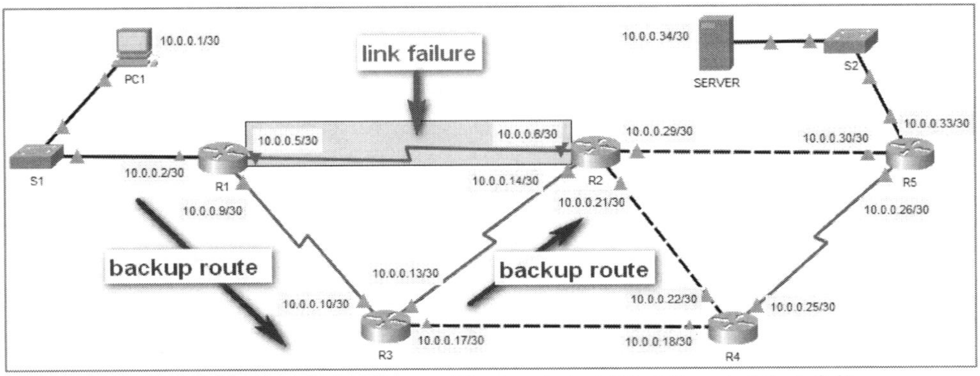

Figure 3.22 Network topology with simulated R1-R2 serial link failure.

To ensure that packets sent by PC1, can take the route via R1-R3-R2, we add two static backup routes:

in router R1:

```
ip route 10.0.0.32 255.255.255.252 10.0.0.10 2
```

in router R2:

```
ip route 10.0.0.0 255.255.255.252 10.0.0.13 2
```

In order for routers to automatically select routes with a default administrative distance of 1 after restoring communication on the R1-R2 link, we need to use an additional parameter in the **ip route** command. This parameter is the value of the administrative distance. In this case, we configure it to 2 (**this number must be greater than the standard value for a static route**).

Once the backup routes are configured and a simulated R1-R2 link failure is performed, the backup routes appear in the routing tables.

```
S        10.0.0.12 [1/0] via 10.0.0.10
S        10.0.0.16 [1/0] via 10.0.0.10
S        10.0.0.32 [2/0] via 10.0.0.10
```

Figure 3.23 Backup route in routing table on router R1.

```
S        10.0.0.0 [2/0] via 10.0.0.13
S        10.0.0.8 [1/0] via 10.0.0.13
S        10.0.0.16 [1/0] via 10.0.0.13
S        10.0.0.24 [1/0] via 10.0.0.22
S        10.0.0.32 [1/0] via 10.0.0.30
```

Figure 3.24 Backup route in routing table on routerR2.

Once the R1-R2 link failure has been corrected, we check the status of the routing tables for R1 and R2.

```
S        10.0.0.12 [1/0] via 10.0.0.10
S        10.0.0.16 [1/0] via 10.0.0.10
S        10.0.0.20 [1/0] via 10.0.0.6
S        10.0.0.24 [1/0] via 10.0.0.6
S        10.0.0.28 [1/0] via 10.0.0.6
S        10.0.0.32 [1/0] via 10.0.0.6
```

Figure 3.25 Routes in the routing table on router R1, once the failure has been repaired.

```
S        10.0.0.0 [1/0] via 10.0.0.5
S        10.0.0.8 [1/0] via 10.0.0.13
S        10.0.0.16 [1/0] via 10.0.0.13
S        10.0.0.24 [1/0] via 10.0.0.22
S        10.0.0.32 [1/0] via 10.0.0.30
```

Figure 3.26 Routes in the routing table on router R2, once the failure has been repaired.

3.8 Configuring the Default Route

Default route is the route, the router will choose when it does not find a route in the routing table that matches the destination network address. The most common use of the default route is to route packets to the gateway of a residual router that is connected to an ISP.

Stub router is a router through which there is only one route to the external (backbone) network adjacent to it. In our case, this is the **ISP** router.

A default route for IPv4 is created using a reserved address of **0.0.0.0** and a mask of **0.0.0.0.**

To find out if a default route is configured on a particular router, we need to run the Cisco IOS **`show ip route`** command and check if the message "**`Gateway of last resort is not set`**" is displayed on the router console. If this message appears, it means that there is no default route.

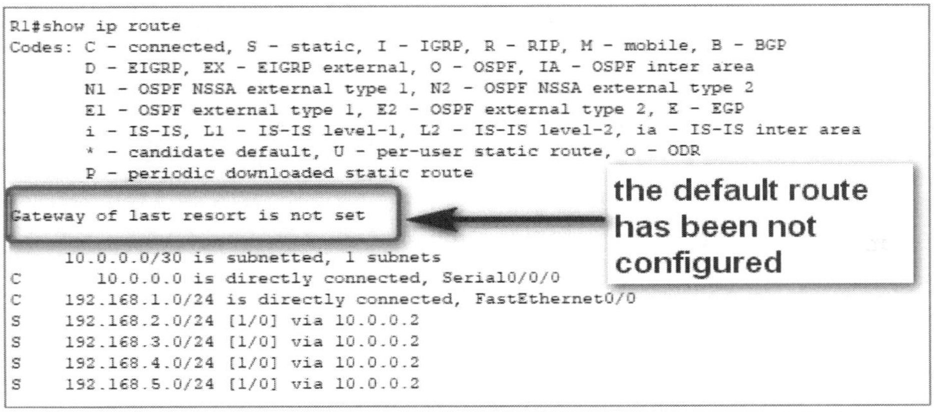

```
R1#show ip route
Codes: C - connected, S - static, I - IGRP, R - RIP, M - mobile, B - BGP
       D - EIGRP, EX - EIGRP external, O - OSPF, IA - OSPF inter area
       N1 - OSPF NSSA external type 1, N2 - OSPF NSSA external type 2
       E1 - OSPF external type 1, E2 - OSPF external type 2, E - EGP
       i - IS-IS, L1 - IS-IS level-1, L2 - IS-IS level-2, ia - IS-IS inter area
       * - candidate default, U - per-user static route, o - ODR
       P - periodic downloaded static route

Gateway of last resort is not set

     10.0.0.0/30 is subnetted, 1 subnets
C       10.0.0.0 is directly connected, Serial0/0/0
C    192.168.1.0/24 is directly connected, FastEthernet0/0
S    192.168.2.0/24 [1/0] via 10.0.0.2
S    192.168.3.0/24 [1/0] via 10.0.0.2
S    192.168.4.0/24 [1/0] via 10.0.0.2
S    192.168.5.0/24 [1/0] via 10.0.0.2
```


Figure 3.27 Result of the command show ip route when there's no default route.

To configure the default routes on routers R1-R5, we will use the following IOS command:

`ip route 0.0.0.0 0.0.0.0 Se0/0/0`

on routers R1-R5.

We first configure the static routes so that the subnets:

- 192.168.1.0/24,
- 192.168.2.0/24,
- 192.168.3.0/24,
- 192.168.4.0/24,
- 192.168.5.0/24,

can communicate between each other.

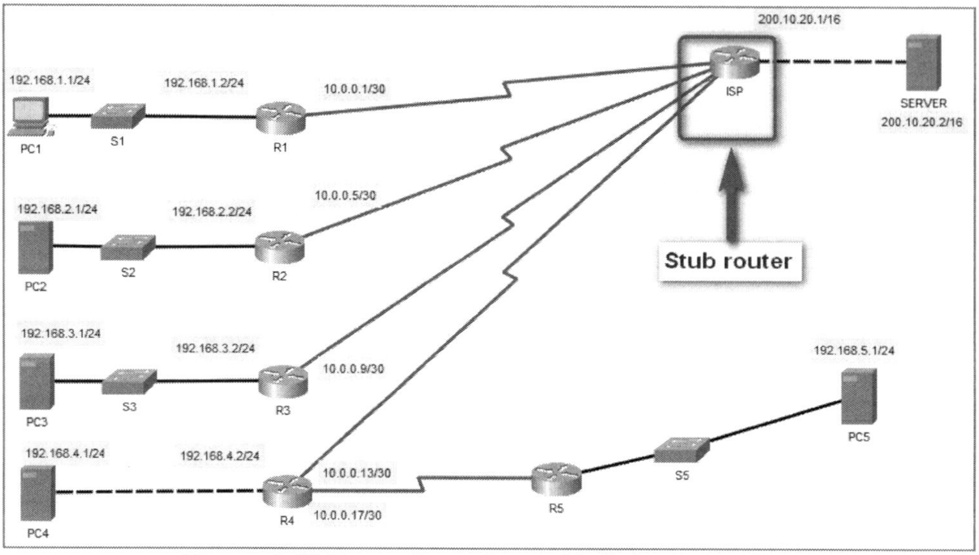

Figure 3.28 Network topology with links to the ISP.

We will then configure the default static routes so that the internal subnets can access the external network **200.10.0.0/16**, located behind the **ISP** router.

To do so we execute command:

```
ip route 0.0.0.0 0.0.0.0 Se0/0/0
```

on each of the internal routers R1-R4. On the other hand, on router R5 we execute the command:

```
ip route 0.0.0.0 0.0.0.0 Se0/0/1
```

Using command **`show ip route static`** we check the status of the static routing tables and whether the default routes have been correctly configured.

```
R1#
R1#show ip route static
S     192.168.2.0/24 [1/0] via 10.0.0.2
S     192.168.3.0/24 [1/0] via 10.0.0.2
S     192.168.4.0/24 [1/0] via 10.0.0.2
S     192.168.5.0/24 [1/0] via 10.0.0.2
S*    0.0.0.0/0 is directly connected, Serial0/0/0
R1#
```

Figure 3.29 A default route in routing table on router R1.

The static default route is indicated by S* (S+star). If we use a more general command, i.e. **`show ip route`**, then we can check whether the IOS console displays the message

„**`Gateway of last resort is 0.0.0.0 to network 0.0.0.0`**". This means that the default route has been configured.

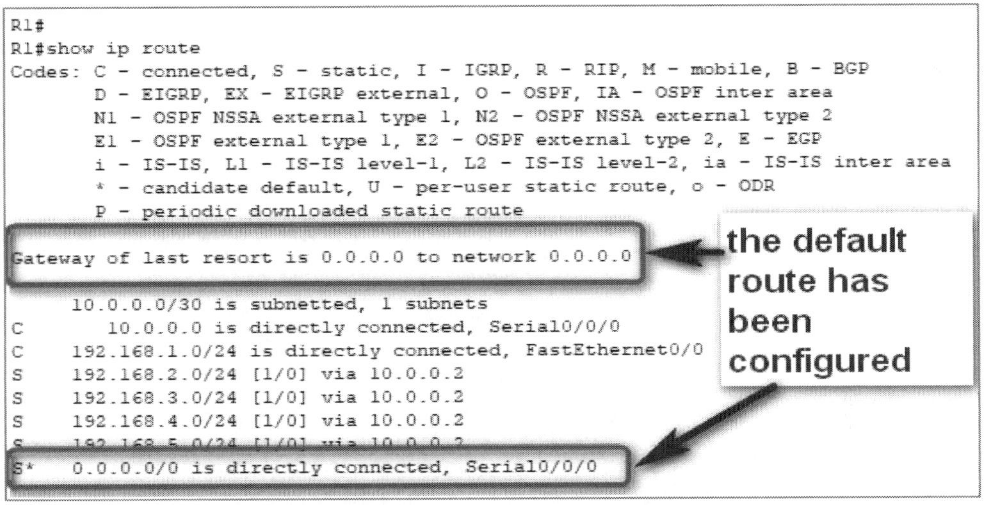

```
R1#
R1#show ip route
Codes: C - connected, S - static, I - IGRP, R - RIP, M - mobile, B - BGP
       D - EIGRP, EX - EIGRP external, O - OSPF, IA - OSPF inter area
       N1 - OSPF NSSA external type 1, N2 - OSPF NSSA external type 2
       E1 - OSPF external type 1, E2 - OSPF external type 2, E - EGP
       i - IS-IS, L1 - IS-IS level-1, L2 - IS-IS level-2, ia - IS-IS inter area
       * - candidate default, U - per-user static route, o - ODR
       P - periodic downloaded static route

Gateway of last resort is 0.0.0.0 to network 0.0.0.0

     10.0.0.0/30 is subnetted, 1 subnets
C       10.0.0.0 is directly connected, Serial0/0/0
C    192.168.1.0/24 is directly connected, FastEthernet0/0
S    192.168.2.0/24 [1/0] via 10.0.0.2
S    192.168.3.0/24 [1/0] via 10.0.0.2
S    192.168.4.0/24 [1/0] via 10.0.0.2
S    192.168.5.0/24 [1/0] via 10.0.0.2
S*   0.0.0.0/0 is directly connected, Serial0/0/0
```


Figure 3.30 The default route on router R1 has been configured.

As above, we check the status of the static routing tables and whether the default routes have been correctly configured on the other routers.

CHAPTER 4

ACCESS CONTROL LISTS

4 ACCESS CONTROL LISTS

4.1 Introduction

The main purpose of using **access control lists** (ACLs) is to control and limit network traffic passing through routers. By using them, we can not only increase the security level of our network, but also improve its performance. Controlling and filtering network traffic is a very responsible task for every administrator, who decides what type of traffic will be allowed through the router and what will be blocked. Therefore, in this chapter of the book we will focus on discussing the configuration of such issues.

Every router may have a large number of **ACLs** configured, but not all of them need to be active, i.e. an access control list created and saved in the router's configuration will only operate if you assign it to the particular interface for which it is to filter traffic and define the direction of operation, i.e. whether the ACL is to filter packets entering or leaving the router. In addition, each ACL can be defined for a particular network protocol, e.g. IP, TCP, UDP, ICMP, as shown in the figure below.

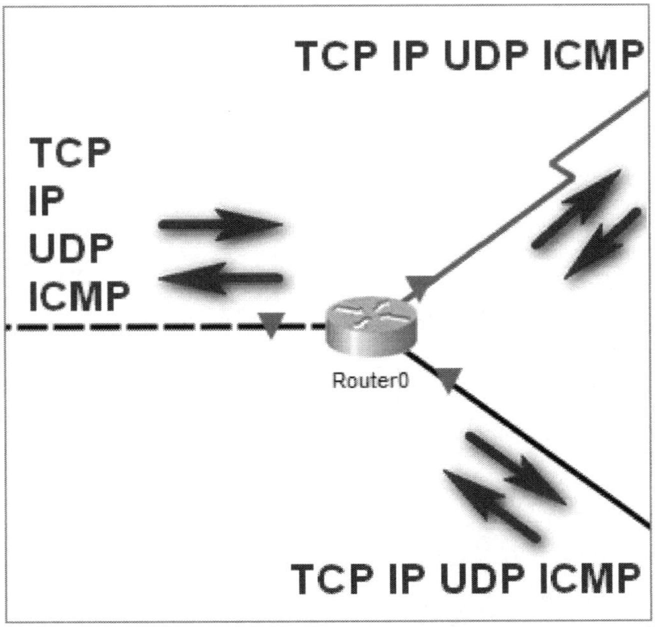

Figure 4.1 Possibilities for the deployment of access control lists, their direction of operation and selected protocols.

Network traffic filtering allows you to control what happens in particular network segments. It is a process that analyses the content of packets in order to decide whether a packet should be allowed into a certain area of the network or blocked.

Packet filtering can be done on the basis of:

- the source IP address,
- the destination IP address,
- protocols (protocol names),
- application type (port numbers).

4.2 Types of ACL

4.2.1 Standard ACL

Features of a **standard** access control list:

- ACLs range from **1 to 99** and **1300 to 1999**
- filters traffic based on the **source IP** address of the packet
- permit or deny based on the **entire protocol,** e.g. IP
- if a given host is blocked by a standard ACL, **all outgoing services** from this host are blocked

Syntax of the IOS command that creates a **standard** list:

```
access-list [access-list-number] [deny|permit] [source address] [source-wildcard] [log]
```

Syntax of the IOS command that removes **ACLs**:

```
no access-list   access-list-number
```

To assign an **ACL** to an interface, use the `ip access-group` command. Each interface can be assigned two lists (for incoming and outgoing traffic). If both lists are assigned, they must be of the same type.

Syntax of the IOS command assigning an **ACL** to an interface:

```
ip access-group access-list-number {in | out}
```

4.2.2 Extended ACL

Features of an **extended** access control list:

- ACLs range from **100 to 199** and from **2000 to 2699**
- filters traffic based on the **source IP** address of the packet and based on the **destination IP** address
- filters traffic on the basis of **protocol** type, **port** number
- permit or deny based on **protocol type,** e.g. TCP, or **application type** (port number)

Syntax of the IOS command that creates the **extended** list:

```
access-list access-list-number {deny | permit protocol
{source-address [source-mask] {destination-address
[destination-mask]} operator service
```

Differences between the standard list and the extended list:

- The standard list permits or blocks based on IP source address.
- The extended list permits or blocks access based on IP source addresses, IP destination addresses, protocol type, port numbers.

4.2.3 Named ACL

Properties of a **named** access control list:

- can be **standard or extended**
- an ACL is **identified by the name** assigned to it
- configuration of named ACLs uses configuration mode (**nacl**)

Starting with Cisco IOS version 11.2, it's possible to create so-called **Named ACLs** (NACLs), i.e. ACLs that have a name instead of a number. They offer the same capabilities as standard and extended lists. The only difference is the syntax.

The name of the list should be unique. By using capital letters in the names it's easier to find them in the router.

Syntax of the IOS command to create a **named ACL**:

```
ip access-list {standard | extended} name
```

After executing this command, the router switches to the **nacl** configuration sub-mode. In this sub-mode, enter the **permit** or **deny** commands.

4.3 Rules for Creating Access Control Lists

When creating access control lists, the order of the defined rules is of great importance. It is the order that plays a huge role when the IOS analyses the lists. Therefore, we must remember a very important point: the IOS system only allows two rules: PERMIT (**permit**) and DENY (**deny**). If we have a network in which the router is connected to, for example, five devices, as shown in the figure below, without enabling any ACLs, the router behaves in such a way that it allows all network traffic in all directions by default.

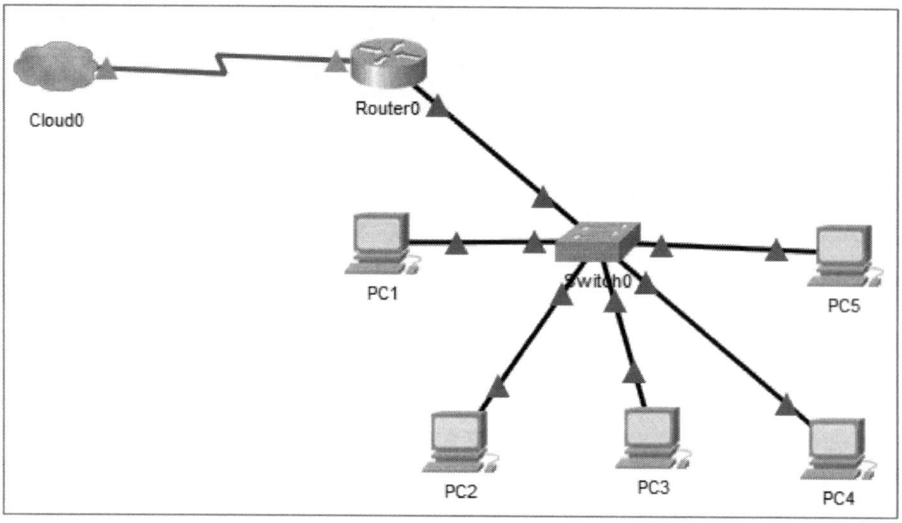

Figure 4.2 Example of topology to describe the rules for creating ACLs.

Let's assume a case like this, where you want to allow PC1 - PC5 access to services on the WAN, which will be symbolized by a cloud icon. In this case, the order in which the ACLs are created is very important: first we need to define the rules in which we will set the access of PC1 - PC5, and then we will allow the others to communicate with the Internet, which here is symbolized by a cloud named **Cloud0**.

All that remains now is the final step, which will be to select the interface on which to operate and define the direction.

4.4 Planning Access Control Lists

Step 1 – specify traffic filtering requirements.

Identify and record the requirements for each subnet. These requirements are likely to be based on user needs, security requirements for the type of network traffic.

Step 2 – select the type of ACL that suits your requirements

Decide whether to use a standard ACL or an extended ACL, depending on your filtering requirements. Choose the type of ACL depending on its flexibility and also on the performance of the routers, network, interface bandwidth.

Standard ACLs are simple to create, but only filter traffic based on **the source address**. When routing to multiple subnets, **you should place standard ACLs as close to the destination as possible** so that traffic **not supported by these ACLs** is not blocked.

When filtering is to be more complex, use **extended ACLs.** These allow filtering based on **source and destination address, as well as layer 3 and 4 and port number.**

Place extended ACLs as close to the source addresses as possible. Packets sent to destination networks can already be blocked before they leave the source router, reducing the load on the network links.

Step 3 – select the router and its interface for the ACL.

Place the ACL in the router and assign it to the interface.

Step 4 – select the direction of the traffic to be filtered.

Try to represent packet routing from the router's perspective. Place the ACL in the router and assign it to an interface as either **in** or **out**. Inbound traffic is traffic coming from outside the router. The router first checks this traffic, i.e. compares it with the list, and then looks for the destination network in the routing table.

The outgoing traffic is inside the router and is already served by the routing table. Before leaving the exit interface, the traffic is checked (compared) against the list, if the result of the comparison is positive, it leaves the interface.

Note: on Cisco routers, an implicit and invisible command is automatically added at the end of each ACL

- for standard lists: **`deny any`**
- for extended lists: **`deny ip any any`**

4.5 Most Common Mistakes

In this chapter, you will find brief advice on how to avoid basic mistakes when configuring ACLs. More often than not, a novice user who wants to learn how to configure ACLs on Cisco routers makes three basic mistakes:

- wrong sequence of introduced router,
- incomplete rules,
- wrong choice of interface or direction of the entered ACL.

4.5.1 Wrong Sequence of Introduced Rules

In the case discussed in the previous chapter, a situation may arise where we first introduce the rule: *allow all* and then *prohibit* PC3 and PC4 computers, a situation that is depicted in the figure below.

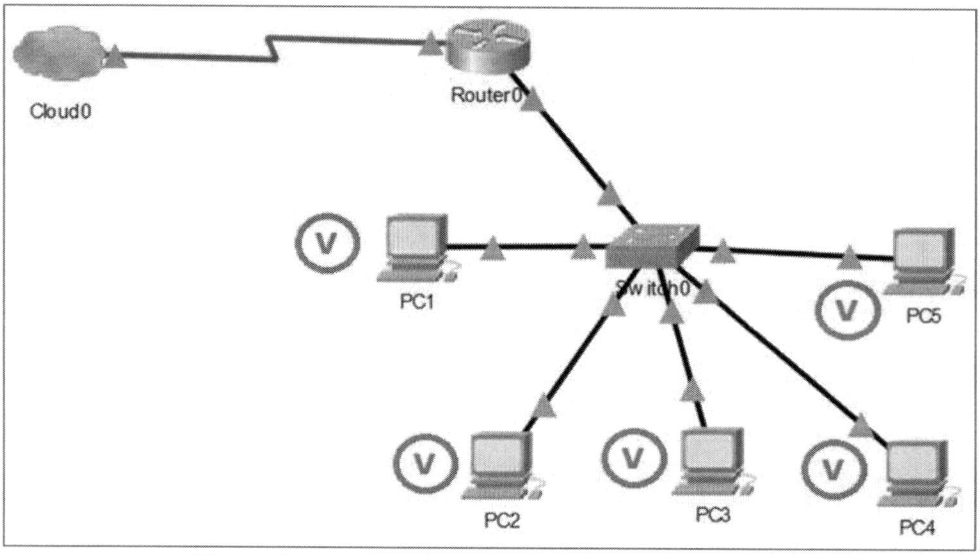

Figure 4.3 Incorrectly entered order of ACL rules.

```
access-list 1 permit any
access-list 1 deny host 192.168.0.4
access-list 1 deny host 192.168.0.5
```

Figure 4.4 Example of an incorrect ACL configuration.

We must remember that when configuring ACLs, rules are not overwritten, i.e. if PC3 and PC4 were allowed traffic the first time (as well as the other computers), then the next rule will not remove the permission and overwrite the rule forbidding traffic.

The same situation can happen if the reverse rules are entered: *first forbid all*, then *allow* PC3 and PC4. Again, the rules will not be overwritten and all PCs will not have permission to traffic as shown in the figure below.

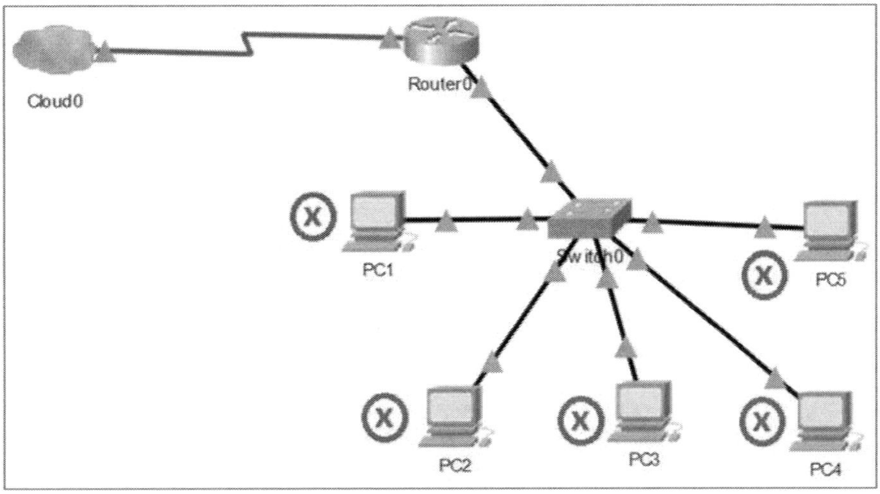

Figure 4.5 Incorrectly entered order of ACL rules.

```
access-list 1 deny any
access-list 1 permit host 192.168.0.4
access-list 1 permit host 192.168.0.5
```

Figure 4.6 Example of incorrect ACL configuration.

4.5.2 Incomplete Rules

Situation like that may also occur in the event that you do not complete entering all rules, i.e. for example enter only one rule: *forbid* PC3 and PC4 and do not enter additional rules. Then the router will not know how to classify the other devices connected to the given interface, as a result of which none of the devices will be able to communicate through the router, as shown in the figure below.

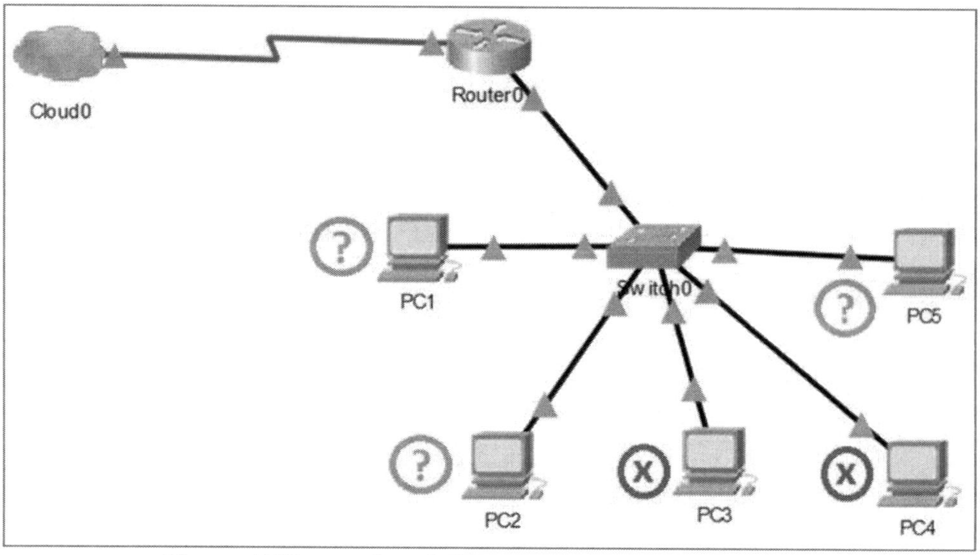

Figure 4.7 Incomplete ACL rules entered on the router.

```
access-list 1 deny host 192.168.0.4
access-list 1 deny host 192.168.0.5
```

Figure 4.8 Example of incomplete ACL configuration.

4.5.3 Wrong Choice of Interface or Direction of the Introduced ACL

Another type of error that can happen to us is that we have correctly defined an access control list on the router, but we have incorrectly set the interface on which it is to operate, or we have incorrectly defined the direction. For example, we want to redefine a rule that prohibits PC3 and PC4 from accessing the cloud. In this case, we make the first entry: *forbid* PC3 and PC4 and then the second: *allow all.*

After that the ACL is defined correctly, but when we enable it on the interface connecting the two routers together, it will block traffic at that point. The traffic between PC3 and PC4 and the cloud will still be allowed through, which is what we intended the router to block. This situation is illustrated in the figure below.

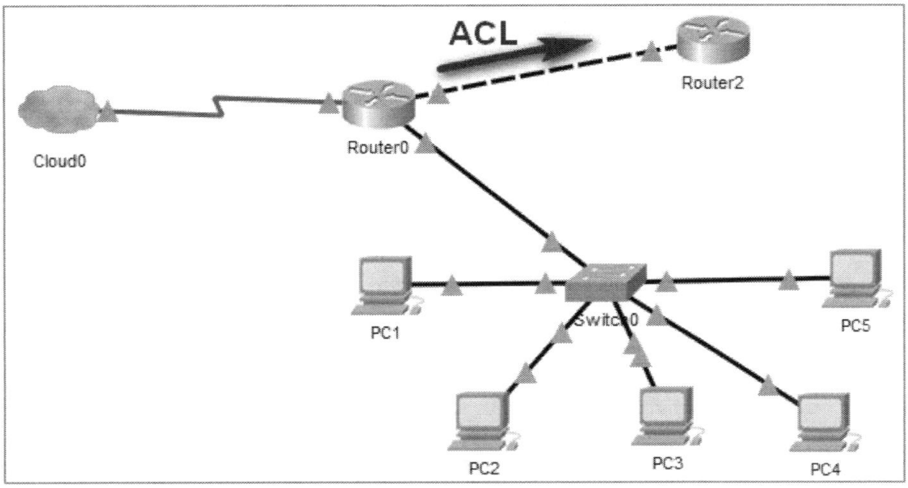

Figure 4.9 Incorrectly selected interface for an ACL.

```
interface FastEthernet0/1
 ip address 200.0.0.5 255.255.255.252
 ip access-group 1 out
```

Figure 4.10 Example of a wrongly selected interface for an ACL list.

After a theoretical introduction to the issues of access control lists, we will now move on to a subsection describing how they are used in practice.

4.6 Access Control List Numbering

The principle adopted in IOS systems is that each ACL has its own unique number. Below are their ranges that can be used in the given list types and their assignment to the given protocols. This manual will only describe the types available for Cisco IOS systems, shown in bold in the table.

Numbers range	ACL type (Protocol)
1 to 99	**Standard (IP)**
100 to 199	**Extended (IP)**
200 to 299	Extended (IP), used on other devices, e.g. TP-Link
700 to 799	Standard(MAC)
800 to 899	Standard(IPX)
900 to 999	Extended (IPX)
1300 to 1999	**Standard (IP)**
2000 to 2699	**Extended (IP)**

Table 4.1 ACL number ranges and the ACL types assigned to them.

4.7 Standard ACL

We will first focus on standard ACLs. In order to demonstrate this with concrete examples, we will first present their syntax. A **standard** ACL **only** permits or blocks network traffic based on the **source IP address**.

4.7.1 Syntax of a Standard ACL

The syntax presented below is the base formula for standard ACLs. Please refer to the legend.

`access-list Number ACTION CONDITION-SOURCES`

Legend:

- **access-list** - command entered in global configuration mode;
- **Number** - ACL number, for simple lists it is a number from the range 1-99;
- **ACTION** - one of two words may be entered here: **`permit`** or **`deny`**;
- **CONDITION-SOURCES** - this is where we specify which source the ACL is to apply to:
- **CONDITION1** - if we want to refer the ACL to one device in the network, we enter: **`host 1.2.3.4`** (where 1.2.3.4 - is the IP address of the device we want to refer to);
- **CONDITION2** - if you want to apply an ACL to a group of devices (e.g. the entire network or a subnet) then you use the so-called inverted mask (also known as a blank mask); For example, if you want to apply an ACL to all devices in the network: 192.168.1.0 with mask 255.255.255.0, you can use the inverted mask **`0.0.0.255;`**
- **CONDITION3** - if the ACL is to apply to all devices on any network - then just enter the word: **`any`**;

4.7.2 Using Standard ACLs

To understand the operation of standard ACLs, we will use a few examples. We will first consider a topology in which two LANs are connected via a router.

Suppose **PC7** and **PC8** cannot communicate with **LAN 1** (network address 200.200.200.0/24) and **PC2** and **PC3** cannot communicate with **LAN 2** (network address 222.222.222.0/24).

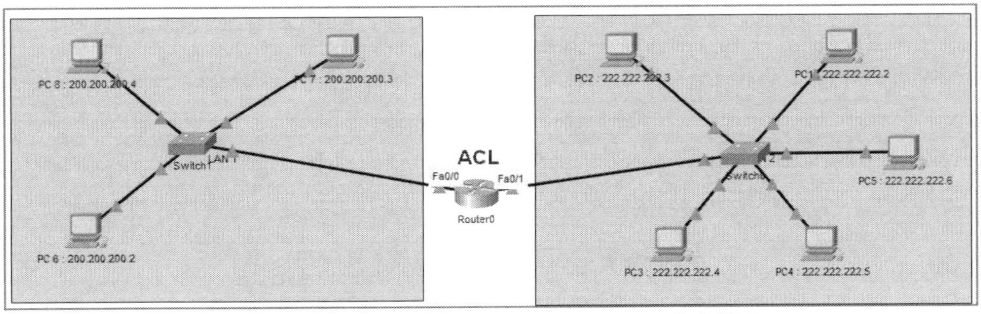

Figure 4.11 Example topology (standard ACL)

In our case, we will need to configure two independent access control lists. We will start with **LAN 1**. We go into global configuration mode in the router, where we define the first ACL. First, we block access to **PC7** (IP: 200.200.200.3) and select, for example, any ACL from the allowed range (e.g. 10).

```
access-list 10 deny host 200.200.200.3
```

Now it is the turn of **PC8** (IP:200.200.200.4). In order for the entry to be in the same ACL, we must specify the same number.

```
access-list 10 deny host 200.200.200.4
```

As **LAN 1** consists of only 3 computers, we only need to allow the last ACL line to access **PC6** (IP:200.200.200.2) remembering that we need to refer to the same ACL number.

```
access-list 10 permit host 200.200.200.2
```

The full access control list is shown in the figure below.

```
Router0(config)#
Router0(config)#access-list 10 deny host 200.200.200.3
Router0(config)#access-list 10 deny host 200.200.200.4
Router0(config)#access-list 10 permit host 200.200.200.2
Router0(config)#
```

Figure 4.12 Access control list configuration

At this point, you still need to enable the ACL on the router interface in question and set the direction of operation. Before doing so, it is worth taking a look at the figure below.

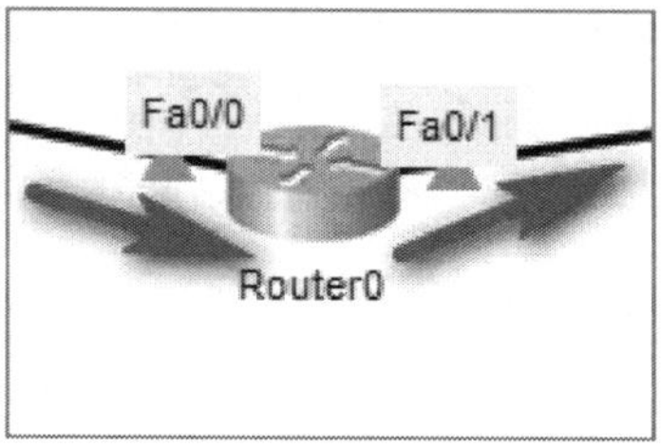

Figure 4.13 Possible ACL directions.

In our very simple topology, we see that we have two possibilities for the location and activation of the ACL. These could be:

- interface FastEthernet0/0 in the inbound (IN) direction;
- the FastEthernet0/1 interface in the outgoing (OUT) direction;

If we want to block traffic from **LAN 1,** we will place an ACL on interface **Fa0/0.** In this case, we have to enter the interface in question and enable the access control list of interest by specifying its number and direction. To do this, we will use the following command.

```
ip access-group 10 in
```

The full process of enabling a given access control list is shown in the figure below.

```
Router0(config)#
Router0(config)#interface FastEthernet 0/0
Router0(config-if)#ip access-group 10 in
Router0(config-if)#
```

Figure 4.14 Enabling ACLs on interface Fa0/0.

Now check the performance of the entire topology, after the first access control list has been entered. We execute the ping command from both **PC7** and **PC8** to any computer on **LAN 2** and, according to our assumptions, the packets are not delivered as shown in the next figure.

```
Packet Tracer PC Command Line 1.0
PC>ping 222.222.222.4

Pinging 222.222.222.4 with 32 bytes of data:

Reply from 200.200.200.1: Destination host unreachable.
Reply from 200.200.200.1: Destination host unreachable.
Reply from 200.200.200.1: Destination host unreachable.
Reply from 200.200.200.1: Destination host unreachable.

Ping statistics for 222.222.222.4:
    Packets: Sent = 4, Received = 0, Lost = 4 (100% loss),
```

Figure 4.15 Undelivered packets after implementation of ACLs.

However, when we execute the **ping** command from **PC6** to the PC located on **LAN 2**, all packets arrive at the indicated destination, as shown in the following figure.

```
PC>ping 222.222.222.6

Pinging 222.222.222.6 with 32 bytes of data:

Reply from 222.222.222.6: bytes=32 time=0ms TTL=127
Reply from 222.222.222.6: bytes=32 time=0ms TTL=127
Reply from 222.222.222.6: bytes=32 time=0ms TTL=127
Reply from 222.222.222.6: bytes=32 time=0ms TTL=127

Ping statistics for 222.222.222.6:
    Packets: Sent = 4, Received = 4, Lost = 0 (0% loss),
Approximate round trip times in milli-seconds:
    Minimum = 0ms, Maximum = 0ms, Average = 0ms
```

Figure 4.16 Delivered packets after implementation of the ACL.

Now, in accordance with the previous assumptions, we need to create a second ACL for **LAN 2**. As we remember, blocked access is to be granted to **PC2** and **PC3**. Therefore, we define a new ACL to which we must assign a new number.

```
access-list 20 deny host 222.222.222.3
access-list 20 deny host 222.222.222.4
```

After locking two computers, we can allow access to the others. Due to the fact that there are more of them than in **LAN 1**, we will not create permissions for each computer separately, we will only apply an inverted mask.

```
access-list 20 permit 0.0.0.255
```

The access control list is shown in the figure below.

```
Router0(config)#access-list 20 deny host 222.222.222.3
Router0(config)#access-list 20 deny host 222.222.222.4
Router0(config)#access-list 20 permit 0.0.0.255
Router0(config)#
```

Figure 4.17 Configuring an access control list.

At this point, you still need to enable the ACL on the router interface in question and specify the direction of operation. Before doing so, it is worth taking a look at the following figure.

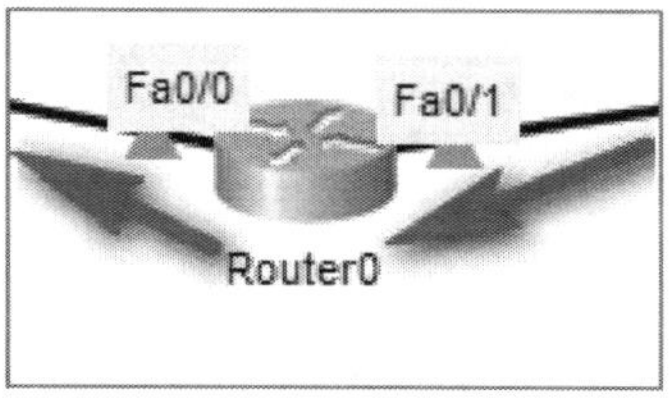

Figure 4.18 Possible directions of ACL operation.

The process of enabling a given access control list is shown in the figure below.

```
Router0(config)#
Router0(config)#interface FastEthernet 0/1
Router0(config-if)#ip access-group 20 in
Router0(config-if)#
```

Figure 4.19 Enabling ACLs on interface Fa0/1.

4.8 Extended ACL

In order to explain the operation of **extended** ACLs, we will first introduce their syntax and then present concrete examples of their use. At the outset, however, let us recall that an extended ACL allows or blocks access based on IP **source addresses**, IP **destination addresses**, **protocol type**, and **port numbers**.

4.8.1 Syntax of the Extended ACLs

The syntax shown below is the base formula for extended ACLs. Refer to the legend.

```
access-list Number ACTION TYPE-PROTOCOL CONDITION-
SOURCES CONDITION-TARGET [PORT-Number]
```

Legend:

- **access-list** - command entered in global configuration mode;
- **Number - ACL** number, in the case of extended lists it is a number from the range 100 199;

- **ACTION** - one of two words can be entered here: permit or deny;
- **PROTOCOL TYPE** - here you specify for which protocol the conditions contained in the ACL will be applied: ip, icmp, tcp, udp;
- **CONDITION-SOURCE** - this is where we specify which source the ACL is to apply to:
- **CONDITION-DESTINATION** - here we specify which destination the ACL is to apply to:
- **CONDITION1** - if we want to refer the ACL to a single device in the network, we enter: `host 1.2.3.4` (where 1.2.3.4 is the IP address of the source device);
- **CONDITION2** - if you want to apply an ACL to a group of devices (for example, the entire network or a subnet) then you use the so-called inverse mask; For example, if you want to apply an ACL to all devices on the network: 192.168.1.0 with a mask of 255.255.255.0, you can use the inverse mask (also known as a blank mask) `0.0.0.255`;
- **CONDITION 3** - if the ACL is to apply to all devices from any network - then just enter the word: `any`;
- **PORT-Number** - here we specify, a filtering condition based on the port number (only if we have selected TCP or UDP protocol type):
- **The PORT-Number option** consists of the operator symbol and the port number or name - we have included a detailed description in the tables later in this subsection;

Protocol types used in extended ACLs:

- IP
- ICMP
- TCP
- UDP

Wildcard mask - a sequence of binary zeros and ones used to filter individual IP addresses or groups of IP addresses. The zeros indicate the bits of the IP address to be matched and the ones indicate the bits to be ignored. For example, a blank mask of **0.0.0.3** means matching the first **30** bits of an IP address.

Operator symbols for options `PORT-Number` used in extended ACLs can be found in the following table:

Operator symbol	***Purpose***
eq	equal
gt	greater than

lt	less than
neg	not equal
range	range of port numbers

Table 4.2 Operator types for the TCP and UDP protocols.

The numbers (names) of the so-called well-known ports for the options: **`PORT-Number`** used in extended ACLs can be found in the following table.

Port number (name)	***Purpose***
21 (ftp)	FTP Protocol
23 (telnet)	Telnet service
25 (smtp)	SMTP Protocol
80 (www)	HTTP Protocol
110 (pop3)	POP version 3. Protocol
0 – 65535	Any port in the specified range

Table 4.3 Port numbers and names for TCP and UDP protocols.

Example:

```
access-list 100 deny tcp host 192.168.1.1 host
192.168.1.3 eq 80
```

4.8.2 Use of Extended ACLs

To understand the operation of **extended** ACLs, we will use several examples. For the following examples, we will use a topology in which three LANs are connected via two routers.

4.8.2.1 Blocking Subnets

Suppose the computers on **LAN2** (network address 222.222.222.0/24) cannot communicate with the computers on **LAN3** (network address 100.100.100.0/24), but the other networks can communicate with each other.

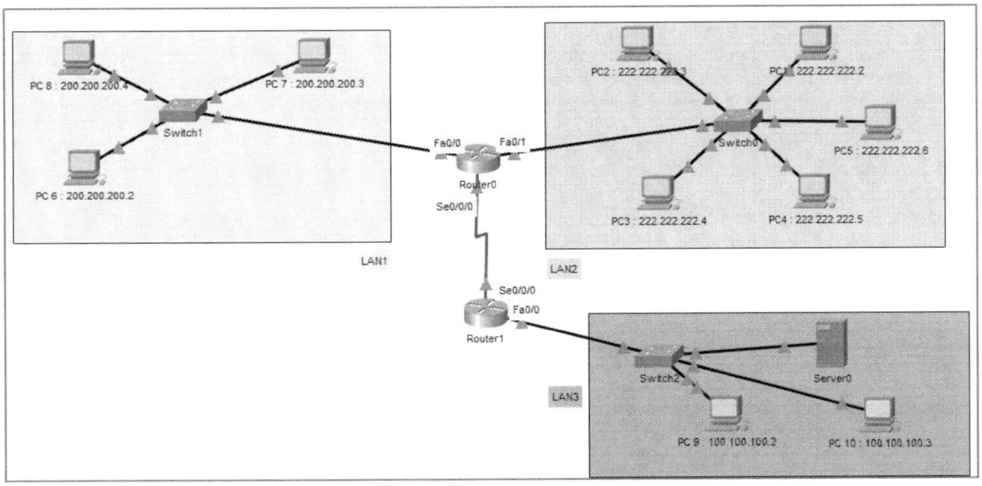

Figure 4.20 Example topology with blocking subnets ACL

In our case, we will only need to configure one access control list. Before we start constructing the list, let's consider where our list should be placed so as not to generate unnecessary network traffic.

Since this will be an extended list, we can make the filtering decision based on the address and mask of the target network. Therefore, it does not make sense to place the list in **Router1**. The list should be placed as close as possible to the source network, i.e. **LAN2**. The best solution would be to place the ACL at the entrance to interface **Fa0/1** in **Router0**.

Go into global configuration mode in **Router0**, where you define an extended ACL (numbered e.g. 100).

```
access-list 100 deny ip 222.222.222.0 0.0.0.255
100.100.100.0 0.0.0.255
access-list 100 permit ip any any
```

Don't forget to add the entry: `access-list 100 permit ip any any` (By default, each extended ACL places an implicit entry at the end: `deny ip any any`) !

In our topology, we can see that the best place to activate the ACL is at the **FastEthernet0/1** interface in the inbound (**IN**) direction.

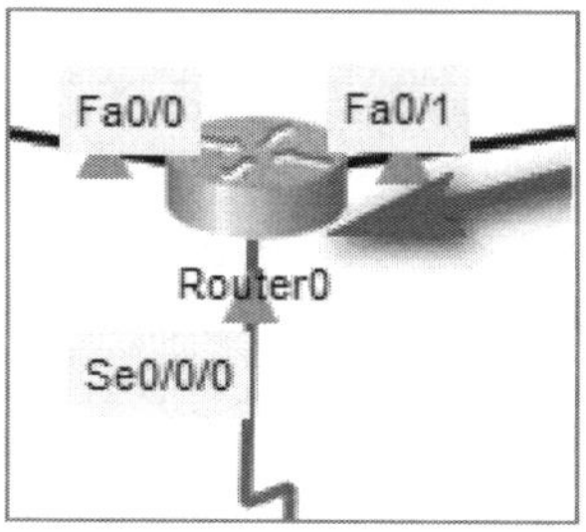

Figure 4.21 Direction of the extended ACL.

Now we enable ACL 100 to the interface and specify the direction of packet filtering.

```
interface FastEthernet 0/1
ip access-group 100 in
```

The full configuration of the access control list is shown in the figure below.

```
Router0>enable
Router0#configure terminal
Enter configuration commands, one per line.  End with CNTL/Z.
Router0(config)#access-list 100 deny ip 222.222.222.0 0.0.0.255 100.100.100.0 0.0.0.255
Router0(config)#access-list 100 permit ip any any
Router0(config)#interface FastEthernet 0/1
Router0(config-if)#ip access-group 100 in
Router0(config-if)#end
Router0#
```

Figure 4.22 Configuration of the extended access control list.

It would now be appropriate to check the performance of the entire topology, once the access control list is in place. We execute the ping command from **PC1-PC5 (LAN2)** to any PC on **LAN3** and, according to our assumptions, packets are not delivered as shown in the figure.

```
Packet Tracer PC Command Line 1.0
PC>ping 100.100.100.2

Pinging 100.100.100.2 with 32 bytes of data:

Reply from 222.222.222.1: Destination host unreachable.
Reply from 222.222.222.1: Destination host unreachable..
Reply from 222.222.222.1: Destination host unreachable.
Reply from 222.222.222.1: Destination host unreachable.

Ping statistics for 100.100.100.2:
    Packets: Sent = 4, Received = 0, Lost = 4 (100% loss),
```

Figure 4.23 Undelivered packets after ACL implementation.

However, when we execute the command: **ping** from **PC6** to any PC on **LAN3**, all packets arrive at the indicated destination, as shown in the figure below:

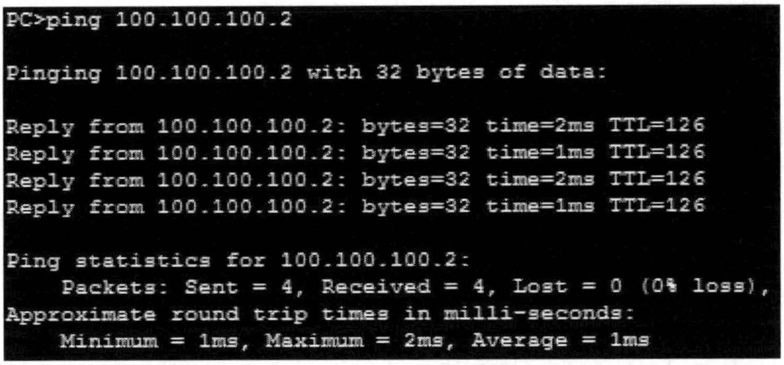

```
PC>ping 100.100.100.2

Pinging 100.100.100.2 with 32 bytes of data:

Reply from 100.100.100.2: bytes=32 time=2ms TTL=126
Reply from 100.100.100.2: bytes=32 time=1ms TTL=126
Reply from 100.100.100.2: bytes=32 time=2ms TTL=126
Reply from 100.100.100.2: bytes=32 time=1ms TTL=126

Ping statistics for 100.100.100.2:
    Packets: Sent = 4, Received = 4, Lost = 0 (0% loss),
Approximate round trip times in milli-seconds:
    Minimum = 1ms, Maximum = 2ms, Average = 1ms
```

Figure 4.24 Delivered packages after implementation of ACLs.

4.8.2.2 Blocking the WWW Service

In this example, we will show how an **extended** ACL works to block the ability to use the **WWW** service for a given network.

Let's assume that only computers located on **LAN1** (network address 200.200.200.0/24) cannot access the Web service located on **Server0** on **LAN3** (network address 100.100.100.0/24), while computers on the other networks can access the Web service.

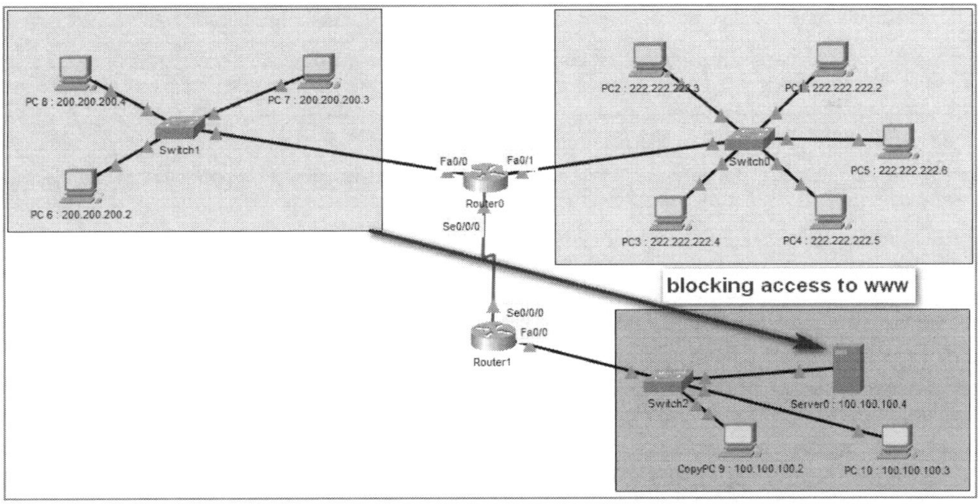

Figure 4.25 Example topology (blocking access to www)

In our case, we will only need to configure one access control list. Before we start constructing the list, let's consider where our list should be placed so as not to generate unnecessary network traffic. Since this will be an extended list, we can make the filtering decision based on the address and mask of the target network. Therefore, it does not make sense to place the list in **Router1**. The list should be placed as close as possible to the source network, i.e. **LAN1**. The best solution would be to place the ACL at the entrance to interface **Fa0/0** in **Router0**.

The second important issue is the choice of transport layer protocol and port number for the web service. In this case, we choose the **TCP** protocol and port number **80** (transport layer supporting HTTP).

We enter global configuration mode in **Router0**, where we define the extended ACL.

```
access-list 100 deny tcp 200.200.200.0 0.0.0.255
100.100.100.0 0.0.0.255 eq 80
access-list 100 permit ip any any
```

Don't forget to add the entry: `access-list 100 permit ip any any` (by default, every extended ACL puts an implicit entry at the end: `deny ip any any`) !

In our topology, we can see that the best place to activate the ACL, is the **FastEthernet0/0** interface in the inbound (**IN**) direction.

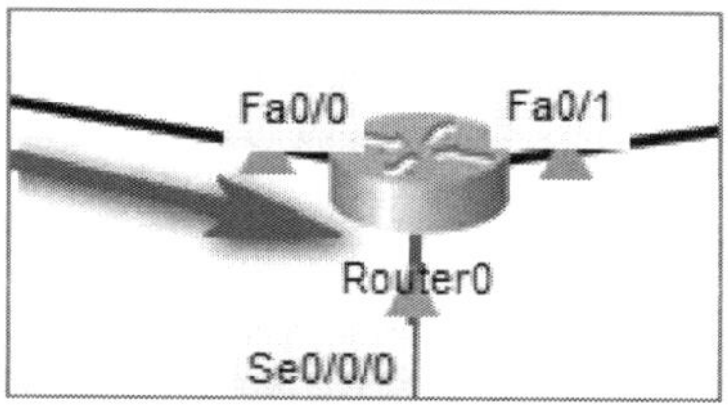

Figure 4.26 Direction of the extended ACL.

Now we enable ACL 100 to the interface and specify the direction of packet filtering.

```
interface FastEthernet 0/0
ip access-group 100 in
```

The full configuration of the access control list is shown in the figure below:

```
Router0>enable
Router0#configure terminal
Enter configuration commands, one per line.  End with CNTL/Z.
Router0(config)#access-list 100 deny tcp 200.200.200.0 0.0.0.255 100.100.100.0 0.0.0.255 eq 80
Router0(config)#access-list 100 permit ip any any
Router0(config)#interface FastEthernet 0/0
Router0(config-if)#ip access-group 100 in
Router0(config-if)#end
Router0#
```

Figure 4.27 Configuration of the extended access control list.

It would now be necessary to check the operation of the entire topology, once the access control list is in place. To do this, we run the **Web Browser** on **PC6 - PC8 (LAN1)**, where we enter the web server address **100.100.100.4** and, according to our assumptions, the web service is not available as shown in the figure.

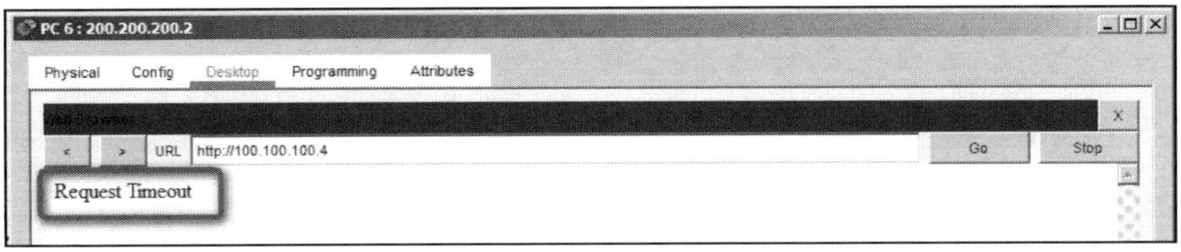

Figure 4.28 The web page with the address 100.100.100.4 is not accessible from PC6.

However, when the same address is used in a browser on **PC2** on **LAN2**, the WWW page is accessible, as shown in the figure below.

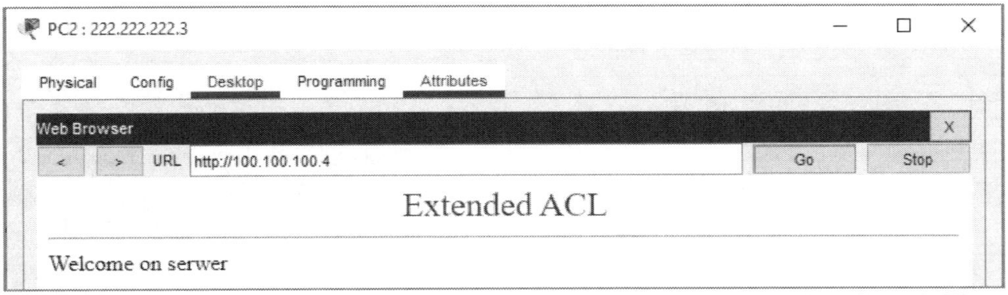

Figure 4.29 The web page with the address 100.100.100.4 is accessible from PC2.

4.8.2.3 Blocking the FTP Service

In this example, we will show how the **extended** ACL works to block the use of the FTP service for a given network.

For the case of blocking the FTP service, the situation is similar to the previous one i.e. blocking the web service. However, in this case, we will use the **port (service) name** instead of the port number. We will use the data from the table below.

Port name	*Application*
ftp	FTP
telnet	TELNET
www	WWW Browser

smtp	SMTP outgoing mail agent
pop3	Received mail agent POP version 3

Table 4.4 Port names for TCP and UDP protocols.

Suppose that only the computers on **LAN1** (network address 200.200.200.0/24) cannot access the FTP service located on **Server0** on **LAN3** (network address 100.100.100.0/24), while the computers on the other networks can access the **FTP** service.

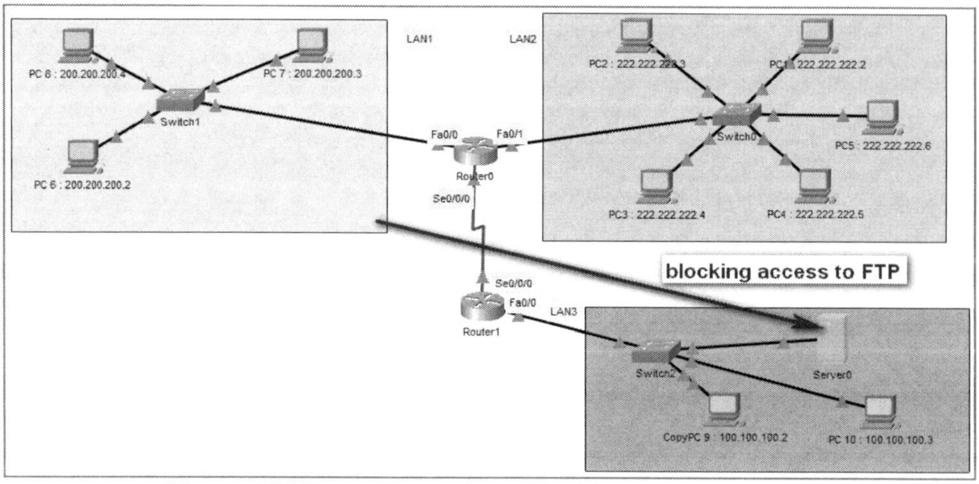

Figure 4.30 Example topology (blocking access to FTP)

In our case, we will only need to configure one access control list. As in the previous example, the list should be placed as close as possible to the source network, i.e. **LAN1**. The best solution would be to place the ACL at the entrance to interface **Fa0/0** on **Router0**.

The second important issue is the choice of transport layer protocol and port number or name for the FTP service. In this case, we choose the **TCP** protocol and the port name **ftp** (we use the name **ftp** instead of the number **21**).

We enter global configuration mode in **Router0**, where we define the extended ACL.

```
access-list 100 deny tcp 200.200.200.0 0.0.0.255
100.100.100.0 0.0.0.255 eq ftp
access-list 100 permit ip any any
```

Don't forget to add an entry: `access-list 100 permit ip any any` (by default, every extended ACL puts an implicit entry at the end: `deny ip any any`) !

In our topology, we can see that the best place to activate the ACL, maybe the **FastEthernet0/0** interface in the inbound (**IN**) direction.

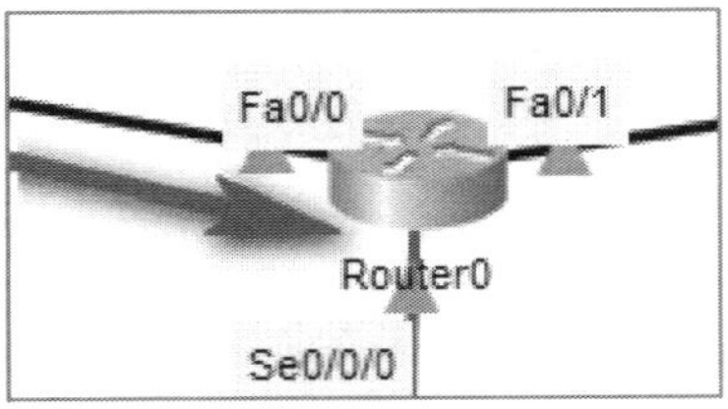

Figure 4.31 Direction of the extended ACL.

Now we enable ACL 100 to the interface and specify the direction of packet filtering.

```
interface FastEthernet 0/0
ip access-group 100 in
```

The full configuration of the access control list is shown in the figure below.

```
Router0>enable
Router0#configure terminal
Enter configuration commands, one per line.  End with CNTL/Z.
Router0(config)#access-list 100 deny tcp 200.200.200.0 0.0.0.255 100.100.100.0 0.0.0.255 eq ftp
Router0(config)#access-list 100 permit ip any any
Router0(config)#
Router0(config)#interface FastEthernet 0/0
Router0(config-if)#ip access-group 100 in
Router0(config-if)#end
Router0#
```

Figure 4.32 Configuration of the extended access control list.

It would now be necessary to check the operation of the entire topology, once the access control list has been entered. To do this, on **PC6-PC8 (LAN1)** we go to the **Command Prompt** where we type **ftp 100.100.100.4** and, according to our assumptions, we get the message that FTP is not available as shown in the figure.

```
PC>
PC>ftp 100.100.100.4
Trying to connect...100.100.100.4

%Error opening ftp://100.100.100.4/ (Timed out)
.
```

Figure 4.33 The FTP server with address 100.100.100.4 isn't accessible from PC6.

However, when we use the same address on the command line on **PC2** on **LAN2**, the FTP server is available, as shown in the figure below.

```
Packet Tracer PC Command Line 1.0
PC>ftp 100.100.100.4
Trying to connect...100.100.100.4
Connected to 100.100.100.4
220- Welcome to PT Ftp server
Username:cisco
331- Username ok, need password
Password:
230- Logged in
(passive mode On)
ftp>
ftp>dir

Listing /ftp directory from 100.100.100.4:
0   : c1841-ipbasek9-mz.124-12.bin                        16599160
1   : c2600-advipservicesk9-mz.124-15.T1.bin              33591768
2   : c2600-i-mz.122-28.bin                               5571584
3   : c2600-ipbasek9-mz.124-8.bin                         13169700
ftp>
```

Figure 4.34. The FTP server with address 100.100.100.4 is accessible from PC2.

To terminate the connection to the FTP server, execute the command: `quit`.

```
ftp>
ftp>quit

Packet Tracer PC Command Line 1.0
PC>221- Service closing control connection.
PC>
```

Figure 4.35 Terminate connection to FTP server.

4.8.2.4 Blocking the Ping Command

In this example, we will show how the **extended** ACL works to block **ping** commands executed from a given network. Since the command: `ping` uses the **ICMP** protocol, we need to familiarize ourselves with this protocol.

Before configuring the blocking of the **ping** command, we will review the basic types of messages regarding this command and the **ICMP** protocol.

ICMP (Internet Control Message Protocol) – an Internet control message protocol. It is described in RFC 792. ICMP is an OSI network layer protocol used for network diagnostics and routing.

The main purpose of this protocol is to control network transmission. On Cisco devices, it is used in the `ping` and `traceroute` commands.

The basic messages in the **ICMP** protocol are:

ICMP message type	***Description***
echo	Request sent to the host
echo-reply	Answer from the host
host-unreachable	Host is unreachable
net-unreachable	Network is unreachable
port-unreachable	Port is unreachable
protocol-unreachable	Protocol is unreachable

Table 4.5 Basic ICMP protocol messages.

For the case of blocking the ping command, we need to consider the network traffic associated with the transmission of ICMP messages. In this case, we will use several entries for the **ACL** list. We will use the table of basic ICMP messages.

Let's assume that only computers located on **LAN1** (network address 200.200.200.0/24) cannot **ping** commands to **LAN3** (network address 100.100.100.0/24).

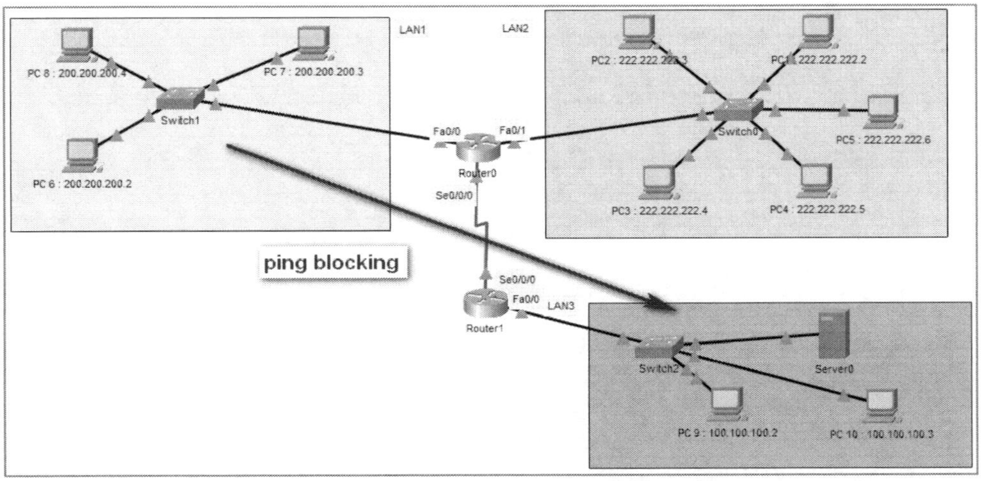

Figure 4.36 Example topology (ping blocking)

In our case, we will only need to configure one access control list. As in the previous example, the list should be placed as close as possible to the source network, i.e. **LAN1**. The best solution would be to place the ACL at the entrance to interface **Fa0/0** on **Router0**.

The protocol selection for the **ping** command is more complicated. In this case, we choose the **ICMP** protocol (we use the word **icmp**). We go into global configuration mode in **Router0**, where we define an extended ACL.

```
access-list 100 deny icmp 200.200.200.0 0.0.0.255
100.100.100.0 0.0.0.255 echo
access-list 100 permit icmp 200.200.200.0 0.0.0.255
100.100.100.0 0.0.0.255 echo-reply
access-list 100 permit icmp 200.200.200.0 0.0.0.255
100.100.100.0 0.0.0.255 host-unreachable
access-list 100 permit ip any any
```

Don't forget to add an entry: `access-list 100 permit ip any any` (by default, every extended ACL puts an implicit entry at the end: `deny ip any any`) !!! In our topology, we can see that the best place to activate the ACL, maybe the **FastEthernet0/0** interface in the inbound (**IN**) direction.

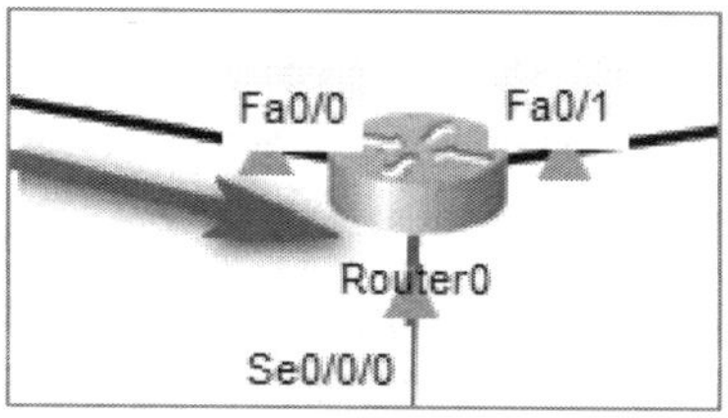

Figure 4.36 The direction of the extended ACL.

Now we enable ACL 100 to the interface and specify the direction of packet filtering.

```
interface FastEthernet 0/0
ip access-group 100 in
```

The full configuration of the access control list is shown in the following figure.

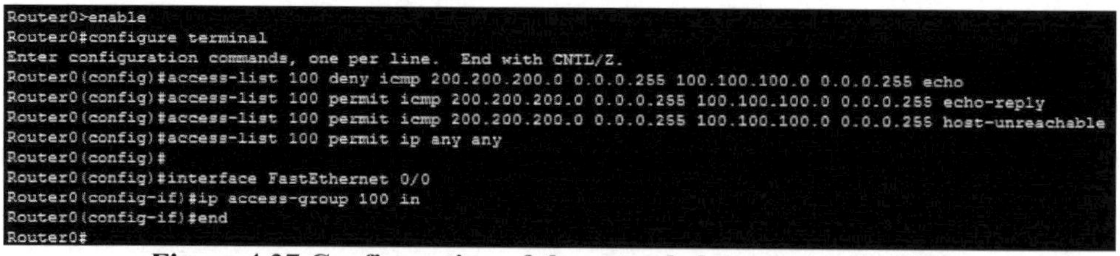

```
Router0>enable
Router0#configure terminal
Enter configuration commands, one per line.  End with CNTL/Z.
Router0(config)#access-list 100 deny icmp 200.200.200.0 0.0.0.255 100.100.100.0 0.0.0.255 echo
Router0(config)#access-list 100 permit icmp 200.200.200.0 0.0.0.255 100.100.100.0 0.0.0.255 echo-reply
Router0(config)#access-list 100 permit icmp 200.200.200.0 0.0.0.255 100.100.100.0 0.0.0.255 host-unreachable
Router0(config)#access-list 100 permit ip any any
Router0(config)#
Router0(config)#interface FastEthernet 0/0
Router0(config-if)#ip access-group 100 in
Router0(config-if)#end
Router0#
```

Figure 4.37 Configuration of the extended access control list.

It would now be necessary to check the operation of the entire topology, once the access control list has been implemented. To do this, on **PC6-PC8 (LAN1)**we go to the

Command Prompt where we type the command **ping100.100.100.4** and, according to our assumptions, we get a message that the host is not accessible as shown in the figure.

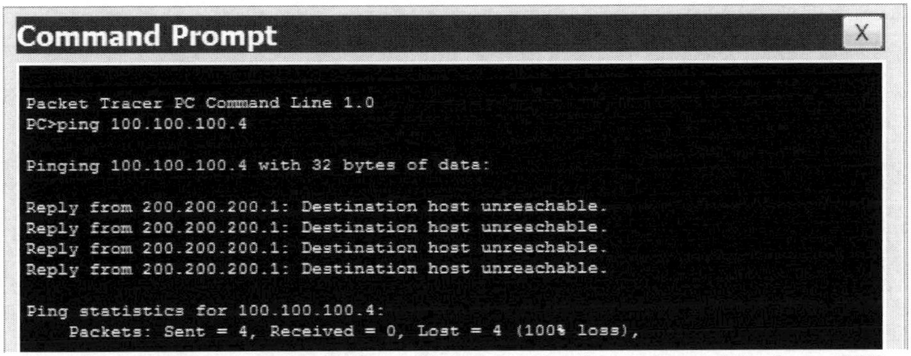

Figure 4.38 The host with address 100.100.100.4 is not accessible from PC8.

However, when the same address is used on the command line on **PC2** on **LAN2**, the host **100.100.100.4** is available, as shown in the following figure.

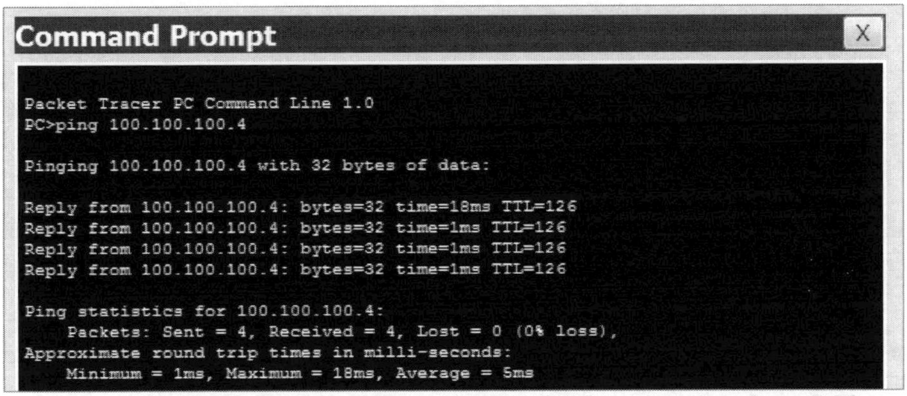

Figure 4.39 The host with address 100.100.100.4 is accessible from PC2.

4.8.2.5 Use of Extended Named ACLs

In this example, we will show how **names** can be used for extended ACL lists. In Cisco IOS, you can create so-called **Named ACLs**, which are ACLs that have a name instead of a number. They offer the same capabilities as standard and extended lists. The only difference is their syntax. The syntax of the IOS command to create a **named** list:

```
ip access-list {standard | extended} name
```

The advantage of these lists is that they are easier to find and to modify in the router. The name of the list should be unique. It is recommended to use **capital** letters in ACL names.

Configuring named ACLs is done in configuration mode (**nacl**). After executing this command, the router enters sub configuration mode **nacl**.

In this sub-tab, enter the commands: **`permit`** or **`deny`**. In this example, we will show how the **called** ACL works to block the possibility of using the TELNET service for all networks. To block the TELNET service, we need to use the extended list to block port **23**. Instead of the port number, we can use the port name (**telnet**).

Let's assume that computers located on **LAN1, LAN2, LAN3** cannot access the **Telnet** service to any network.

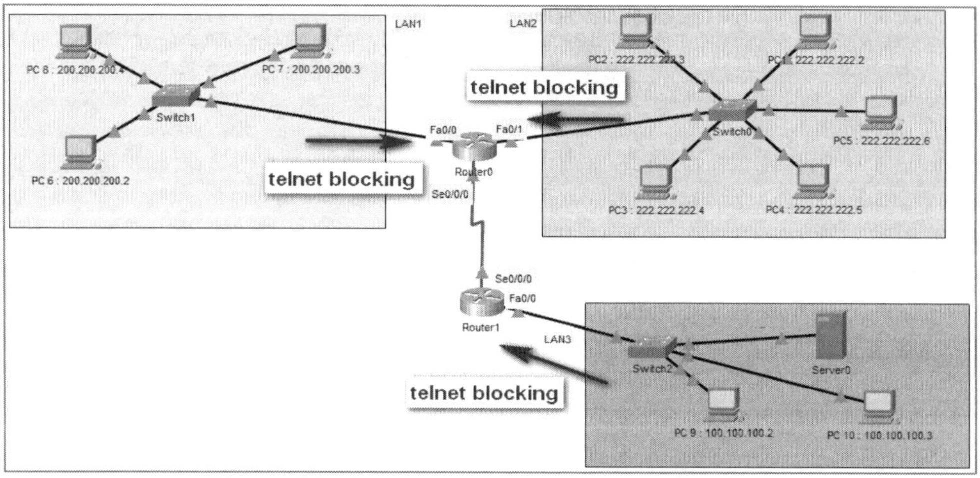

Figure 4.40 Example topology (telnet blocking).

In our case, we will configure three access control lists: two on **Router0** and one on **Router1**. The full configuration of the first two access control lists (named **LAN1, LAN2**) on **Router0** is shown in the figure below.

```
Router0(config)#
Router0(config)#ip access-list extended LAN1
Router0(config-ext-nacl)#remark LISTA-LAN1
Router0(config-ext-nacl)#deny tcp 200.200.200.0 0.0.0.255 any eq telnet
Router0(config-ext-nacl)#permit ip any any
Router0(config-ext-nacl)#
Router0(config-ext-nacl)#ip access-list extended LAN2
Router0(config-ext-nacl)#remark LISTA-LAN2
Router0(config-ext-nacl)#deny tcp 222.222.222.0 0.0.0.255 any eq telnet
Router0(config-ext-nacl)#permit ip any any
Router0(config-ext-nacl)#
Router0(config-ext-nacl)#interface FastEthernet 0/0
Router0(config-if)#ip access-group LAN1 in
Router0(config-if)#interface FastEthernet 0/1
Router0(config-if)#ip access-group LAN2 in
Router0(config-if)#end
Router0#
```

Figure 4.41 ACL configuration in Router0.

The full configuration of the third access control list (named **LAN3**) in **Router1** is shown in the following figure.

```
Router1(config)#
Router1(config)#ip access-list extended LAN3
Router1(config-ext-nacl)#remark LISTA-LAN3
Router1(config-ext-nacl)#deny tcp 100.100.100.0 0.0.0.255 any eq telnet
Router1(config-ext-nacl)#permit ip any any
Router1(config-ext-nacl)#
Router1(config-ext-nacl)#interface FastEthernet 0/0
Router1(config-if)#ip access-group LAN3 in
Router1(config-if)#end
Router1#
```

Figure 4.42 Configuration of ACLs in Router1.

Now we check access to the TELNET service. To do this, on all computers we go to the **Command Prompt** command line, where we type the commands:

```
telnet 100.100.100.1
telnet 200.200.200.1
telnet 222.222.222.1
```

We get a message that the remote host is not available, as shown in the following figure.

```
Packet Tracer PC Command Line 1.0
PC>telnet 100.100.100.1
Trying 100.100.100.1 ...
% Connection timed out; remote host not responding
PC>
PC>telnet 200.200.200.1
Trying 200.200.200.1 ...
% Connection timed out; remote host not responding
PC>telnet 222.222.222.1
Trying 222.222.222.1 ...
% Connection timed out; remote host not responding
PC>
```

Figure 4.43 The TELNET service has been blocked.

CHAPTER 5

THE VoIP TECHNOLOGY

5 THE VOIP TECHNOLOGY

5.1 Introduction to the VoIP Technology

VoIP (Voice over Internet Protocol) technology is a technique for transmitting speech over data communication links using the IP protocol (packet switching).

The main advantages of **VoIP** over traditional telephony are:

- low cost of cabling (a working IP network is sufficient),
- free calls on the internal network,
- integration with services such as data or video transmission.

The main disadvantages **VoIP** over traditional telephony are:

- greater unreliability of services,
- need for dedicated hardware and software,
- communications are more exposed to the possibility of eavesdropping.

5.2 IP Phone End Device

An IP phone (IP Phone) is a terminal device with the ability to communicate via voice and the existing IP network. Therefore, the IP Phone has an Ethernet port marked **Switch**. In addition, it must be connected to a power supply.

There is only one model of IP Phone available in Packet Tracer, namely the 7960. In order to start building a telephone network, we must first insert the phone into the program's main board.

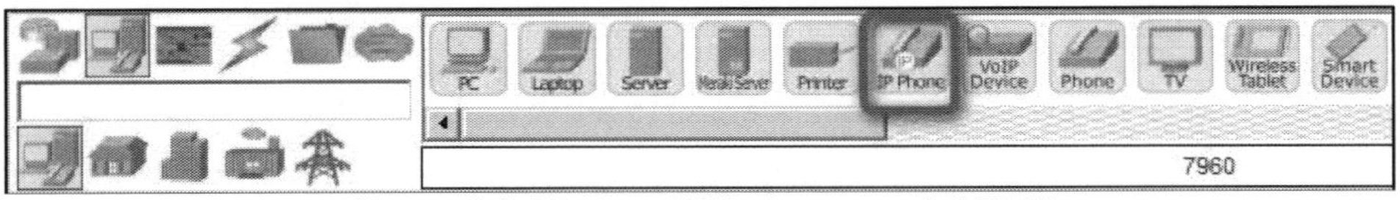

Figure 5.1 Choice of IP phone model 7960

In the bottom left corner of the program, find the "**End Devices**" device group, click on it and then select "**IP Phone**" and move the device to the board. The IP Phone will be represented as the following icon:

Figure 5.2 IP phone model 7960

Before we move on to describing how to prepare the phone for operation, it is worthwhile for us to be able to simulate the dialing and busy tones.

To enable this, go to the Packet Tracer main menu and select **Options → Preferences**, then under "**Interface**" select "**Play Telephony Sound**".

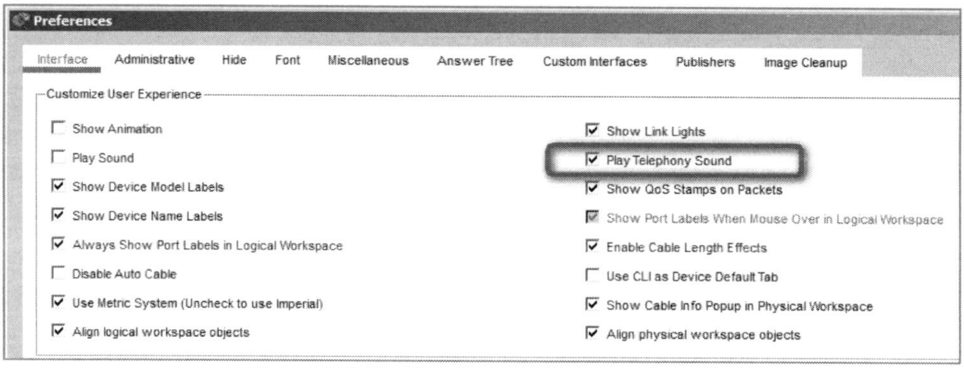

Figure 5.3 Option Play Telephony Sound

Now we can move on to the section describing how to prepare the IP phone for operation.

5.3 Preparing the IP Telephone for Operation

The IP Phone must be connected to an external voltage source. To do this, click on the **IP Phone**. A window appears with the **Physical** tab, where you use the mouse to connect (drag) the power supply (VoIP power adapter) to the socket indicated by the arrow in the figure.

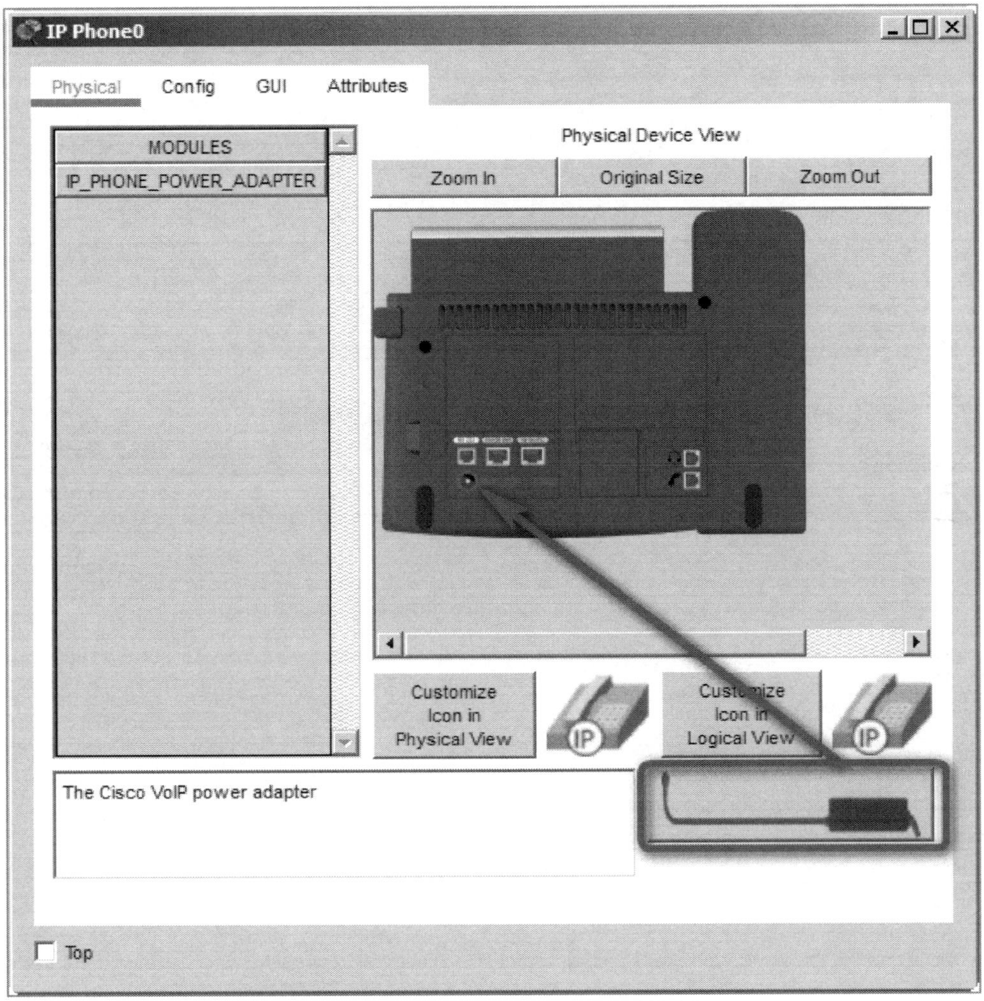

Figure 5.4 Connecting power to an IP phone.

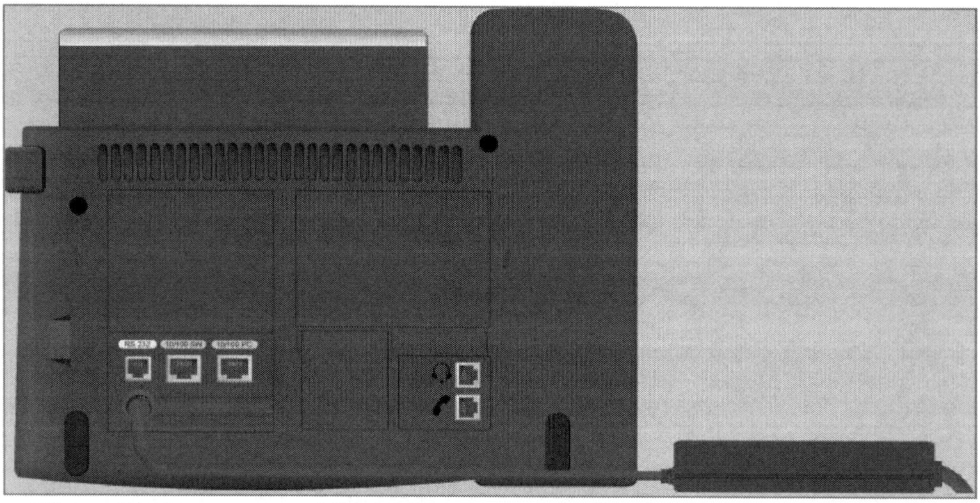

Figure 5.5 Appearance of the bottom part of the IP phone after connecting the power supply

In the "**Config**" tab, we can change the **Display Name** for the telephone.

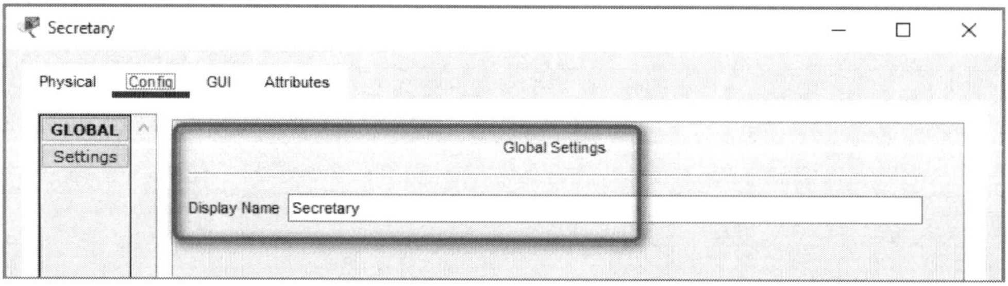

Figure 5.6 Changing the IP phone name

The "**GUI**" tab contains the view of the IP telephone (handset, display panel and keypad). We will use this tab only after configuring the IP network, telephone numbers and when testing connectivity.

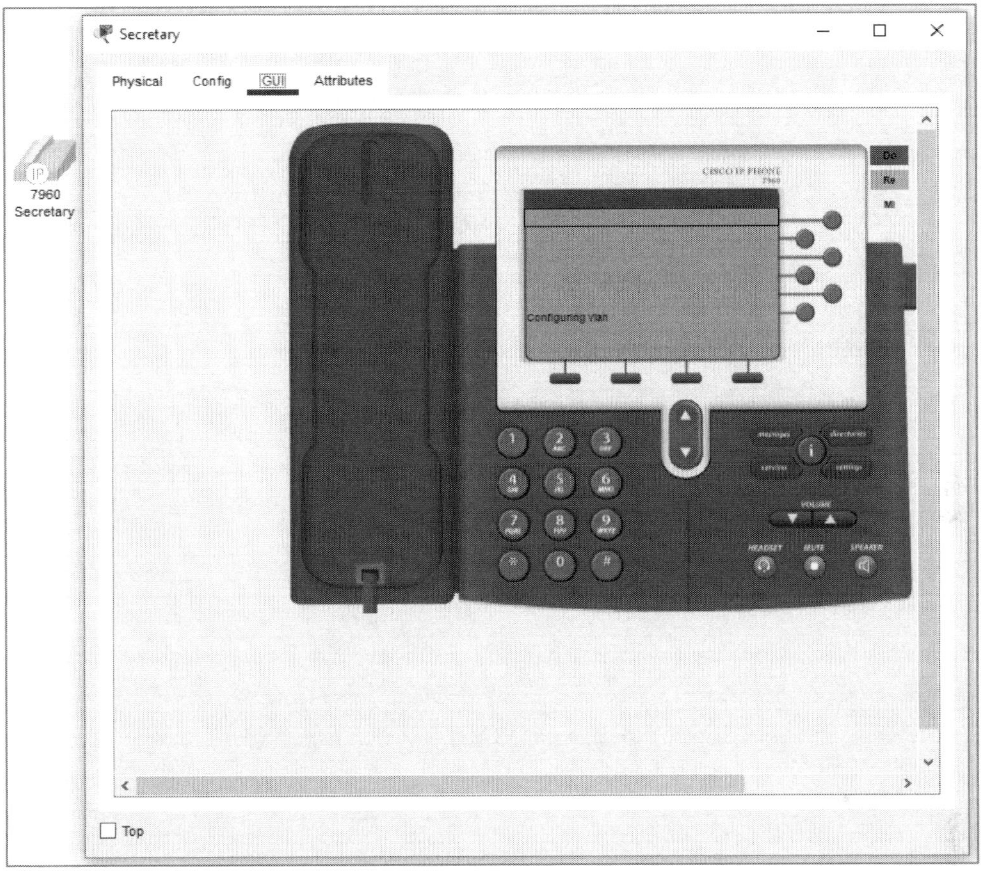

Figure 5.7 View of the IP phone on the GUI tab

To run a simple IP-based telephone network, you need a minimum of one router, one switch and two IP phones.

However, not every router has the necessary software to become a telephone exchange. In Packet Tracer, the **2811** meets this requirement. The VoIP PBX management software for Cisco routers is called **Call Manager Express**.

5.4 Call Manager Express

Call Manager Express (CME) software runs on Cisco routers and acts as a virtual PBX for IP telephony. For the description of **Voice over IP** technology in this chapter, the **2811** was chosen because in Packet Tracer only this model supports IP telephony.

5.5 Configuring a Simple VoIP Network

In order to set up and configure a simple VOIP network, we will select the following devices:

- router model **2811** (works as Call Manager Express),
- a switch model **2960** (works as a switch),
- and two IP telephones (model **7960**).

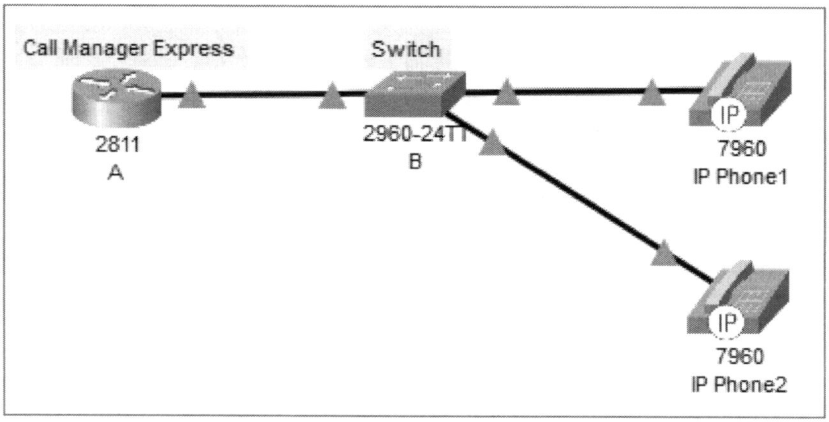

Figure 5.8 Simple VOIP network topology

Configuring a simple VOIP network takes place in the following steps:

Step 1. Connect the power supplies to both phones.

In addition, we change the names of the phones to: **IP Phone1, IP Phone2.**

Step 2. Connect router A to switch B.

We connect the router interface **Fa0/0** to the **Fa0/24** interface of the switch with an Ethernet cable.

Step 3. Connect IP Phone 1 to switch B.

Connect the phone's **Fa** interface (**note**: two ports will appear on the screen, one named **Switch** and the other **PC** - choose either one) to the switch's **Fa0/1** interface using an Ethernet cable.

Step 4. We configure the IP address for interface Fa0/0 of router A.

To do this, we execute the following commands:

```
conf t
hostname A
int Fa0/0
ip address 192.168.1.1 255.255.255.0
no shutdown
```

Step 5. We configure the DHCP service on router A.

To do this, we run the following commands:

```
conf t
ip dhcp pool POOL
network 192.168.1.0 255.255.255.0
default-router 192.168.1.1
option 150 ip 192.168.1.1
```

Note: in order for the router to use VoIP technology, it is necessary to use option 150 in the DHCP configuration.

Step 6. We configure the Call Manager Express telephony service on the router

To do this, we enter global configuration mode (execute the following commands):

```
en
conf t
```

Assuming that a maximum of 5 phones will be supported on our network. We enter the telephone service configuration mode using the command:

```
telephony-service
```

In the telephone service configuration mode, the following options are set:

```
max-dn 5
max-ephones 5
ip source-address 192.168.1.1 port 2000
```

Below we can read a brief description of the purpose of the commands:

- **max-dn** – is used to set the maximum number of directory entries (so-called **directory names)** that will store information about telephone numbers,
- **max-ephones** – is used to set the maximum number of IP phones,
- **ip source-address <source_address> port <port_no> - defines IP address** and the source port number for telephone services,

Step 7. We configure the VLAN on switch B.

Since we established in the previous step that we will support a maximum of 5 phones, we need 5 ports on the switch.

need to configure them to carry voice on **VLAN 1**. To do this, we run the commands:

```
conf t
hostname B
interface range fa0/1-fa0/5
switchport mode access
switchport voice vlan 1
```

Step 8. On router A, we assign telephone numbers to both phones.

Now we create directory entries (called **directory names**). To perform this step we will use the commands:

```
en
conf t
ephone-dn 1
number 101
exit
ephone-dn 2
number 102
end
```

```
A(config)#ephone-dn  1
A(config-ephone-dn)#number  101
A(config-ephone-dn)#exit
A(config)#ephone-dn  2
A(config-ephone-dn)#number  102
A(config-ephone-dn)#end
```

Figure 5.9 Configuring phone numbers in Call Manager Express

Step 9. We check that IP Phone1 has received an IP address and number.

Note: the process of receiving the line number address can take up to several minutes. **Call Manager Express** needs to register the configured phones. Correct registration manifests itself in the form of messages in the router. This is shown in the following figure.

```
%IPPHONE-6-REGISTER: ephone-2 IP:192.168.1.2 Socket:2
DeviceType:Phone has registered.

%IPPHONE-6-REGISTER: ephone-1 IP:192.168.1.3 Socket:2
DeviceType:Phone has registered.
```

Figure 5.10 Correct registration of telephone numbers in Call Manager Express

To check whether **IP Phone1** has been given the correct IP address and line number, move the mouse pointer over the phone and check the data that appears.

```
Port     Link    IP Address          MAC Address
Vlan1    Up      192.168.1.3/24      0009.7C34.D69D
Switch   Up      <not set>           0050.0FB9.7501
PC       Down    <not set>           0050.0FB9.7502

Gateway: 192.168.1.1
Line Number: 101
```

Figure 5.11 Current configuration of IP Phone1.

Step 10. Connect IP Phone 2 to switch B.

We connect the **Fa** interface of the phone to the **Fa0/2** interface of the switch using an Ethernet cable. Check that the **IP Phone2** has obtained the correct IP address and line number. To do this, move the mouse pointer to the phone and check the data that appears.

```
Port     Link    IP Address          MAC Address
Vlan1    Up      192.168.1.2/24      0001.4379.5EA3
Switch   Down    <not set>           0001.96A5.CE6D
PC       Up      <not set>           0001.6343.A1D7

Gateway: 192.168.1.1
Line Number: 102
```

Figure 5.12 Current configuration of IP Phone2.

In addition, on the console of router **A** using the command: **`show ip dhcp binding`**, we can check the status of the assigned IP addresses.

```
A#show ip dhcp binding
IP address       Client-ID/              Lease expiration        Type
                 Hardware address
192.168.1.2      0001.4379.5EA3           --                     Automatic
192.168.1.3      0009.7C34.D69D           --                     Automatic
```

Figure 5.13 Status of dynamically assigned IP addresses

Step 11. We check the connectivity between the IP phones.

We have reached the last step, which is to check if it is possible to call number 102 from number 101 and vice versa. To do this, we click **IP Phone1**. The phone number (**101**) appears in the top right corner on the display panel.

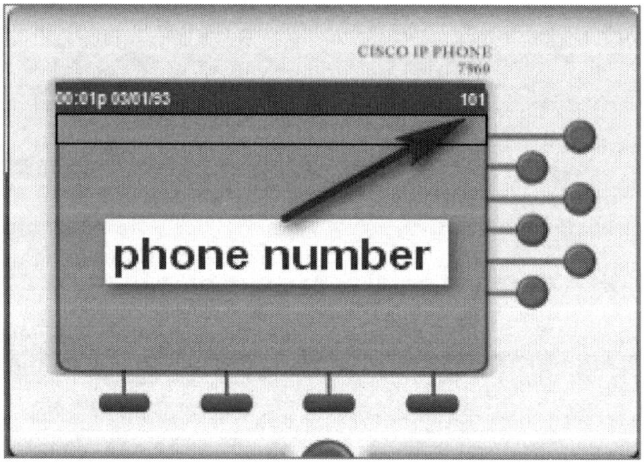

Figure 5.14 Display panel on phone number 101

If we want to call the number of the second telephone 102, we remove the handset (simply click it). You will hear a continuous tone confirming the call to the telephone exchange.

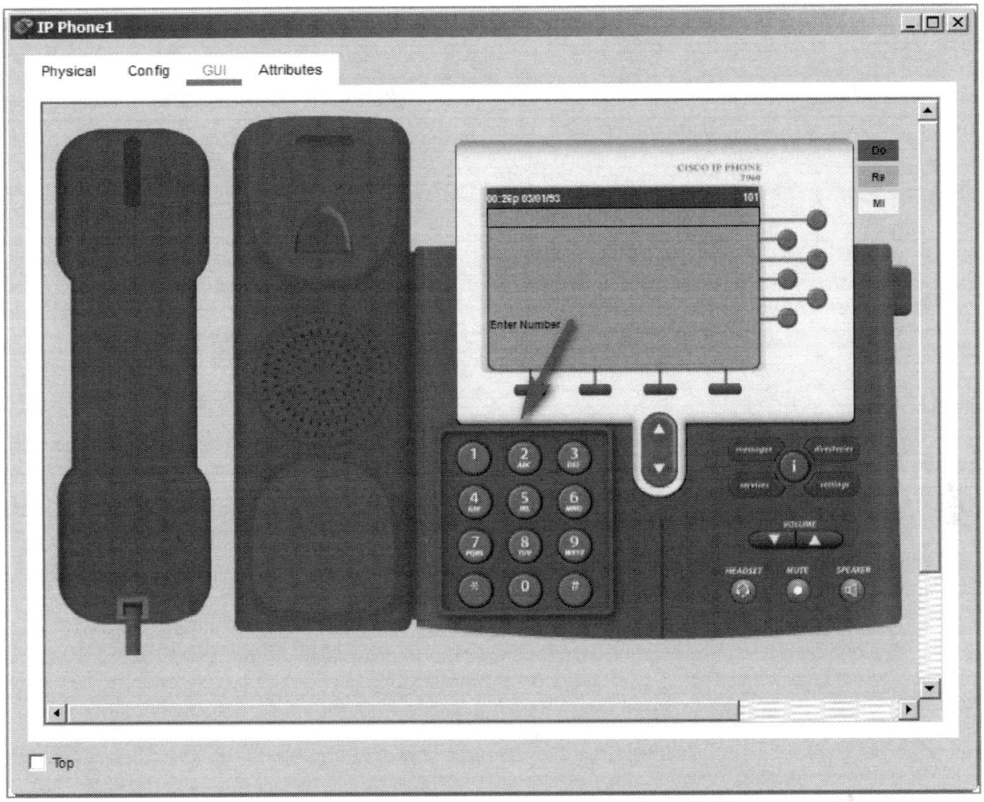

Figure 5.15 The phone is now ready for dialing.

The display will show "**Enter number**". We proceed to dial the number. On **IP Phone1** you dial **102**, on **IP Phone2** you hear a ring tone.

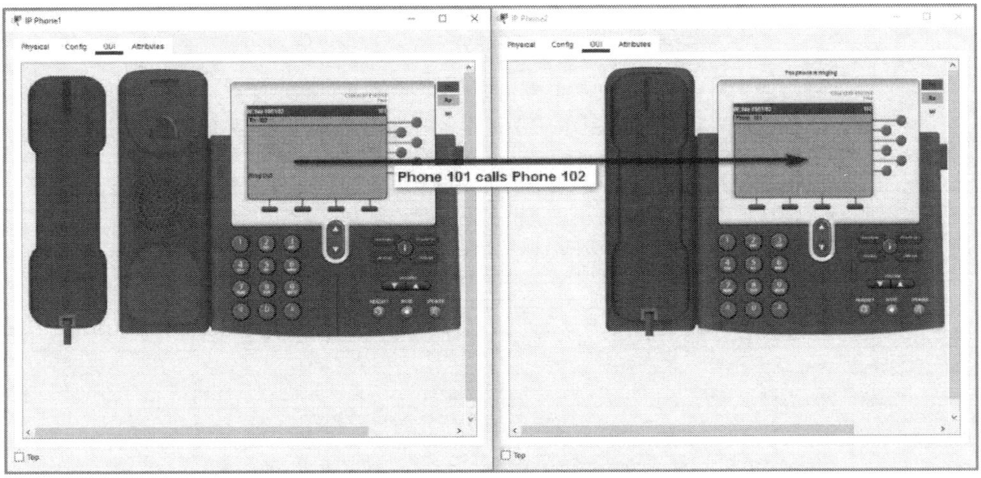

Figure 5.16 Phone 101 calls Phone 102.

Now we can hang up and call from the second phone (number **102**) to the number of the first phone, i.e. **101**. At the same time, on display of **Phone 102** we can observe that the message "**From: 101**". This message informs us that this is an incoming call from the number 101.

5.6 Communication between Two VoIP Exchanges

In order to set up and configure two VOIP networks (exchanges), connected between each other, we will first perform the following topology:

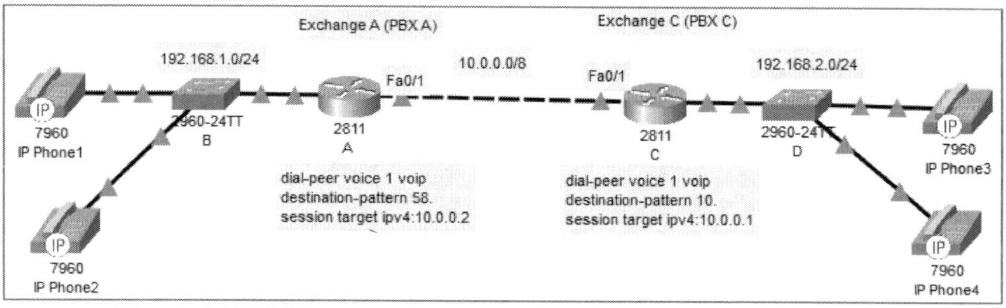

Figure 5.17 VoIP network topology with two exchanges A and C.

To create the topology, we choose:

- two routers (model **2811**),
- two switches (model **2960**),
- four IP telephones (model **7960**).

Assumptions for the configuration:

The assumptions for this example are shown in the table below.

PBX A	Internal network 192.168.1.0/24	Exchange network 10.0.0.0/8	IP of destination network : 10.0.0.2
PBX A	IP Phone 1	Prefix number 10	Number **101**
PBX A	IP Phone 2	Prefix number 10	Number **102**
PBX C	Internal network 192.168.2.0/24	Exchange network 10.0.0.0/8	IP of destination network 10.0.0.1
PBX C	IP Phone 3	Prefix number 58	Number **581**
PBX C	IP Phone 4	Prefix number 58	Number **582**

Table 5.1 Assumptions for the configuration of a VoIP network with two PBXs.

We will configure two VoIP PBXs in two stages :

- Stage 1 – internal (local) configuration of phones and exchanges.
- Stage 2 - configuring the link between the exchanges.

Stage 1 - Configuring the phones and PBXs.

We will carry out Stage 1 using the following steps:

Step 1. We connect the power supplies to the telephones at PBXs A and C.

Step 2. We connect PBX A to switch B.

Step 3. Connect PBX C to switch D.

Step 4. Connect IP Phone 1 and IP Phone 2 to switch B.

Step 5. Connect IP Phone 3 and IP Phone 4 to switch D.

Step 6. We configure the IP address for interface Fa0/0 of PBX A.

To do this, perform the following commands:

```
conf t
hostname A
int Fa0/0
ip address 192.168.1.1 255.255.255.0
no shutdown
```

Step 7. We configure the IP address for interface Fa0/1 of PBX A.

To do this, we execute the following commands:

```
conf t
hostname A
int Fa0/1
ip address 10.0.0.1 255.0.0.0
no shutdown
```

Step 8. We configure the DHCP service on PBX A with option 150.

To do this, we execute the following commands:

```
conf t
ip dhcp pool VOICE1
network 192.168.1.0 255.255.255.0
default-router 192.168.1.1
```

```
option 150 ip 192.168.1.1
```

Step 9. We configure the IP address for interface Fa0/0 of panel C.

To do this, we execute the following commands:

```
conf t
hostname C
int Fa0/0
ip address 192.168.2.1 255.255.255.0
no shutdown
```

Step10. We configure the IP address for interface Fa0/1 of the C panel.

To do this, we execute the following commands:

```
conf t
hostname C
int Fa0/1
ip address 10.0.0.2 255.0.0.0
no shutdown
```

Step 11. We configure the DHCP service on PBX C with option 150.

To do this, we execute the following commands:

```
conf t
ip dhcp pool VOICE2
network 192.168.2.0 255.255.255.0
default-router 192.168.2.1
option 150 ip 192.168.2.1
```

Step 12. We configure the Call Manager Express telephony service on PBX A.

To do this, we enter global configuration mode and execute the following commands:

```
en
conf t
telephony-service
```

```
max-dn 5
max-ephones 5
ip source-address 192.168.1.1 port 2000
```

Step 13. We configure the Call Manager Express telephony service on PBX C.

To do this, we enter global configuration mode and execute the following commands:

```
en
conf t
telephony-service
max-dn 5
max-ephones 5
ip source-address 192.168.2.1 port 2000
```

Step 14. On PBX A, we assign telephone numbers.

Note: In the event of misconfiguration of directory entries, when telephones cannot obtain line numbers, it is best to delete router A, then add it again, correctly connect to the devices in the topology and configure it.

We now create directory entries (so-called **directory names**) for PBX **A**, using the commands: `ephone-dn` and `number`. We then create the phone line assignments for the directory entries.

We assign telephone line 1 of the first telephone found by DHCP to directory entry **ephone-dn 1** (i.e. number 101). We assign phone line 2 of the second phone found by DHCP to the **ephone-dn 2** directory entry (i.e. number 102).

We will use commands to perform this step:

```
en
conf t
ephone-dn 1
number 101
ephone-dn 2
number 102
end
```

Step 15. On PBX C we assign telephone numbers.

Note: in case of misconfiguration of directory entries, when phones cannot obtain line numbers, it is best to remove the C router, then add it again, correctly connect to the devices in the topology and configure it.

As with PBX A, we now create directory entries (so-called **directory names**) for PBX **C,** using the **ephone-dn** and **number** commands. We then create the phone line assignments for the directory entries.

We assign telephone line number 1 of the first telephone found by DHCP to directory entry **ephone-dn 1** (i.e. number 581). We assign phone line 1 of the second phone found by DHCP to the **ephone-dn 2** directory entry (that is, number 582).

To perform this step we will use the commands:

```
en
conf t
ephone-dn 1
number 581
ephone-dn 2
number 582
end
```

Step 16. We configure the VLAN on switches B and D.

To do this, we execute the commands:

```
conf t
hostname B
interface range fa0/1-fa0/5
switchport mode access
switchport voice vlan 1

conf t
hostname D
interface range fa0/1-fa0/5
switchport mode access
switchport voice vlan 1
```

Stage 2 – configuring the link between A and C exchanges

We will carry out stage two, the configuration of the inter-panel link, using the following steps.

Step 1. At PBX A, we configure a static route to PBX C.

To do this, we execute the commands:

```
en
conf t
ip route 192.168.2.0 255.255.255.0 FastEthernet0/1
```

```
A#
A#show ip route static
S    192.168.2.0/24 is directly connected, FastEthernet0/1
```

Figure 5.18 Static routes in router A.

Step 2. At PBX A, we configure the processing of VoIP traffic to PBX C.

To do this, we execute the commands:

```
en
conf t
dial-peer voice 1 voip
destination-pattern 58.
session target ipv4:10.0.0.2
end
```

Note: here we also configure the number prefix to PBX C (**58**). The **dot** that follows the prefix is important - it stands for a single digit from 0 to 9.

```
A>en
A#conf  t
Enter configuration commands, one per line.  End with CNTL/Z.
A(config)#dial-peer voice 1 voip
A(config-dial-peer)#destination-pattern 58.
A(config-dial-peer)#session target ipv4:10.0.0.2
A(config-dial-peer)#end
```

Figure 5.19 Configuring VoIP traffic from router A to router C.

Step 3. At PBX C, we configure a static route to PBX A.

To do this, we execute the commands:

```
en
conf t
ip route 192.168.1.0 255.255.255.0 FastEthernet0/1
```

```
C#show ip route static
S    192.168.1.0/24 is directly connected, FastEthernet0/1
```

Figure 5.20 Static routes in router C .

Step 4. In PBX C, we configure the processing of VoIP traffic to PBX A.

To do this, we execute the commands:

```
en
conf t
dial-peer voice 1 voip
destination-pattern 10.
session target ipv4:10.0.0.1
end
```

Note: here we also configure the number prefix to PBX C (**10**). The **dot** that follows the prefix is important - it stands for a single digit from 0 to 9.

```
C>en
C#conf  t
Enter configuration commands, one per line.  End with CNTL/Z.
C(config)#dial-peer voice 1 voip
C(config-dial-peer)#destination-pattern 10.
C(config-dial-peer)#session target ipv4:10.0.0.1
C(config-dial-peer)#end
```

Figure 5.21 Configuring VoIP traffic from router C to router A.

Step 5. We check the communication between IP phones belonging to different exchanges.

We can now check whether phones located in different exchanges can call each other. To carry out a communication check of the phone located in PBX A (**101**) to the phone located in PBX C (**582**), we will dial the phone number **101**, which will call the phone number **582**.

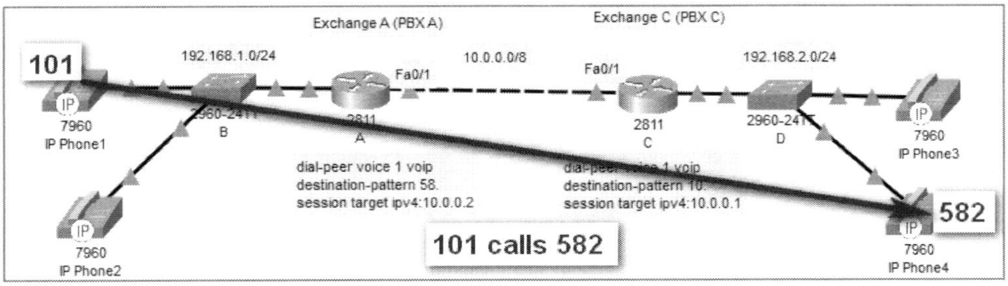

Figure 5.22 Phone 101 is calling Phone 582.

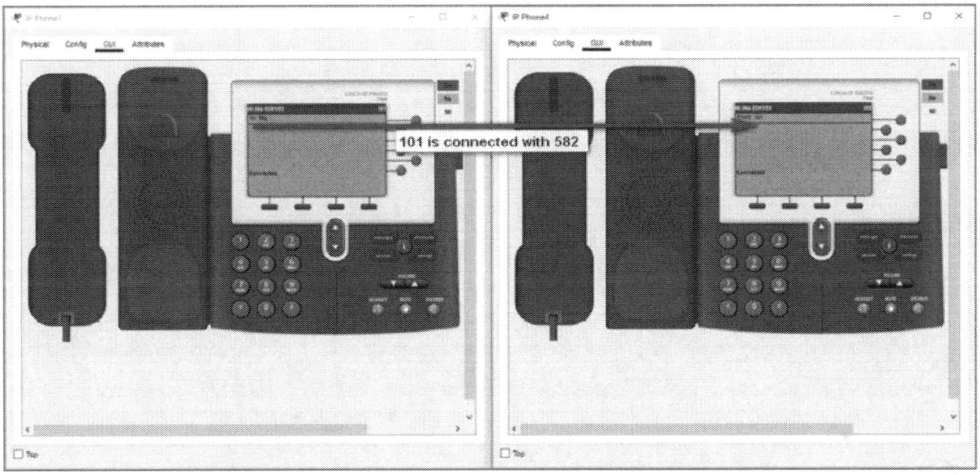

Figure 5.23 Phone 101 is connected with phone 582.

CHAPTER 6

STP PROTOCOL

6 STP PROTOCOL

The chapter describes the basic concepts of the STP and RSTP protocols and the main problems encountered in networks built with switches.

6.1 Introduction to STP Protocol

Networks built from multiple switches are usually characterized by redundancy, which, as well as increasing the reliability of the network, can result in partial or complete network failure. A simple example would be the distribution of a broadcast frame (with destination address **FF:FF:FF:FF:FF**), causing a so-called **broadcast storm**.

Spanning Tree Protocol is defined in the IEEE 802.1(d) standard and operates on the second layer of the ISO/OSI model. The purpose of the STP protocol is to determine which ports on the switch must be blocked so that network frame traffic does not cause loops in the layer two, the so-called broadcast domain. The STP protocol uses the Spanning-Tree Algorithm (**STA**). The purpose of the algorithm is to establish only one communication path between two stations. The STA algorithm sets each switch port to either the active state or the blocking state. Frames can only be transmitted via the active ports. The STP protocol is automatically enabled on each Cisco switch.

6.2 Basic STP concepts

Broadcast domain – A group of network devices in which devices can transmit information to other devices on a network segment without passing through a routing device.

Switch port states - Ports on a switch can have the following states:

BLK (*blocking*) – A blocked port assumes the role of an alternate port (***alternate port***) and doesn't participate in the transmission of Ethernet frames. In the blocked state, the port only receives BPDU frames and processes them with the corresponding switch module to select the best path to the root switch and establishes port roles: **root port** and **designated port**.

LSN (*Listening*) – The port is in the listening state. In the listening state, the port receives BPDU frames and forwards them to the corresponding switch module.

After 15 seconds, the port enters the LRN (Learning) state.

LRN (*Learning*) – The port changes state from LSN to LRN (MAC address learning). The port receives and processes BPDU frames. An update of the MAC address table (*mac address table*) is performed.

After 15 seconds, the port enters the FWD (Forwarding) state.

FWD (*Forwarding*) – the port forwards frames (sends and receives BPDU frames) and Ethernet frames.

Root Bridge – Main switch, is a term that defines the role of a switch in STP. The master switch is the reference point in the STP topology of the LAN. There can only be one master switch in an STP topology.

BPDU Frame (*Bridge Protocol Data Unit*) – a frame containing Spanning Tree Protocol (STP) information. Switches send **BPDU** frames to the multicast MAC address **01:80:C2:00:00:00** to implement the STA algorithm. The most important fields contained in a BPDU frame are: **Root BID, Root Patch Cost, Sender BID, Port ID**.

BID (*Bridge Identifier*) – the switch ID is a numeric value determined by the switch priority (value 32768), the extended system identifier **sys-id-ext** (value 1) and the MAC address of the port sending the BPDU frame. The default **BID** value is **32769**.

Root BID (*Root Bridge Identifier*) – Root Bridge ID (Root Bridge ID), dependent on the switch priority (default value 32769) and the MAC address of the port sending the BPDU frame.

Root Path Cost – the contractual distance to the master switch given as a cost value (*patch cost*). The default port cost is determined by the link speed - see the cost table.

Link speed	Cost (IEEE 802.1d)
10 Gb/s	2
1 Gb/s	4
100 Mb/s	19
10 Mb/s	100

Table 6.1 IEEE 802.1d cost table

Sender BID (*Sender Bridge Identifier*) – BPDU frame sender identifier,

STP Port Priority (*Port Priority*) – switch port priority (default value 128),

Port ID (*Port Identifier*) – switch port identifier consisting of port priority and port number.

Root port – the role of a switch port in the STP protocol (on a switch other than the root switch) that has the lowest cost connection leading to the root switch (has the shortest path to the root bridge). The switch has only one root port. The selection of the root port is determined by the **STA algorithm**.

Designated port – a designated port is a port that can forward network traffic but is not a master port. On the master switch, all ports are designated ports.

Alternate port or **Blocked port** – an alternate blocked port through which you can connect to the master switch in the event of a failure of the existing operational links.

6.3 Main Principles of the STA

6.3.1 Determining the BID and Root BID Sent by the Switches

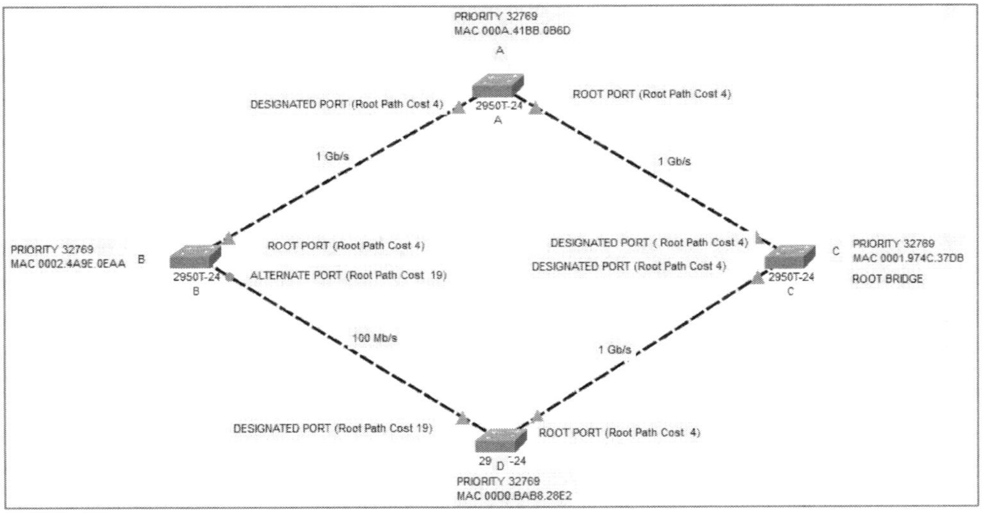

Figure 6.1 Example topology.

For example, switch A has a priority of 32769 and a MAC address of **000A.41BB.0B6D**. The switch will send a BPDU frame with the field values:

- BID: **32769.000A.41BB.0B6D**
- Root BID: **32769. 000A.41BB.0B6D**

For example, switch B has priority 32769 and MAC address **0002.4A9E.0EAA**. The switch will send a BPDU frame with the field values:

- BID: **32769.0002.4A9E.0EAA**
- Root BID: **32769.0002.4A9E.0EAA**

Switch C has priority 32769 and MAC address **0001.974C.37DB**. The switch will send a BPDU frame with the field values:

- BID: **32769.0001.974C.37DB**
- Root BID: **32769.0001.974C.37DB**

Switch D has priority 32769 and MAC address **00D0.BAB8.28E2**. The switch will send a BPDU frame with the field values:

- BID: **32769.00D0.BAB8.28E2**
- Root BID: **32769.00D0.BAB8.28E2**

6.3.2 Root Bridge Switch Election.

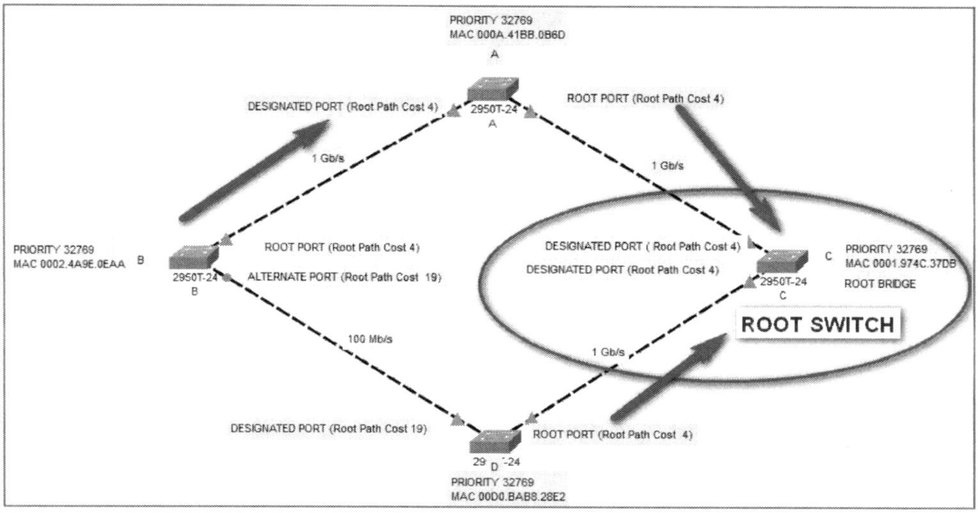

Figure 6.2 Election of the root switch in the STP topology.

At the beginning of the **STA algorithm**, the STP main root switch election must take place. The main switch becomes the switch with the smallest **Root BID** value. For this purpose, the switches exchange BPDU frames between each other (frames are sent every 2 seconds) and determine which switch has the smallest **Root BID** value from among the received frames, for example:

- **32769.000A.41BB.0B6D,**
- **32769.0002.4A9E.0EAA,**
- **32769.0001.974C.37DB,** *(lowest value)*
- **32769.00D0.BAB8.28E2.**

In the topology shown, the switch with the smallest **Root BID** field value has been selected, i.e. switch **C**. Note: all ports on the master switch assume the role of Designated (**Desg**) ports.

6.3.3 Establishing the Role of the Root

Once the root switch has been selected, the other switches must select their **root port**, i.e. the port through which it is possible to reach the root switch at the lowest cost.

In order to select the root port for a switch, the BDPU frames are analyzed and the port that will have (**conditions must be met in the order listed**) is selected:

1. the smallest **Root Path Cost**,
2. the smallest BID of the sending device (**Sender BID**),
3. the lowest number (**Port ID**),

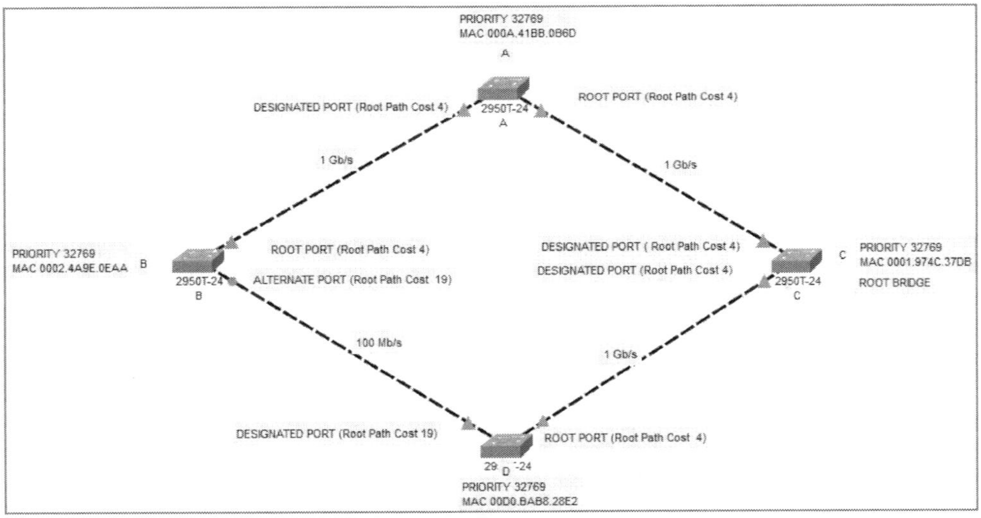

Figure 6.3 Root port election.

- For switch A it will be the port of switch C.
- For switch B it will be the port of switch C.
- For switch D it will be the port of switch C.

6.3.4 Determining the Role of a Designated Port

If the sum of the lowest accumulated path cost between two switches is the same, the port selected is the port that is not the root port and is set as the designated port.

Any port that has not been selected as a root or designated port will be set to **BLK** (*blocking*) mode and will become an alternate port for the STP protocol, designated as **Altn** (*alternate port*).

6.4 Observation of the STP Protocol Operation

On each switch, the STP protocol is enabled by default (no special command is required). Let us analyze an example topology in which three switches (SW1, SW2, SW3) are connected in a triangle, for the following three cases:

- all links between the switches are operational,
- the link between switches SW2 and SW3 is faulty,
- the link between switches SW1 and SW3 is faulty.

If all links are operational, SW3 is elected to be the **Root Bridge** based on the MAC address (switch SW3 has the smallest address). The link between switch SW1 and SW2 becomes a secondary link, as indicated by the role of the Gig0/2 (**Altn**) port. In this situation, Ethernet frames communicate through switch SW3.

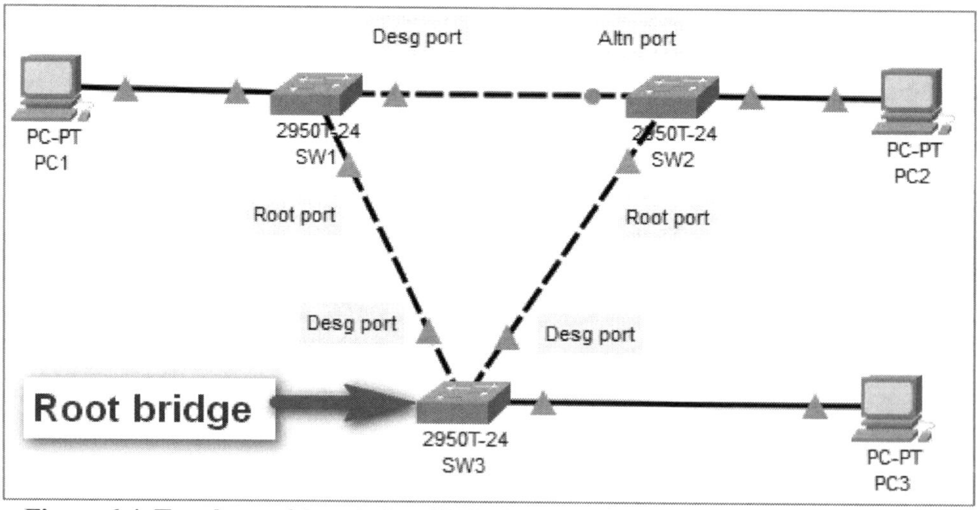

Figure 6.4 Topology with switches SW1, SW2 and SW3 connected in a triangle.

We can check it using command: `show spanning-tree`.

```
SW3#show spanning-tree
VLAN0001
  Spanning tree enabled protocol ieee
  Root ID     Priority     32769
              Address      0001.C918.C0B1
              This bridge is the root
              Hello Time   2 sec  Max Age 20 sec  Forward Delay 15 sec
```

Figure 6.5 Checking the role of switch SW3.

6.4.1 First Case of Link Failure

If the link between SW2 and SW3 is faulty (e.g. damaged), SW3 will also be elected to the role of **Root Bridge** - in this sense nothing changes. However, the corresponding ports between SW2 and SW3 will be blocked (enter the **BLK** state) and will lose the possibility of elevation to the role of Designated or Root Ports.

The **Gi0/2** port on SW2 will take on the role of the **root port**, thus bypassing the faulty link. In this situation, the Ethernet frames communicate via the faulty links.

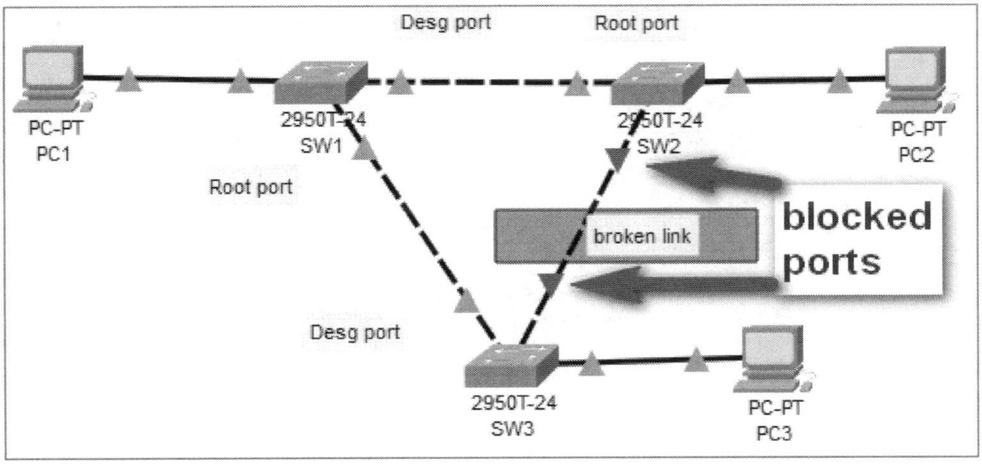

Figure 6.6 Topology with broken link between SW2 and SW3.

```
SW2#show spanning-tree
VLAN0001
  Spanning tree enabled protocol ieee
  Root ID    Priority    32769
             Address     0001.C918.C0B1
             Cost        8
             Port        26(GigabitEthernet0/2)
             Hello Time  2 sec  Max Age 20 sec  Forward Delay 15 sec

  Bridge ID  Priority    32769  (priority 32768 sys-id-ext 1)
             Address     00E0.F97E.9161
             Hello Time  2 sec  Max Age 20 sec  Forward Delay 15 sec
             Aging Time  20

Interface        Role Sts Cost      Prio.Nbr Type
---------------- ---- --- --------- -------- --------------------------------
Fa0/1            Desg FWD 19        128.1    P2p
Gi0/2            Root FWD 4         128.26   P2p
```

Figure 6.7 Checking the status of the ports on switch SW2.

```
SW3#show spanning-tree
VLAN0001
  Spanning tree enabled protocol ieee
  Root ID    Priority    32769
             Address     0001.C918.C0B1
             This bridge is the root
             Hello Time  2 sec  Max Age 20 sec  Forward Delay 15 sec

  Bridge ID  Priority    32769  (priority 32768 sys-id-ext 1)
             Address     0001.C918.C0B1
             Hello Time  2 sec  Max Age 20 sec  Forward Delay 15 sec
             Aging Time  20

Interface        Role Sts Cost      Prio.Nbr Type
---------------- ---- --- --------- -------- --------------------------------
Gi0/1            Desg FWD 4         128.25   P2p
Fa0/1            Desg FWD 19        128.1    P2p
```

Figure 6.8 Checking the status of the ports on switch SW3.

In order to explain the status of the STP protocol in detail, we will again use the command: **`show spanning-tree`**. on the switch acting as the so-called **root**. The execution of this command will result in the following information (at the top):

- switch priority,
- MAC address of the switch,
- the information "**This bridge is the root**" (this switch is the root in STP),
- and at the bottom, port detail information:
- interface name (**Interface** field),
- port role (**Role** field),
- port status (field **Sts**),
- port cost (field **Cost**),
- port priority (field **Prio**),
- port number (field **Nbr**).

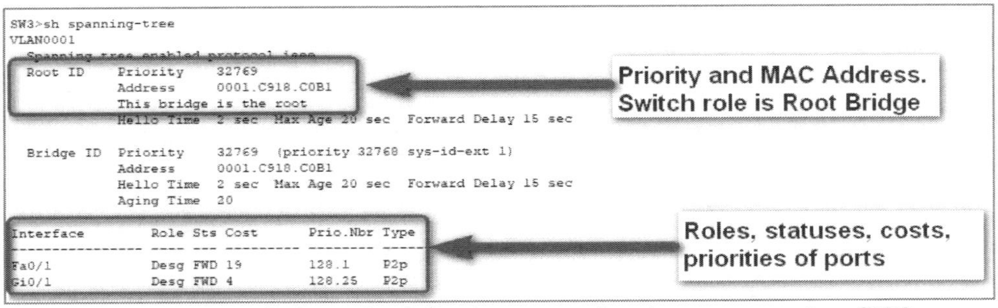

Figure 6.9 Detailed result of the show spanning-tree command on SW3

The **Gi0/2** port on switch SW3 is not displayed because it has been set as blocked (**BLK**), so it does not currently belong to the STP tree.

6.4.2 Second Case of Link Failure

In the case where the link between SW1 and SW3 is faulty (e.g. damaged), this also elects SW3 to the role of **Root Bridge** - in this sense nothing changes. On the other hand, the corresponding ports between switches SW1 and SW3 will be blocked (enter the **BLK** state) and will lose their ability to be elected as Designated or Root ports.

The port **Gi0/1** on SW1, will enter the role of the **root port** and the port **Gi0/2** on SW2 will enter the role of **designated port**, thus bypassing the failed link.

In this situation, Ethernet frames communicate over the faulty link.

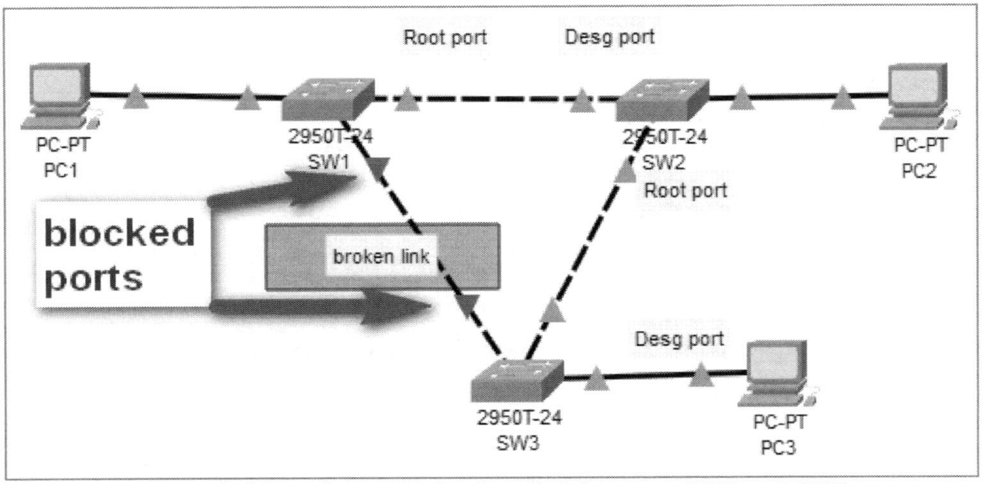

Figure 6.10 Topology with broken link between SW1 and SW3

Port **Gi0/1** on switch SW3 is not displayed because it has been set as blocked (**BLK**), so it does not currently belong to the STP tree.

```
SW3#show spanning-tree
VLAN0001
  Spanning tree enabled protocol ieee
  Root ID    Priority    32769
             Address     0001.C918.C0B1
             This bridge is the root
             Hello Time  2 sec  Max Age 20 sec  Forward Delay 15 sec

  Bridge ID  Priority    32769  (priority 32768 sys-id-ext 1)
             Address     0001.C918.C0B1
             Hello Time  2 sec  Max Age 20 sec  Forward Delay 15 sec
             Aging Time  20

Interface        Role Sts Cost      Prio.Nbr Type
---------------- ---- --- --------- -------- --------------------------------
Fa0/1            Desg FWD 19        128.1    P2p
Gi0/2            Desg FWD 4         128.26   P2p
```

Figure 6.11 Result of command `show spanning-tree` on SW3.

6.5 Description of the RSTP

The *Rapid Spanning Tree Protocol* (**RSTP**) is actually an amendment introduced to the STP protocol (according to the 802.1w standard). RSTP improves the operation of the STP protocol by providing mechanisms for rapid network convergence.

The RSTP protocol reduces the number of port states, limiting them to the following states:

- frame **discarding** (*blocked*) - BLK,
- MAC address learning - LRN,
- frame **forwarding** - FWD.

Unlike the STP protocol, where only the master switch generated BPDU frames, in RSTP, **each switch generates BPDU frames at all times.** These act as connection control between neighboring switches. As a result, the maximum time required to exchange BPDU frames between switches has been reduced from 20 to six seconds.

6.6 Comparison of RSTP and STP Performance

The main difference between the STP and RSTP protocols is the time it takes for a network at layer two of the ISO/OSI model to become a converged network. If one of the connections fails or the network topology unexpectedly changes, it takes the STP protocol approximately 30 to 60 seconds to detect the failure and reconfigure the STP protocol. In the **RSTP** protocol, only a few seconds are needed for this.

6.6.1 Enabling the RSTP Protocol

To enable the **RSTP** protocol (i.e. to activate the **802.1w** standard extension), we need to execute the commands on each switch:

```
enable
configure terminal
spanning-tree mode rapid-pvst
```

After executing the above commands in the example topology, we can see that the effects of **RSTP** are observed immediately.

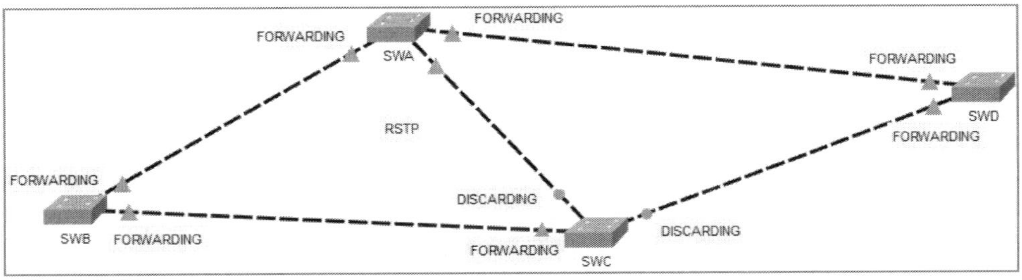

Figure 6.12 The state of the topology immediately after the topology is created (activating the RSTP protocol).

6.6.2 Disabling the RSTP Protocol

To disable the operation of the **RSTP** protocol (i.e. to restore the operation of STP without extension according to the **802.1w** standard), we need to execute the commands on each switch:

```
enable
configure terminal
no spanning-tree mode rapid-pvst
```

After executing the above commands in the example topology, we can see that the effects are only observed after a long time.

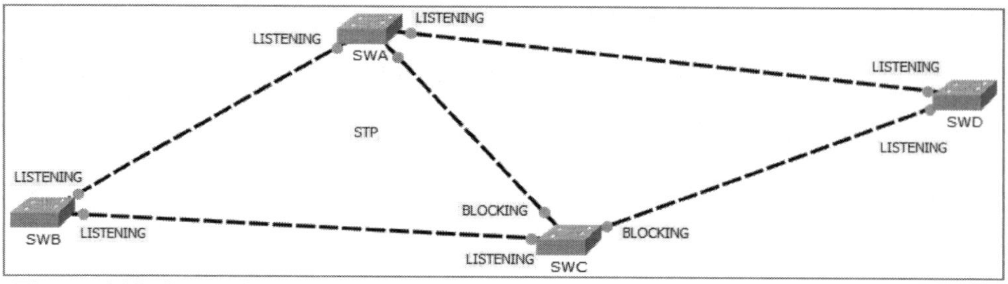

Figure 6.13 State of the topology at some time after the topology has been created (STP protocol start-up).

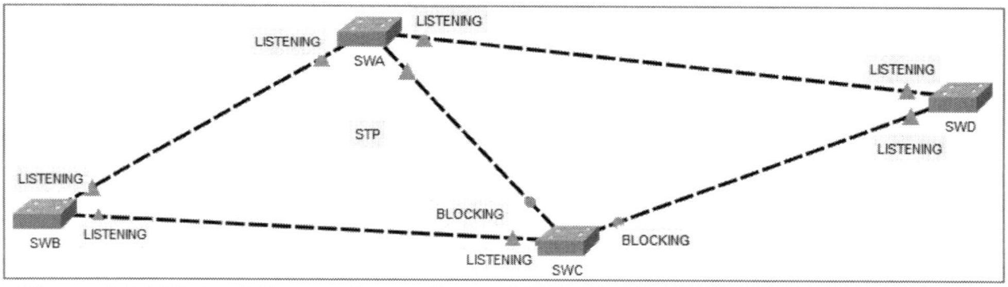

Figure 6.14 State of the topology after waiting a few seconds (STP protocol start-up).

Conclusion: the topology states in both cases (STP and RSTP) are the same, but the advantage of RTSP is that the RSTP protocol executes faster.

CHAPTER 7

VTP PROTOCOL

7 VTP PROTOCOL

This chapter describes the basic concepts of the VTP protocol and VLAN management.

7.1 Introduction to VTP Protocol

The VTP protocol (***VLAN Trunking Protocol***) is a protocol that operates in layer two of the ISO/OSI network model. This protocol is used to manage multiple VLANs.

The protocol facilitates configuration changes regarding VLANs, in networks with multiple switches. When using this protocol, we need to determine which switch will contain the primary VLAN base for the entire physical network. We call this switch the VTP server. All switches must operate in the same VTP domain.

The other switches can act as either a VTP client or be transparent (only transmit information about changes in the VLAN configuration). The table below shows the modes of switches in the VTP protocol and their detailed capabilities

Mode	In a VTP domain, the switch can:	In a VTP domain, the switch cannot:
Server	store VLAN information for the entire VTP domain. Create, modify, delete VLANs; determine the VTP version;, propagate the VTP configuration and synchronize the configuration across the domain. propagate changes to the VTP configuration; store configuration about VLANs; create local VLANs	-
Client	-	create, modify, delete VLANs, VTPs on other switches.
Transparent	propagate VTP configuration changes; create local VLANs	create, modify, delete VLANs; determine the version of VTP; on other switches; store the VTP configuration.

Table 7.1 Description of the switch modes in the VTP protocol.

7.2 Configuring of VTP and RSTP Protocol.

7.2.1 Configuring the RSTP Protocol without Using VTP

In order to compare the configuration without VTP with the configuration with VTP, we will first present the configuration without using VTP.

Step 1. Creating the network topology

We will first create a network consisting of:

- five switches (S1, S2, S3, S4, S5),
- eleven computers,
- and five VLANs (TEACHERS, STUDENTS, GUESTS, THEORY, MANAGEMENT)

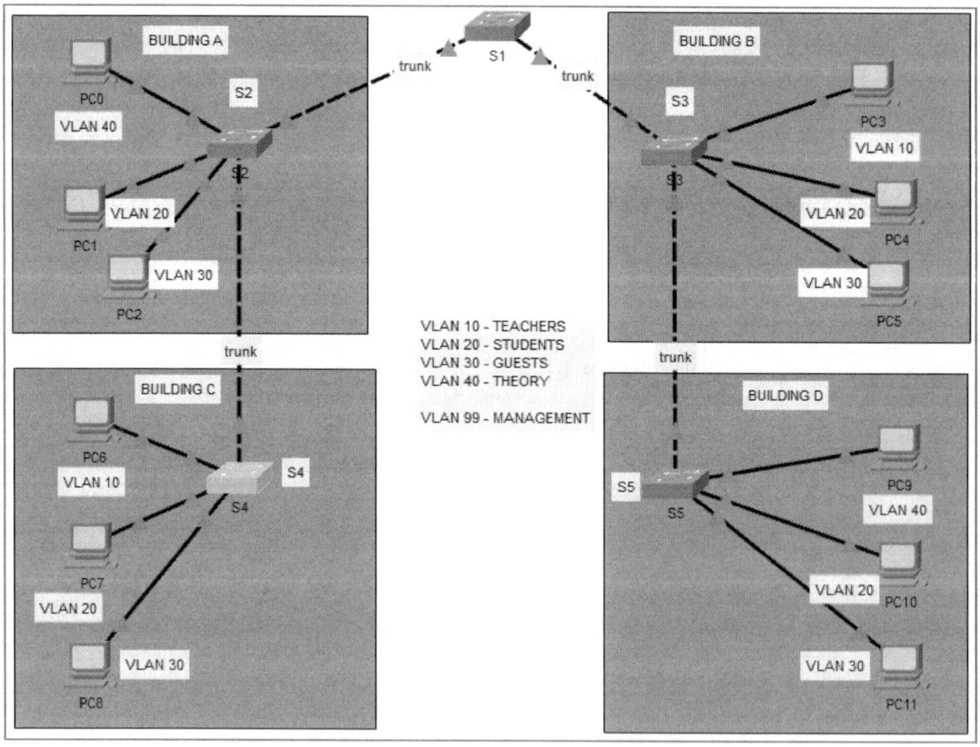

Figure 7.1 Network topology without VTP.

Step 2. We configure the addresses of network devices

Next, we will configure the addresses of the end devices according to the following tables.

Device(VLAN)	Address / Mask / Gateway to VLAN
PC0 (VLAN 40)	172.17.40.21 / 255.255.255.0 / 172.17.40.1
PC1 (VLAN 20)	172.17.20.21 / 255.255.255.0 / 172.17.20.1
PC2 (VLAN 30)	172.17.30.21 / 255.255.255.0 / 172.17.30.1

Table 7.2 Addressing of computers (BUILDING A).

Device (VLAN)	Address / Mask / Gateway to VLAN
PC3 (VLAN 10)	172.17.10.22 / 255.255.255.0 / 172.17.10.1
PC4 (VLAN 20)	172.17.20.22 / 255.255.255.0 / 172.17.20.1
PC5 (VLAN 30)	172.17.30.22 / 255.255.255.0 / 172.17.30.1

Table 7.3 Addressing of computers (BUILDING B).

Device (VLAN)	Address / Mask / Gateway to VLAN
PC6 (VLAN 10)	172.17.10.23 / 255.255.255.0 / 172.17.10.1
PC7 (VLAN 20)	172.17.20.23 / 255.255.255.0 / 172.17.20.1
PC8 (VLAN 30)	172.17.30.23 / 255.255.255.0 / 172.17.30.1

Table 7.4 Addressing of computers (BUILDING C).

Device (VLAN)	Address/ Mask / Gateway to VLAN
PC9 (VLAN 40)	172.17.40.24 / 255.255.255.0 / 172.17.40.1
PC10 (VLAN 20)	172.17.20.24 / 255.255.255.0 / 172.17.20.1
PC11 (VLAN 30)	172.17.30.24 / 255.255.255.0 / 172.17.30.1

Table 7.5 Addressing of computers (BUILDING D).

Step 3. We configure switches S1, S2, S3, S4, S5 into RSTP mode.

On each switch, we execute the command (in global configuration mode)

```
spanning-tree mode rapid-pvst
```

Step 4. We configure the VLANs on the switches.

We configure the VLAN base according to the following table.

VLAN network	Name of VLAN network	VLAN network description
10	**TEACHERS**	Teachers in buildings B and C
20	**STUDENTS**	Students in buildings A, B, C, D
30	**GUESTS**	Guests in buildings A, B, C, D
40	**THEORY**	Scientists in buildings A and D, working on new networking technologies

99	**MANAGEMENT**	**This network is used for VLAN management only.**

Table 7.6 VLAN network description

In global configuration mode, on each of the switches: **S1, S2, S3, S4, S5** we execute the following commands (where **n** is the switch number):

```
Sn(config)#vlan 10
Sn(config-vlan)#name TEACHERS
Sn(config-vlan)#vlan 20
Sn(config-vlan)#name STUDENTS
Sn(config-vlan)#vlan 30
Sn(config-vlan)#name GUESTS
Sn(config-vlan)#vlan 40
Sn(config-vlan)#name THEORY
Sn(config-vlan)#vlan 99
Sn(config-vlan)#name MANAGEMENT
```

Step 5. We configure VLAN access on switch ports.

We configure the access ports on all end switches: **S2, S3, S4, S5** , according to the following template.

```
interface <interface>
switchport mode access
switchport access vlan <vlan_no>
```

Ports on switches S2, S3: **Fa 0/1, Fa 0/24** are reserved for trunk links only - do not use them for VLAN access.

Step 6.We configure VLAN access on switch S2.

For port Fa0/11 (**PC0**), we set the configuration:

```
switchport access vlan 40
switchport mode access
```

For port Fa0/18 (**PC1**), we set the configuration:

```
switchport access vlan 20
switchport mode access
```

For port Fa0/6 (**PC3**) we set the configuration:

```
switchport access vlan 30
switchport mode access
```

Step 7. We configure VLAN access on switch S3.

For port Fa0/11 (**PC3**), we set the configuration:

```
switchport access vlan 10
switchport mode access
```

For port Fa0/18 (**PC4**), we set the configuration:

```
switchport access vlan 20
switchport mode access
```

For port Fa0/6 (**PC5**), we set the configuration:

```
switchport access vlan 30
switchport mode access
```

Fa 0/24 ports on switches S4, S5 are reserved for trunk links only - do not use them for VLAN access.

Step 8. We configure VLAN access on switch S4.

For port Fa0/11 (**PC6**), we set the configuration

```
switchport access vlan 10
switchport mode access
```

For port Fa0/18 (**PC7**), we set the configuration:

```
switchport access vlan 20
switchport mode access
```

For port Fa0/6 (**PC8**) we set the configuration:

```
switchport access vlan 30
switchport mode access
```

Step 9. We configure VLAN access on switch S5.

For port Fa0/11 (**PC9**), we set the configuration:

```
switchport access vlan 40
switchport mode access
```

For port Fa0/18 (**PC10**), we set the configuration:

```
switchport access vlan 20
switchport mode access
```

For port Fa0/6 (**PC11**) we set the configuration:

```
switchport access vlan 30
switchport mode Access
```

Step 10. Verification of the STP protocol on switch S1.

To verify the status of the STP protocol on switch S1, the following commands are executed:

```
enable
show spanning-tree
```

```
S1#show spanning-tree
VLAN0001
  Spanning tree enabled protocol rstp
  Root ID    Priority    24577
             Address     0001.42D2.8B30
             This bridge is the root
             Hello Time  2 sec  Max Age 20 sec  Forward Delay 15 sec

  Bridge ID  Priority    24577  (priority 24576 sys-id-ext 1)
             Address     0001.42D2.8B30
             Hello Time  2 sec  Max Age 20 sec  Forward Delay 15 sec
             Aging Time  20

Interface        Role Sts Cost      Prio.Nbr Type
---------------- ---- --- --------- -------- --------------------------------
Fa0/1            Desg FWD 19        128.1    P2p
Fa0/3            Desg FWD 19        128.3    P2p
```

Figure 7.2 Verify STP status on switch S1.

Command results:

- STP protocol used: **RSTP**.
- The STP priority for this switch is **24577**.
- Switch role: **root**.

Switch S1 is the primary STP (**root**) device at Layer 2. The other switches store the same VLAN information as S1.

Step 11. Verify the STP protocol on switch S5.

To verify the status of the STP protocol on switch S5, we run the following commands:

```
enable
show spanning-tree
```

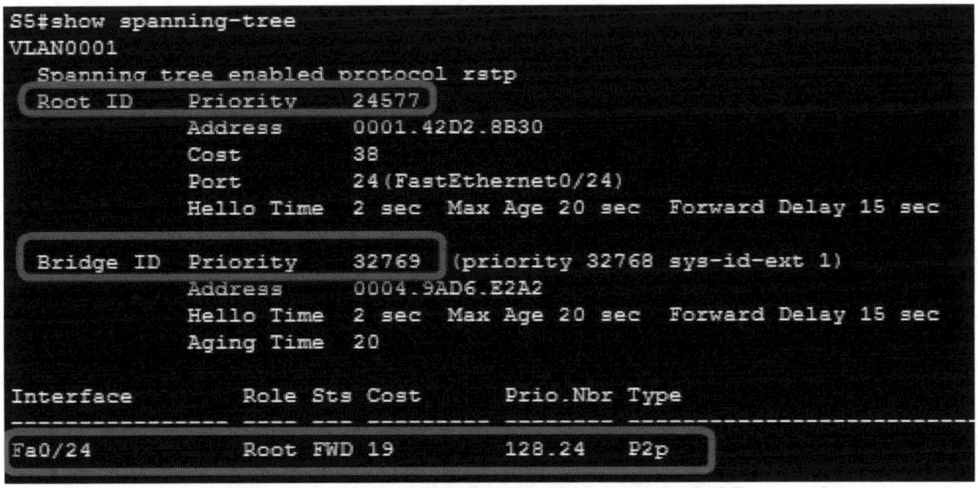

```
S5#show spanning-tree
VLAN0001
  Spanning tree enabled protocol rstp
  Root ID    Priority    24577
             Address     0001.42D2.8B30
             Cost        38
             Port        24(FastEthernet0/24)
             Hello Time  2 sec  Max Age 20 sec  Forward Delay 15 sec

  Bridge ID  Priority    32769  (priority 32768 sys-id-ext 1)
             Address     0004.9AD6.E2A2
             Hello Time  2 sec  Max Age 20 sec  Forward Delay 15 sec
             Aging Time  20

Interface        Role Sts Cost      Prio.Nbr Type
---------------- ---- --- --------- -------- --------------------------------
Fa0/24           Root FWD 19        128.24   P2p
```

Figure 7.3 Checking STP status on switch S5.

Command results:

- STP protocol used: **RSTP**.
- The STP priority for this switch is **24769**.
- The switch communicates with the master switch S1 via port Fa0/24.

Step 12. Checking the VLAN base on switch S5.

To check the status of the VLAN base on switch S5, run the command:

```
show vlan
```

```
S5#show vlan

VLAN Name                             Status    Ports
---- -------------------------------- --------- -------------------------------
1    default                          active    Fa0/1, Fa0/2, Fa0/3, Fa0/4
                                                Fa0/5, Fa0/7, Fa0/8, Fa0/9
                                                Fa0/10, Fa0/12, Fa0/13, Fa0/14
                                                Fa0/15, Fa0/16, Fa0/17, Fa0/19
                                                Fa0/20, Fa0/21, Fa0/22, Fa0/23
                                                Gig0/1, Gig0/2
10   TEACHERS                         active
20   STUDENTS                         active    Fa0/18
30   GUESTS                           active    Fa0/6
40   THEORY                           active    Fa0/11
99   MANAGEMENT                       active
1002 fddi-default                     active
1003 token-ring-default               active
1004 fddinet-default                  active
1005 trnet-default                    active
```

Figure 7.4 Check VLAN base status on switch S5.

All switches share the same VLAN database, configured separately on each switch. However, a more convenient solution, in networks with a large number of switches and many VLANs, is the VTP protocol, which offers central management of these networks (VLANs).

7.2.2 Configuring RSTP without Using VTP

This example is a modification of the example in the previous section. Therefore, we will focus on configuring the primary VLAN base on switch **S1** and the VTP protocol in the **VTP** domain.

Step 1. Creating the network topology

We will first create a network consisting of:

- five switches (S1, S2, S3, S4, S5),
- eleven computers,
- and five VLANs (TEACHERS, STUDENTS, GUESTS, THEORY, MANAGEMENT)

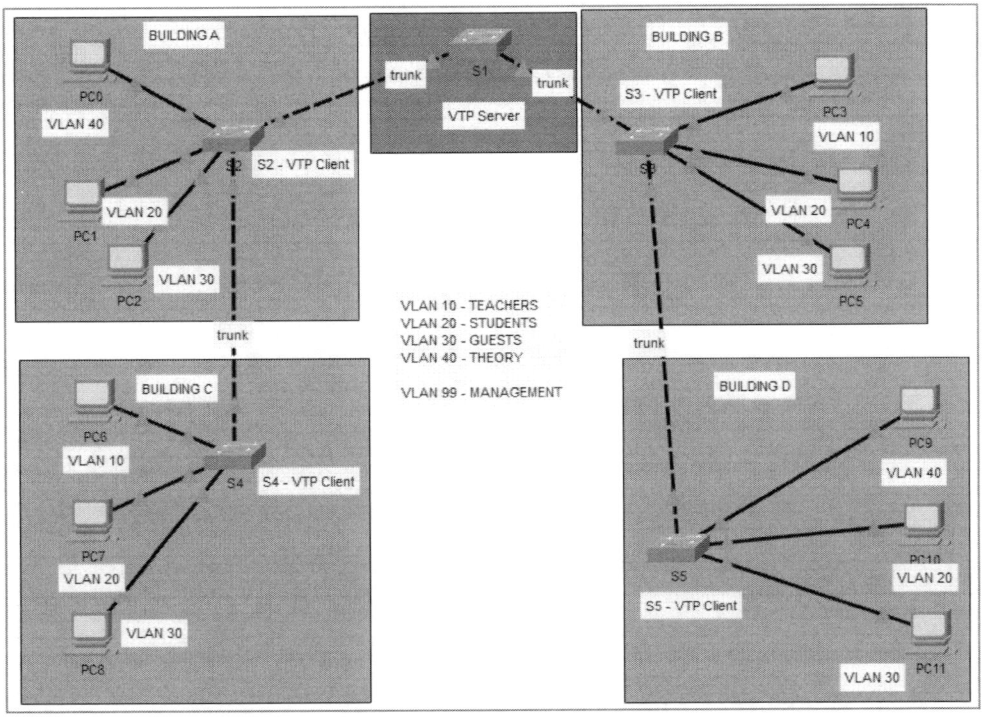

Figure 7.5 Network topology with VTP protocol.

Step 2. Removing the VLAN base configuration on the switches.

We delete the VLAN base on all switches: **S1, S2, S3, S4, S5,** using the commands:

```
enable
delete vlan.dat
```

Step 3. We configure VLAN access on the switch ports.

We configure the access ports on all end switches: **S2, S3, S4, S5** , according to the following template.

```
interface <interface>
switchport mode access
switchport access vlan <vlan_no>
```

Step 4. We configure switches S1, S2, S3, S4, S5 into RSTP mode.

On each switch we execute the command (in global configuration mode)

```
spanning-tree mode rapid-pvst
```

Step 5. We configure the primary VLAN base on switch S1.

We configure the primary VLAN base on **S1** according to the following table.

VLAN network	VLAN network name	VLAN network description
10	**TEACHERS**	Teachers in buildings B and C
20	**STUDENTS**	Students in buildings A, B, C, D
30	**GUESTS**	Guests in buildings A, B, C, D
40	**THEORY**	Scientists in building A and D, working on new networking technologies
99	**MANAGEMENT**	**This network is used for VLAN management only**

Table 7.7 VLAN base.

In global configuration mode, we execute the following commands on switch **S1**:

```
S1(config)#vlan 10
S1(config-vlan)#name TEACHERS
S1(config-vlan)#vlan 20
S1(config-vlan)#name STUDENTS
S1(config-vlan)#vlan 30
S1(config-vlan)#name GUESTS
S1(config-vlan)#vlan 40
S1(config-vlan)#name THEORY
S1(config-vlan)#vlan 99
S1(config-vlan)#name MANAGEMENT
```

Step 6. We configure the VTP domain on the switches.

We now configure the VTP domain on all switches: **S1, S2, S3, S4, S5**, according to the following pattern.

```
enable
conf t
vtp domain <domain_name>
vtp mode <mode>
```

`vtp password <password_for_domain>`

- VTP domain name: **itstart**
- VTP domain password: **itstart**
- Domain server: **S1**
- Domain clients: **S2, S3, S4, S5**

Step 7. We check switch S1 to see if it is as a server in the VTP protocol.

We check the configuration with the command: **`show vtp status`**

```
S1#show vtp status
VTP Version                        : 2
Configuration Revision             : 0
Maximum VLANs supported locally : 255
Number of existing VLANs           : 10
VTP Operating Mode                 : Server
VTP Domain Name                    : itstart
```

Figure 7.6 Configure the VTP server on switch S1.

Step 8. We check switch S2 if it is as a VTP client.

We check the configuration with the command: **`show vtp status`**.

```
S2#show vtp status
VTP Version                        : 2
Configuration Revision             : 0
Maximum VLANs supported locally : 255
Number of existing VLANs           : 10
VTP Operating Mode                 : Client
VTP Domain Name                    : itstart
VTP Pruning Mode                   : Disabled
VTP V2 Mode                        : Disabled
VTP Traps Generation               : Disabled
MD5 digest                         : 0x1C 0x90 0x7C 0x47 0xC0 0x15 0xEA 0x12
Configuration last modified by 0.0.0.0 at 3-1-93 00:25:06
```

Figure 7.7 Configuration of the VTP client on the S2 switch.

Step 9. We check switch S3 to be as a VTP client.

We check the configuration using the command: **`show vtp status.`**

```
S3#show vtp status
VTP Version                     : 2
Configuration Revision          : 0
Maximum VLANs supported locally : 255
Number of existing VLANs        : 10
VTP Operating Mode              : Client
VTP Domain Name                 : itstart
VTP Pruning Mode                : Disabled
VTP V2 Mode                     : Disabled
VTP Traps Generation            : Disabled
MD5 digest                      : 0x1C 0x90 0x7C 0x47 0xC0 0x15 0xEA 0x12
Configuration last modified by 0.0.0.0 at 3-1-93 00:25:06
```

Figure 7.8 VTP client configuration on S3.

Step 10. We check switch S4 to be as a VTP client.

We check the configuration using the command: **`show vtp status`**

```
S4#show vtp status
VTP Version                     : 2
Configuration Revision          : 0
Maximum VLANs supported locally : 255
Number of existing VLANs        : 10
VTP Operating Mode              : Client
VTP Domain Name                 : itstart
VTP Pruning Mode                : Disabled
VTP V2 Mode                     : Disabled
VTP Traps Generation            : Disabled
MD5 digest                      : 0x1C 0x90 0x7C 0x47 0xC0 0x15 0xEA 0x12
Configuration last modified by 0.0.0.0 at 3-1-93 00:25:06
```

Figure 7.9 VTP client configuration on S4.

Step 11. We check the switch S5 to be as a VTP client.

We check the configuration using the command: **`show vtp status`**

```
S5#show vtp status
VTP Version                     : 2
Configuration Revision          : 0
Maximum VLANs supported locally : 255
Number of existing VLANs        : 10
VTP Operating Mode              : Client
VTP Domain Name                 : itstart
VTP Pruning Mode                : Disabled
VTP V2 Mode                     : Disabled
VTP Traps Generation            : Disabled
MD5 digest                      : 0x1C 0x90 0x7C 0x47 0xC0 0x15 0xEA 0x12
Configuration last modified by 0.0.0.0 at 3-1-93 00:25:06
```

Figure 7.10 VTP client configuration in S5.

Conclusion: on each switch belonging to the **VTP domain named itstart,** there is the same VLAN base configuration.

CHAPTER 8

FRAME RELAY TECHNOLOGY

8 FRAME RELAY TECHNOLOGY

The chapter describes the basic concepts of Frame Relay technology, the Frame Relay frame format, the purpose of CIR, CBIR parameters in FR, address mapping in FR, the role of the **Inverse ARP** protocol and also basic FR configuration commands.

8.1 Brief Description of Frame Relay Technology

Frame Relay (**FR**) is the name of a technology and a protocol that combines circuit switching technology and packet switching technology.

The **FR** protocol operates at layers two and one of the OSI/ISO model. The main advantages of networks based on FR technology are their relatively low maintenance cost and easy configuration of end devices.

Application areas for FR technology are:

- transferring large data files requiring low latency and high bandwidth in WANs,
- connecting different types of remote local networks,
- creating access to ATM networks,
- data and voice transmission,
- videoconferencing and teleconferencing.

A **Frame Relay** network consists of various types of terminal equipment (PCs, servers or workstations), the equipment that provides access to this network (e.g. routers, modems) and the devices typical of Frame Relay technology (FR switches, CSU/DSU devices and multiplexers). The user-side equipment is called *Data Terminal Equipment* (**DTE**), while the equipment that provides the DTE equipment with a connection to the WAN is called *Data Circuit-terminating Equipment* (**DCE**).

The connections between two **DTE** devices in an FR network are called virtual circuits. A **Virtual Circuit** is called a logical circuit created to ensure reliable communication between two network devices. We can distinguish between two types of circuits:

- Switched Virtual Circuits (SVC),
- Permanent Virtual Circuits (PVC)

SVCs are virtual circuits created dynamically, set up when the network sends a connection request and then disconnected when the transmission is completed.

Communication over an SVC circuit consists of three phases:

1. *circuit establishment phase* - a circuit is established between the source and destination devices.
2. *data transfer phase* - data is transferred via a virtual circuit.
3. *circuit disconnection phase* - the virtual circuit is decommissioned between the source and target device.

8.2 Frame Relay Operating Principle

8.2.1 Frame Relay Operating Principle

The Frame Relay wide area network binds local LANs together. Routers located at the edge of the LAN act as DTE devices. Serial links connect the routers to a central **FR Switch,** which in this case acts as a DCE device.

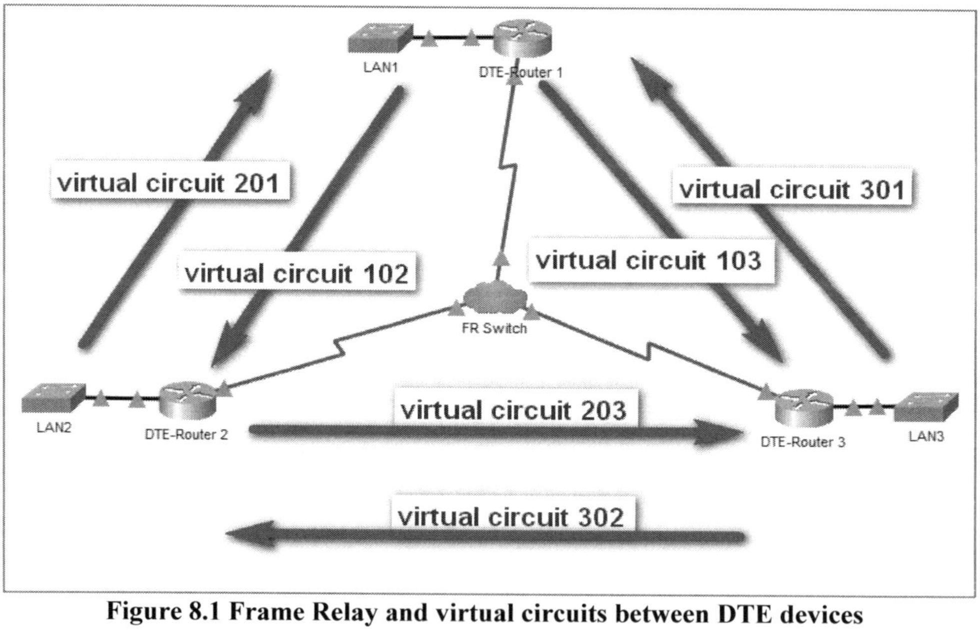

Figure 8.1 Frame Relay and virtual circuits between DTE devices

Frames are sent from the distant router (DTE device), through the **FR Switch** (DCE device) and are delivered to the destination router (DTE device).

In a **Frame Relay** network, permanent **PVC** virtual circuits are set up between DTE devices. The **PVC** virtual circuit is configured and stored permanently in the switch memory. These are the actual mappings between the input port and the output port of the switch.

When multiple virtual circuits are configured in the access links of one local network, there must be a mechanism to distinguish between them. This mechanism is called the *Data Link Connection Identifier* (**DLCI**). The DLCI is an **identifier defined locally by the operator (service provider)**, which means that it can be different at both ends of the PVC circuit. DLCI numbers must be unique, but only in the physical link in which they are located.

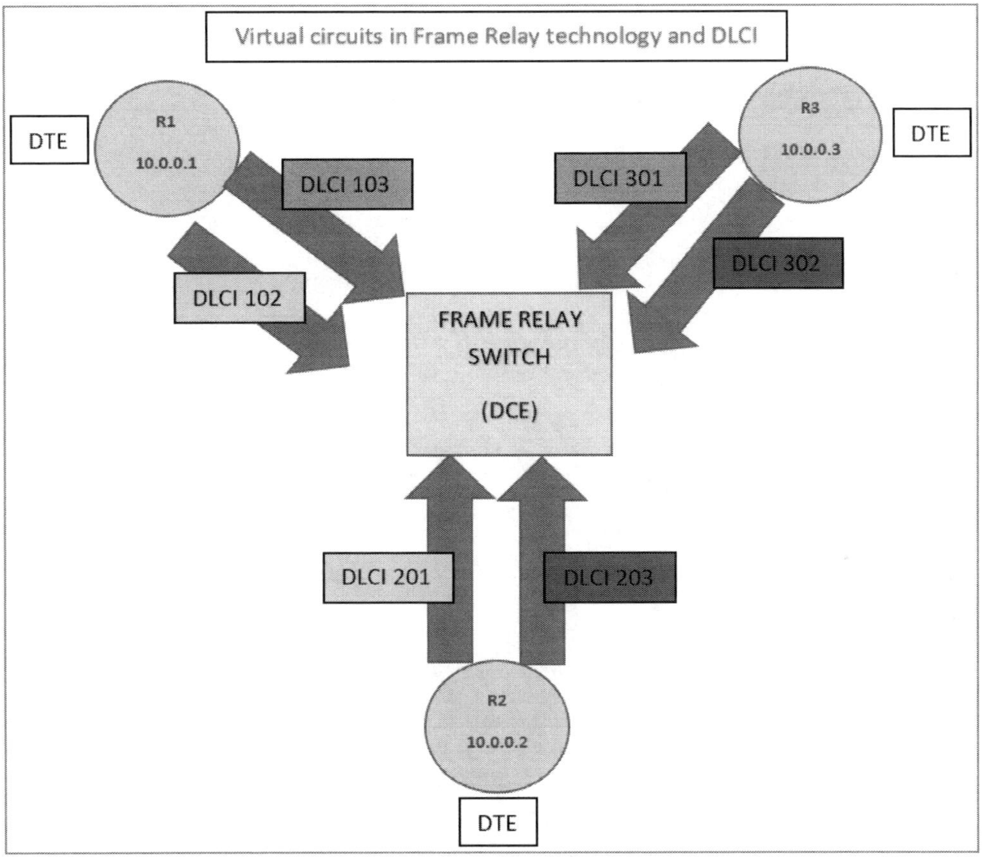

Figure 8.2 Examples of virtual circuits between DTE devices.

The end devices providing the connection between the LAN and the Frame Relay WAN are of the **DTE** type and we call them **FRAD** (*Frame Relay Access Device*). In this example, these devices are GDAŃSK, GDYNIA, SOPOT.

The edge interfaces in the Frame Relay WAN (cloud) are of type **DCE** and we call them **FRS** (*Frame Relay Switch*). The connection between two DTE devices in a Frame Relay network is called a virtual circuit (VC). It is a logical connection inside a physical link.

8.2.2 Frame Relay Frame Format

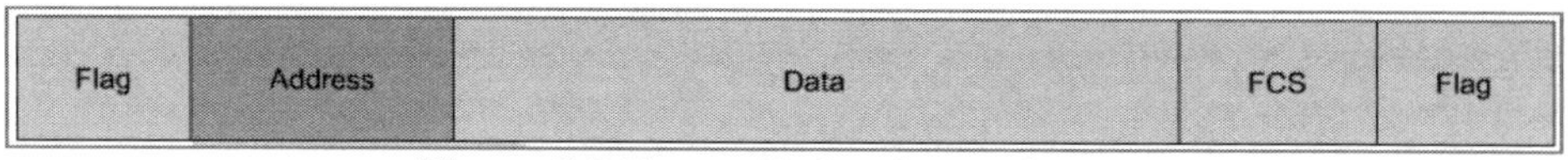

Figure 8.3 Frame Relay frame format

The same binary values **01111110 (7E hex)** are set in both **Flag** fields. They mark the beginning and the end of the frame.

The **Address** field consists of the following data:

- **DLCI** - a 10-bit DLCI identifier representing the virtual connection between the DTE device and the FR Switch,
- **C/R** - currently not defined (not used),and information about controlling the congestion notification mechanism:
- **FECN** - Forward Explicit Congestion Notification,
- **BECN** - Backward Explicit Congestion Notification,
- **DE** - if Discard Eligibility DE = 0 frames cannot be discarded, if DE = 1, frames can be discarded if congestion occurs on the link.

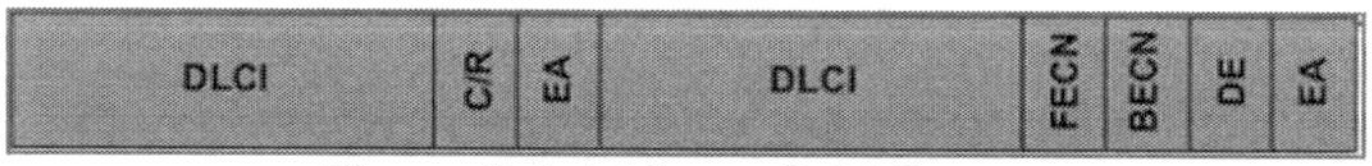

Figure 8.4 Address field format

8.2.3 Network Congestion and the Role of CIR, CBIR Parameters in the FR

The delivery charges for Frame Relay service mainly depend on the so-called agreed **CIR** (*Committed Information Rate*) for each circuit separately. The service provider guarantees in the contract to the customer that it can send data at the **CIR** rate. (There is a fee for this service, specified in the contract).Service providers sometimes sell higher speeds than they can provide, assuming that not everyone will be using the physical link at the same time. When the sum of CIR speeds from multiple VC circuits is greater than the port speed, congestion or traffic rejection can result.

An excessive amount of data per second is denoted by the parameter **BE** (*Burst Excess*). An excessive approved data rate per second is denoted by the **CBIR** (*Committed Burst Information Rate*) parameter. An example of the situation for specific link data is shown in the following figure.

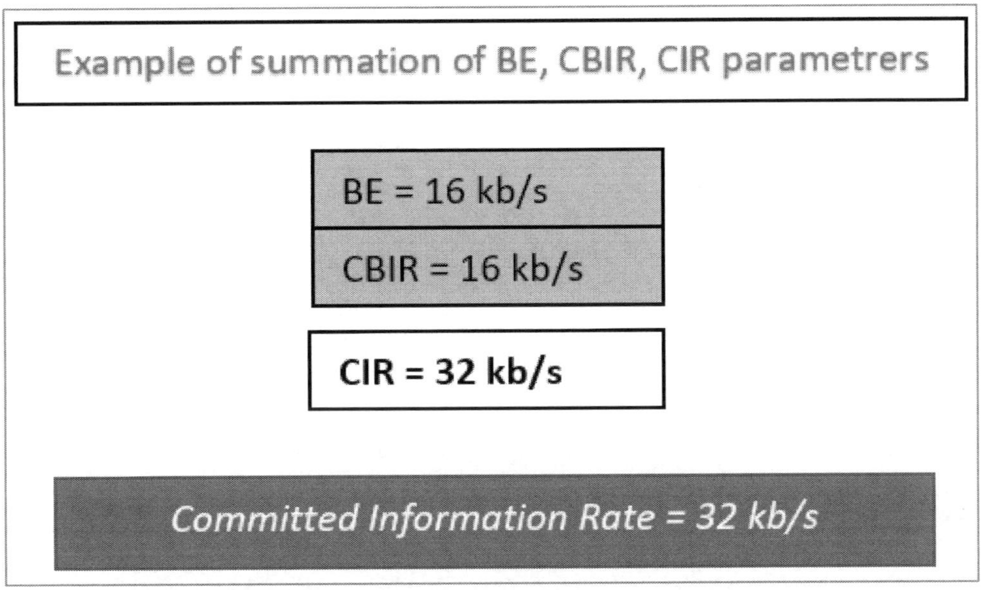

Figure 8.5 Example of summation of BE, CBIR , CIR parameters.

If the frame transmission is from:

- rate <= CIR, then bit DE=0 and the frame will be passed through the link,
- rate > CIR and <= CIR+CBIR, then bit DE=1. In this situation, the frame may be discarded if there is congestion.
- rate > CIR+CBIR, then bit DE=1. The frame is discarded.

8.3 Frame Relay Address Mapping

Before a Cisco router can send data over Frame Relay, it needs to know the associations of local **DLCI** numbers with destination IP addresses. IP addresses are associated using what is known as mapping.

8.3.1 Inverse ARP Protocol

The Inverse ARP (*Inverse Address Resolution Protocol*) converts addresses in the Data Link Layer (e.g. **DLCI**) into addresses in the Network Layer (e.g. **IP**).

Dynamic mapping

Dynamic mapping uses the **Inverse ARP** protocol.

On Cisco routers, the **Inverse ARP** protocol is enabled by default.

Static mapping

When the router on the other side of the Frame Relay network does not support dynamic **Inverse ARP**, then we must use static mapping. The syntax of the command that configures the mapping is as follows.

```
Router (config-if)# frame-relay map <protocol>
<address> <dlci> [broadcast] [ietf] [cisco]
```

For routers not manufactured by Cisco, we use the **ietf** option.

A sample mapping configuration for Cisco devices is shown below:

```
Router (config)# interface Serial0/0/0
Router (config-if)# ip address  10.0.0.1 255.0.20.0
Router (config-if)# encapsulation  frame-relay
Router (config-if)# no frame-relay  inverse-arp
Router (config-if)# frame-relay map ip  10.0.0.2 102
broadcast cisco
Router (config-if)# no shutdown
```

8.3.2 Frame Relay Connection Status

The Local Management Interface (**LMI**) provides a mechanism to report the status of the Frame Relay connection between the router (**DTE**) and the Frame Relay Switch (**DCE**). The mechanism is that every 10 seconds, the end device polls the network requesting information on the status of the channel. When the network responds with a **FULL STATUS** message, it means that the channel contains status information about the DLCI numbers associated (mapped) with the channel under investigation.

We can obtain detailed FR status information by executing the commands:

```
show frame-relay lmi
show frame-relay map
```

8.3.3 DLCI Reserved Numbers

The following numbers for DLCI identifiers are reserved for special purposes, so we will not use them in the examples and exercises:

- 0 – 15,
- 1008 – 1023.

8.4 Configuring Frame Relay Networks

In this chapter we'll show how to configure an example **Frame Relay** network. Our **Frame Relay** network will consist of three LANs and three WANs, as well as three routers and one cloud-emulated **FR Switch**.

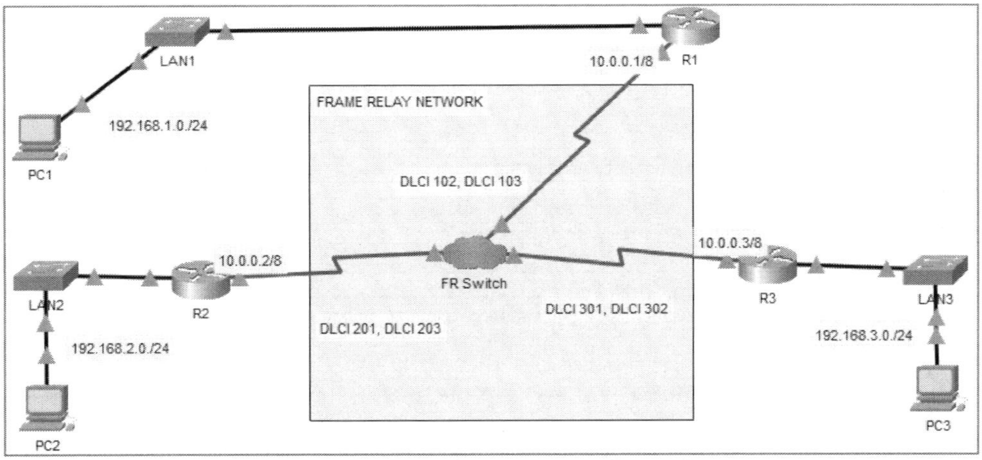

Figure 8.6 Frame Relay network topology

Step 1. We're creating a Frame Relay network topology.

Step 2. We configure the IP addresses of LANs and WANs.

Step 3. We configure the R1 router interface for Frame Relay network operation.

On the outbound interface to the **FR Switch** cloud, we enter serial interface configuration mode **Se0/0/0.** We set **frame-relay** encapsulation and disable the **Inverse ARP** protocol and create a static mapping of DLCI circuits.

```
R1(config)# interface Se0/0/0
R1 (config-if)# ip address 10.0.0.1  255.0.0.0
R1 (config-if)# encapsulation frame-relay
R1 (config-if)# no frame-relay inverse-arp
R1 (config-if)# frame-relay map ip 10.0.0.2 102
broadcast cisco
R1(config-if)# frame-relay map ip 10.0.0.3 103
broadcast cisco
```

```
R1 (config-if)# no shutdown
```

Step 4. We configure the R2 router interface for Frame Relay operation.

On the outbound interface to the **FR Switch** cloud, we enter serial interface configuration mode **Se0/0/0.** We set **frame-relay** encapsulation and disable the **Inverse ARP** protocol and create a static mapping of DLCI circuits.

```
R2 (config)# interface Se0/0/0
R2 (config-if)# ip address 10.0.0.2  255.0.0.0
R2 (config-if)# encapsulation frame-relay
R2 (config-if)# no frame-relay inverse-arp
R2 (config-if)# frame-relay map ip 10.0.0.1 201
broadcast cisco
R2 (config-if)# frame-relay map ip 10.0.0.3 203
broadcast cisco
R2 (config-if)# no shutdown
```

Step 5. We configure the R3 router interface for Frame Relay networking.

On the outbound interface to the **FR Switch** cloud, we enter serial interface configuration mode **Se0/0/0**. We set **frame-relay** encapsulation and disable the **Inverse ARP** protocol and create a static mapping of DLCI circuits.

```
R3 (config)# interface Se0/0/0
R3 (config-if)# ip address 10.0.0.3 255.0.0.0
R3 (config-if)# encapsulation frame-relay
R3 (config-if)# no frame-relay inverse-arp
R3 (config-if)# frame-relay map ip 10.0.0.1 301
broadcast cisco
R3 (config-if)# frame-relay map ip 10.0.0.3 302
broadcast cisco
R3 (config-if)# no shutdown
```

Step 6. We configure the **FR Switch** (interface-DLCI mapping).

To configure the virtual circuits on the Frame Relay switch, we need to perform the following steps:

- mapping the internal physical interface to the DLCI number,
- mapping the internal physical interfaces on the Frame Relay switch.

We are creating internal assignments (mapping) of physical ports to **DLCI** circuits. Since all the devices we are using are from Cisco, some parameters will be default (e.g. LMI). For this purpose, we will use the following table.

Interface FR	DLCI	Circuit name
Serial0	102	R1---R2
Serial0	103	R1---R3
Serial	201	R2---R1
Serial1	203	R1---R3
Serial2	301	R3---R1
Serial2	302	R3---R2

Table 8.1 Internal DLCI assignments in FR Switch.

We open the **FR Switch** cloud and go to the **Config** tab. We then select the **Serial0** series interface in the **INTERFACE** section.

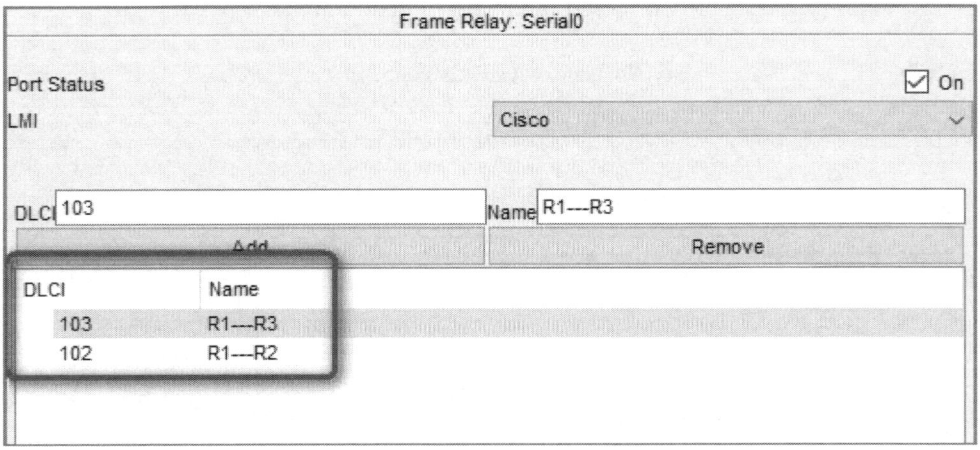

Figure 8.7 Mapping the DLCI circuits on the Serial0 interface.

Similar operations are performed for the other serial interfaces: **Serial1, Serial2,** making sure to use the correct data found in the table of internal DLCI assignments in the **FR Switch.**

Step 7. We configure the **FR Switch** (mapping of physical interfaces).

In the **FR Switch** cloud, we go to the **Config** tab. In the **CONNECTIONS** section, we select the **Frame Relay** option. In Frame Relay, using the drop-down lists and the **Add** button, we add connection mappings between the internal physical interfaces.

From interface	Circuit name	To interface	Circuit name
Serial0	R1---R2	Serial1	R2---R1
Serial1	R2---R3	Serial2	R3---R2
Serial2	R3---R1	Serial0	R1---R3

Table 8.2 Mappings between internal physical interfaces.

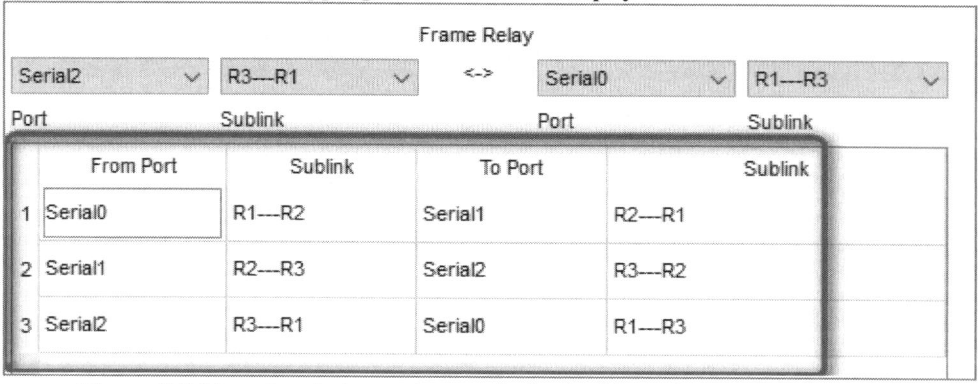

Figure 8.8 Mapping between internal physical interfaces in FR Switch.

Step 8. We configure the RIP V2 routing protocol on routers R1, R2, R3.

Step 9. We check the status of DLCI mapping on routers R1, R2, R3.

To do this, we run the commands on router R1:

```
show frame-relay map
show frame-relay lmi
```

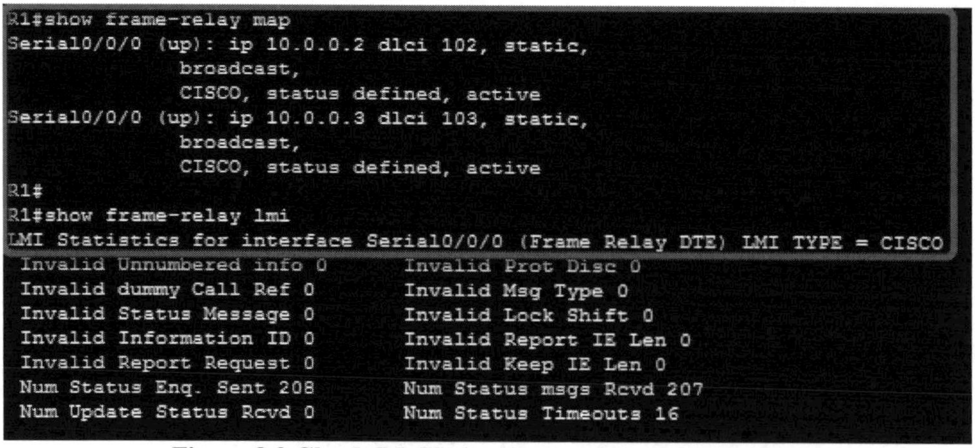

```
R1#show frame-relay map
Serial0/0/0 (up): ip 10.0.0.2 dlci 102, static,
              broadcast,
              CISCO, status defined, active
Serial0/0/0 (up): ip 10.0.0.3 dlci 103, static,
              broadcast,
              CISCO, status defined, active
R1#
R1#show frame-relay lmi
LMI Statistics for interface Serial0/0/0 (Frame Relay DTE) LMI TYPE = CISCO
 Invalid Unnumbered info 0          Invalid Prot Disc 0
 Invalid dummy Call Ref 0           Invalid Msg Type 0
 Invalid Status Message 0           Invalid Lock Shift 0
 Invalid Information ID 0           Invalid Report IE Len 0
 Invalid Report Request 0           Invalid Keep IE Len 0
 Num Status Enq. Sent 208           Num Status msgs Rcvd 207
 Num Update Status Rcvd 0           Num Status Timeouts 16
```

Figure 8.9 Check DLCI circuit mapping status on R1.

Similarly also on router R2 we execute the commands:

```
show frame-relay map
show frame-relay lmi
```

```
R2#show frame-relay map
Serial0/0/0 (up): ip 10.0.0.1 dlci 201, static,
              broadcast,
              CISCO, status defined, active
Serial0/0/0 (up): ip 10.0.0.3 dlci 203, static,
              broadcast,
              CISCO, status defined, active
R2#show frame-relay lmi
LMI Statistics for interface Serial0/0/0 (Frame Relay DTE) LMI TYPE = CISCO
 Invalid Unnumbered info 0        Invalid Prot Disc 0
 Invalid dummy Call Ref 0         Invalid Msg Type 0
 Invalid Status Message 0         Invalid Lock Shift 0
 Invalid Information ID 0         Invalid Report IE Len 0
 Invalid Report Request 0         Invalid Keep IE Len 0
 Num Status Enq. Sent 280         Num Status msgs Rcvd 279
 Num Update Status Rcvd 0         Num Status Timeouts 16
```

Figure 8.10 Check status of DLCI circuit mapping on R2.

On router R3, we execute the commands:

```
show frame-relay map
show frame-relay lmi
```

```
R3#
R3#show  frame-relay  map
Serial0/0/0 (up): ip 10.0.0.1 dlci 301, static,
              broadcast,
              CISCO, status defined, active
Serial0/0/0 (up): ip 10.0.0.2 dlci 302, static,
              broadcast,
              CISCO, status defined, active
R3#show  frame-relay  lmi
LMI Statistics for interface Serial0/0/0 (Frame Relay DTE) LMI TYPE = CISCO
 Invalid Unnumbered info 0        Invalid Prot Disc 0
 Invalid dummy Call Ref 0         Invalid Msg Type 0
 Invalid Status Message 0         Invalid Lock Shift 0
 Invalid Information ID 0         Invalid Report IE Len 0
 Invalid Report Request 0         Invalid Keep IE Len 0
 Num Status Enq. Sent 314         Num Status msgs Rcvd 313
 Num Update Status Rcvd 0         Num Status Timeouts 16
```

Figure 8.11 Check DLCI circuit mapping status on R3.

Step 10. We check the communication between LANs

Finally, we check the communication between PC1, PC2, PC3. To do this, we use the **ping** command, executed on the command line for each computer.

```
Packet Tracer PC Command Line 1.0
PC>ping 192.168.3.2

Pinging 192.168.3.2 with 32 bytes of data:

Reply from 192.168.3.2: bytes=32 time=2ms TTL=126
Reply from 192.168.3.2: bytes=32 time=3ms TTL=126
Reply from 192.168.3.2: bytes=32 time=2ms TTL=126
Reply from 192.168.3.2: bytes=32 time=2ms TTL=126
```

Figure 8.12 Checking communication from PC1 to PC3.

CHAPTER 9

PPP PROTOCOL

9 PPP PROTOCOL

The chapter describes the basic concepts of the *Point-to-Point-Protocol* (PPP) and its authorization and authentication methods.

9.1 Introduction to PPP Protocol

9.1.1 PPP Protocol Characteristics

The *Point-to-Point Protocol* (PPP) is a protocol that supports layer two (the data link layer) and layer three (the network layer) in the OSI/ISO model.

The **PPP** protocol operates in two sub-layers:

- NCP (*Network Control Protocol*),
- LCP (*Link Control Protocol*).

9.1.2 NCP Sublayer (NCP Protocol)

The **NCP** sublayer, which uses the *Network Control Protocol* (**NCP**), is responsible for authorizing and communicating PPP with layer three (the network layer) in the OSI/ISO model and communicating with the **LCP** sublayer.

9.1.3 LCP Sublayer (LCP Protocol)

The **LCP** sublayer using the *Link Control Protocol* (**LCP**) is responsible for communicating with the **NCP** sublayer and communicating with layer two of the network (**data link layer**) in the OSI/ISO model.

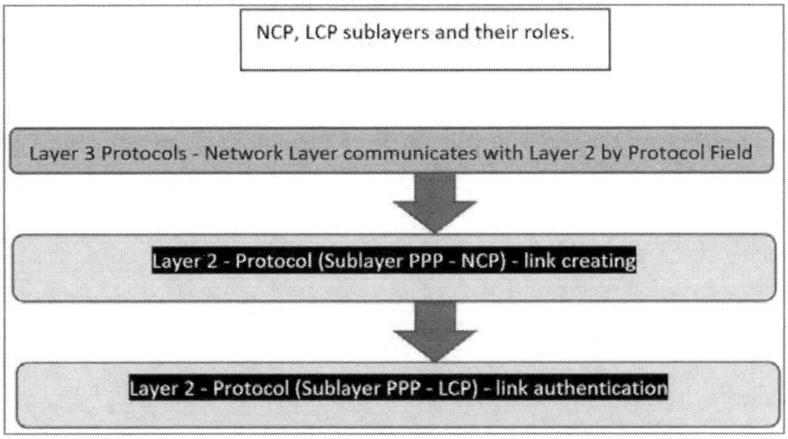

Figure 9.1 NCP, LCP sublayers and their roles.

9.2 Authentication Types in the PPP Protocol

We can use two types of authentication in the PPP protocol:

- **PAP** (*Password Authentication Protocol*),
- **CHAP** (*Challenge-Handshake Authentication Protocol*).

The main disadvantage of **PAP** authentication is that passwords are sent in open text. The password is only checked the first time the router is logged in. The only advantage of this type of authentication is its simple configuration.

The main advantage of **CHAP** authentication is that authentication between routers is based on a three-step reconciliation, and it takes place each time a connection is attempted to the router. In addition, passwords are hashed using the MD5 algorithm. The disadvantage of this type of authentication is its more advanced configuration.

9.2.1 Configuring PPP with PAP Authentication

We'll make a simple topology containing point-to-point links. We will configure PPP with **PAP** authentication at each end of the link.

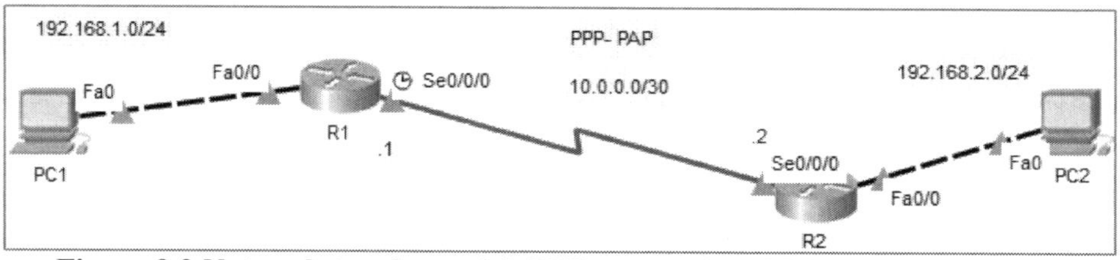

Figure 9.2 Network topology with PPP protocol and PAP authentication.

Step 1. We create the network topology.

Step 2. We configure the IP addresses.

Step 3. We configure the RIP protocol on routers R1 and R2.

For R1:

```
rip router
version 2
network 10.0.0.0
network 192.168.1.0
```

For R2:

```
rip router
version 2
network 10.0.0.0
network 192.168.2.0
```

Step 4. We configure the R1 router.

We configure the hostname:

```
hostname R1
```

We configure the username and password for R2:

```
username R2 password cisco
```

On the **Serial0/0/0** interface, we configure encapsulation and PAP authentication:

```
encapsulation ppp
ppp pap sent-username R2 password cisco
```

Step 5. We configure the router R2.

We configure the hostname:

```
hostname R2
```

We configure the username and password for R2:

```
username R1 password cisco
```

On interface **Serial0/0/0** we configure encapsulation and PAP authentication:

```
encapsulation ppp
ppp pap sent-username R1 password cisco
```

Step 6. We verify the PPP protocol parameters on router R1.

To verify the PPP protocol parameters, we run the command

```
show interfaces se 0/0/0
```

```
R1#show  interfaces  se0/0/0
Serial0/0/0 is up, line protocol is up (connected)
  Hardware is HD64570
  Internet address is 10.0.0.1/30
  MTU 1500 bytes, BW 128 Kbit, DLY 20000 usec,
     reliability 255/255, txload 1/255, rxload 1/255
  Encapsulation PPP, loopback not set, keepalive set (10 sec)
  LCP Open
  Open: IPCP, CDPCP
  Last input never, output never, output hang never
  Last clearing of "show interface" counters never
  Input queue: 0/75/0 (size/max/drops); Total output drops: 0
  Queueing strategy: weighted fair
```

Figure 9.3 Excerpt from the command result: `show interfaces se 0/0/0`

The selected encapsulation is **PPP**. The **LCP** sublayer is open (i.e. it is operational). The **NCP** sublayer has enabled two sub-protocols (**IPCP, CDPCP**), i.e. it communicates with the network layer protocols: **IP, CDP**.

Step 7. We verify the PPP protocol parameters on the R2 router.

To check the PPP protocol parameters, we run the command:

`show interfaces se0/0/0`

```
R2#show  interfaces  se0/0/0
Serial0/0/0 is up, line protocol is up (connected)
  Hardware is HD64570
  Internet address is 10.0.0.2/30
  MTU 1500 bytes, BW 128 Kbit, DLY 20000 usec,
     reliability 255/255, txload 1/255, rxload 1/255
  Encapsulation PPP, loopback not set, keepalive set (10 sec)
  LCP Open
  Open: IPCP, CDPCP
  Last input never, output never, output hang never
  Last clearing of "show interface" counters never
```

Figure 9.4 Fragment of the command result: `show interfaces se 0/0/0`

The selected encapsulation is **PPP**. The **LCP** sublayer is open (i.e. it is operational). The **NCP** sublayer has enabled two sub-protocols (**IPCP, CDPCP**), i.e. it communicates with the network layer protocols: **IP, CDP**.

9.2.2 Configuring PPP with CHAP Authentication

We will make a simple topology containing point-to-point links. We will configure PPP with **CHAP** authentication at each end of the link.

Assumptions:

Access from router	for router (**user name**)	password
R1	**R2**	**cisco**
R2	**R1**	**cisco**

Table 9.1 CHAP configuration for router access.

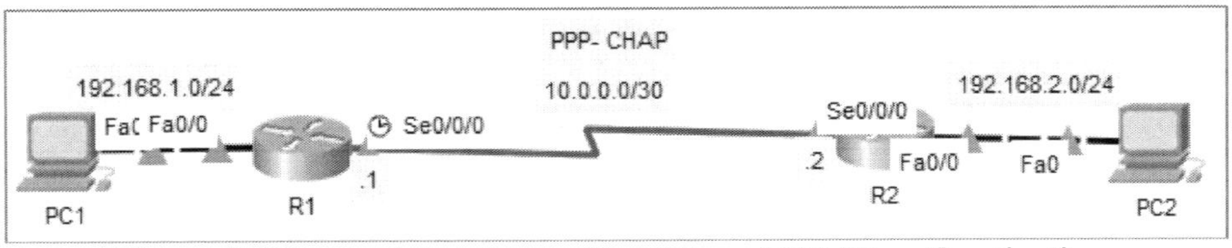

Figure 9.5 Network topology with PPP and CHAP authentication.

Step 1. Creating network topology.

Step 2. Configuring IP address.

Step 3. Configuring RIP protocols on routers R1 and R2.

For R1:

```
rip router
version 2
network 10.0.0.0
network 192.168.1.0
```

For R2:

```
rip router
version 2
network 10.0.0.0
network 192.168.2.0
```

Step 4. We are configuring router R1.

We are configuring the hostname:

```
hostname R1
```

Configuring username and password for R2:

```
username R2 password cisco
```

On the **Serial0/0/0** interface, we configure encapsulation and CHAP authentication:

```
encapsulation ppp
ppp authentication chap
```

Step 5. We configure the R2 router.

We configure hostname:

```
hostname R2
```

Configuring username and password for R2:

```
username R1 password cisco
```

On the **Serial0/0/0** interface, we configure encapsulation and CHAP authentication:

```
encapsulation ppp
ppp authentication chap
```

Step 6. We verify the PPP protocol parameters on router R1.

To verify the PPP protocol parameters, we run the command:

```
show interfaces se 0/0/0
```

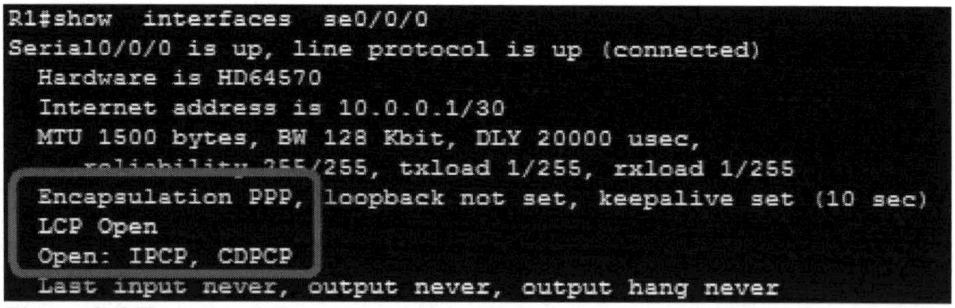

Figure 9.6 Excerpt of the command result: `show interfaces se 0/0/0`

The selected encapsulation is **PPP**. The **LCP** sublayer is open (i.e. it is operational). The **NCP** sublayer has enabled two sub-protocols (**IPCP, CDPCP**), i.e. it communicates with the network layer protocols: **IP, CDP**.

Step 7. We verify the parameters of the PPP protocol on the R2 router.

To check the parameters of the PPP protocol, we run the command:

`show interfaces se 0/0/0`

```
R2#show  interfaces  se0/0/0
Serial0/0/0 is up, line protocol is up (connected)
  Hardware is HD64570
  Internet address is 10.0.0.2/30
  MTU 1500 bytes, BW 128 Kbit, DLY 20000 usec,
     reliability 255/255, txload 1/255, rxload 1/255
  Encapsulation PPP, loopback not set, keepalive set (10 sec)
  LCP Open
  Open: IPCP, CDPCP
  Last input never, output never, output hang never
  Last clearing of "show interface" counters never
  Input queue: 0/75/0 (size/max/drops); Total output drops: 0
  Queueing strategy: weighted fair
  Output queue: 0/1000/64/0 (size/max total/threshold/drops)
```

Figure 9.7 Fragment of the command result: `show interfaces se 0/0/0`

The selected encapsulation is **PPP**. The **LCP** sublayer is open (i.e. it is operational). The NCP sublayer has enabled two sub-protocols (**IPCP, CDPCP**), i.e. it communicates with the network layer protocols: **IP, CDP**.

CHAPTER 10

RADIUS PROTOCOL

10 RADIUS PROTOCOL

The chapter describes RADIUS protocol configurations.

10.1 Short Introduction to RADIUS Protocol

RADIUS (*Remote Authentication Dial-In User Service*) is a network protocol that enables centralized management of users who connect to network services. Integrated management includes the following services:

- authentication
- authorization,
- control of access to network resources.,

Management that integrates authentication, authorization and control of access to network resources is called **AAA** (short for ***Authentication, Authorization and Accounting***).

The **RADIUS** protocol is a client-server protocol that operates at the **application** layer of the OSI/ISO model and uses the TCP and UDP transport protocols, from *Network Access Servers* (**NAS**).

10.2 Configuring RADIUS Protocol

To demonstrate the operation of the **RADIUS** network protocol, we will create the following network topology.

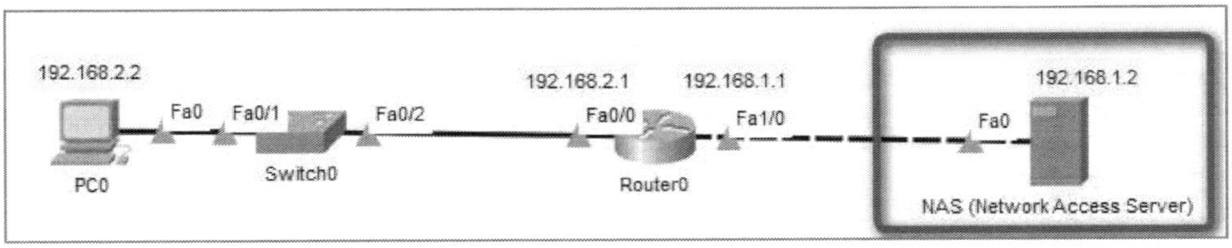

Figure 10.1 Network topology with NAS server.

Next we will then configure the IP address of the network:

- Address PC0: 192.168.2.2/24, gateway address: 192.168.2.1
- Address Fa0/0 in Router0: 192.168.2.1/24
- Address Fa1/0 in Router0: 192.168.1.1/24
- Address of NAS server: 192.168.1.2/24, gateway address: 192.168.1.1

In **Router0**, we perform the following steps.

Step 1. We change the password for privileged mode in the router.

We change its name to **Router0** and the password (**cisco**) to privileged mode using the commands:

```
enable
conf t
hostname R0
enable secret cisco
end
```

Step 2. We configure AAA services on the router.

On **Router0**, we configure AAA services by setting the IP address of the NAS server (**192.168.1.2**) and the default key (**test**), using the commands:

```
enable
conf t
aaa new-model
radius-server host 192.168.1.2 key test
aaa authentication login default group radius local
end
```

Step 3. We configure the telnet service on the router.

We configure the secure **telnet** service using the commands:

```
enable
conf t
line vty 0 5
login authentication default
end
```

Step 4. We configure the AAA service in the NAS server

On the NAS server, we select the **Services** tab, and the **AAA** section, as the RADIUS protocol on **Router0** communicates with the **AAA** service located on the server. We leave the default configuration as shown in the following figure.

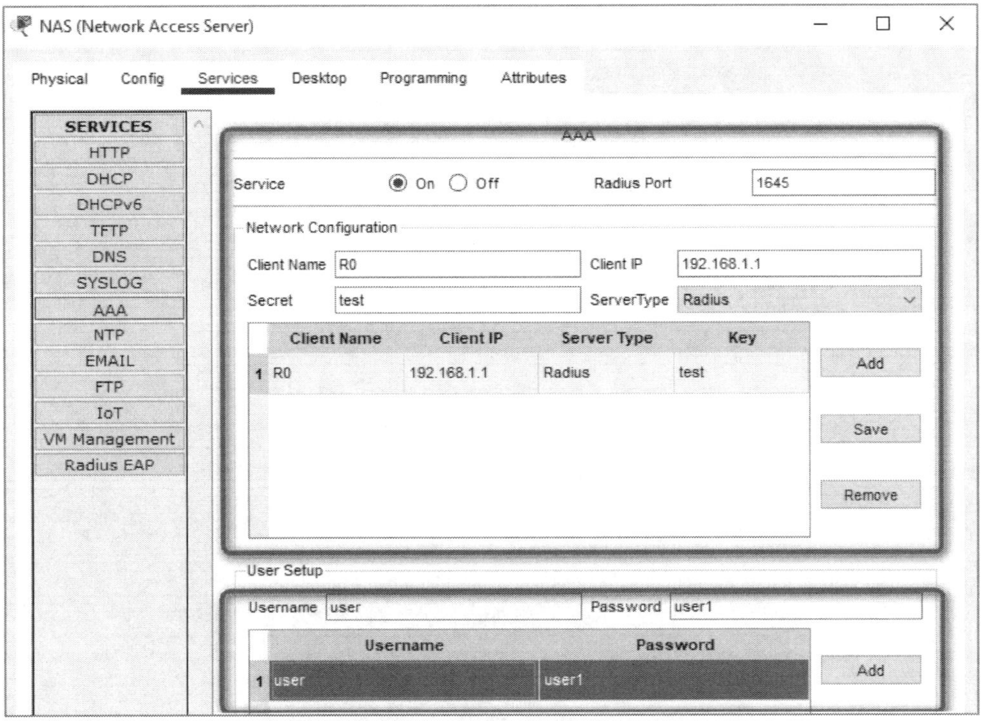

Figure 10.2 AAA section in the NAS server.

Step 5. We check the AAA security for access to the telnet service.

At the command line on **PC0**, we execute the telnet command to Router0. Router Router0 has the password set for privileged mode: **cisco**.

```
telnet 192.168.2.1
```

Figure 10.3 Logging into the telnet service from PC0.

Step 6. We check the AAA security for access to the Router0 console.

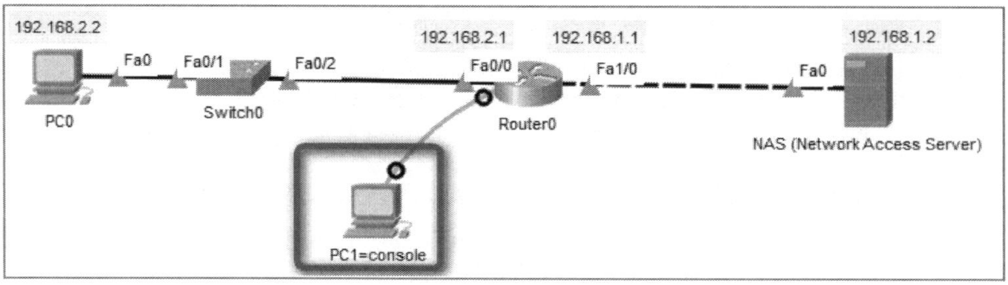

Figure 10.4 Network topology with NAS server and console connection.

We are trying to log on to the Router0 console

Login to console: **user**

Password to console **user1**

Password for privileged mode: **cisco**

Figure 10.5 Router0 Router console login.

CHAPTER 11

NETFLOW TECHNOLOGY

11 NETFLOW TECHNOLOGY

The chapter describes the technology and configuration of the NETFLOW protocol.

11.1 Introduction to NETFLOW Technology

NETFLOW is a Cisco IOS technology and protocol that provides statistics on packets passing through a Cisco router or multilayer switch. **NETFLOW** technology allows network traffic to be monitored and analyzed.

Monitoring and analyzing the network, enables the administrator to plan the network more effectively. The latest version of NETLOW technology is what is known as **Flexible NetFlow**. Flexible NetFlow extends the capabilities of the original NETFLOW, as it can create a more comprehensive analysis of data traffic by reusing configuration sets.

Notes:

The NETFLOW protocol should be completely transparent to applications and devices on the network.

NETFLOW does not need to be run and configured on all devices to function properly.

11.2 NETFLOW Operation

The operation of the **NETFLOW** protocol relies on continuous examination of TCP/IP communications to collect statistical information about data streams. We define a data stream (flow) as a unidirectional flow of packets between a specified source and destination system.

The original **NETFLOW** protocol involves defining a data flow as a combination of seven fields. The main premise of NETFLOW is the following.

If one of the following fields **differs** in value from an analogous field in another packet, it is safe to assume that they come from **different** flows:

- source IP address,
- destination IP address,
- source port number,
- destination port number,
- Layer 3 protocol type,
- service type tag (ToS),
- logical input interface. IP address,

11.3 Configuring NETFLOW

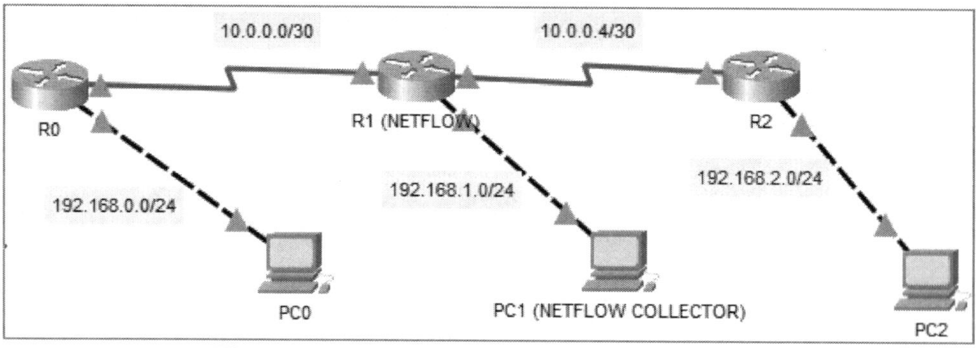

Figure 11.1 Network topology for NETFLOW.

Step 1. We select the Cisco 2811 router with IOS 12.4(15) T1.

Step 2. Configuring IP addresses.

Step 3. We configure the RIP protocol on the routers.

For R0:

```
rip router
version 2
network 10.0.0.0
network 192.168.0.0
```

For R1:

```
rip router
version 2
network 10.0.0.0
network 10.0.0.4
network 192.168.1.0
```

For R2:

```
rip router
version 2
network 10.0.0.4
network 192.168.2.0
```

Step 4. We configure the telnet service on router R1

```
line vty 0 4
password cisco
login
```

Step 5. Check connectivity between PC0 , PC1, PC2

```
Packet Tracer PC Command Line 1.0
PC>ping 192.168.2.2

Pinging 192.168.2.2 with 32 bytes of data:

Reply from 192.168.2.2: bytes=32 time=14ms TTL=125
Reply from 192.168.2.2: bytes=32 time=13ms TTL=125
Reply from 192.168.2.2: bytes=32 time=11ms TTL=125
Reply from 192.168.2.2: bytes=32 time=2ms TTL=125
```

Figure 11.2 The result of the ping command from PC0 to PC2 (ping 192.168.2.2**).**

Configuring NETFLOW on R1 involves the following steps.

Step 6. We configure NTFLOW data capture on R1.

We configure **NETFLOW** data capture on both serial interfaces on router R1, using the commands:

```
R1(config)# interface s0/0/0
R1(config-if)# ip flow ingress
R1(config-if)# ip flow egress
R1(config-if)# interface s0/0/1
R1(config-if)# ip flow ingress
R1(config-if)# ip flow egress
```

```
R1(config)#interface Serial0/0/0
R1(config-if)#ip flow egress
R1(config-if)#ip flow ingress
R1(config-if)#ip address 10.0.0.2 255.255.255.252
R1(config-if)#
R1(config-if)#interface Serial0/0/1
R1(config-if)#ip flow egress
R1(config-if)#ip flow ingress
R1(config-if)#ip address 10.0.0.5 255.255.255.252
```

Figure 11.3 Configuring NETFLOW on R1.

Step 7. We configure NETFLOW data export to the collector.

We configure the export of **NETFLOW** data to the PC1 collector.

Use command: **`ip flow-export destination`** to specify the **IP** address and **UDP** port number for the NETFLOW collector to which the router will send NETFLOW data.

Data:

- Collector IP address: 192.168.1.2
- Collector UDP port: 9996

Command:

```
R1(config)# ip flow-export destination 192.168.1.2
9996
```

Step 8. We configure the export version of the NETFLOW data.

We are configuring the export version of **NETFLOW** data.

Use command: **`ip flow-export version`** to specify the NETFLOW data export version.

Command:

R1(config)# **ip flow-export version 9**

Step 9. Performing a network traffic simulation

We perform a simulation of some network traffic, e.g.:

```
PC>ping 192.168.2.2
PC>telnet 10.0.0.6
```

```
C:\>ping 192.168.2.2

Pinging 192.168.2.2 with 32 bytes of data:

Reply from 192.168.2.2: bytes=32 time=3ms TTL=125
Reply from 192.168.2.2: bytes=32 time=4ms TTL=125
Reply from 192.168.2.2: bytes=32 time=4ms TTL=125
Reply from 192.168.2.2: bytes=32 time=11ms TTL=125

Ping statistics for 192.168.2.2:
    Packets: Sent = 4, Received = 4, Lost = 0 (0% loss),
Approximate round trip times in milli-seconds:
    Minimum = 3ms, Maximum = 11ms, Average = 5ms
```

Figure 11.4 Network traffic simulation ping.

```
C:\>telnet 10.0.0.6
Trying 10.0.0.6 ...Open

[Connection to 10.0.0.6 closed by foreign host]
C:\>
```

Figure 11.5 Telnet network traffic simulation.

Step 10. Displaying network traffic statistics.

We display statistics using the command:

`R1# show ip cache flow`

```
R1#show ip cache flow
IP packet size distribution (82 total packets):
   1-32   64   96  128  160  192  224  256  288  320  352  384  416  448  480
   .000 .634 .000 .366 .000 .000 .000 .000 .000 .000 .000 .000 .000 .000 .000

    512  544  576 1024 1536 2048 2560 3072 3584 4096 4608
   .000 .000 .000 .000 .000 .000 .000 .000 .000 .000 .000

IP Flow Switching Cache, 278544 bytes
  1 active, 4095 inactive, 47 added
  4 ager polls, 0 flow alloc failures
  Active flows timeout in 30 minutes
  Inactive flows timeout in 15 seconds
IP Sub Flow Cache, 34056 bytes
  0 active, 1024 inactive, 0 added, 0 added to flow
  0 alloc failures, 0 force free
  1 chunk, 1 chunk added
  last clearing of statistics never
Protocol         Total    Flows   Packets Bytes  Packets Active(Sec) Idle(Sec)
--------         Flows     /Sec     /Flow  /Pkt     /Sec     /Flow     /Flow
ICMP                 4      0.0         7   128      0.1      10.0      14.8
TCP-TELNET           2      0.0         3    41      0.0       0.0      15.0
TCP-other            2      0.0         3    41      0.0       0.0      14.5
UDP-RIP             38      0.1         1    52      0.1       0.0      15.0
Total:              46      0.1         1    78      0.2       0.9      15.0

SrcIf         SrcIPaddress    DstIf         DstIPaddress    Pr SrcP DstP  Pkts
Se0/0/0       10.0.0.1        Null          224.0.0.9       11 0208 0208     1
R1#
```

Figure 11.6 Result of the command: `show ip cache flow` for R1.

CHAPTER 12

ADDRESS TRANSLATION USING NAT

12 ADDRESS TRANSLATION USING NAT

This chapter describes the NAT (***Network Address Translation***) technique and the basics of configuring network address translation using NAT.

12.1 Introduction to NAT

12.1.1 Reasons for Using the NAT Technique

We mainly use NAT translation for several reasons, these include:

- Depletion of public IPv4 address resources - a single public address as seen by the Internet can be used for multiple local IP addresses on the LAN.
- The NAT technique allows internal addresses on the local network to be hidden by replacing them with a single internal address with a global address (we call this address masquerading).
- The NAT technique is commonly used in firewall devices (NAT works with ACLs).

12.1.2 NAT Technique Terminology

When determining which type of address is used, it is important to remember that NAT terminology is always used from the perspective of the device for which the translation is being performed.

- **Internal address** - the address of the source device.
- **External address** - the address of the destination device.
- **Local address** - address present on the internal side of the network.
- **Global address** - address present on the external side of the network.
- **Local internal address** - the address of the source as seen from inside the network.
- **Internal global address** - the address of the source as seen from outside the network.
- **External global address** - the destination address as seen from outside the network. Is an IPv4 globally routed address assigned to a computer on the Internet.
- **External local address** - the destination address as seen from inside the network.

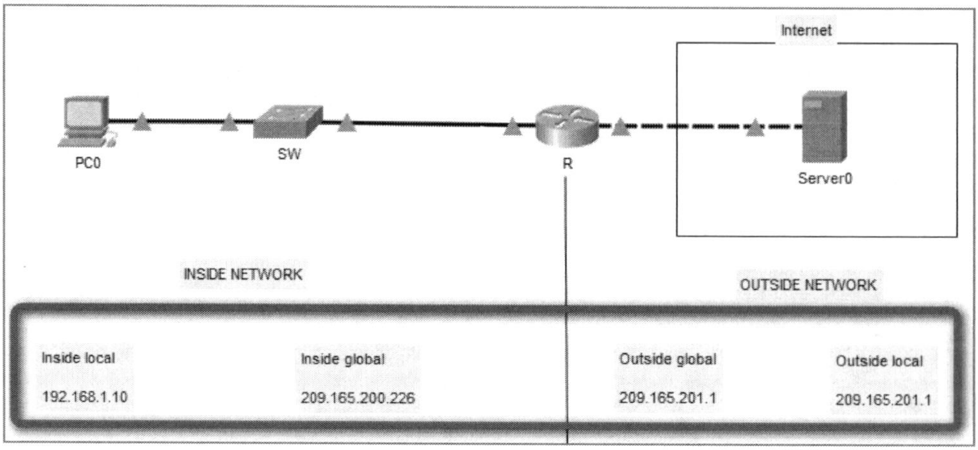

Figure 12.1 NAT terminology.

12.2 NAT Operating Diagram

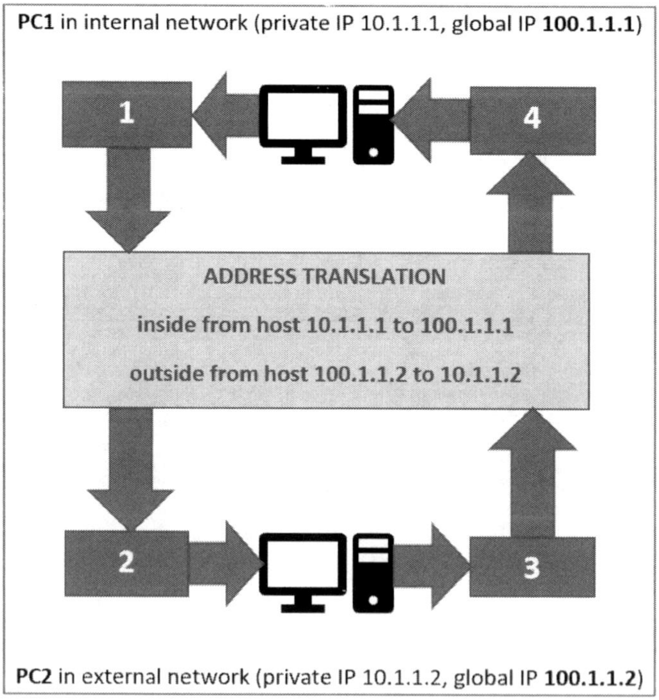

Figure 12.2 NAT operating diagram.

12.3 NAT Translation Types

12.3.1 Static Translation (Static NAT)

Static NAT is usually used when a client, located on an external network (e.g. the Internet) wants to connect to servers on an internal network. The translation process begins when a client attempts to connect to a server using the **Inside global** address as the destination address.

The operation of static translation is based on the transformation of one-to-one addresses, between local addresses and global addresses. Static NAT translation enables the creation of a one-to-one mapping between local and global addresses. These transformations are configured by the network administrator and remain constant.

Inside local	Inside global	Outside global	Outside local
192.168.10.254	209.165.201.5	-	-

Table 12.1 Example of static NAT translation.

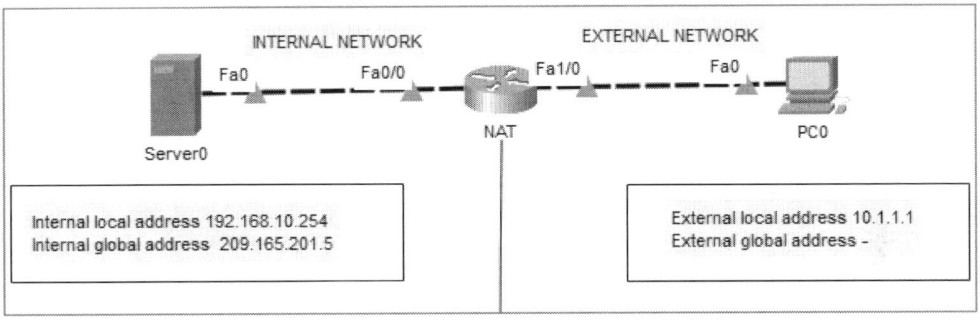

Figure 12.3 Example of NAT static translation.

We convert network traffic from PC0 to Server0 (from 10.1.1.1. to 209.165.201.5) into traffic from 10.1.1.1. to 192.168.10.254 in the NAT router.

```
NAT#sh ip nat translations
Pro  Inside global      Inside local       Outside local      Outside global
---  209.165.201.5      192.168.10.254     ---                ---
```

Figure 12.4 The result of the sh ip nat translations command for NAT static translation.

12.3.2 Dynamic NAT Translation

The operation of dynamic translation involves the transformation of many-to-many addresses, between local addresses and global addresses. Dynamic NAT uses a pool of IPv4 public addresses for translation. It requires the configuration of internal and external interfaces participating in NAT and one simple standard ACL assigned to the address pool, e.g. NAT-POOL.

The following example demonstrates the use of a Pv4 address pool in the range 209.165.200.226 to 209.165.200.230.

Inside local	Inside global	Outside global	Outside local
192.168.1.11 192.168.1.12 192.168.1.13	od 209.165.200.226 do 209.165.200.230	10.0.0.1	-

Table 12.2 Example of NAT dynamic translation.

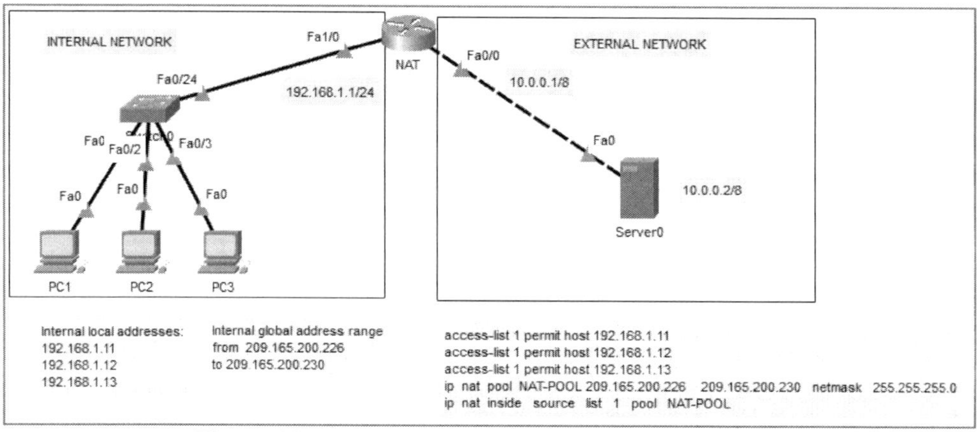

Figure 12.5 Example of NAT dynamic translation.

To configure dynamic NAT, there are four steps to follow:

1. Create an ACL with the IP addresses required for translation
2. Create a pool of global IP addresses available for NAT
3. Associate ACLs with the NAT pool 4.
4. Define which interfaces act as internal and external for NAT.

Step 1. Creating ACL No.1.

We configure ACLs with host addresses (PC1, PC2, PC3) using the commands:

```
access-list 1 permit host 192.168.1.11
access-list 1 permit host 192.168.1.12
access-list 1 permit host 192.168.1.13
```

```
NAT(config)#access-list 1 permit host 192.168.1.11
NAT(config)#access-list 1 permit host 192.168.1.12
NAT(config)#access-list 1 permit host 192.168.1.13
```

Figure 12.6 Create ACL No. 1.

Step 2. We create an address pool named NAT-POOL.

We create NAT-POOL for addresses 209.165.200.226/24 through 209.165.200.230/24 using the command

```
ip nat pool NAT-POOL 209.165.200.226 209.165.200.230
netmask 255.255.255.0
```

```
NAT(config)#
NAT(config)#ip nat pool NAT-POOL 209.165.200.226 209.165.200.230 netmask 255.255.255.0
NAT(config)#
```

Figure 12.7 Creating NAT-POOL.

Step 3. We associate ACL No. 1 with an address pool named NAT-POOL.

We associate ACL No. 1 with the address pool named NAT-POOL using the command:

```
ip nat inside source list 1 pool NAT-POOL
```

```
NAT(config)#
NAT(config)#ip nat inside source list 1 pool NAT-POOL
NAT(config)#
```

Figure 12.8 Creating an association between ACL and NAT-POOL.

Step 4. We define the internal and external interfaces.

In this case, the internal interface is Fa1/0 and the external interface is Fa0/0. Run the following commands:

```
interface FastEthernet1/0
ip nat inside
interface FastEthernet0/0
ip nat outside
```

```
NAT(config)#
NAT(config)#interface FastEthernet1/0
NAT(config-if)#ip nat inside
NAT(config-if)#
NAT(config-if)#interface FastEthernet0/0
NAT(config-if)#ip nat outside
NAT(config-if)#
```

Figure 12.9 Define internal and external interfaces.

To check the translation status, use the commands:

```
sh ip nat statistics
sh ip nat translations
```

```
NAT#sh ip nat statistics
Total translations: 1 (0 static, 1 dynamic, 1 extended)
Outside Interfaces: FastEthernet0/0
Inside Interfaces: FastEthernet1/0
Hits: 8  Misses: 95
Expired translations: 3
Dynamic mappings:
-- Inside Source
access-list 1 pool NAT-POOL refCount 0
 pool NAT-POOL: netmask 255.255.255.0
      start 209.165.200.226 end 209.165.200.230
      type generic, total addresses 5 , allocated 0 (0%), misses 0
```

Figure 12.10 Result of command sh ip nat statistics.

```
NAT#sh ip nat translations
Pro  Inside global      Inside local       Outside local      Outside global
tcp 209.165.200.227:1025192.168.1.11:1025  10.0.0.2:80        10.0.0.2:80
```

Figure 12.11 Result of command sh ip nat translations.

CHAPTER 13

ADDRESS TRANSLATION USING L2NAT

13 ADDRESS TRANSLATION USING L2NAT

This chapter describes the **L2NAT** (***Layer 2 Network Address Translation***) technique and the basics of configuring network address translation using L2NAT.

13.1 Introduction to L2NAT

L2NAT (*Layer 2 Network Address Translation*) allows a unique public IP (global) address to be assigned to an existing private IP address, providing the ability to communicate private subnets with public subnets.

L2NAT supports two translation tables: one stores the translation definitions of private addresses to public (global) addresses, and the other stores the translation definitions of public (global) addresses to private addresses. The translations are defined based on the **physical addresses** of the end devices.

The limitations of the L2NAT service are as follows:

- Cisco IOS version15.0 (2)EB minimum required,
- only IPv4 addresses can be translated,
- if L2NAT translation is configured for a host, it should not be configured as a DHCP client.

Requirements:

- you must use a switch that includes the L2NAT service (in Packet Tracer, this is the **IE 2000** switch),
- you must configure so-called instances that define address translations,
- L2NAT instances must be assigned to an interface or VLAN.

13.2 L2NAT Operating Diagram

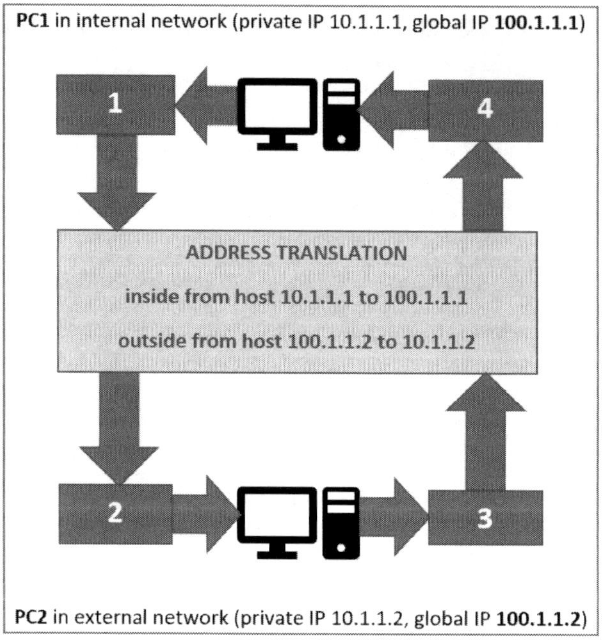

Figure 13.1 L2NAT operating diagram.

Assumption: PC1 performs a ping to the global address of PC2.

```
ping 10.1.1.2
```

Step-by-step analysis of the L2NAT translation operation:

1 – packet in the direction from PC1 to PC2 before translation

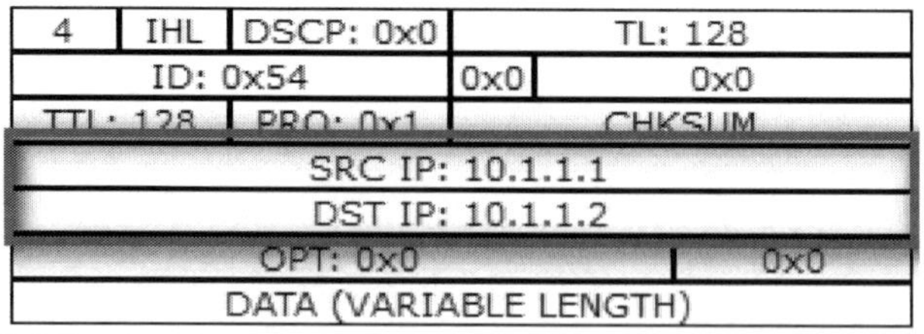

Figure 13.2 Packet from PC1 to PC2 before translation is performed.

2 – Packet in the direction from PC1 to PC2 after translation

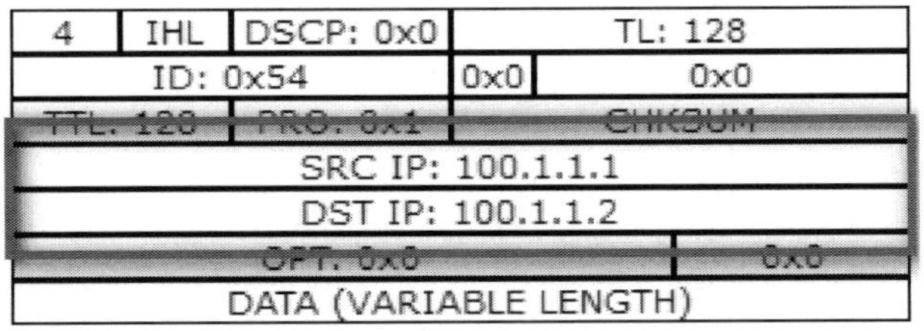

Figure 13.3 Packet from PC1 to PC2 after translation.

3 - Return packet in the direction from PC2 to PC1 before translation.

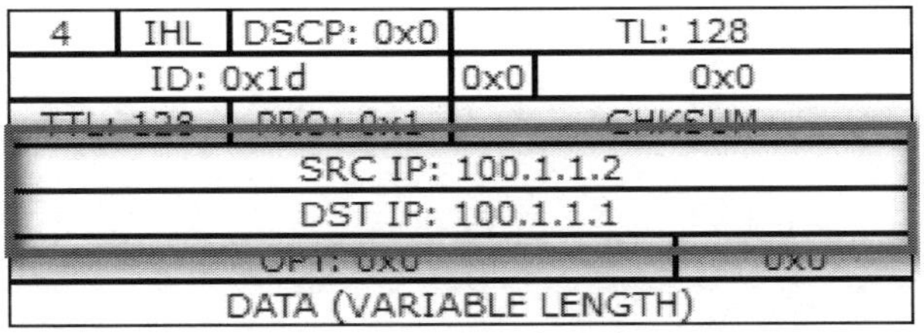

Figure 13.4 Packet from PC2 to PC1 before translation.

4 - Return packet in PC2 to PC1 direction after translation

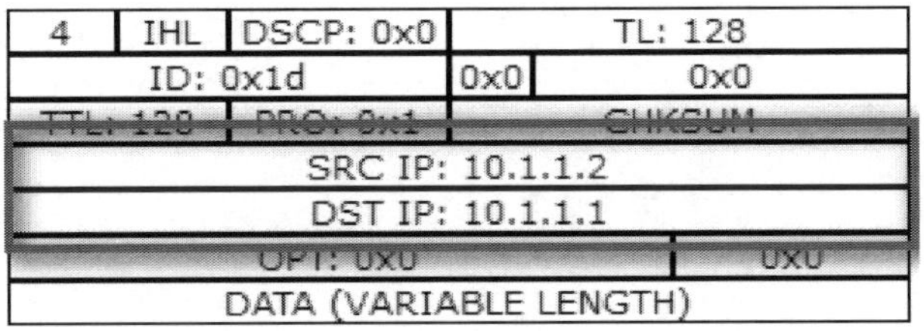

Figure 13.5 Packet from PC2 to PC1 after translation.

Operations in the direction from PC1 to PC2:

- A frame arrives from the **internal** network and is to be forwarded to the external network.
- The switch searches the Layer 2 NAT table.
- The Layer 2 NAT table contains an entry that matches the local source address
- inside from host 10.1.1.1 to 100.1.1.1
- The switch converts the local address to a global address, which is 100.1.1.1 .
- The switch searches the Layer 2 NAT table.
- The Layer 2 NAT table contains an entry that matches the global destination address
- outside from host 100.1.1.2 to 10.1.1.2
- The switch converts the global address to the local address, which is 10.1.1.2 .

Operations in the direction from PC2 to PC1:

- A frame arrives from the external network and is to be forwarded to the internal network.
- The switch searches the Layer2 NAT table.
- The Layer 2 NAT table contains an entry that matches the local source address
- outside from host 100.1.1.2 to 10.1.1.2
- The switch converts the local address to a global address, which is 100.1.1.2 .
- The switch searches the Layer2 NAT table.
- The Layer 2 NAT table contains an entry that matches the global destination address.
- inside from host 10.1.1.1 to 100.1.1.1
- The switch converts the global address to a local address, that is, to 10.1.1.1 .

13.2.1 Example of the Simple L2NAT Configuration

Addressing table

Device	Interface	Private IP address	Global IP address	MAC Address
PC1	Fa0	10.0.0.1/8	100.1.1.1/8	000B.BE46.A9DA
PC2	Fa0	100.1.1.2/8	10.1.1.2/8	0009.7C65.8782
IE2000	Gi1/1	-	-	-
IE2000	Gi1/2	-	-	-

Table 13.1 Addressing table.

Topology

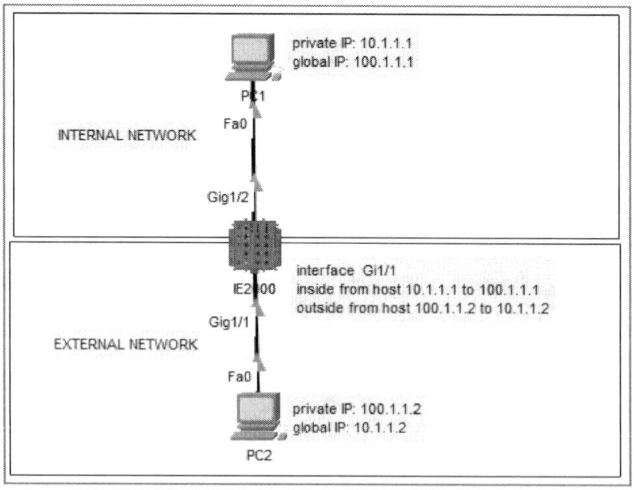

Figure 13.6 L2NAT topology.

Configuring a simple topology with L2NAT is done in the following steps.

Step 1. Connect two computers to the IE 2000 switch according to the topology.

Step 2. Configure the IP addresses of the computers according to the addressing table

Step 3. Configure an L2NAT instance named OUTSIDE on the IE 2000 switch.

```
enable
conf t
l2nat instance OUTSIDE
inside from host 10.1.1.1 to 100.1.1.1
outside from host 100.1.1.2 to 10.1.1.2
```

Step 4. Assign the OUTSIDE instance to an interface on the IE 2000

```
interface Gi1/1
l2nat OUTSIDE
```

Step 5. Check with the ping command the communication between the computers

From the command line of PC1 (global address of PC2), execute:

```
ping 10.1.1.2
```

From the command line of PC2 (global address PC1), execute:

```
ping 100.1.1.1
```

13.2.2 Handling repeating IP addresses in L2NAT

The following example shows how, using the L2NAT service, you can configure repeating IP addresses (duplicate IP addresses). Here we will use two IE **2000** switches and one **2950** switch.

Addressing table

Device	Interface	Private IP address	Internal subnetwork	MAC address
PC-A1	Fa0	192.168.1.1/24	A	000B.BEBB.383D
PC-A2	Fa0	192.168.1.2/24	A	00E0.B09B.8EBD
PC-A3	Fa0	192.168.1.3/24	A	00D0.D302.A2B0

PC-B1	Fa0	192.168.1.1/24	B	0050.0FD7.BB14
PC-B2	Fa0	192.168.1.2/24	B	0040.0B67.3CA9
PC-B3	Fa0	192.168.1.3/24	B	0030.A39E.6A03

Table 13.2 Addressing table.

Switch configuration table - Part 1

Device	Device type	Interface(s)	VLAN	Address	Notes
SW-0	2950-24	Vlan1	1	10.1.1.254/24	-
SW-A	IE-2000	Vlan1	1	10.1.1.100/8	-
SW-B	IE-2000	Vlan1	1	10.1.1.101/8	-
Subnet-a	2950-24	Fa0/1, Fa0/2, Fa0/3	-	-	connected to computers
Subnet-a	2950-24	Fa0/4	-	-	connected to SW-A
Subnet-b	2950-24	Fa0/1, Fa0/2, Fa0/3	-	-	connected to computers
Subnet-b	2950-24	Fa0/4	-	-	connected to SW-B

Table 13.3 Switch configuration table - Part 1.

Switch configuration table – Part 2

Device	Installation name	Interface	Working port mode	Translations for internal subnetwork	Translations for external subnetwork
SW-A	-	Fa1/1	trunk	-	-
SW-A	Subnet-a	Gi1/1	trunk	inside from network 192.168.1.0 to 10.1.1.16 mask 255.255.255.240	outside from host 10.1.1.254 to 192.168.1.254 outside from network 10.1.1.32 to 192.168.1.32 mask 255.255.255.240
SW-B	-	Fa1/1	trunk	-	-
SW-B	Subnet-b	Gi1/1	trunk	inside from network 192.168.1.0 to 10.1.1.32 mask 255.255.255.240	outside from host 10.1.1.254 to 192.168.1.254 outside from network 10.1.1.32 to 192.168.1.0

					mask 255.255.255.240 outside from network 10.1.1.16 to 192.168.1.16 mask 255.255.255.240

Table 13.4 Switch configuration table - Part 2.

Topology

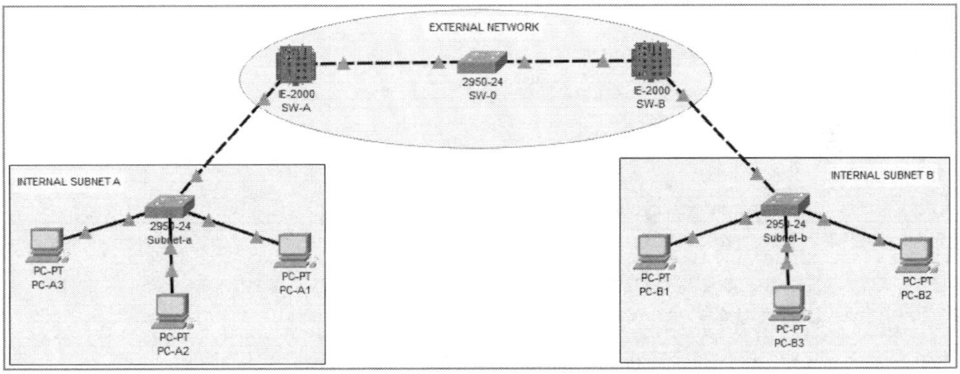

Figure 13.7 Network topology.

Configuring the above topology with L2NAT is done in the following steps.

Step 1. Connect the devices according to the topology.

Step 2. Configure the IP addresses of the computers according to the addressing table, switch configuration tables (Part 1, 2).

Step 3. Configure the L2NAT service named A-Subnet on the SW-A switch according to the switch configuration table (Part 2).

```
enable
conf t
l2nat instance A-Subnet
inside from network 192.168.1.0 to 10.1.1.16 mask
255.255.255.240
outside from host 0.1.1.254 to 192.168.1.254
outside from network 10.1.1.32 to 192.168.1.32 mask
255.255.255.240
```

Step 4. Assign the A-Subnet instance to an interface on the SW-A switch.

```
interface Gi 1/1
l2nat A-Subnet
```

Step 5. Configure the L2NAT service named B-Subnet on switch SW-B according to the switch configuration table (Part 2).

```
en
conf t
l2nat instance B-Subnet
inside from network 192.168.1.0 to 10.1.1.32 mask
255.255.255.240
outside from host 10.1.1.254 to 192.168.1.254
outside from network 10.1.1.32 to 192.168.1.0 mask
255.255.255.240
outside from network 10.1.1.16 to 192.168.1.16 mask
255.255.255.240
```

Step 6. Assign the B-Subnet instance to an interface on switch SW-B.

```
interface Gi1/1
l2nat B-Subnet
```

Step 7. Check that PC-A1 → PC-B1, PC-A2 → PC-B2, PC-A3 → PC-B3, can ping each other.

CHAPTER 14

VIRTUAL PRIVATE NETWORKS

14 VIRTUAL PRIVATE NETWORKS

This chapter describes the technology and configuration of ***Virtual Private Networks*** (VPNs).

VPN technology allows traffic to be transferred in an encrypted manner between computers on a private or public network, such as the Internet.

A full description of the encryption and authentication methods and algorithms used in VPN technology is very extensive and complex, so this chapter is narrowed down to the basics, such as: types of VPNs, basic protocols and types of encryption and authentication.

14.1 Basic concepts

There are two main types of VPNs:

- **Remote Access VPN**
- **Site-to-Site VPN**

Remote access VPNs are used to connect individual hosts, teleworkers, contractors, needing to use secure access to the company network via the Internet. Each user, is usually equipped with a VPN software client or uses a web application.

Site-to-Site Virtual Private Networks connect all networks to each other, for example, they may connect a branch office to the main company network. Each site is equipped with a VPN gateway, which can be, a router, firewall, VPN hub or other security device. The remote office uses a site-to-site VPN connection to connect to the company headquarters.

Tunnelling is the establishment of a connection between two distant computers so as to create the impression that they are directly connected. The rationale for tunneling is:

- enabling a connection between computers hidden in private networks (behind a firewall, or with private addresses - a condition one of the hosts involved in creating the tunnel must have a public address,
- security - encryption of the connection,
- possibility to speed up transmission - use of compression on slow connections.

Security Association (SA) is to establish the security relationships needed to create a tunnel using IPsec.

14.2 Basic Protocols, Encryption and Authentication Methods

The main protocols used in VPNs are:

- **SSH**
- **IPsec**
- **AH**
- **ESP**
- **IKE**
- **ISAKMP**

SSH (Secure SHell) are a family of protocols used in TCP/IP networks for user recognition and for encrypting data transfer.

Internet Protocol Security (IPsec) secures the IP protocol by means of session authentication and encryption of each packet during the connection.

AH (Authentication Header) protocol provides encryption, authentication and data integrity, but does not provide confidentiality like **ESP**.

ESP (Encapsulating Security Payload) protocol provides encryption, authentication and data integrity.

IKE (Internet Key Exchange) is a protocol for establishing a secure SA (***Security Association***) between two hosts. IKE has two versions: IKEv1 and IKEv2.

The IKE protocol is based on the Diffie-Hellman algorithm, which allows a secure session key to be determined in a secure manner. Establishing a secure IKE session consists of two phases.

- phase 1 - **ISAKMP** phase 1 during which an **IKE SA** security relationship is established,
- phase 2 - during which the **IPSEC SA** security relationship is established.

ISAKMP (Internet Security Association and Key Management Protocol) is used to establish security associations (Security Association) using the IKE protocol. Encryption methods ensure the confidentiality of transmitted data. Methods used include AES, DES, 3DES, among others.

AES (Advanced Encryption Standard)

The original name is **Rijndael**. A standard adopted in 2001 in the USA. The block algorithm was designed by Joan Daemen and Vincent Rijmen. The length of the block as well as the key can be chosen as 128, 192 or 256 bits. The Rijmen standard is generally available.

DES (Data Encryption Standard)

DES is a symmetric block cipher with blocks of 64 bits. It was designed in 1975 by IBM.

A 56-bit key is used to encrypt and decrypt data, which is stored as a 64-bit string, in which every 8 bits is a check bit and can be used for parity checking. Several of the keys are considered weak keys and semi-weak keys.

A **weak key of the DES algorithm** is a cryptographic key that results in the generation of an identical subkey in subsequent steps of the encryption algorithm.

3DES (Triple DES)

3DES is a symmetric encryption algorithm that involves processing a message three times with the DES algorithm:

- encryption with the first key
- decryption with the second key
- encryption with a third key

RADIUS (Remote Authentication Dial In User Service) is a protocol for remote user authentication. It is described in a separate chapter.

14.3 Configuring Remote Access VPN

To demonstrate the operation of **Remote Access VPN**, we will create the network topology shown below. This topology consists of a Radius **AAA** server (used to authenticate a user named **user**), a **VPN** server (router named VPN), an **RTR** router, and two computers (**PC1, PC2**) acting as VPN clients.

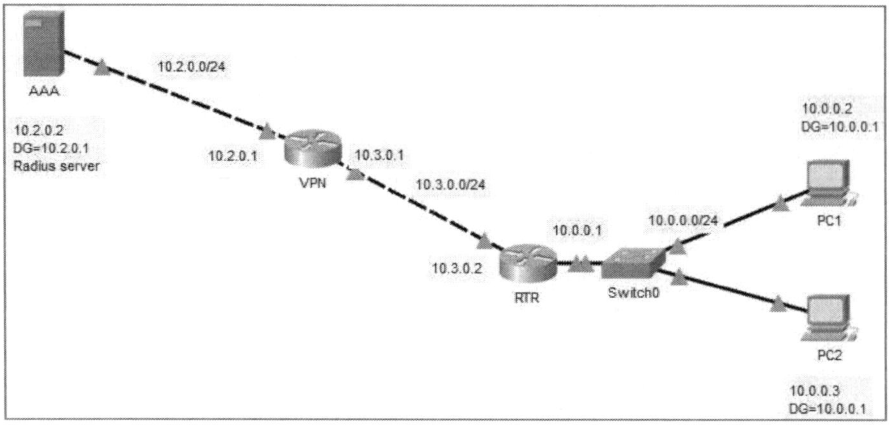

Figure 14.1Remote Access VPN topology.

Step 1. Connect the devices together according to the diagram shown in the figure.

Step 2. Configure their IP address as shown in the figure.

Step 3. Configure static routes:

- Configure a static route in the RTR router to network 10.2.0.0/24 via address 10.3.0.1
- Configure static route in RTR router to network 10.1.0.0/24 via address 10.3.0.1
- Configure a static route in the RTR router to network 10.1.1.0/24 via address 10.3.0.1.

```
ip route 10.2.0.0 255.255.255.0 10.3.0.1
ip route 10.1.0.0 255.255.255.0 10.3.0.1
ip route 10.1.1.0 255.255.255.0 10.3.0.1
```

Configure a static route in the VPN router to network 10.0.0.0/24 via address 10.3.0.2.

```
ip route 10.0.0.0 255.255.255.0 10.3.0.2
```

Step 4. Perform connection tests (ping) from PC1 and PC2 to the AAA server.

```
C:\>ping 10.2.0.2

Pinging 10.2.0.2 with 32 bytes of data:

Reply from 10.2.0.2: bytes=32 time=11ms TTL=126
Reply from 10.2.0.2: bytes=32 time<1ms TTL=126
Reply from 10.2.0.2: bytes=32 time<1ms TTL=126
Reply from 10.2.0.2: bytes=32 time<1ms TTL=126
```

Figure 14.2 Positive connection test from PC1 to AAA.

```
C:\>ping 10.2.0.2

Pinging 10.2.0.2 with 32 bytes of data:

Reply from 10.2.0.2: bytes=32 time=12ms TTL=126
Reply from 10.2.0.2: bytes=32 time<1ms TTL=126
Reply from 10.2.0.2: bytes=32 time=10ms TTL=126
Reply from 10.2.0.2: bytes=32 time<1ms TTL=126
```

Figure 14.3 Positive connection test from PC2 to AAA.

Step 5. In the AAA server, configure the AAA RADIUS service and enter the address of the VPN server, which here is the client of the AAA server.

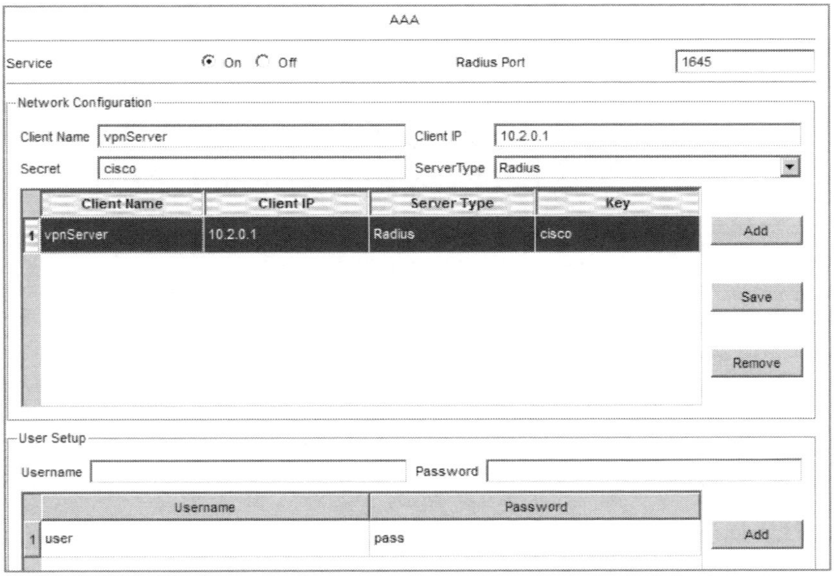

Figure 14.4 Configuring the AAA service.

Step 6. On the VPN router, activate and configure the AAA service parameters. Use the following commands (AAA stands for **Authentication, Authorization, Accounting**):

```
aaa new-model
aaa authentication login VPNAUTH group radius local
aaa authorization network VPNAUTH local
```

```
VPN(config)#aaa new-model
VPN(config)#aaa authentication login VPNAUTH group radius local
VPN(config)#aaa authorization network VPNAUTH local
```

Figure 14.5 Activate AAA services in the VPN.

Step 7 On the VPN router, activate SSH version 1. Use the following commands.

```
ip ssh version 1
```

```
VPN(config)#ip ssh version 1
```

Figure 14.6 Activation of SSH in VPN.

Step 8. On the VPN router, configure ISAKMP AES. Use the following commands.

```
crypto isakmp policy 10
encr aes 256
authentication pre-share
group 2
```

```
VPN(config)#crypto isakmp policy 10
VPN(config-isakmp)#encr aes 256
VPN(config-isakmp)#authentication pre-share
VPN(config-isakmp)#group 2
VPN(config-isakmp)#
```

Figure 14.7Activation of the ISAKMP AES in VPN.

Step 9 On the VPN router, configure further ISAKMP parameters: group, key, address pool. Use the following commands.

```
crypto isakmp client configuration group ciscogroup
key ciscogroup
pool VPNCLIENTS
netmask 255.255.255.0
```

```
VPN(config-isakmp)#crypto isakmp client configuration group ciscogroup
VPN(config-isakmp-group)#key ciscogroup
A key already exists for groupciscogroup
VPN(config-isakmp-group)#pool VPNCLIENTS
VPN(config-isakmp-group)#netmask 255.255.255.0
VPN(config-isakmp-group)#
```

Figure 14.8 Configurating ISAKMP in VPN.

Step 10. In the VPN router, configure further IPsec parameters. Use the following commands:

```
crypto ipsec transform-set mytrans esp-3des esp-sha-
hmac
```

```
VPN(config-isakmp-group)#
VPN(config-isakmp-group)#crypto ipsec transform-set mytrans esp-3des esp-sha-hmac
VPN(config)#
```

Figure 14.9 Configuring IPsec in VPN.

Step 11. In the VPN router, configure further mapping parameters. Use the following commands.

```
crypto dynamic-map mymap 10
set transform-set mytrans
reverse-route
```

```
VPN(config)#crypto dynamic-map mymap 10
VPN(config-crypto-map)#set transform-set mytrans
VPN(config-crypto-map)#reverse-route
VPN(config-crypto-map)#
```

Figure 14.10 Configure the mapping in VPN.

Step 12. In the VPN router, configure further mapping parameters. Use the following commands.

```
crypto map mymap client authentication list VPNAUTH
crypto map mymap isakmp authorization list VPNAUTH
crypto map mymap client configuration address respond
crypto map mymap 10 ipsec-isakmp dynamic mymap
```

```
VPN(config-crypto-map)#crypto map mymap client authentication list VPNAUTH
VPN(config)#crypto map mymap isakmp authorization list VPNAUTH
VPN(config)#crypto map mymap client configuration address respond
VPN(config)#crypto map mymap 10 ipsec-isakmp dynamic mymap
VPN(config)#
```

Figure 14.11 Configure the mapping in VPN.

Step 13. On the VPN router, configure the address pool for the VPN clients. Use the following command.

```
ip local pool VPNCLIENTS 10.1.1.100 10.1.1.200
```

```
VPN(config)#ip local pool VPNCLIENTS 10.1.1.100 10.1.1.200
VPN(config)#
```

Figure 14.12 Configure the address pool in the VPN.

Step 14. On the VPN router, configure the address of the RADIUS server. Use the following command.

```
radius-server host 10.2.0.2 auth-port 1645 key cisco
```

```
VPN(config)#radius-server host 10.2.0.2 auth-port 1645 key cisco
VPN(config)#
```

Figure 14.13 Configure the address of the RADIUS server in the VPN.

Step 15. On the VPN router on interface Fa0/0, configure the crypto map. Use the following command:

```
crypto map mymap
```

```
VPN(config)#interface FastEthernet0/0
VPN(config-if)#ip address 10.3.0.1 255.255.255.0
VPN(config-if)#crypto map mymap
*Jan  3 07:16:26.785: %CRYPTO-6-ISAKMP_ON_OFF: ISAKMP is ON
```

Figure 14.14 Map configuration for Fa0/0 interface in VPN.

Step 16. On PC1, start the VPN application.

Figure 14.15 VPN application.

Step 17. Perform the configuration of the VPN application on PC1.

Enter the following data in the appropriate fields:

```
Group name: ciscogroup
Group Key: ciscogroup
Server IP: 10.3.0.1
Username: user
Password: pass
```

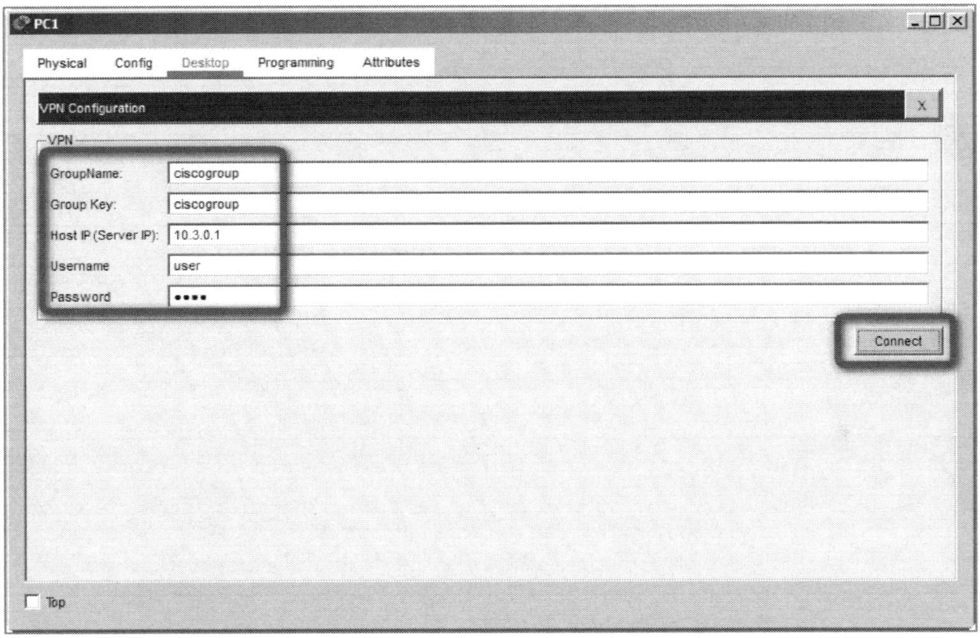

Figure 14.16 Configuration of the VPN application on PC1.

Step 18. To log in, click the **[Connect]** button.

A message will appear indicating that the VPN connection is active.

Figure 14.17 The VPN connection is active.

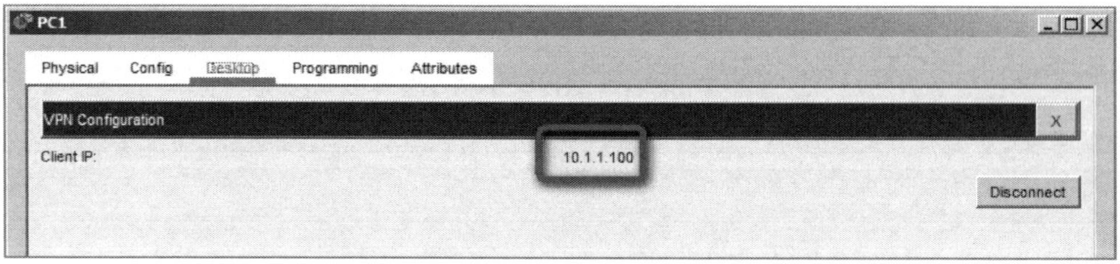

Figure 14.18 PC1 has been assigned the address 10.1.1.100.

Step 19. In simulation mode, observe the routing of an ICMP packet (ping) from PC1 to PC2.

Perform a ping from 10.0.0.2 to 10.0.0.3 and observe the window: **Simulation Panel**.

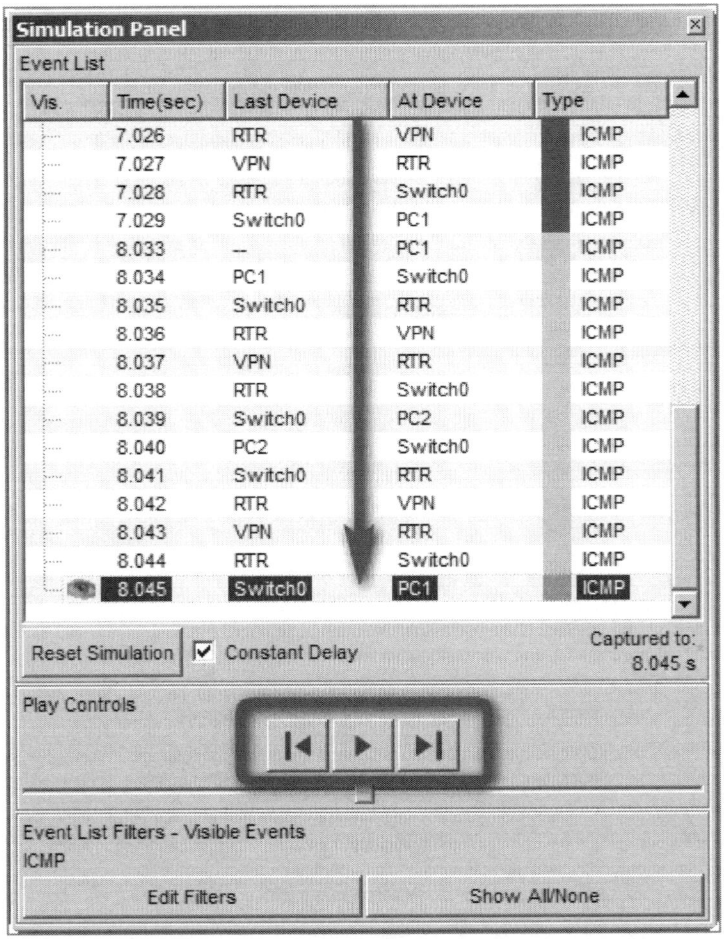

Figure 14.19 Observation of an ICMP packet route (ping) from PC1 to PC2 in simulation mode.

To demonstrate the operation of a VPN tunnel between two routers, without IPsec, we will create the network topology shown below.

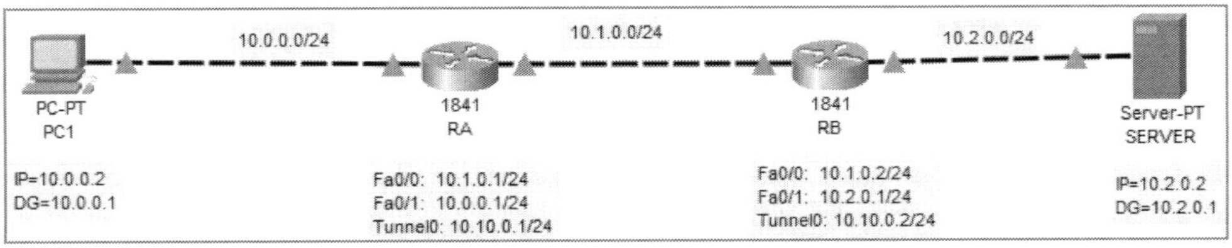

Figure 14.20 Site-to-Site VPN network topology without IPsec.

To establish a Site-to-Site VPN tunnel between the RA and RB routers, perform the following steps:

Step 1. Connect the devices together according to the diagram shown in the figure.

Step 2. Configure their IP addresses as shown in the diagram.

Step 3. Configure the virtual interface for the tunnel on the RA router.

To do this, in the **RA** router, execute the commands:

```
interface Tunnel 0
ip address 10.10.0.1 255.255.255.0
tunnel source FastEthernet 0/0
tunnel destination 10.1.0.2
exit
```

```
!
interface Tunnel0
 ip address 10.10.0.1 255.255.255.0
 mtu 1476
 tunnel source FastEthernet0/0
 tunnel destination 10.1.0.2
!
```

Figure 14.21 The configured tunnel from RA side.

Step 4. Configure the virtual interface for the tunnel in the RB router.

To do this, in the RB router execute the commands:

```
interface Tunnel0
ip address 10.10.0.2 255.255.255.0
tunnel source FastEthernet0/0
tunnel destination 10.1.0.1
exit
```

```
!
interface Tunnel0
 ip address 10.10.0.2 255.255.255.0
 mtu 1476
 tunnel source FastEthernet0/0
 tunnel destination 10.1.0.1
!
```

Figure 14.22 The configured tunnel from the RB side.

Step 5. Configure static routes in the tunnel.

Configure a static route in the RA router to network 10.2.0.0/24 via address 10.10.0.2 (tunnel edge in RB) using the command.

```
ip route 10.2.0.0 255.255.255.0 10.10.0.2
```

Configure static route in RB router to network 10.0.0.0/24 via address 10.10.0.1 (tunnel edge in RA) using command.

```
ip route 10.0.0.0 255.255.255.0 10.10.0.1
```

Step 6. Check the path of the packet from PC1 to the SERVER (10.2.0.2).

Execute command: **`tracert 10.2.0.2`** and observe its results.

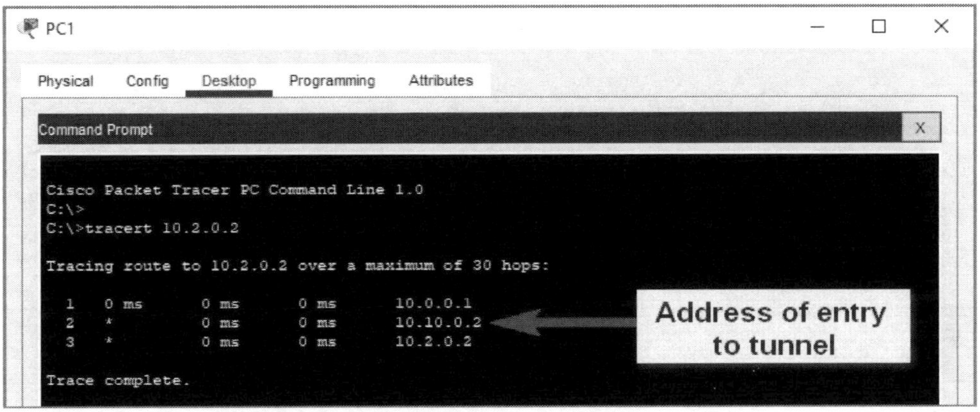

Figure 14.23 Results of the tracert command.

Observations:

The packet 'sees' only the source and destination addresses, and the internal address of the tunnel entrance. It does not see the addresses of the routers it passes through.

14.4 Configuring a Site-to-Site VPN Tunnel Using IPsec

To demonstrate the operation of a Site-to-Site VPN tunnel using the ISAKMP protocol and the IPsec protocol, we will create the network topology shown below.

The topology shown contains two local networks **A** and **B**, which for simplicity are represented by the so-called Loopback interfaces (addresses 172.16.1.1 and 172.16.2.1 respectively). In addition, a Site-to-Site VPN tunnel will be established between the routers R1 and R3, which are connected via the router R2 and the switch SW12. All routers should support EIGRP dynamic routing.

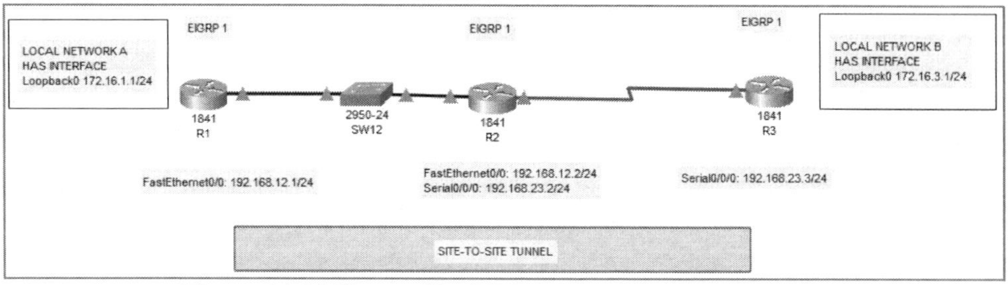

Figure 14.24 Site-to-Site VPN topology without IPsec.

To establish a Site-to-Site VPN tunnel between the R1 and R3 routers, perform the following steps:

Step 1. Connect the devices together according to the diagram shown in the figure.

Step 2. Configure their IP addresses as shown in the diagram.

Step 3. Create the Loopback0 interface and its IP address on the R1 router using the appropriate commands.

```
interface Loopback0
ip address 172.16.1.1 255.255.255.0
```

Step 4. Create the Loopback0 interface and its IP address in the R3 router using the appropriate commands.

```
interface Loopback0
ip address 172.16.3.1 255.255.255.0
```

Step 5. Configure the EIGRP dynamic protocol on each router.

For the R1 router, use the commands:

```
router eigrp 1
network 172.16.0.0
network 192.168.12.0
```

For the R2 router use command:

```
router eigrp 1
network 192.168.12.0
network 192.168.23.0
```

For the R3 router use command:

```
router eigrp 1
network 192.168.23.0
network 172.16.0.0
```

Step 6. Perform the VPN configuration for the **R1** router.

Use the following commands to configure a VPN tunnel using IPsec and ISAKMP and an extended ACL:

```
crypto isakmp policy 10
encr aes 256
authentication pre-share
group 5
crypto isakmp key cisco address 192.168.23.3
crypto ipsec transform-set 50 ah-sha-hmac esp-aes 256
esp-sha-hmac
crypto map MYMAP 10 ipsec-isakmp
set peer 192.168.23.3
set pfs group5
set security-association lifetime seconds 900
set transform-set 50
match address 101
interface FastEthernet0/0
crypto map MYMAP
access-list 101 permit ip 172.16.1.0 0.0.0.255
172.16.3.0 0.0.0.255
```

Step 7. Perform VPN configuration for router **R3**.

Use the following commands to configure a VPN tunnel using IPsec and ISAKMP and an extended ACL:

```
crypto isakmp policy 10
encr aes 256
authentication pre-share
group 5
lifetime 3600

crypto isakmp key cisco address 192.168.12.1
crypto ipsec security-association lifetime seconds
1800
crypto ipsec transform-set 50 ah-sha-hmac esp-aes 256
esp-sha-hmac
crypto map MYMAP 10 ipsec-isakmp
set peer 192.168.12.1
set pfs group5
set security-association lifetime seconds 900
set transform-set 50
match address 101
interface Serial0/0/0
crypto map MYMAP
access-list 101 permit ip 172.16.3.0 0.0.0.255
172.16.1.0 0.0.0.255
```

Step 8. Check ISAKMP security on the R1 router.

```
R1#SHOW CRYPTO ISAKMP SA
IPv4 Crypto ISAKMP SA
dst             src             state           conn-id slot status

IPv6 Crypto ISAKMP SA
```

Figure 14.25 The result of the show crypto isakmp sa command.

Step 9. Check the IPsec configuration on the R1 router.

```
R1#SHOW CRYPTO IPSEC SA

interface: FastEthernet0/0
    Crypto map tag: MYMAP, local addr 192.168.12.1

   protected vrf: (none)
   local  ident (addr/mask/prot/port): (172.16.1.0/255.255.255.0/0/0)
   remote  ident (addr/mask/prot/port): (172.16.3.0/255.255.255.0/0/0)
   current_peer 192.168.23.3 port 500
    PERMIT, flags={origin_is_acl,}
   #pkts encaps: 0, #pkts encrypt: 0, #pkts digest: 0
   #pkts decaps: 0, #pkts decrypt: 0, #pkts verify: 0
   #pkts compressed: 0, #pkts decompressed: 0
   #pkts not compressed: 0, #pkts compr. failed: 0
   #pkts not decompressed: 0, #pkts decompress failed: 0
   #send errors 0, #recv errors 0

     local crypto endpt.: 192.168.12.1, remote crypto endpt.:192.168.23.3
     path mtu 1500, ip mtu 1500, ip mtu idb FastEthernet0/0
     current outbound spi: 0x0(0)

     inbound esp sas:
```

Figure 14.26 Result of command show crypto ipsec sa.

Step 10. Check the path of the packet from the R1 router to the Loopback0 interface on the R3 router (172.16.3.1).

Use command: `traceroute`. Observe results.

```
R1#traceroute 172.16.3.1
Type escape sequence to abort.
Tracing the route to 172.16.3.1

  1   192.168.12.2      0 msec     1 m...     ... msec
  2   192.168.23.3      ...        1 msec     5 msec
R1#
```

R3 Address

Figure 14.27 Result of command: `traceroute 172.16.3.1` from router R1.

Step 11. Check the packet travel path from the R3 router to the Loopback0 interface on the R1 router (172.16.1.1).

Use command: `traceroute` . Observe results.

```
R3#traceroute 172.16.1.1
Type escape sequence to abort.
Tracing the route to 172.16.1.1

  1   192.168.23.2      7 msec     1 msec     1 ...
  2   192.168.12.1      ...        1 msec     1 msec
R3#
```

R1 Address

Figure 14.28 Result of command: `traceroute 172.16.1.1` from router R3.

Observations

The packet "doesn't see" the source or destination address or internal addresses, but only the address of the destination router through which it is passing.:

CHAPTER 15

MULTILAYER SWITCHES

15 MULTILAYER SWITCHES

This chapter describes multilayer access switches (***Multilayer Switches***) and their basic configuration. The descriptions contained herein apply to the switches available in Packet Tracer, operating in layer three of the ISO/OSI model: **3560** and **3650**.

15.1 Introduction to Network Layer Switching

A Layer 3 switch has wider capabilities compared to a switch operating only at Layer 2 of the ISO/OSI model; it can operate at Layer 3 of the ISO/OSI model (the same as the router).

Generally speaking, a ***Switch Layer 3*** switch is a device that works in a similar way to a router, but also has certain limitations.

The main advantages of a **Layer 3 switch** are:

- is faster than a traditional router,
- supports static routing,
- supports basic dynamic routing protocols.

The main disadvantages of the **third layer switch** are:

- it is usually more expensive than a traditional router,
- it may have limitations regarding address translation (NAT),
- may have limitations regarding security mechanisms.

15.2 Multilayer Switch Models in Packet Tracer

Two multilayer switch models are available in Packet Tracer: **3560-24PS** and **3650-24PS**.

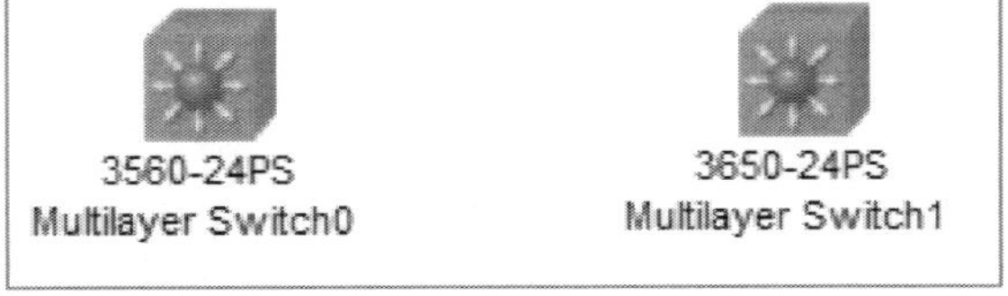

Figure 15.1 Switch symbols 3560-24PS and 3650-24-PS

The **3560-24PS** has 24 Fast Ethernet interfaces at 10/100 Mbps, numbered **Fa0/1** to **Fa0/24**, and two Gigabit Ethernet interfaces at 10/100/1000 Mbps, numbered **Gi0/1** to **Gi0/2**. All interfaces are non-replaceable, meaning that they cannot be replaced.

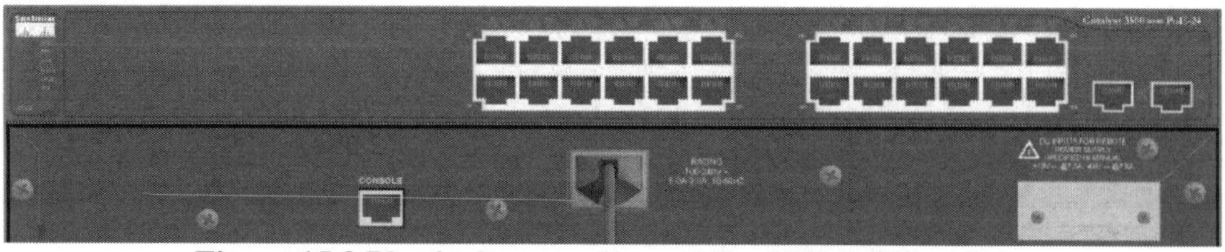

Figure 15.2 Physical appearance of the 3560-24PS switch

The **3650-24PS** has 24 10/100/1000 Mbps Gigabit Ethernet interfaces (RJ-45 type sockets), numbered **Gi1/0/1** to **Gi1/0/24**. These interfaces are non-replaceable. On the right-hand side of the chassis, there are four 10/100/1000 Mbps Gigabit Ethernet interfaces (type sockets), numbered **Gi1/1/1** to **Gi1/1/4**. The last four interfaces are interchangeable.

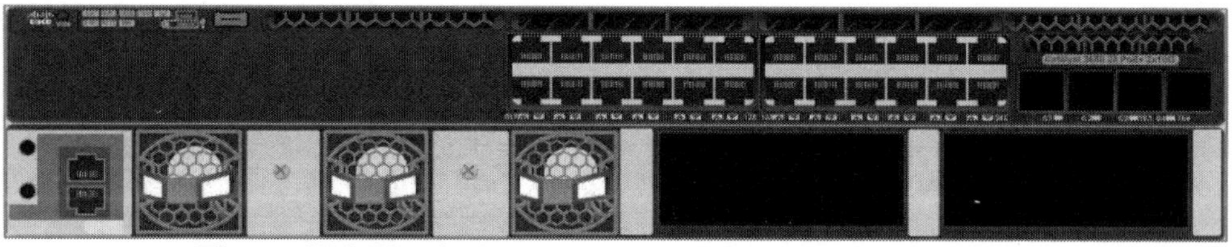

Figure 15.3 Physical appearance of the 3650-24PS switch

Possible modules to be fitted are:

- GLC-LH-SMD
- GLC-T

The **GLC-LH-SMD** module allows a Gigabit Ethernet connection to be established using single-mode optical fiber.

Figure 15.4 GLC-LH-SMD Module

The **GLC-T** module allows a Gigabit Ethernet connection to be established using an unscreened CAT 5 Ethernet cable with a length of up to 100 m.

Figure 15.5 GLC-T Module

The switch also has two interchangeable power supplies.

Figure 15.6 The appearance of the power supplies in the 3650-24PS switcher

15.3 Resetting the Switch

To reset the switch configuration, perform the following steps:

1. Navigate to the **[CLI]** tab.
2. Execute the **enable** command.
3. Execute the **delete flash:vlan.dat** command.
4. Confirm the delete operation twice (with the Enter key).
5. Execute the **erase startup-config** command.
6. Confirm the erase operation (by pressing the Enter key).
7. Restart the switch with the **reload** command.
8. Confirm the restart operation (by pressing the Enter key).

Figure 15.7 Deleting the VLNs database.

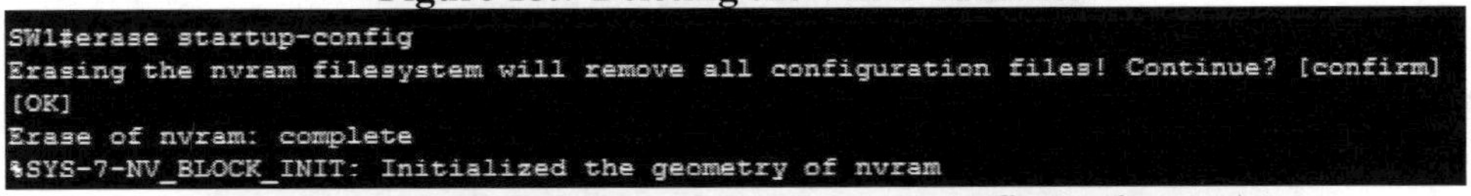

Figure 15.8 Deletion of the start-up configuration.

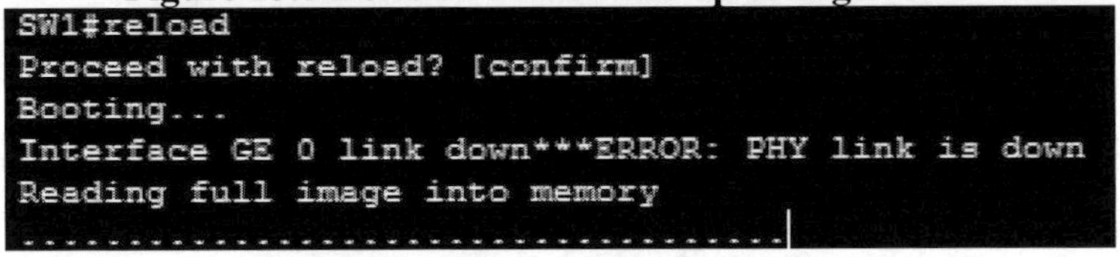

Figure 15.9 Restarting the device.

15.4 Configuration of the 3560 24PS Multilayer Switch

Note on routing in the 3560-24PS switch.

The routing process in a Layer 3 switch is between VLANs, so a basic knowledge of VLANs is necessary.

15.4.1 Example of the Router-Switch Topology

When connecting local networks to a router using the 3560-24PS switch, configuration of the multilayer switch will require the following steps:

1. In the router, configure the router interface IP for the switch connection.
2. In the router, creating a default static route to the switch.
3. On the switch, configuring the interface IP for the router connection and no switchport mode.
4. On the switch, enabling IP routing.
5. On the switch, creating as many VLANs as there are local networks.
6. On the switch, assigning VLANs to access interfaces.
7. On the switch, configuring IP addresses for the VLANs.
8. On the switch, configuring the default gateway.

Note: Access devices located on local networks must have a default gateway that matches the VLAN number. The next configuration steps are shown for an example whose topology is included in the figure.:

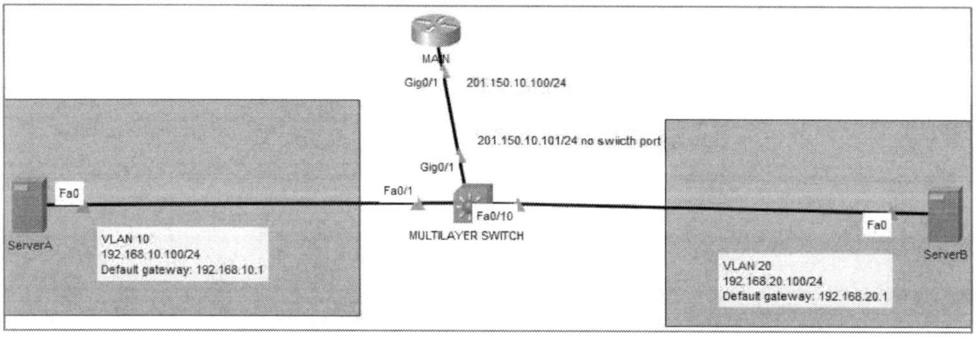

Figure 15.10 Multilayer Switch 3560 example network topology.

Step 1. Create a network topology containing: a type 1941 router, a type 3560 24PS switch and two servers. Then configure the IP 201.150.10.100/24 on the MAIN router for the Gi0/1 interface.

Step 2. On the MAIN router, create a default static route using the command

```
ip route 0.0.0.0 0.0.0.0 201.150.10.101
```

Step 3. On the switch, configure IP 201.150.10.101/24 for interface Gi0/1, and no switchport mode, using the commands.

```
interface Gi 0/1
no switchport
```

```
ip address 201.150.10.101 255.255.255.0
no shutdown
```

Note: the switch must ensure communication between the VLANs and the MAIN router port, so the Gi0/1 port is not an access port

Step 4. Enable IP routing on the switch, using the command.

```
ip routing
```

Step 5. Create two VLANs, numbered 10 and 20, using the commands:

```
vlan 10
vlan 20
```

Step 6. Assign VLANs to access interfaces, using the commands:

```
int Fa 0/1
switchport mode access
switchport access vlan 10
int Fa0/10
switchport mode access
switchport access vlan 20
```

Step 7. Set the IP addresses for the VLANs, according to the given table, using the commands:

```
interface vlan 10
ip address 192.168.10.1 255.255.255.0
no shutdown
interface vlan 20
ip address 192.168.20.1 255.255.255.0
no shutdown
```

VLAN	IP	Mask
10	192.168.10.1	255.255.255.0
20	192.168.20.1	255.255.255.0

Table 15.1 VLANs addressing.

Step 8. Set the default gateway for the switch, using the following command:

```
ip default-gateway 201.150.10.100
```

Step 9. Configure the local networks (use the configurations for servers: ServerA, ServerB according to the table).

Device	IP	Default Gateway
ServerA	192.168.,10.100	192.168.10.1
ServerB	192.168.20.100	192.168.20.1

Table 15.2 Addressing of end devices.

Step 10. Check communication between VLANs and VLAN 10 and the MAIN router.

Check communication between VLANs.

```
SERVER>ping 192.168.20.100

Pinging 192.168.20.100 with 32 bytes of data:

Reply from 192.168.20.100: bytes=32 time=1ms TTL=127
Reply from 192.168.20.100: bytes=32 time=0ms TTL=127
Reply from 192.168.20.100: bytes=32 time=0ms TTL=127
Reply from 192.168.20.100: bytes=32 time=0ms TTL=127

Ping statistics for 192.168.20.100:
    Packets: Sent = 4, Received = 4, Lost = 0 (0% loss),
Approximate round trip times in milli-seconds:
    Minimum = 0ms, Maximum = 1ms, Average = 0ms
```

Figure 15.11 Response for PING from ServerA to ServerB.

Check the communication from VLAN 10 to the MAIN router.

```
SERVER>ping 201.150.10.100

Pinging 201.150.10.100 with 32 bytes of data:

Reply from 201.150.10.100: bytes=32 time=0ms TTL=254
Reply from 201.150.10.100: bytes=32 time=0ms TTL=254
Reply from 201.150.10.100: bytes=32 time=0ms TTL=254
Reply from 201.150.10.100: bytes=32 time=0ms TTL=254

Ping statistics for 201.150.10.100:
    Packets: Sent = 4, Received = 4, Lost = 0 (0% loss),
Approximate round trip times in milli-seconds:
    Minimum = 0ms, Maximum = 0ms, Average = 0ms
```

Figure 15.12 Response for PING from ServerA to the MAIN router.

15.4.2 Example of L3 Switch - L2 Switch topology.

When connecting local networks with multiple 3560-24PS switches and access switches, the configuration of the switches is more complicated. This example also demonstrates the configuration of the DHCP service on the 3560-24PS switches. To perform this example configuration, the following steps will be required:

1. Create a topology.
2. Setting up dynamic addressing on PC0-PC5.
3. On the ATL and BST access switches, creating the appropriate VLANs.
4. On ATL and BST access switches, assigning VLANs to access interfaces.
5. On the ATLANTA and BOSTON switches, create the corresponding VLANs.
6. On the ATLANTA and BOSTON switches, do assignment of VLANs to the access interfaces.
7. On the ATLANTA and BOSTON switches, configure the IP addresses for the VLANs.
8. On the ATLANTA and BOSTON switches, enable IP routing.
9. On the ATLANTA switch, create a static route to the local network in Boston.
10. On the BOSTON switch, create a static route to the local network in Atlanta.
11. Configure the DHCP server on the ATLANTA switch.
12. Configure the DHCP server in the BOSTON switch.
13. Checking the configuration of the ATLANTA switch.
14. Checking the configuration of the BOSTON switch.

For the specific example, an additional VLAN will be needed to ensure communication between the ATLANTA and BOSTON switches. The intermediate VLAN will be number 12 (12.0.0.0/8).

Addressing of the VLAN interfaces.

Device	VLAN	IP	Mask	Interface
ATLANTA	10	192.168.1.1	255.255.255.0	Fa0/24
ATLANTA	12	12.0.0.1	255.0.0.0	Gi0/1
BOSTON	20	192.168.2.1	255.255.255.0	Fa0/24
BOSTON	12	12.0.0.2	255.0.0.0	Gi0/1

Table 15.3 Addressing of the VLAN interfaces.

The next configuration steps are shown for a topology with two Layer 3 switches. The topology is presented in the figure.

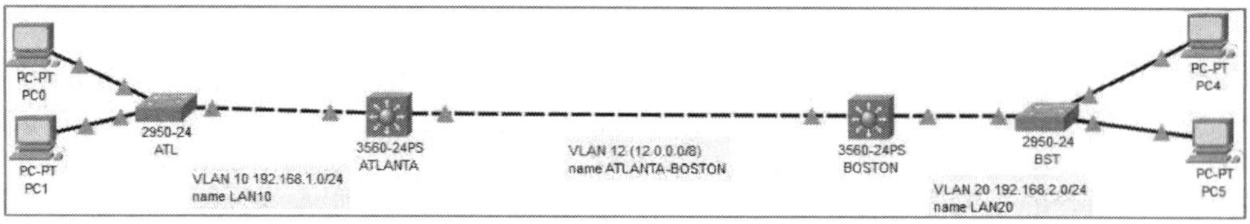

Figure 15.13 Multilayer Switches example network topology.

Step 1. Create a topology according to the figure, with two type 2950-24 switches named: **ATL**, **BST**. and two switches of type 3560-24PS named: **ATLANTA, BOSTON.** On PC0 - PC5 set up a dynamic address, taken from the DHCP server.

Step 2. On the access switch ATL, create a VLAN 10 named LAN10. To do this, use the commands:

```
vlan 10
name LAN10
```

On the BST access switch, create a VLAN 20 named LAN20. To do this, use the commands:

```
vlan 20
name LAN20
```

Step 3. On access switch GD, assign interfaces Fa0/1, Fa0/2, Fa0/24 to VLAN 10.

To do this, use the commands:

```
interface Fa 0/1
sw mode access
sw access vlan 10
interface Fa0/2
sw mode access
sw access vlan 10
interface Fa0/24
sw mode access
sw access vlan 10
```

On the access switch GA, assign the interfaces Fa0/1, Fa0/2, Fa0/24 to VLAN 20.

To do this, use the commands:

```
interface Fa 0/1
sw mode access
sw access vlan 20
interface Fa 0/2
sw mode access
sw access vlan 20
interface Fa 0/24
sw mode access
sw access vlan 20
```

Step 4. On the ATLANTA switch, create the following VLANs: 10 named LAN10, 12 named ATLANTA-BOSTON. To do this, use the commands:

```
vlan 10
name LAN10
vlan 12
name ATLANTA-BOSTON
```

On the BOSTON switch, create the following VLANs: 20 named LAN20, 12 named ATLANTA-BOSTON. To do this, use the commands:

```
vlan 20
name LAN20
vlan 12
name ATLANTA-BOSTON
```

Step 5. On the ATLANTA switch, make the assignment of interface Fa0/24 to VLAN 10 and Gi0/1 to VLAN 12. To do this, use the commands:

```
interface Fa 0/24
sw mode access
sw access vlan 10
interface Gi 0/1
sw mode access
sw access vlan 12
```

On the BOSTON switch, make the assignment of interface Fa0/24 to VLAN 20 and Gi0/1 to VLAN 12. To do this, use the commands:

```
interface Fa 0/24
sw mode access
sw access vlan 20
interface Gi 0/1
sw mode access
sw access vlan 12
```

Step 6. On the ATLANTA switch, configure the IP for VLAN 10 and VLAN 12, using the commands:

```
interface vlan10
ip address 192.168.1.1 255.255.255.0
interface vlan12
ip address 12.0.0.1 255.0.0.0
```

On the BOSTON switch, configure the IP for VLAN 20 and VLAN 12. To do so, use the commands:

```
interface vlan20
ip address 192.168.2.1 255.255.255.0
interface vlan12
ip address 12.0.0.2 255.0.0.0
```

Step 7. On the ATLANTA and BOSTON switches, enable IP routing. To do this, use the command:

```
ip routing
```

Step 8. On the ATLANTA switch, create static routes to the local network in BOSTON (VLAN 20).

To do this, use the command:

```
ip route 192.168.2.0 255.255.255.0 12.0.0.2
```

Step 9. On the BOSTON switch, create static routes to the local network in ATLANTA (VLAN 10).
To do this, use the command

```
ip route 192.168.1.0 255.255.255.0   12.0.0.1
```

Step 10. Perform the configuration of the DHCP server on the ATLANTA switch. To do this, use the following commands:

```
ip dhcp excluded-address 192.168.1.1
ip dhcp pool LAN10
network 192.168.1.0 255.255.255.0
default-router 192.168.1.1
```

Step 11. Perform the configuration of the DHCP server on the BOSTON switch. To do this, use the following commands:

```
ip dhcp excluded-address 192.168.2.1
ip dhcp pool LAN20
network 192.168.2.0 255.255.255.0
default-router 192.168.2.1
```

15.5 Configuration of the 3650-24PS Multilayer Switch

Basic rules for configuring the 3650-24PS switch.

15.5.1 Introductory Note for the 3650-24PS Switch.

To start configuring this switch, you need to install a power supply (possibly two power supplies) in the switch chassis. To do this, we will perform the following steps:

1. change to the **[Physical]** tab.
2. use the mouse to move the **AC-POWER-SUPPLY** module(s) to the empty slot(s) of the device - see illustration.

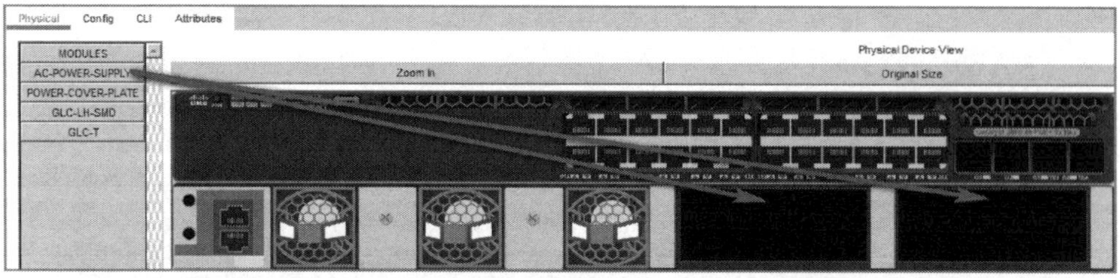

Figure 15.14 Installing power supplies in the 3650-24PS switch.

Figure 15.15 The appearance of the installed power supplies in the 3650-24PS switch.

3. go to the [CLI] tab and check that the IOS on the switch has been started.

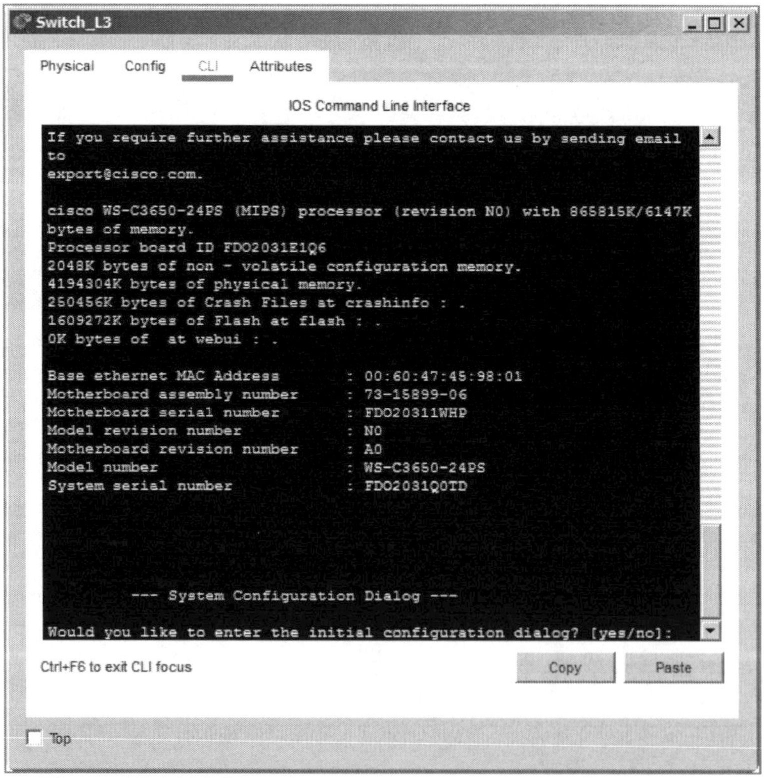

Figure 15.16 IOS has been started on the 3650-24PS switch.

15.5.2 Example of L3 Switch - L2 Switches Topology

In this example, there are two Layer 2 switches 2960-24TT (Switch1_L2, Switch2_L2), one Layer 3 switch (Switch_L3) 3650-24PS and four laptops operating in VLANs.

Step 1. Create a network topology containing the devices, name them according to the figure.

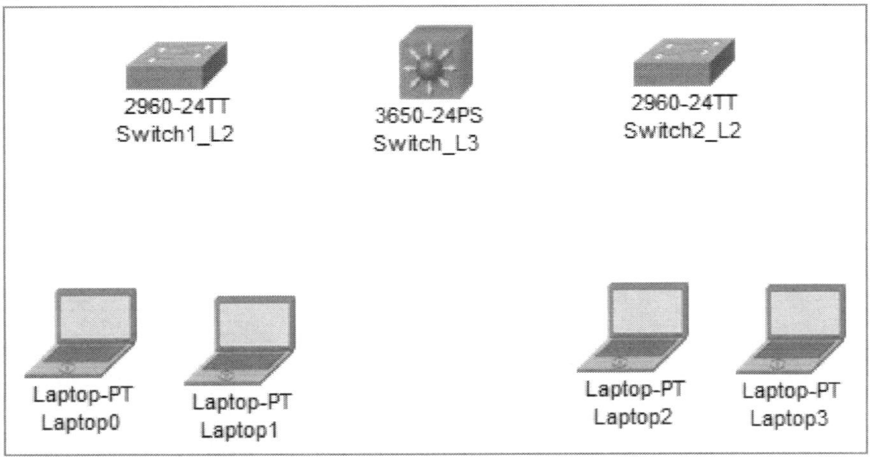

Figure 15.17 Example network topology without cabling.

Step 2. Connect the devices with the appropriate cables, remembering that switch to switch is connected with a crossover cable.

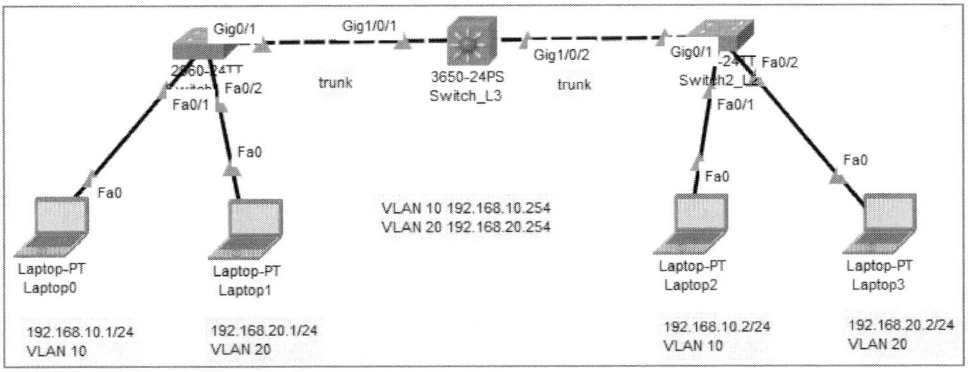

Figure 15.18 Example of network topology with cabling.

Step 3. Perform IP addressing on the laptops, according to the table below.

Name	IP	Mask	Default gateway
Laptop0	192.168.10.1	255.255.255.0	192.168.10.254
Laptop1	192.168.20.1	255.255.255.0	192.168.20.254
Laptop2	192.168.10.2	255.255.255.0	192.168.10.254

Laptop3	192.168.20.2	255.255.255.0	192.168.20.254

Table 15.4 Laptops addressing.

Step 4. On both Layer 2 switches, create and configure VLANs, using the commands:

```
conf t
interface vlan 10
ip address 192.168.10.254 255.255.255.0
no shutdown
interface vlan 20
ip address 192.168.20.254 255.255.255.0
no shutdown
```

Step 5. On both Layer 2 switches, assign VLANs to access interfaces, using the commands

```
conf t
int Fa0/1
switchport mode access
switchport access vlan 10
int Fa0/2
switchport mode access
switchport access vlan 20
```

Step 6. On both Layer 2 switches, configure interface Gi0/1 as a trunk, using the commands

```
conf t
int Gi0/1
switchport mode trunk
(switchport trunk encapsulation dot1q)
```

Step 7. On the Layer 3 switch (**Switch_L3**), create and configure VLANs, using the commands

```
conf t
vlan 10
vlan 20
```

```
exit
interface vlan 10
ip address 192.168.10.254 255.255.255.0
no shutdown
interface vlan 20
ip address 192.168.20.254 255.255.255.0
no shutdown
```

Step 8. Check the network status, can Laptop0 PING Laptop2 and Laptop1 can PING Laptop3?

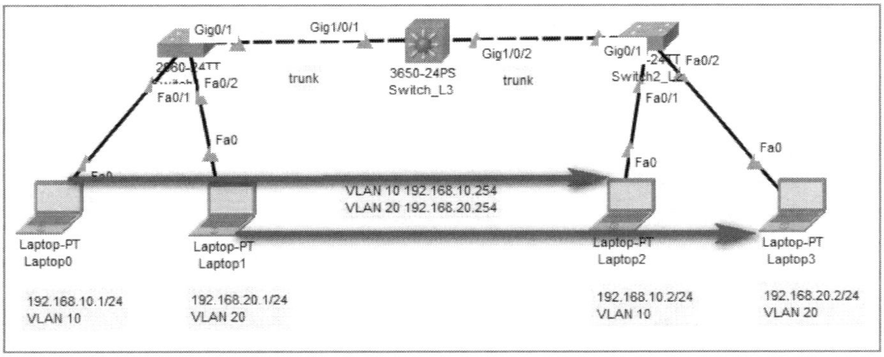

Figure 15.19 Communication within VLANs.

The pinging results should be positive for laptops that are in the same VLAN subnet.

Step 9. On the Layer 3 switch (**Switch_L3**), enable communication between VLANs, using the commands

```
conf t
ip routing
```

Step 10. Check the routing table in the Layer 3 switch (**Switch_L3**), using the command

```
show ip route
```

```
Switch_L3#show ip route
Codes: C - connected, S - static, I - IGRP, R - RIP, M - mobile, B - BGP
       D - EIGRP, EX - EIGRP external, O - OSPF, IA - OSPF inter area
       N1 - OSPF NSSA external type 1, N2 - OSPF NSSA external type 2
       E1 - OSPF external type 1, E2 - OSPF external type 2, E - EGP
       i - IS-IS, L1 - IS-IS level-1, L2 - IS-IS level-2, ia - IS-IS inter area
       * - candidate default, U - per-user static route, o - ODR
       P - periodic downloaded static route

Gateway of last resort is not set

C    192.168.10.0/24 is directly connected, Vlan10
C    192.168.20.0/24 is directly connected, Vlan20
```

Figure 15.Result of the command show ip route.

Step 11. Check network status, can Laptop0 PING Laptop1 and Laptop3?

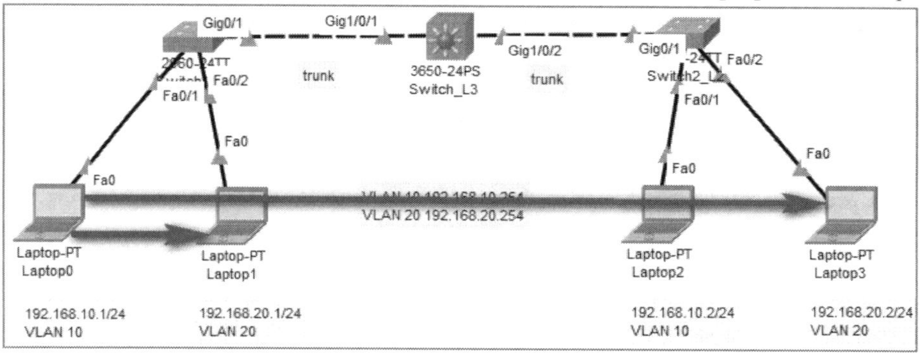

Figure 15.20 Communication between VLANs.

```
C:\>ping 192.168.20.1

Pinging 192.168.20.1 with 32 bytes of data:

Reply from 192.168.20.1: bytes=32 time=1ms TTL=127
Reply from 192.168.20.1: bytes=32 time<1ms TTL=127
Reply from 192.168.20.1: bytes=32 time<1ms TTL=127
Reply from 192.168.20.1: bytes=32 time<1ms TTL=127
```

Figure 15.21 The result of a ping command from Laptop0 to Laptop1.

```
C:\>ping 192.168.20.2

Pinging 192.168.20.2 with 32 bytes of data:

Reply from 192.168.20.2: bytes=32 time=1ms TTL=127
Reply from 192.168.20.2: bytes=32 time<1ms TTL=127
Reply from 192.168.20.2: bytes=32 time=1ms TTL=127
Reply from 192.168.20.2: bytes=32 time=10ms TTL=127
```

Figure 15.22 The result of a ping command from Laptop0 to Laptop3.

The ping results should be positive for laptops located in different VLAN subnets.

15.5.3 Example of Topology with Fiber-based L3 Switches

In this example, there are six 3650-24PS Layer 3 switches (SW1, SW2, SW3, SW12, SW13, SW23) and three computers (PC10, PC20, PC30) operating in VLANs.

Step 1. Create a network topology containing the devices, name them according to the drawing.

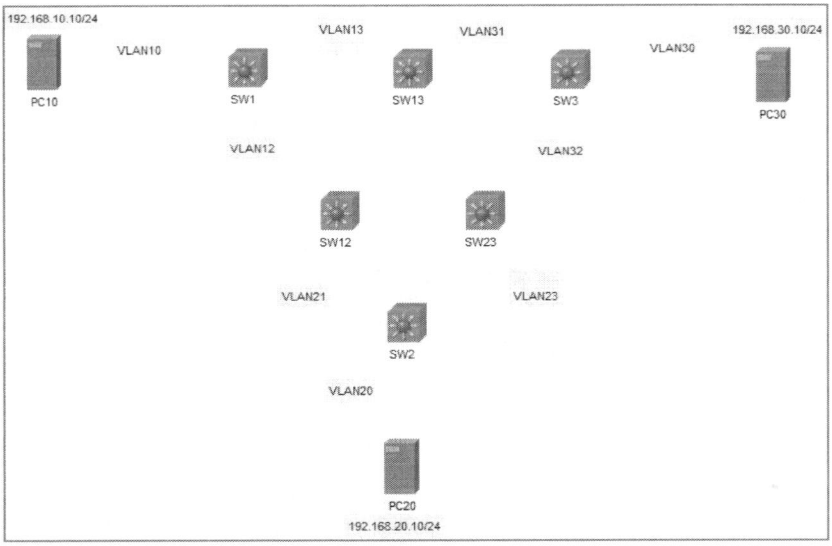

Figure 15.23 Example network topology without cabling.

Step 2. In each computer, replace the network modules from **PT-HOST-NM-1CFE** with **PT-HOST-NM-1FGE**.

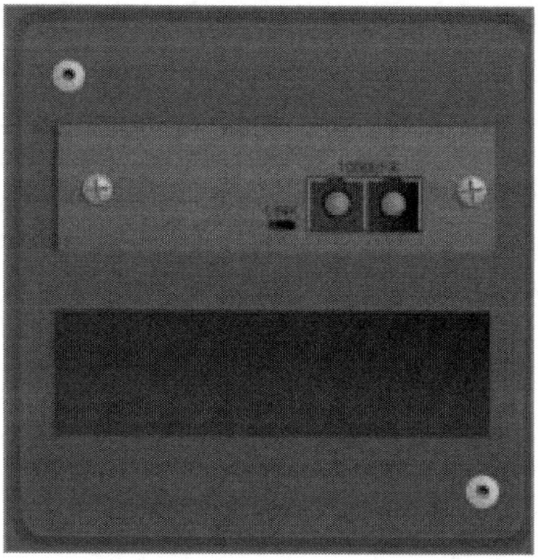

Figure 15.24 Module PT-HOST-NM-1FGE.

Step 3. In each switch, add four **GLC-LH-SMD** network modules.

Figure 15.25 Modules GLC-LH-SMD.

Step 4. Connect the devices via fiber optic cables.

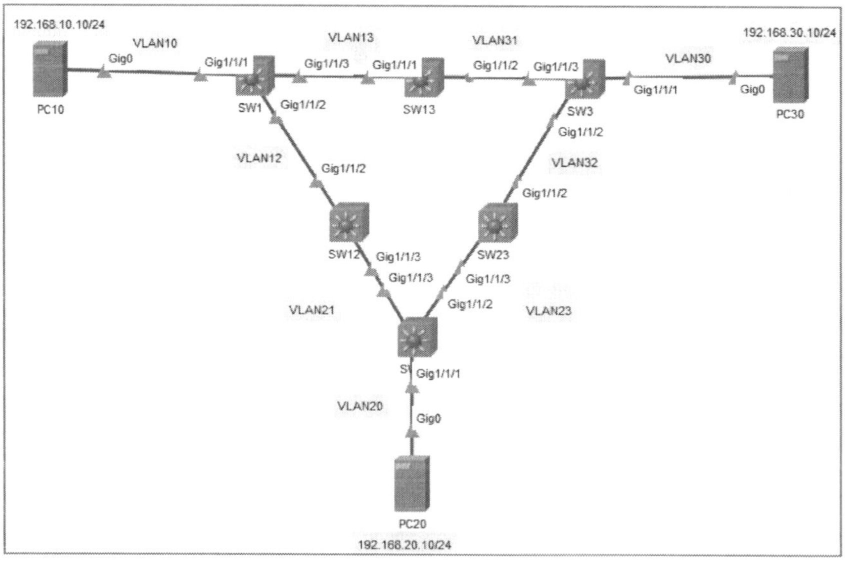

Figure 15.26 Example of network topology with cabling.

Switch	Interface	VLAN	VLAN IP
SW1	Gi1/1/1	10	192.168.10.1
SW1	Gi1/1/2	12	192.168.12.1
SW1	Gi1/1/3	13	192.168.13.1
SW12	Gi1/1/2	12	192.168.12.2
SW12	Gi1/1/3	21	192.168.21.2
SW2	Gi1/1/1	20	192.168.20.1
SW2	Gi1/1/2	23	192.168.23.1
SW2	Gi1/1/3	21	192.168.21.1
SW23	Gi1/1/2	32	192.168.32.2
SW23	Gi1/1/3	23	192.168.23.2
SW3	Gi1/1/1	30	192.168.30.1
SW3	Gi1/1/2	31	192.168.31.1
SW3	Gi1/1/3	32	192.168.32.1

Table 15.5 VLANs addressing.

Step 5. Perform IP addressing on the computers, according to the following table.

Name	IP	Mask	Default gateway
PC10	192.168.10.10	255.255.255.0	192.168.10.1
PC20	192.168.20.10	255.255.255.0	192.168.20.1
PC30	192.168.30.10	255.255.255.0	192.168.30.1

Table 15.6 Computers addressing.

Step 6. On switch SW1, create and configure VLANs (VLAN addressing), using the commands:

```
enable
conf t
hostname SW1
vlan 10
vlan 12
vlan 13
exit
interface vlan 10
ip address 192.168.10.1 255.255.255.0
no shutdown
interface vlan 12
ip address 192.168.12.1 255.255.255.0
no shutdown
interface vlan 13
```

```
ip address 192.168.13.1 255.255.255.0
no shutdown
end
write
```

Step 7. On switch SW12, create and configure VLANs (VLAN addressing), using the commands:

```
enable
conf t
hostname SW12
vlan 12
vlan 21
exit
interface vlan 12
ip address 192.168.12.2 255.255.255.0
no shutdown
interface vlan21
ip address 192.168.21.2 255.255.255.0
no shutdown
end
write
```

Step 8. On switch SW2, create and configure VLANs (VLAN addressing), using the commands:

```
enable
conf t
hostname SW2
vlan 20
vlan 21
exit
interface vlan 20
ip address 192.168.20.1 255.255.255.0
no shutdown
interface vlan 21
ip address 192.168.21.1 255.255.255.0
no shutdown
```

```
interface vlan 23
ip address 192.168.23.1 255.255.255.0
no shutdown
end
write
```

Step 9. On switch SW23, create and configure VLANs (VLAN addressing), using the commands:

```
enable
conf t
hostname SW23
vlan 2
vlan 21
exit
interface vlan 23
ip address 192.168.23.2 255.255.255.0
no shutdown
interface vlan 32
ip address 192.168.32.2 255.255.255.0
no shutdown
end
write
```

Step 10. On the SW3 switch, create and configure VLANs (VLAN addressing), using the commands:

```
enable
conf t
hostname SW3
vlan 30
vlan 31
vlan 32
exit
interface vlan 30
ip address 192.168.30.1 255.255.255.0
no shutdown
interface vlan 31
```

```
ip address 192.168.31.1 255.255.255.0
no shutdown
interface vlan 32
ip address 192.168.32.1 255.255.255.0
no shutdown
end
write
```

Step 11. On switch SW13, create and configure VLANs (VLAN addressing), using commands

```
enable
conf t
hostname SW13
vlan 13
vlan 31
exit
interface vlan 13
ip address 192.168.13.2 255.255.255.0
no shutdown
interface vlan 31
ip address 192.168.31.2 255.255.255.0
no shutdown
end
write
```

Step 12. On switch SW1, assign **VLAN 10** to access interface **Gi1/1/1, VLAN 12** to access interface **Gi1/1/2, VLAN 13** to access interface **Gi1/1/3**, using the commands:

```
enable
conf t
interface Gi1/1/1
switchport mode access
switchport access vlan 10
interface Gi1/1/2
switchport mode access
switchport access vlan 12
interface Gi1/1/3
```

```
switchport mode access
switchport access vlan 13
end
write
```

Step 13. On switch SW12, assign **VLAN 12** to access interface **Gi1/1/2, VLAN 21** to access interface **Gi1/1/3**, using the commands:

```
enable
conf t
interface Gi1/1/2
switchport mode access
switchport access vlan 12
interface Gi1/1/3
switchport mode access
switchport access vlan 21
end
write
```

Step 14. On switch SW2, assign **VLAN 20** to access interface **Gi1/1/1, VLAN 21** to access interface **Gi1/1/3, VLAN 23** to access interface **Gi1/1/2**, using the commands:

```
enable
conf t
interface Gi 1/1/1
switchport mode access
switchport access vlan 20
interface Gi 1/1/3
switchport mode access
switchport access vlan 21
interface Gi 1/1/2
switchport mode access
switchport access vlan 23
end
write
```

Step 15. On the SW23 switch, assign **VLAN 23** to access interface **Gi1/1/3, VLAN 32** to access interface **Gi1/1/2**, using the commands:

```
enable
conf t
interface Gi1/1/3
switchport mode access
switchport access vlan 23
interface Gi1/1/2
switchport mode access
switchport access vlan 32
end
write
```

Step 16. On switch SW3, assign **VLAN 30** to access interface **Gi1/1/1, VLAN 31** to access interface **Gi1/1/3, VLAN 32** to access interface **Gi1/1/2**, using the commands:

```
enable
conf t
interface Gi1/1/1
switchport mode access
switchport access vlan 30
interface Gi1/1/3
switchport mode access
switchport access vlan 31
interface Gi1/1/2
switchport mode access
switchport access vlan 32
end
write
```

Step 17. On switch SW13, assign **VLAN 13** to access interface **Gi1/1/1, VLAN 31** to access interface **Gi1/1/2**, using the commands:

```
enable
conf t
interface Gi1/1/1
```

```
switchport mode access
switchport access vlan 13
interface Gi1/1/2
switchport mode access
switchport access vlan 31
end
write
```

Step 18. On switch SW1, configure static routing, using the commands:

```
enable
conf t
ip routing
ip route 192.168.20.0 255.255.255.0 Vlan 12
ip route 192.168.30.0 255.255.255.0 Vlan 13
end
write
```

On switch SW1, verify static routing, using the command:

```
show ip route static
```

```
SW1#show ip route static
S     192.168.20.0/24 is directly connected, Vlan12
S     192.168.30.0/24 is directly connected, Vlan13
```

Figure 15.27 Result of the command: `show ip route static`.

Step 19. On switch SW12, configure static routing, using the commands

```
enable
conf t
ip routing
ip route 192.168.10.0 255.255.255.0 Vlan 12
ip route 192.168.20.0 255.255.255.0 Vlan 21
end
write
```

On switch SW12, check static routing, using the command:

```
show ip route static
```

```
SW12#sh ip route static
S     192.168.10.0/24 is directly connected, Vlan12
S     192.168.20.0/24 is directly connected, Vlan21
```

Figure 15.28 Results of the command: `show ip route static`.

Step 20. On switch SW2, configure static routing, using commands:

```
enable
conf t
ip routing
ip route 192.168.10.0 255.255.255.0 Vlan 21
ip route 192.168.30.0 255.255.255.0 Vlan 23
end
write
```

On switch SW2,check the static routing, using command:

```
show ip route static
```

```
SW2#show ip route static
S     192.168.10.0/24 is directly connected, Vlan21
S     192.168.30.0/24 is directly connected, Vlan23
```

Figure 15.29 Results of the command: `show ip route static`.

Step 21. On switch SW3, configure static routing, using the commands:

```
enable
conf t
ip routing
ip route 192.168.10.0 255.255.255.0 Vlan 31
ip route 192.168.20.0 255.255.255.0 Vlan 32
end
write
```

On switch SW3, check static routing, using command:

```
show ip route static
```

```
SW3#show ip route static
S     192.168.10.0/24 is directly connected, Vlan31
S     192.168.20.0/24 is directly connected, Vlan32
```

Figure 15.30 Result of the command show ip route static.

Step 22. On switch SW13, configure static routing, using the commands:

```
enable
conf t
ip routing
ip route 192.168.10.0 255.255.255.0 Vlan 13
ip route 192.168.30.0 255.255.255.0 Vlan 31
end
write
```

On switch SW13, verify static routing, using the command:

```
show ip route static
```

```
SW13#show ip route static
S     192.168.10.0/24 is directly connected, Vlan13
S     192.168.30.0/24 is directly connected, Vlan31
```

Figure 15.31 Result of the command `show ip route static`.

Step 23. Check communication (PINGing) from PC10 to PC20 and from PC20 to PC30.

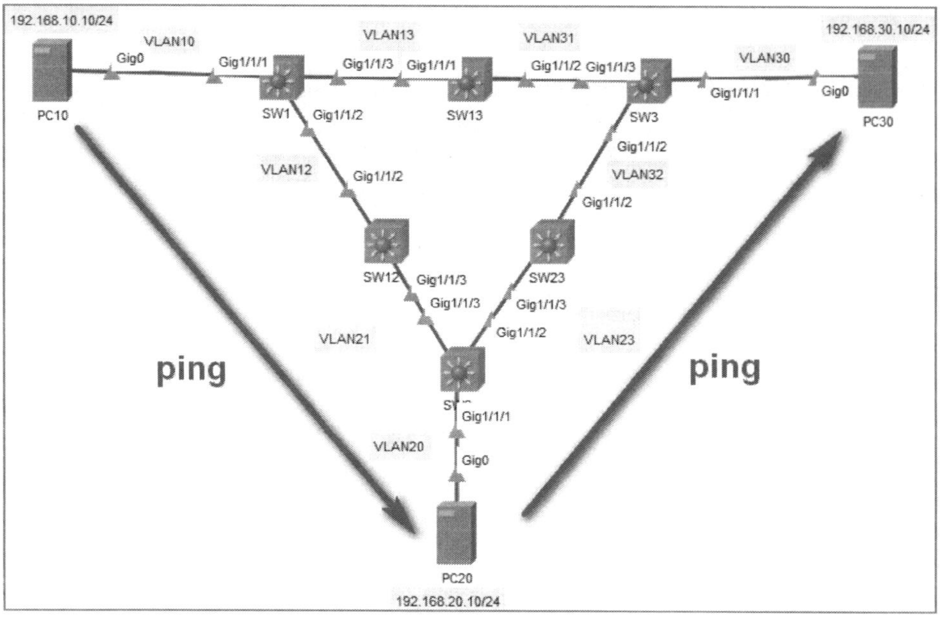

Figure 15.32 Performing check pings.

```
C:\>ping 192.168.20.10

Pinging 192.168.20.10 with 32 bytes of data:

Reply from 192.168.20.10: bytes=32 time=14ms TTL=125
Reply from 192.168.20.10: bytes=32 time=20ms TTL=125
Reply from 192.168.20.10: bytes=32 time=13ms TTL=125
Reply from 192.168.20.10: bytes=32 time=10ms TTL=125
```

Figure 15.33 The result of the ping 192.168.20.10 command executed from PC10.

```
C:\>ping 192.168.30.10

Pinging 192.168.30.10 with 32 bytes of data:

Reply from 192.168.30.10: bytes=32 time=14ms TTL=125
Reply from 192.168.30.10: bytes=32 time=12ms TTL=125
Reply from 192.168.30.10: bytes=32 time=22ms TTL=125
Reply from 192.168.30.10: bytes=32 time=14ms TTL=125
```

Figure 15.34 The result of the ping 192.168.30.10 command executed from PC20.

CHAPTER 16

EXERCISES

e

16 EXERCISES

16.1 RIP Protocol

This chapter contains practical exercises for the RIP protocol.

Remember to save the status of the file periodically (keyboard shortcut CTRL+S) while performing exercises.

16.1.1 Exercise (No. 1) – Configuring RIP v2.

The diagram below shows the network on which we will carry out this exercise. Interconnect the devices according to the diagram shown below. All the necessary modules are already installed in the devices shown below. Address the device interfaces as required and configure the RIP protocol version 1 on the routers. Create your own HTML page on the ***server***, which can be accessed via the IP address of the device.

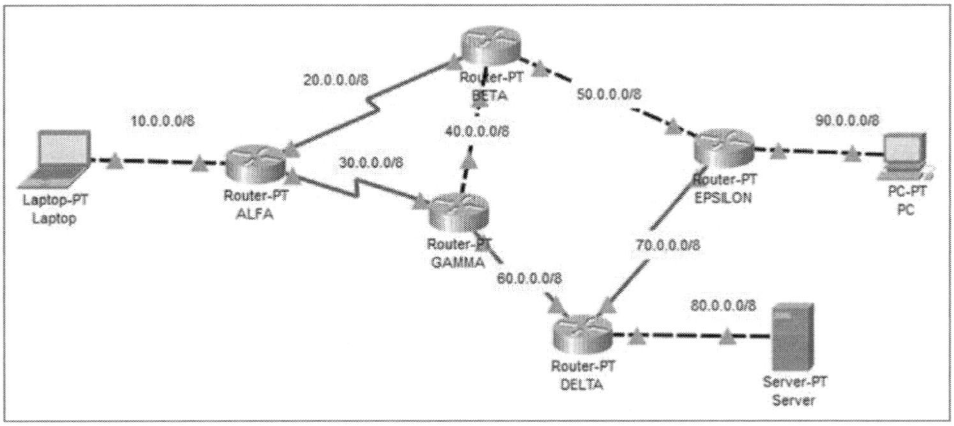

Figure 16.1 Exercise – Topology scheme.

Solution:

1. Create a topology as in the diagram above - use the same cable types and device types. You may also want to make appropriate notes (e.g. network addressing) to make the configuration easier.
2. Address the interfaces of the devices - routers and end devices - as appropriate and enable them.
3. Configure the RIP routing protocol version one on the routers. Consider all neighboring networks.
4. On the Server device, configure the HTTP page required for network testing.

5. Address and enable the interfaces of the devices - routers and end devices - as appropriate.
6. Configure RIP routing protocol version one on the routers. Take all neighboring networks into account.
7. On the ***Server*** device, configure the HTTP page needed for network testing.
8. Using the ***Laptop*** device and the ***PC***, try to access the http page of the ***Server*** device as part of the network tests. Enter the IP address of the ***Server*** device in the URL field.

16.1.2 Exercise (No. 2) – Configuring RIP v2

The diagram below shows the network on which, we will carry out this exercise. The addressing of the devices should match the addressing in the diagram. The ***DNS server*** acts as the DNS server for ***PC0***. The entry that should be present is the IP address of the ***HTTP Server*** available under the name ***www.isp.com.*** The end device ***PC0*** can communicate with ***HTTP Server*** thanks to the RIP routing protocol version two.

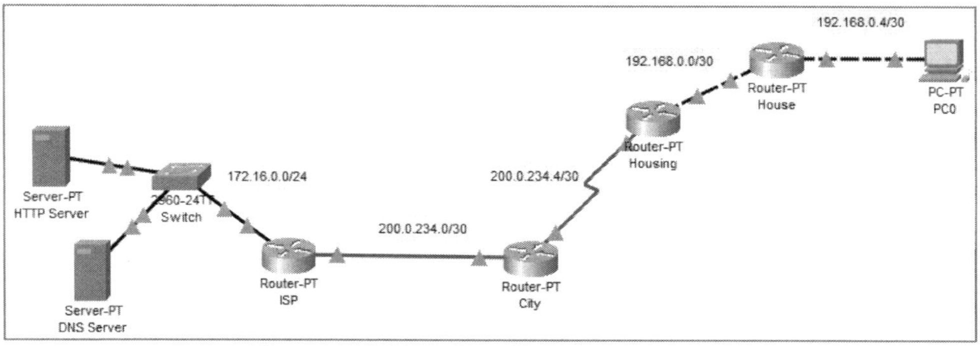

Figure 16.2 Exercise – Topology scheme.

Solution:

1. Create a logical topology the same as in the diagram. The cabling must match that shown in the diagram.
2. Address the device interfaces - the addressing must match the addresses given in the diagram. Remember that the IP address of the ***DNS server*** device is the DNS server address for **PC0**.
3. On the routers, configure the RIP routing protocol version 2.
4. On the ***DNS Server*** device, create an entry for the IP address of the ***HTTP Server*** device so that it is available under the name ***www.isp.com*** .
5. Configure the http page on ***HTTP Server*** so that it displays an ISP-related message.

6. As part of the network test, try to access ***HTTP Server*** using the name www.isp.com from the end device ***PC0***.

16.1.3 Exercise (No. 3) – Configuring RIP v2 with Static Routing

Using the diagram below, create a logical network topology consisting of four routers, two switches and two terminal devices. The ***INTERNET*** router simulates the Internet; using static routing, all traffic not covered by the LAN should be routed to this router. The network addressing is included in the figure and should match these assumptions. Once the interfaces have been correctly addressed and enabled and traffic redirected to ***INTERNET***, configure the RIP protocol version two.

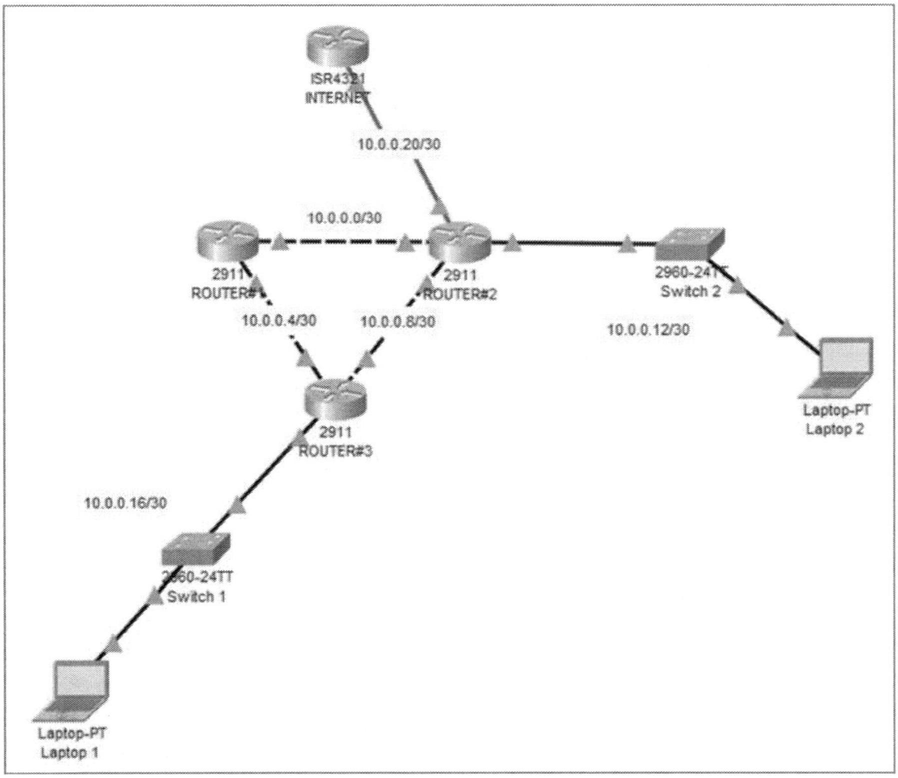

Figure 16.3 Exercise – Topology scheme.

Solution:

1. Create a logical network topology based on the diagram above. If the device in question does not have a corresponding module - add it.
2. Address the interfaces of the devices accordingly and switch them on.

3. Configure static routing on the routers (not including the ***INTERNET*** router) with one entry - the default route to ***INTERNET***.
4. Configure RIP version two routing protocol on each router.
5. Test the communication between the two laptop end devices, and in simulation mode, verify that packets whose destination network is not on our LAN are routed through the correct route to the ***INTERNET*** router.

16.1.4 Exercise (No. 4) – Exporting the RIP v2 Protocol Configuration

Create a simple logical topology consisting of two end devices and three routers. RIP protocol version two will be running on the routers. We will use this topology to check the RIP protocol configuration on it and to export the finished router configuration to the server. Change the administrative distance of the RIP protocol to 10. Check the configuration on each router, using the commands we learned earlier, and then copy the correct configurations to the ***Server***.

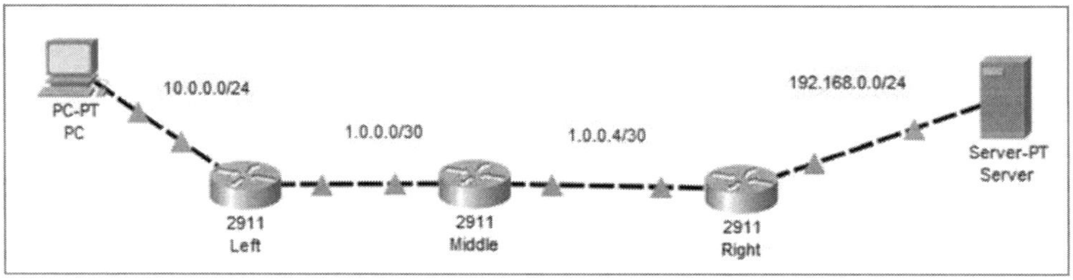

Figure 16.4 Exercise – Topology scheme.

Solution:

1. Create a configuration according to the diagram, using the same connection cables and devices.
2. Address the device interfaces according to the diagram.
3. Configure the RIP protocol version two on the routers. The administrative distance is to be 10.
4. Check that the ***PC*** can communicate with the ***server***.
5. Copy the configuration of each router to ***Server*** with the appropriate name (router name = file name).

16.1.5 Exercise (No. 5) – Incorrect Local Subnet Addressing

Your task is to fix the errors of the network described below.

In the logical topology shown in the figure below (it is downloadable from the publisher's website), there are three errors through which the network is not able to work properly, i.e. as intended. Find these three errors and perform the appropriate actions to make the network work in the correct way.

Assumptions: The entire network is based on a dynamic routing protocol - RIP v2. Each user (***Laptop A, Laptop B, Laptop C*** and ***Server***) are able to communicate with each other The network test is performed by accessing the following page in your browser *www.test.com* .

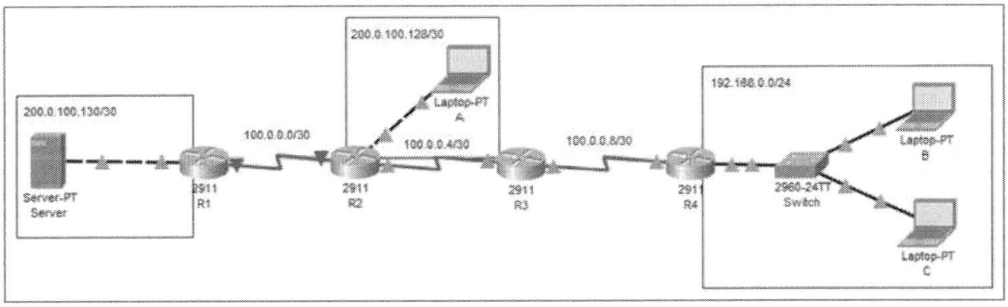

Figure 16.5 Problematic situation – Incorrect addressing.

Solution:

1. Check the routing tables on any router. If all the networks are in it, it means that the routers have exchanged information with each other and theoretically the router should be able to route the packet to the destination route (within the LAN).
2. As we can see, one route (**200.0.100.132/30**) is missing from the routing table. This is due to a disabled interface on router **R2** - enable it. (Error #1)
3. The next error we will see after reviewing the configuration of the individual routers (using the *show running-config* command) is that the IP address assigned to the interface on router **R1** is missing, and there is an error in the network description on the left. The network **200.0.100.130/30** cannot exist due to subnetting rules. (Error #2)
4. Now perform an access test on the ***Server*** device using ***www.test.com.*** Three devices will pass this test - ***Laptop A, Laptop b*** and the ***Server*** itself. This is because ***Laptop C*** has been incorrectly addressed and even such a small error is already a huge problem for the network. After changing the IP configuration on ***Laptop C***, the whole network will work as intended. (Error #3)

16.1.6 Exercise (No. 6) – Incorrect Protocol Configuration

Your task is to repair the errors of the network described below.

As in the previous exercise, there is a problem situation. This time the addressing matches, but the problem is the configuration of the RIP protocol. It is likely that the network administrator, during the configuration, misspelled the routes or used the wrong versions of the protocol on the devices, which is why the network is not working correctly. Find three configuration errors, using the commands you learned earlier, and eliminate these errors. Test the network using the PING and TRACERT commands. Every device should communicate with every device, and the routing table of the routers should contain all networks shown in the logical topology.

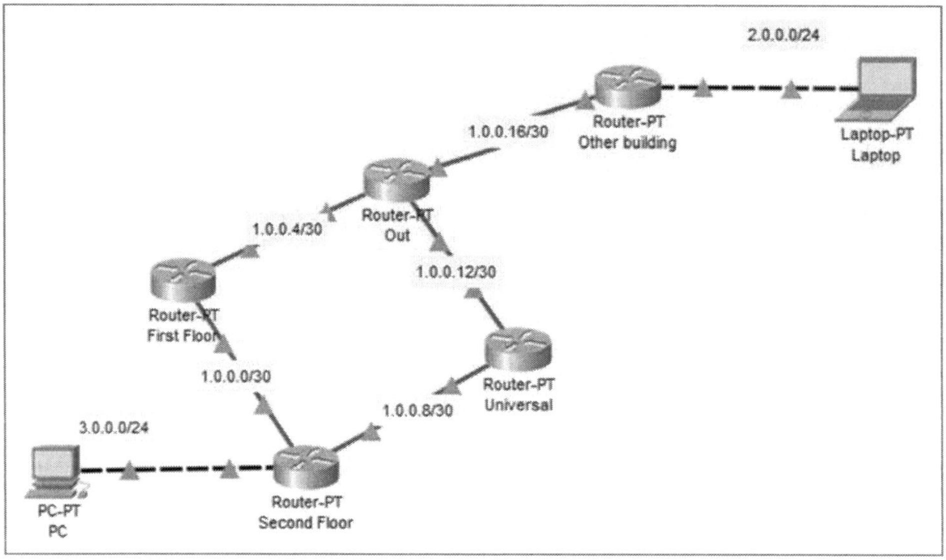

Figure 16.6 Problematic situation – Misconfiguration of the RIP protocol.

Solution:

1. Check the configuration that is currently running on each router. As you can see, on some routers the commands are misspelled, or some configuration options are missing.
2. The first thing you should do is configure the protocol itself. The absence of this configuration is noticeable on router Out. (Error #1)
3. Next, you can see that not all routes are being broadcast. This is due to an incorrect route being broadcast on the **Other building** router. (Error #2)
4. The last thing that is missing for the correct configuration of the whole network is that the **First Floor** router is not participating in the routing protocol. This is due to the fact that both interfaces are set as passive interfaces. Remove these commands and the problem will be solved. (Error #3)
5. Perform a network test using the *PING* and *TRACERT* commands.

16.1.7 Exercise (No. 7) – Incorrect Configuration of Interfaces and RIP Vers

Your task is to fix the errors of the network described below.

The diagram shows a network that is assumed to work and allow devices ***Texas PC*** and ***California PC*** to access **www.resources.com**, whose server is located in MONTANA. When you test such a connection it will be negative due to the three errors found in this simulation, which relate to the misconfiguration of the interfaces and the RIP version. Find these three errors and eliminate them. After eliminating the errors, save the configuration to *startup-config* and switch the network devices on and off. Perform a connection test of the end devices to the server.

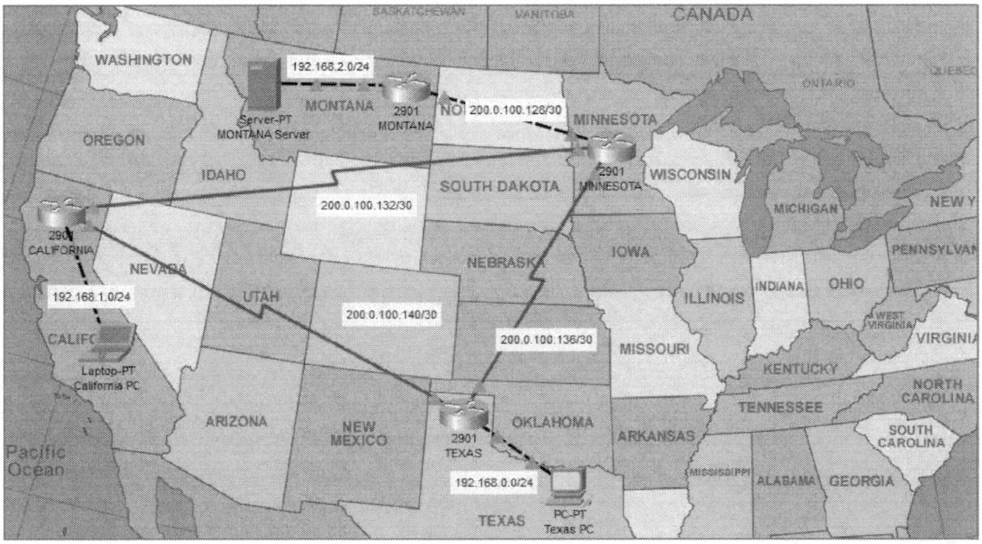

Figure 16.7 Problematic situation– Misconfiguration of interfaces and RIP versions.

Solution:

1. Check the configuration of each router. See what is missing and whether routes are properly propagated to other routers.
2. Once you have found three different problems on three different routers, proceed to fix the errors - start with the **TEXAS** router and change the routing protocol version from RIP v1 to RIP v2. (Error #1)
3. The next error is the "split horizon" option disabled on both interfaces of the ***CALIFORNIA*** router. (Error #2)
4. Last thing that disturbs us is three interfaces of the router ***MINESSOTA*** , which were switched into passive mode, i.e. no information about routing table of the router is broadcasted through these interfaces. Once these interfaces have been switched using the *no passive-interface<interface>* command, you can proceed with network testing.
5. Save the correct configuration of the routers to *startup-config* and reset the devices.

6. Try using the PING command to communicate with **www.resources.com** from two devices : ***Texas PC*** and ***California PC***.

16.2 EIGRP Protocol

The chapter contains practical exercises for the EIGRP protocol.

Remember to save the status of the file periodically (keyboard shortcut CTRL+S) while performing the exercises.

16.2.1 Exercise (No. 8) – Configuring EIGRP

Based on the diagram in the picture below, build a LAN. This consists of two bridges, four CGR1240 version routers (these have *ip routing* disabled and each port is a switching port by default) and two laptops. Configure this network so that laptop ***L*** and laptop ***P*** can communicate with each other. The routers are to use the EIGRP dynamic routing protocol (AS 10). The IP addressing is shown in the diagram below.

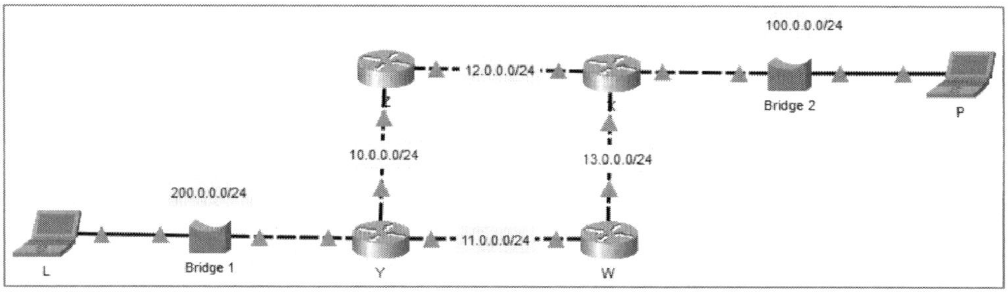

Figure 16.8 Exercise – Topology scheme- Configuring EIGRP

Solution:

1. Create a logical network topology according to the diagram. Use the same connection cables and devices.
2. Address the interfaces of the routers so that they are in the networks described in the diagram. Switch the interfaces to the appropriate mode using the *no switchport* command.
3. Address the interfaces of the end devices - laptop ***L*** and laptop ***P***.
4. Configure the basics of the EIGRP routing protocol on the routers. AS is equal to 10. Before configuring EIGRP, enable routing on the routers using the *ip routing* command.
5. Perform network tests using the PING command from device ***L*** to device ***P***.

16.2.2 Exercise (No. 9) – EIGRP Configuring and Testing

In Packet Tracer, create a diagram, shown in the figure below, which will simulate a small business with a warehouse in a different location to the main office. The routers between the two areas will run the EIGRP protocol (AS 100). Each router will have its own router-id assigned by you. There will be a ***DNS*** server in the main office, whose DNS service will have an entry for the IP address of the ***warehouse.xyz*** device available under the same name. Conduct a network test by first checking the routing table of each router, the EIGRP neighbors and the interfaces that participate in routing using the EIGRP protocol. The last command you should perform is to get from the ***ADMIN*** device to the *warehouse.xyz* website.

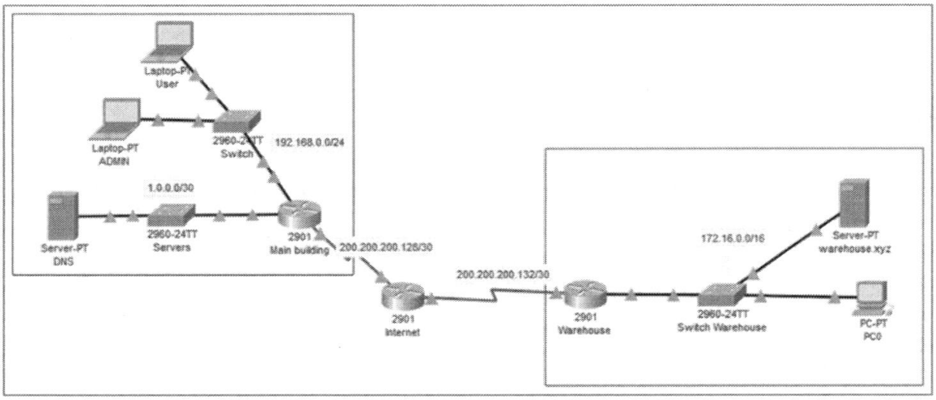

Figure 16.9 Exercise – Topology scheme – EIGRP configuring and verifying

Solution:

1. Following the topology diagram shown above, create the same logical topology.
2. Address and enable the device interfaces - starting with the routers and ending with the end devices.
3. Configure the DNS service on the ***DNS*** server and the HTML page on the ***warehouse.xyz*** device.
4. Configure the EIGRP routing protocol (AS 100) on each router. Set your own *eigrp router-id* values for each router. For example : ***Main building - 1.1.1.1, Internet - 2.2.2.2, Warehouse - 3.3.3.3.***
5. Check on each router their routing table, EIGRP neighbor tables and interfaces that are involved in EIGRP broadcasting.
6. Access *warehouse.xyz* from the ***ADMIN*** device.

16.2.3 Exercise (No. 10) – Configuring and Verifying Secure EIGRP

The logical topology below shows a simulated LAN using three routers, three switches and three terminal devices. According to the assumptions, this network should work all the time and each end device can send a message to another. The routing protocol in this case is EIGRP (AS 1). Each router has its own *eigrp router-id*, which is unique and set by you. In this network, the EIGRP protocol is secured by a key (key-chain 1) called *KEY*. The key that secures the protocol is the word ***eigrp12345***. The encryption is provided by the MD5 algorithm.

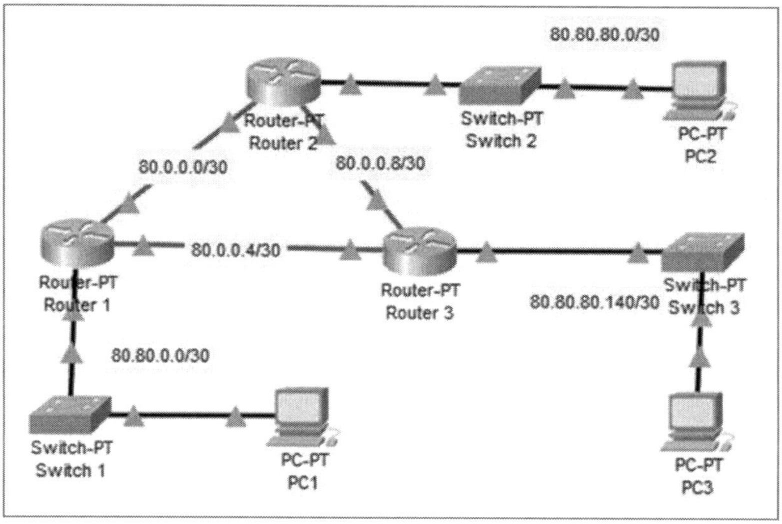

Figure 16.10 Exercise – Configuring and verifying secure EIGRP

Solution:

1. Create a logical topology as shown above for your computer network simulation. Use the same connection cables and devices. If the task requires it, change the device modules.
2. Address and enable the device interfaces starting with the routers and ending with the end devices.
3. Configure the basics of the EIGRP routing protocol (AS 1). Include all networks adjacent to a given router. Distinguish each router with a manually assigned eigrp router-id.
4. Test the connection between the two selected end users, e.g. using the PING command.
5. If the previous step was successful then start securing the EIGRP protocol. Create a key-chain with the name KEY and the keyword ***eigrp12345*** assigned to key number 1. Then provide encryption using MD5 algorithm and activate security on each interface leading to another router.

6. Repeat step 4 again, but between all three end devices.

16.2.4 Exercise (No. 11) – Configuring Packet Metrics and Path in EIGRP

Using the knowledge you gained earlier, create a topology as in the figure below and configure the EIGRP routing protocol (AS 5) so that packets travel the route you have chosen. In our case, we will want packets from ***User 1*** to ***User 2*** to travel the route ***R1→ R4→R5→R6→R3*** (vice versa). With the default configuration, packets travel along a route built from fibre connections. To change this, use your own delay and bandwidth settings on each interface of each router so that the final topology matches. Then test the network by sending a PING command in simulation mode from one end device to another.

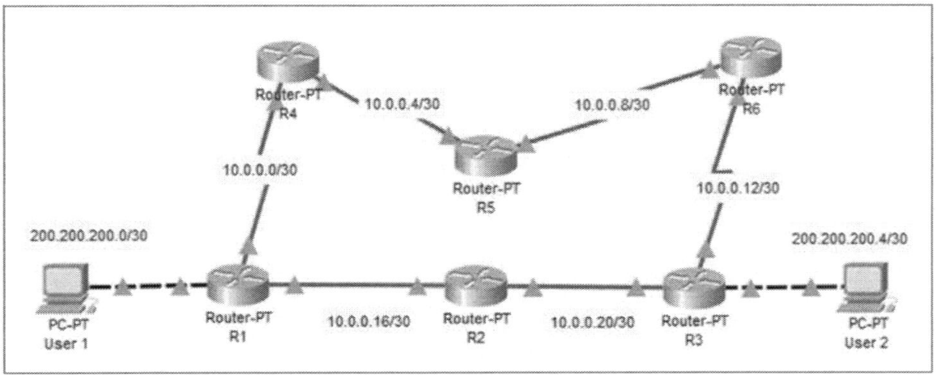

Figure 16.11 Configuring packet metrics and path in EIGRP

Solution:

1. Create a network topology as shown above. Use the same connection cables and network and terminal devices.
2. Address and enable device interfaces using the IP addressing in the diagram.
3. Configure the basics of the EIGRP routing protocol (AS 5) on the routers.
4. In the simulation, test with the PING command the route that packets take from one end device to another.
5. As you can see, they do not take the route we want them to take. The easiest way to change this is to introduce a delay on the respective interfaces of the devices : ***R1, R2 and R3***.
6. Although a sufficiently high delay is enough to change the routing of packets, for practice we will also change the throughput of these links on the same devices.
7. Repeat point no. 4 and observe that, when done correctly, the packets travel along the correct path.

16.2.5 Exercise (No. 12) – Incorrect Configuration of Adjacent Networks

Your task is to fix the errors of the network described below.

In the exercise below, we have the EIGRP routing protocol (AS 1) configured so that **LAN 1** should be able to communicate with **LAN 2**. Unfortunately, after much testing, this has proved impossible and the reason for this is the misconfiguration of the networks adjacent to the routers. Find three errors in this configuration and fix them so that the two areas can communicate with each other. Once the network has been fixed, check the communication by entering the name of the other server in the URL field of the browser of any server, e.g. on device ***lan1*** enter the name of lan2.

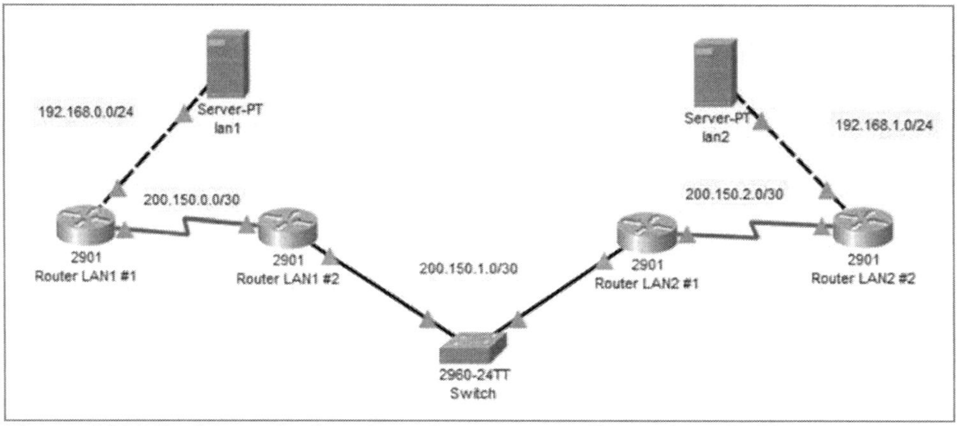

Figure 16.12 Problematic situation – Incorrect configuration of adjacent networks

Solution:

1. The basic thing that should match is the addressing. Check the IP address on each router interface and see if it matches the assumptions in the diagram.
2. After looking at each router, you will notice that on ***Router LAN1 #2*** the addressing does not agree on interface Se0/3/0. (Error #1).
3. The next step is to check the routing tables on each Layer 3 network device. As you can see the route 200.150.2.0 is not broadcast by ***Router LAN2 #1*** due to the fact that it is not among the broadcast networks at all. (Error #2)
4. We are at the step where our network should theoretically work properly, but after exchanging information between routers we are still missing one very important network. This is the network that should be shared by ***Router LAN2 #2*** . It turns out that the Gig0/0 interface is a passive interface. (Error #3)
5. You can now access lan2 from ***lan1*** and you should see LAN2 written.

16.2.6 Exercise (No. 13) – Wrong Wildcard Mask

Your task is to fix the network errors described below.

The problem in this case is misconfigured blank masks on three routers. Review the configuration and routing tables on the routers to find out exactly where the error is and eliminate it. Then carry out a test using the PING command between all end devices.

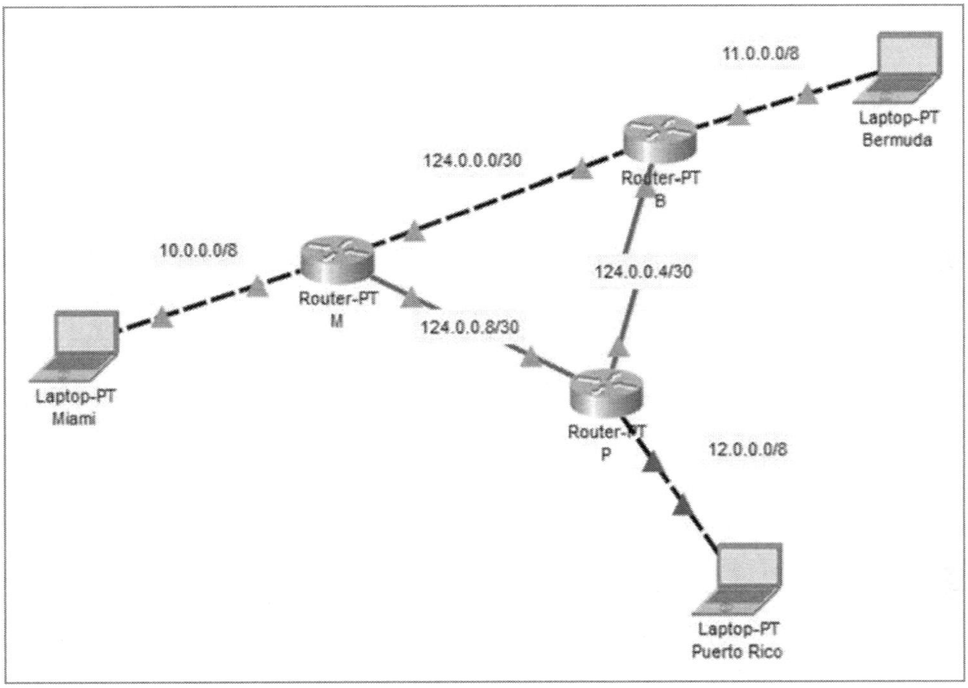

Figure 16.13 Problematic situation – Wrong wildcard mask

Solution:

1. Review the configuration that is running on the routers and the current routing tables. Deduce, what is not as intended and correct it.
2. On router ***M*** we see that the wrong wildcard mask is specified for the network 124.0.0.0/30.(Error #1)
3. On router ***B*** two networks 11.0.0.0.0 are specified and both have the wrong wildcard mask which does not match the assumptions. (Error #2)
4. On router ***P***, network 12.0.0.0/8 has a wildcard mask for the network with mask /30. (Error #3)
5. Using the PING command (after a timeout - you need to wait a while for the routers to exchange information), test the connections between the end devices.

16.2.7 Exercise (No. 14) – Incorrect EIGRP Process Number

Your task is to fix the errors of the network described below.

The problem situation you will face is the following: the network is running the EIGRP routing protocol (AS 5) and the configuration on all routers agrees as intended, except for the EIGRP process number. This is a small detail, but it completely changes the topologies and the way the routers work. On the two routers that have the wrong AS number for the EIGRP protocol, change this number to the number as intended (AS 5). Then check the routing table on one of the three routers and send a PING command from one end device to the other.

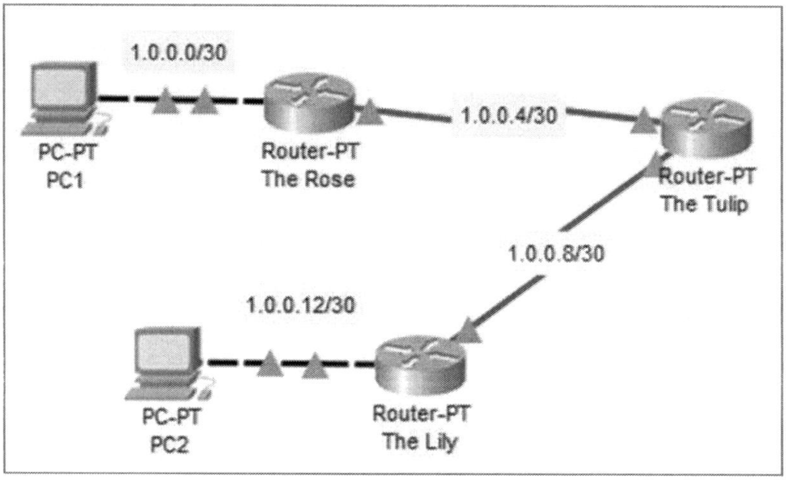

Figure 16.14 Problematic situation – Incorrect EIGRP process number

Solution:

1. The first step will be to check the current configurations on the routers. We are only looking for the process number because the configuration is almost correct, but EIGRP is not working properly.
2. After looking at the configuration for a while, you will find that the process numbers do not match on two of the routers - ***The Tulip*** and ***The Lil***y, change these numbers to the correct ones and save the configuration.
3. After a while, check the routing tables of one of the routers and the EIGRP neighbor tables. If the configuration matches, carry out a test using the PING command.

16.3 OSPF Protocol

The chapter contains practical exercises for the OSPF protocol.

Remember to save the state of the file periodically (keyboard shortcut CTRL+S) during the exercises.

16.3.1 Exercise (No. 15) – Basic Configuration of OSPF

Build the logical topology as shown in the figure below. The addressing is also dissected and, as intended, the corresponding interfaces belong to the corresponding networks. Once the network device interfaces have been addressed and enabled, configure the basics of the OSPF routing protocol (AS 10). Do not change the default *router-id* or anything like that. After configuring the protocol on each router and waiting a while (so that the routers can communicate), perform a network test using the PING tool between the end devices (***PC, Printer, Server***).

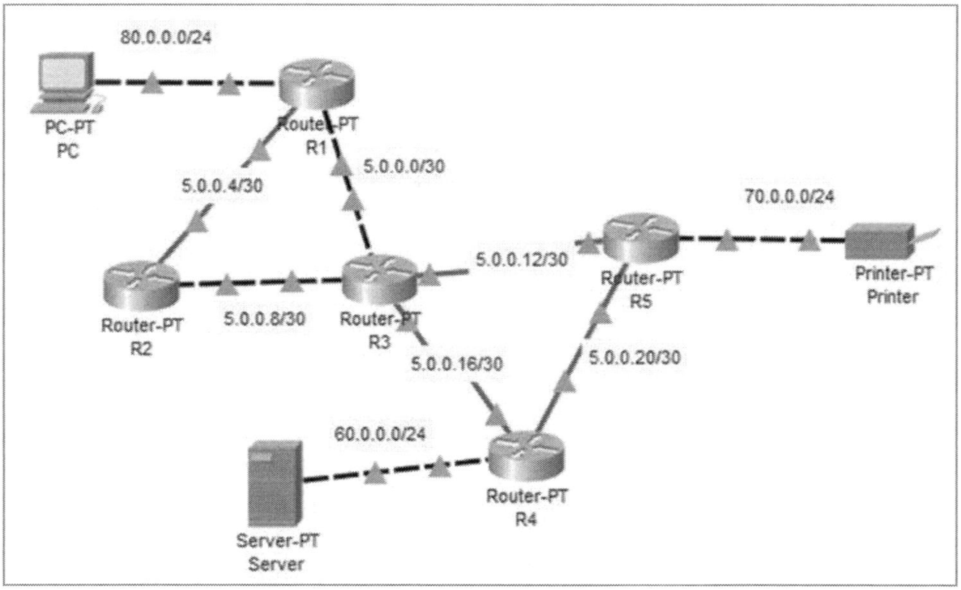

Figure 16.15 Basic configuration of OSPF

Solution:

1. Based on the figure above, build a logical network topology using the same devices and connection cables.
2. Address and enable the interfaces of the network and end devices as specified.
3. Configure the OSPF routing protocol (AS 10) on the routers, considering only the neighboring networks of the routers.

4. Wait a moment and carry out a network test using the PING command between end devices, e.g. from ***PC*** to ***Server*** or ***Printer***.

Exercise (No. 16) – Configuring Secure OSPF with router-id

This time our logical topology will be consist five the capital cities in Europe. We are dealing with five network devices (routers) located in different location in Europe. According to the assumptions, the IP addressing should match the one in the figure below. The routing protocol is OSPF (AS 100 and area 0) and it is secured using *message-digest* encryption and the key word "OSPF123". Each router is also assigned its own *router-id* given by you (the numbers are arbitrary). When the network conforms to these assumptions you can run a test using the simulation option in Packet Tracer.

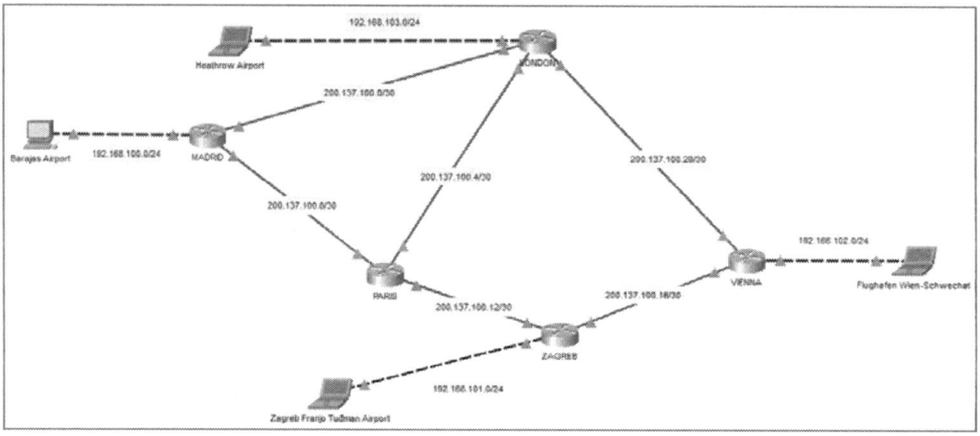

Figure 16.16 Configuring secure OSPF including router-id

Solution:

1. Create the same network simulation as shown above.
2. Address and enable the network and end device interfaces as specified.
3. Configure the OSPF routing protocol (AS 100) on the routers taking into account the neighboring networks of the routers and give each router a unique *router-id.*
4. Secure the OSPF protocol using the keyword "OSPF123" and *message-digest* encryption on each interface.
5. Wait for the network to converge and then run network tests in Packet Tracer simulation.

16.3.2 Exercise (No. 17) – OSPF Configuration with Change of Link Costs

In this case, we have two end devices with six routers in between, set up in such a way that ***R1*** or ***R6*** has to choose whether the packet goes along the path "at the bottom" or "at the top". The default will usually be to choose the path at the bottom due to the fact that there is a fiber connection there, which is faster than a crossover connection (at the top). Build a network similar to this one and configure it so that packets are always routed via the path at the top (via OSPF protocol AS 50, area 0) Change the link cost on both routes accordingly, and then check in simulation which path the OSPF protocol chooses. Then check the working configuration on the routers, their routing tables and the OSPF database

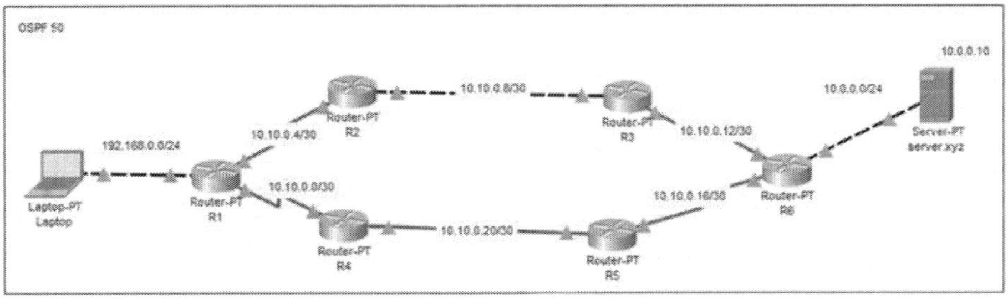

Figure 16.17 OSPF configuration with change of link costs

Solution:

1. Build a network similar to the one in the figure above. Use the same devices and connection cables.
2. Address and enable the interfaces of the network and end devices as intended.
3. Configure the OSPF protocol (AS 50) taking into account the neighboring networks of the routers.
4. Change the cost of the links as appropriate so that the network works as intended - e.g. links at the top will have a cost of 1 and those at the bottom 54000.
5. Check the routing tables, current configuration and OSPF database on each router. If anything is out of line - try to correct it.
6. Test the connection between one and the other end device using simulation or the *tracert* command.

16.3.3 Exercise (No. 18) – Configuring OSPF Based on the Loopback Address

The inspiration for this configuration came from the Croatia, specifically two cities - **ZAGREB** and **SPLIT**. Our small network has two routers for each city and one end device. The difference between this exercise and the others is that in this case we will not be directly specifying the *router-id* for a particular router, but the device itself will designate such an ID as we wish.

To do this, give a unique IP address for *loopback* interface 1 on each router. In this case, it can be an IP address with a mask of /32, because it characterizes only one host (itself) and is not used in the network. The routing protocol running on this network is OSPF (AS 1, area 0). Once you have configured the IP address, protocol and interfaces, test the connection between the two end devices and review the OSPF database to ensure that the *router-id* matches.

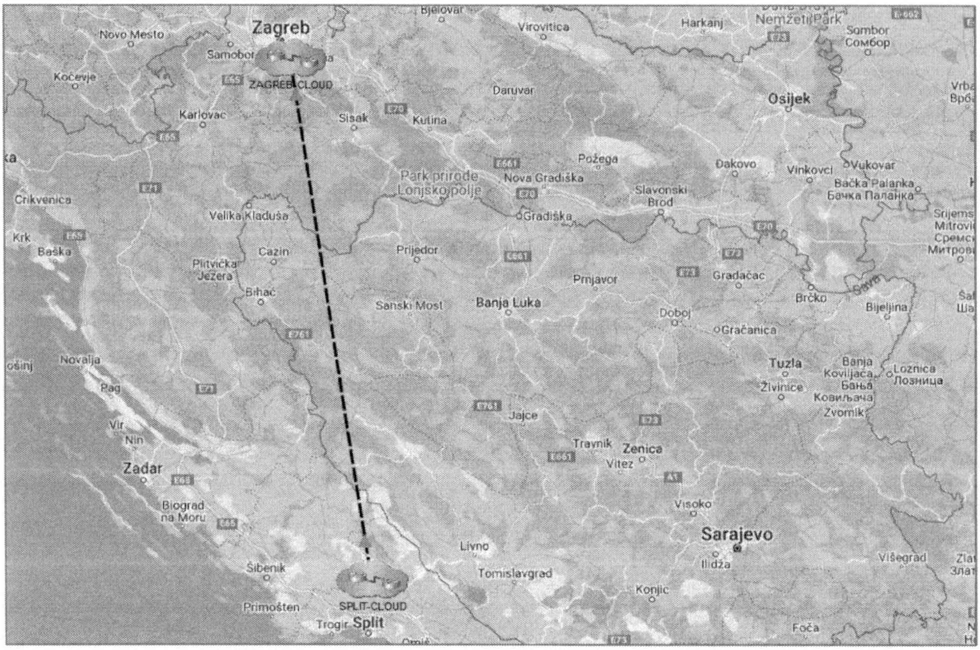

Figure 16.18 Connection between ZAGREB and SPLIT clusters.

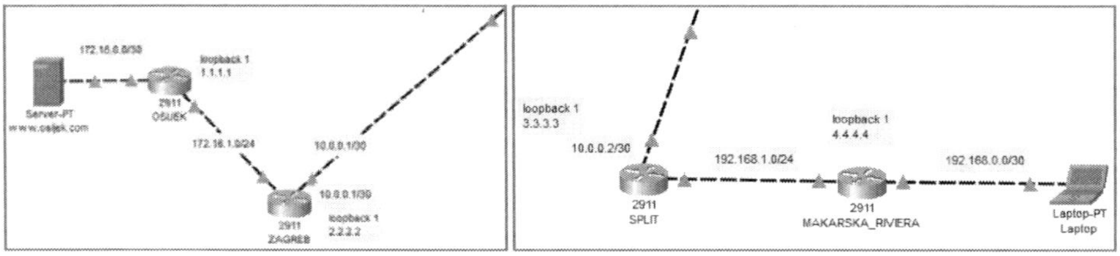

Figure 16.19 Configuring OSPF based on a loopback address

Solution:

1. Following the figure above, build a logical network topology using the same devices and interconnecting cables.
2. Address and switch on the interfaces of the network devices and terminal equipment according to the assumptions. 3. address one loop interface each.
3. Address one loopback interface on each router (for example, *loopback 1* interfaces and IP addresses such as 1.1.1.1/32, 2.2.2.2/32, etc.).
4. Cluster the devices into two separate clusters.

5. Configure the OSPF protocol (AS 1, area 0) considering the neighboring networks.
6. Check the routing table and the OSPF database to confirm the configuration.
7. Test the connection between the two end devices using e.g. simulation.

16.3.4 Exercise (No. 19) – Configuring OSPF Based on Priority

We are now faced with a similar exercise to the link cost change exercise, but this time we will change the priority of the interfaces for the OSPF protocol. First create a logical topology, as shown in the figure, and then, after addressing and enabling the interfaces, configure the OSPF protocol (AS 2, area 0). Once the protocol is configured, it will calculate for itself the best route between the end devices and this will be the top route. Using the priority of the interfaces, set them up so that the routers always take the route that goes through router **T3**. Then carry out the test using simulation.

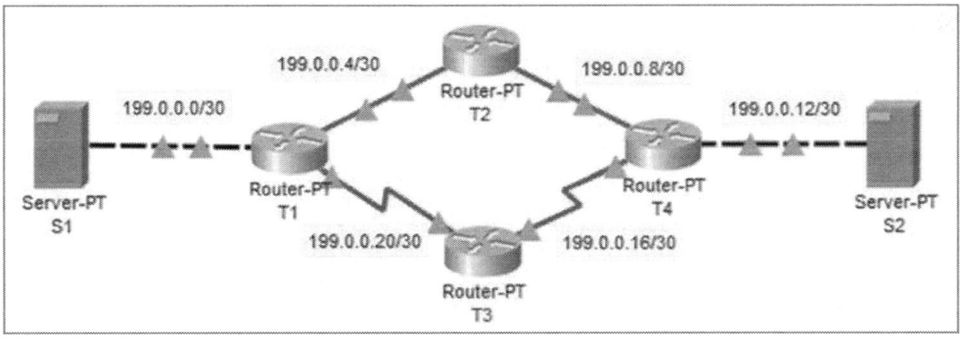

Figure 16.20 Configuring OSPF based on priority

Solution:

1. Build a network similar to the one in the figure above. Use the same devices and connection cables.
2. Address and enable the network and end device interfaces as specified.
3. Configure the OSPF protocol (AS 2, area 0) taking into account the neighboring networks.
4. Set the OSPF priority on the two interfaces (leading to routers **T2** and **T3**) on both routers adjacent to the end devices in such a way that the priority for the path you want to route the packets is higher.
5. Using a simulation, test the connection between the two end-devices and check that the packets go, as intended, down the route.

16.3.5 Exercise (No. 20) – Wrong Area Number

Your task is to fix the errors of the network described below.

The problem situation you are facing is one where the network is running the OSPF routing protocol (AS 1, area 0) and the configuration on all routers is correct except for the OSPF process number. This is a small detail, but it completely changes the topologies and the way our routers work. On the two routers that have the wrong AS number for the OSPF protocol, change this number to the number as intended (AS 1). Then check the routing table on one of the three routers and send a PING command from one end device to the other.

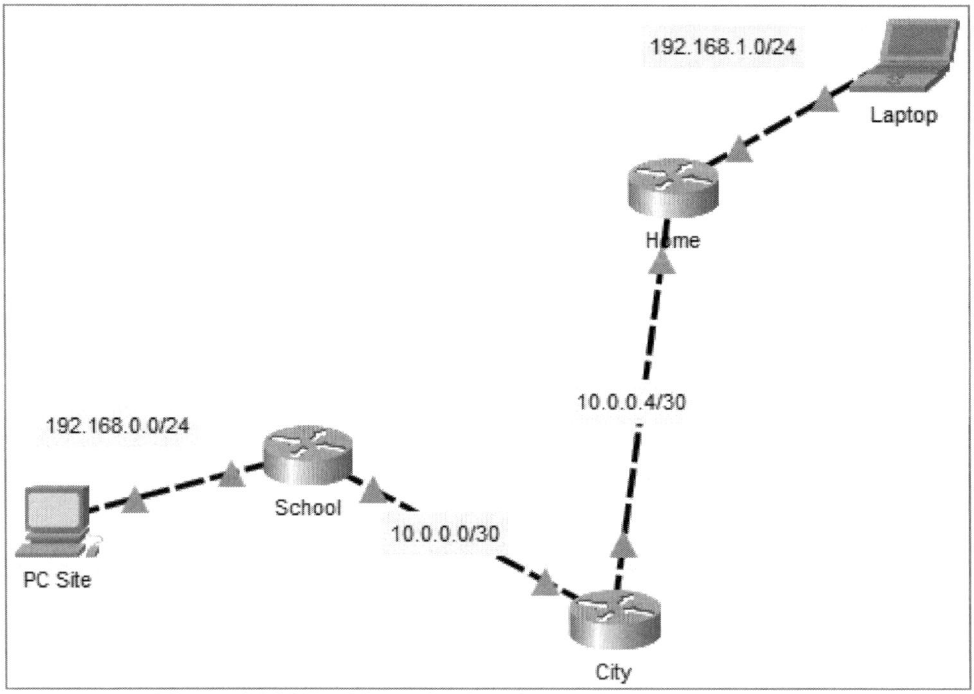

Figure 16.21 Problematic situation - Wrong area number

Solution:

1. The first step will be to check the current configurations on the routers. We are only looking for the process number because, as already written - the configuration is correct, apart from this minor detail.
2. After a while of looking through the configuration, it turns out that the process numbers do not match on two routers - ***City*** and ***Home***, change these numbers to the correct ones and save the configuration.(Errors #1 and #2)

3. After some time, check the routing tables of one of the routers and the OSPF database. If the configuration agrees with the assumptions conduct a test using the PING command.

16.3.6 Exercise (No. 21) – Wrong Wildcard Mask

Your task is to fix the network errors described below.

Another problem situation that you may encounter on a daily basis when doing exercises is an incorrect wildcard mask. Anyone can make a mistake, and it often happens that we don't look a second time to see if the blank mask has been entered correctly, and then we have a communication problem in the network. In the task whose topology we have shown below, there is just such a problem. The errors are in three places - look at the configuration of the routers (the network is based on OSPF (AS 5, area 0) and the routing tables to find out where and replace those blank masks with the correct ones. Then wait a moment for the routers to exchange information and use the PING command to perform a packet exchange between the end users - ***Helsinki*** and ***Madrid***.

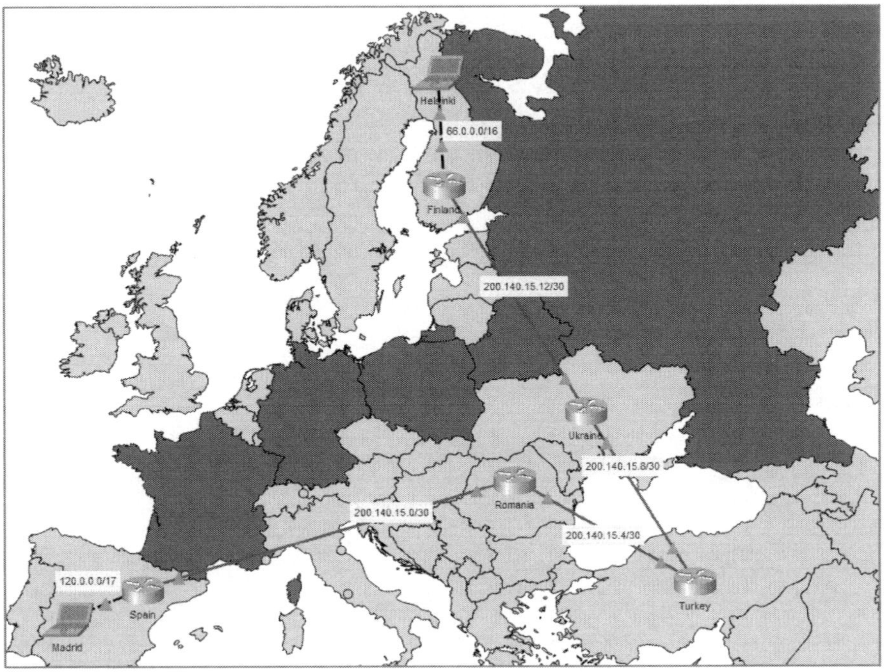

Figure 16.22 Problematic situation – wrong wildcard mask

Solution:

1. Let's start by reviewing all the configurations current on the routers - check that the IP addressing matches.
2. As expected - the IP addressing is as intended from the diagram, but another thing should catch our eye. Well, on the three routers ***Spain, Turkey*** and ***Finland*** in the configuration details of the OSPF protocol we have entered strange wildcard masks. These are masks that are not necessarily the inverse of the masks in the diagram.
3. Start from the left - on the ***Spain*** router remove the wrong entry and replace it with the network 120.0.0.0 with a blank mask of 0.0.127.255 . (Error #1).
4. Next we have the router ***Turkey*** where the problem occurs with the network 200.140.15.8 and where the mask should be 0.0.0.3 (Error #2).
5. The last router to be misconfigured is the ***Finland*** router. The blank mask should be 0.0.255.255 for a network of 66.0.0.0/16 (Error #3).
6. After fixing the network errors, clear the current OSPF processes (***clear ip ospf process*** command) on each router and wait for the network to converge.
7. Test the connection between end users and check the routing table on one of the routers.

16.3.7 Exercise (No. 22) – Incorrect Interface Configuration

Your task is to fix the network errors described below.

Another problem situation we discuss with the OSPF protocol is an environment where an error can occur with the configuration of network device interfaces. This is one of the common errors and can occur in various forms, be it a bad IP address assigned to an interface, or accidentally enabling passive mode for an interface. In the exercise below, we have three problems related to misconfiguration of interfaces on network devices. Find these four problems and solve them, then check the network convergence and connectivity between network devices.

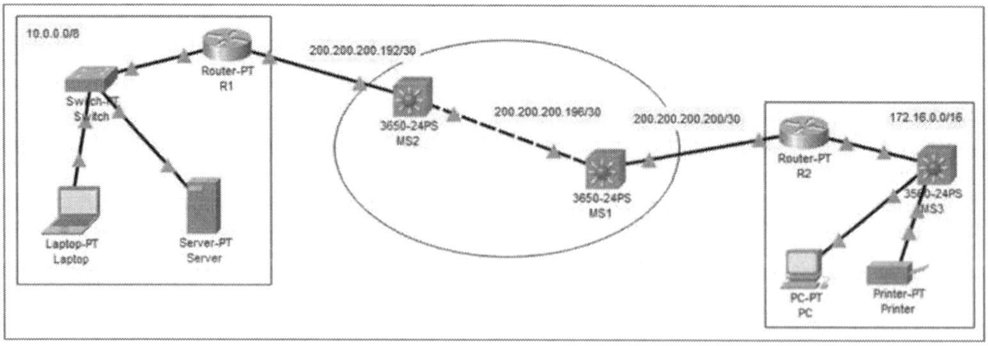

Figure 16.23 Problematic situation - Incorrect interface configuration

Solution:

1. As always - the easiest way is to look at the configurations of each router one at a time, as they are the ones we have a problem with in this case. See what configurations are in the routers at this point and what networks the OSPF protocol (AS 15, area 0) sees on each router.
2. You can already see on the first router on the left that something is not right. The network administrator must have accidentally placed interface Fa0/0 into the cluster of passive interfaces that was configured for network security. Remove this interface from there so that this router can broadcast its networks. (Error #1).
3. The next error occurs on router ***MS1***, which loses OSPF convergence all the time with the router that is on its left (interface Gig1/0/1). When we look at the configuration we see that the *hello-interval* and *dead-interval* values for the OSPF protocol have been changed from their default values to other values. Restore these values to the defaults using the no command . (Error #2).
4. The final piece of the puzzle is the error located on network device ***R2*** . When we access the ***PC*** device and try to connect to its default gateway we find that it does not exist for this PC. This is due to an incorrect IP address on the ***R2*** router. Change the IP address for the interface leading to ***MS3*** so that it matches the default gateways on the ***PC*** and ***Printer*** devices. (Error #3).
5. After fixing the network errors, clear the current OSPF processes (***clear ip ospf process*** command) on each router and wait for the network to converge.
6. Test with simulation the connections between different end devices and check the routing table of network device ***MS2***.

16.4 eBGP Protocol

16.4.1 Exercise (No. 23) – Configuring eBGP with the Loopback Address

We have now moved on to exercises that focus on the last dynamic routing protocol, BGP, more precisely its eBGP variant. In this exercise we have a very simple logical topology consisting of three routers (appropriately named after their BGP identifier) and two end users. According to the assumptions, the IP addressing should follow the scheme and each router should have one loopback interface configured. The IP address of this interface should be the same as the router name. The BGP protocol should be configured on each router. The AS numbers can be found on the diagram right next to the IP address. Once the routing protocol is configured correctly, check the routing table of each router and the BGP neighbor tables. Finally, check that the ***Server*** can send a PING command to the ***Laptop***.

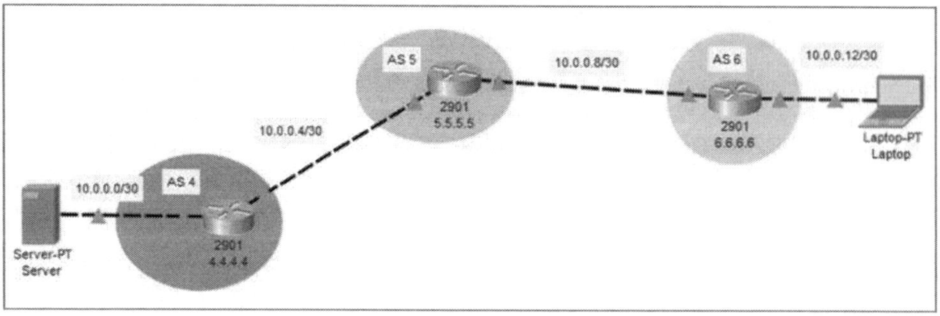

Figure 16.24 Configuring eBGP with a loopback address

Solution:

1. Create the same logical topology as in the diagram above. Use the same devices and connection cables.
2. Following the IP addressing in the diagram above, address and enable the interfaces of the network devices.
3. Address one loopback interface on each router so that the IP address is the same as the name of the router.
4. On each router, configure the BGP protocol (AS 4, AS5 and AS6) taking into account the neighboring networks, the networks from which the IP address of the loopback interface is derived and the neighbors from other instances (AS).
5. After the network has converged, check the routing table and BGP neighbor tables on at least one router.
6. Perform a network test using the PING command between end devices.

16.4.2 Exercise (No. 24) – Configuring eBGP with the Router ID

This time we will focus on configuring eBGP similarly to the exercise before, but the BGP IDs of the routers will result from their manual setup. Create a network as shown in the figure below and address and enable the network device interfaces. Configure the eBGP protocol with four different instance numbers and assign a unique identifier number for each router. This will be derived from its name, e.g. router ***1*** will have an ID of *1.1.1.1*, router 2 an ID of *2.2.2.2* etc. Then check the routing table and the table with summarized information about the BGP protocol running on the router. Also carry out some tests in simulation to see if the end devices are reachable.

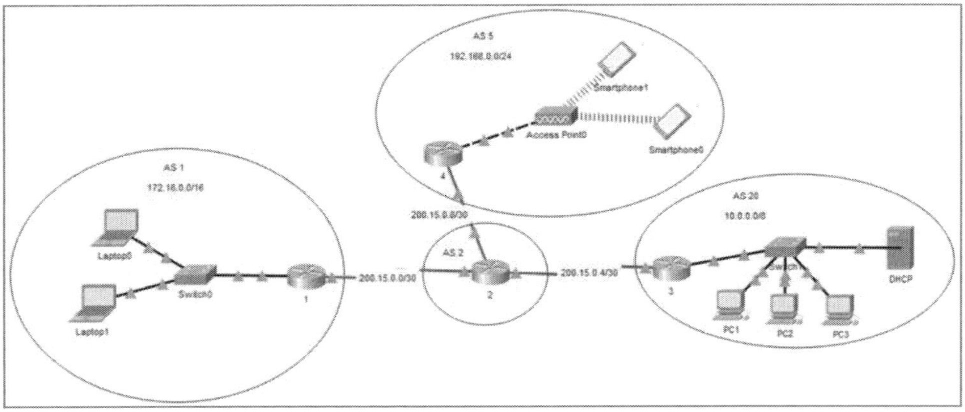

Figure 16.25 Configuring eBGP with a router ID

Solution:

1. Create a topology as in the diagram above - use the same cable types and device types. You may also want to make appropriate notes (e.g. network addressing) to make the configuration easier.
2. Address the interfaces of the devices - routers and end devices - in the appropriate way and enable them.
3. Configure the eBGP routing protocol on the routers. Consider all neighboring networks and neighboring routers.
4. Instead of configuring addresses on the loopback interfaces, manually configure a BGP identifier on each router. It needs to be unique, so follow the naming of the routers e.g. router ***1*** should have an ID of *1.1.1.1* .
5. Check the routing table and the BGP summary table.
6. In the simulation, carry out network tests between end users.

16.4.3 Exercise (No. 25) – No Entries for BGP Neighbors

Your task is to fix the network errors described below.

The first eBGP problem situation we will face will be where the eBGP configuration is missing entries for routers and neighbor instances. This is an element that is not mandatory in the configuration of other dynamic routing protocols and is therefore often forgotten by novice administrators. Check the current configuration of the routers and see which entries are missing. Complete them and check the network convergence.

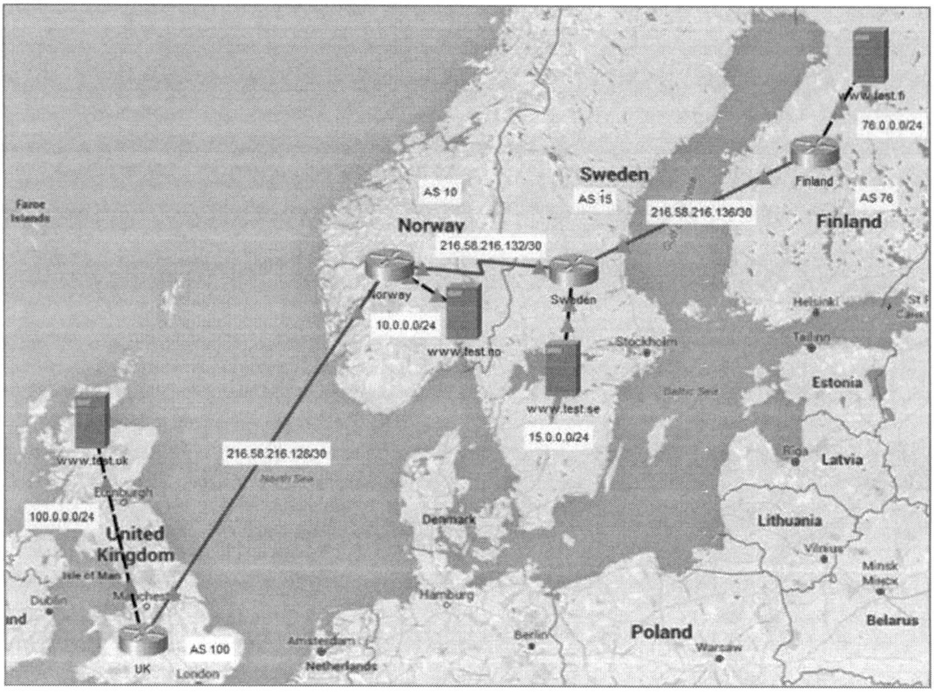

Figure 16.26 Problematic situation – No entries for BGP neighbors

Solution:

1. Open the relevant file and see if you can get from one server to every other server's site.
2. The first thing that catches your eye is that you cannot access two or any servers. This is due to eBGP configuration errors on two routers.
3. Review the current configuration of the routers and look for errors in the eBGP configuration.
4. There is an entry missing on the ***Norway*** router for the existence of a ***UK*** neighbor with IP address *216.58.216.129* and remote-as 100. (Error #1)
5. When you now run the network test the only server that cannot be accessed is *www.test.fi*.
6. This is due to an error in the configuration of the ***Finland*** router. The entry for the neighbor ***Sweden*** with IP address *216.58.216.137* and remote-as 15 is missing (Error #2).
7. Check the routing table on the routers and try to access each server's site from one of the routers.

16.4.4 Exercise (No. 26) – No Entry for Local Network

Your task is to fix the errors of the network described below.

In this case, the assumption of the network is that each end user can communicate with each other. For this to be the case, the eBGP protocol must be correctly configured in the ***Internet*** area. The ***Internet*** area consists of six routers with correctly configured interfaces. The only problem with this network is the lack of entries in the routing table. This is probably due to missing neighboring network entries on some routers. Find which routers are misconfigured and make the routing tables match the network. Then run a test in a simulation between each user.

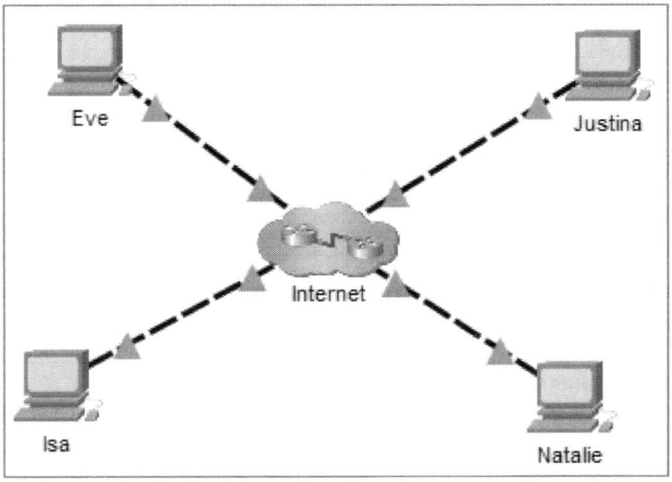

Figure 16.27 Problematic situation– overall topology

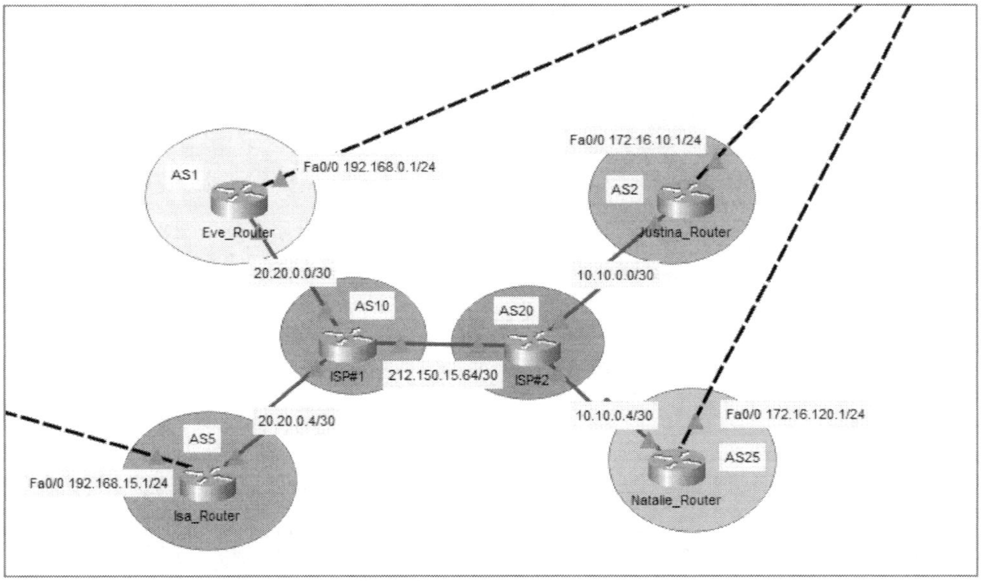

Problematic situation– no entry for local network

Solution:

1. Open the appropriate file and check whether you can send a PING command from any computer to any other terminal device.
2. If the result is negative, it means that our network is misconfigured. As it was written in the introduction - the interfaces are configured correctly, and the error is in the lack of entries for neighboring networks on routers.
3. Go to one of the routers and use the routing table to check which entries are missing.
4. Then go into the appropriate routers and enter the missing networks.
5. The first router we'll look at is ***Isa's router*** which is missing an entry for the *192.168.15.0/24* network (Error #1).
6. The next router we will deal with is ***Justina's router*** where there is no entry for the network *172.16.10.0/24* (Error #2).
7. The last problem we have is that there is no network *212.150.15.64/30* on both routers ***ISP#1*** and ***ISP#2***. (Error #3)
8. Once you have configured the routers appropriately, perform a network test in the simulation between the end users.

16.5 Static Routing

16.5.1 Exercise (No. 27) – Static Routing Using the Next Hop

In the exercises in this chapter, we will deal with logical topologies in which no dynamic routing protocol will work. Communication between end devices will be based entirely on static entries on routers. We will start with a simple exercise where only two routers and two end devices are running on the network. Address and enable the interfaces as appropriate, as shown in the diagram, and on each router identify one path that will follow the IP address of the next hop to the destination network (not adjacent to the router in question). Conduct a test using a simple PING command between ***User 1*** and ***User 2***.

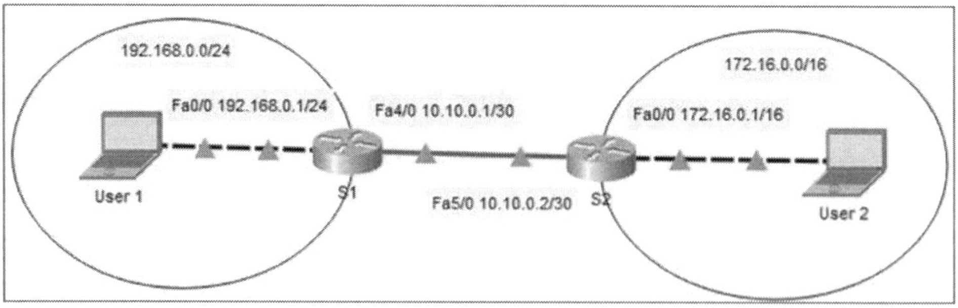

Figure 16.28 Exercise - Configuring static routing using simple hopping, simple topology.

Solution:

1. Following the figure above, create the same logical topology.
2. Address and enable the appropriate device interfaces.
3. For each router, add one static entry that leads to a network that the router is not adjacent to. For example: on router ***S1***, the entry should lead to network *172.16.0.0/16* via address 10.10.0.2.
4. Perform a network test using the PING command between ***User 1*** and ***User 2.***

16.5.2 Exercise (No. 28) – Static Routing Using the Output Interface

The next exercise we will focus on is also a simple logical topology where you need to configure static routing (two entries per router), but this time looking at which interface the data will be sent to, rather than which IP address. Once you have configured the IP addresses on the interfaces and the static routing on the routers, try, in simulation mode, to send a couple of packets between the end users and see if they go the way you planned.

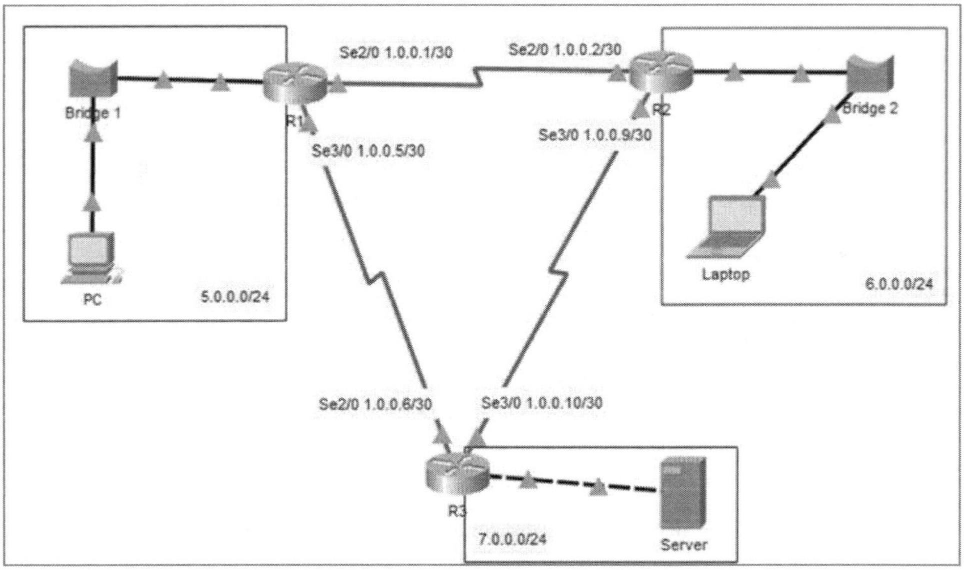

Figure 16.29 Exercise - Configuring static routing using an output interface, simple topology.

Solution:

1. Create the same network simulation as in the figure above.
2. Address and enable the interfaces of the network devices and end devices following the IP addressing spread - figure above.
3. Configure two static routing entries on each router, for example: on router ***R1*** there should be entries that route packets to networks *6.0.0.0/24 (int se2/0)*and

7.0.0.0/24 (int se3/0). These are to be entries that route packets through a given interface, not to a given IP address.

4. Check the current configuration of the routers and their routing tables.
5. If the information obtained from step 4 agrees with your assumptions conduct a network test - send packets between end devices in simulation.

16.5.3 Exercise (No. 29) – Packet Routing (Static Routing)

This time we will focus not only on configuring static routing (using the output interface), but also on tracing the path of packets using a device called a sniffer. Such a device is sandwiched between two network devices and examines the packets passing through it without affecting them (which is why it has only two input/output interfaces). The topology in this exercise consists of four routers and three networks with end devices. Configure the network interfaces of all devices and insert a ***Sniffer*** device between the ***Server_Room*** and the ***School_Room***.

Next, take care of configuring the static routing - on some routers two entries are enough, and in the case of the ***School_Room*** router it is three entries. As mentioned earlier use the static routing configuration using the exit interface rather than the next hop. In order to test our network, we will send PING commands between the end devices (which will show if there is a connection between them) and then we will check this information in the ***GUI*** tab on the ***Sniffer*** device.

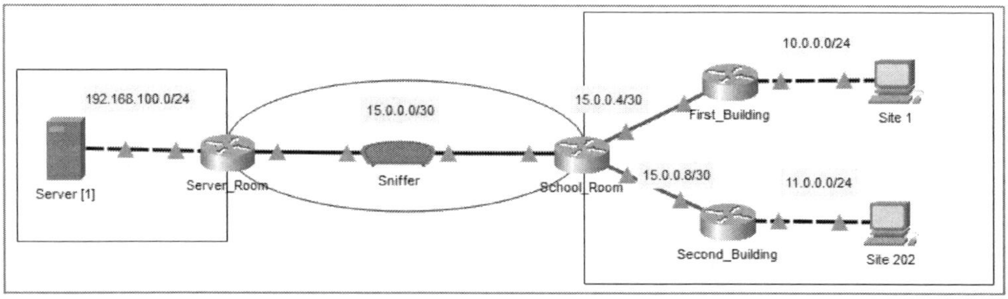

Figure 16.30 Exercise - Packet tracing with a sniffer using static routing.

Solution:

1. In your simulation program, create the same logical topology as shown above. Use the same connection cables between devices.
2. Configure the interfaces of the devices according to the diagram above.
3. Provide the routers with static entries for the network with the end devices (*192.168.100.0/24, 10.0.0.0/24* and *11.0.0.0/24*). Use the output interfaces in the entries.
4. Check that the end devices are connected to each other using the PING command from one end device to another,

5. After a couple of such commands to/from the ***Server [1]*** device, enter the **GUI** tab of the ***Sniffer*** device and analyze the ICMP packets that the device has captured. If the information matches, then the exercise has been done correctly and the network has achieved convergence.

16.5.4 Exercise (No. 30) – Creating Routing Using the Next Hop

This exercise, which will revolve around static routing and whose configuration you will have to do yourself, is a logical topology against a map of Germany. Here we have six routers, which are named after major cities in the country. In two places there are sniffers with Fast Fiber Ethernet modules that analyze traffic between these parts of Germany. IP addressing is, as usual, dissected in the figure below and should be followed. As we are in the chapter dealing with static routing, there should be at least three static entries on each router (using the next hop) leading to end devices in a different topology area (we have four such areas).

Once all the devices are configured, you can test in simulation mode which path the packets take (if it is not the path you have planned - check what goes wrong in the configuration) and check the routing table of each router. The next step is to change the packet filtering on the Sniffers - get rid of all protocols except TCP and ICMP. Next, access the ***Server Kiel*** server page and display it from the ***Admin Dusseldorf*** device. The final step is to go into one of the sniffers and analyze the packets for IP addresses and content.

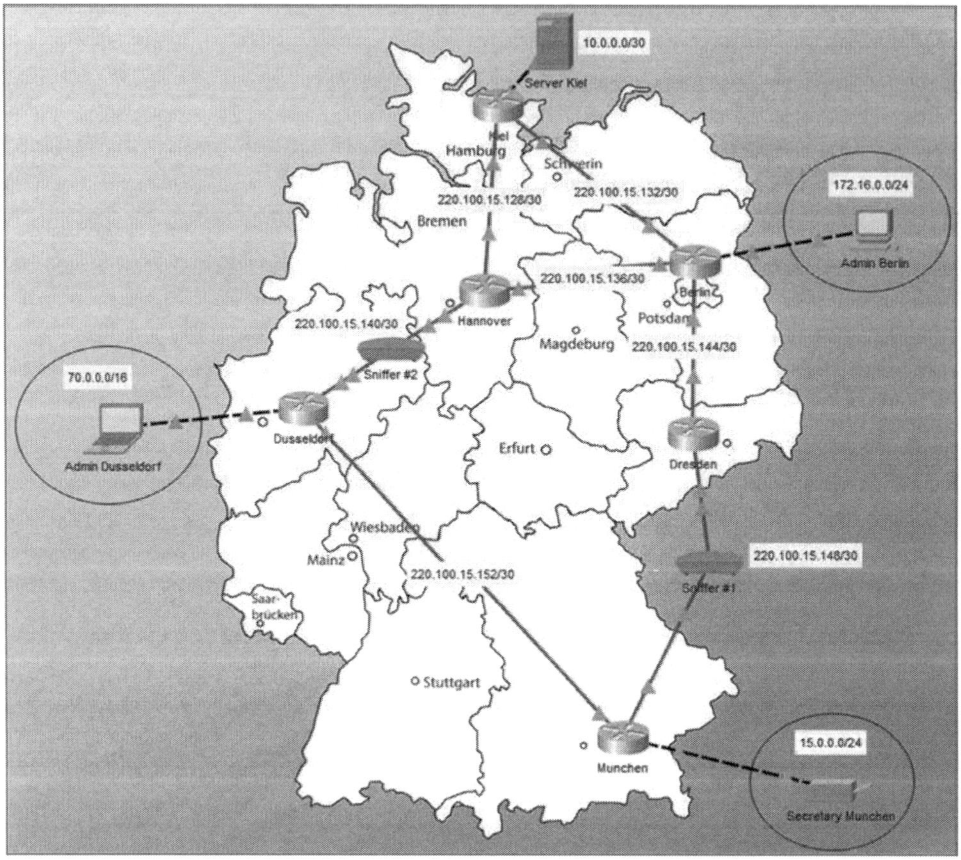

Figure 16.31 Exercise - Configuring static routing using next hop (advanced topology) and packet analysis using sniffer

Solution:

1. Following the German map above, create the same logical topology.
2. Address and enable the interfaces of the network devices and end devices following the IP addressing spread - figure above.
3. On the routers, configure a minimum of three static entries (in some cases it has to be four entries) that lead to the target networks with the end devices. We have these four networks : *10.0.0.0/30, 70.0.0.0/16, 15.0.0.0/24* and *172.16.0.0/24.* These are to be static entries considering the IP address of the next hop, not the output interface.
4. Check the routing table of each router and, in simulation mode, observe whether the packets follow the path you have planned. Also avoid loops in the network, so if any appear - eliminate them.
5. Change the protocols that are filtered by the sniffers - only ICMP and TCP should remain.

6. From the ***Admin Dusseldorf*** device, access the ***Server Kiel*** site and use the PING command to check the communication between the two end devices.
7. On the ***Sniffer#2*** device, carry out an analysis of the ICMP and TCP packets that originate from the ***Admin Dusseldorf*** computer.

16.5.5 Exercise (No. 31) – Incorrect Subnet Mask

Your task is to fix the network errors described below.

Often when configuring static routing, we can get a wrong look or simply make a mistake when entering the address / mask of the destination network. This is a typical mistake and can happen to anyone. The most important thing is to check the current configuration of a device again after it has been configured. In the problem situation we are facing in this exercise, we have two errors that prevent our two end users, ***House*** and ***Work***, from communicating. Find these two errors and erase them from the configuration by replacing them with valid entries. Then run the test using the *tracert* command.

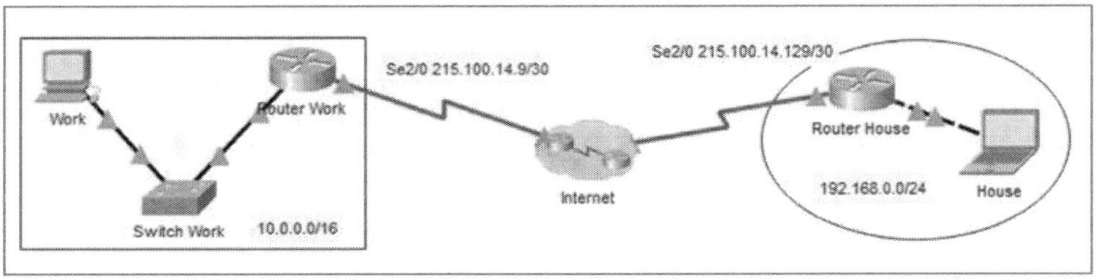

Figure 16.32 Exercise - Problem situation, incorrect subnet mask when configuring a static routing entry

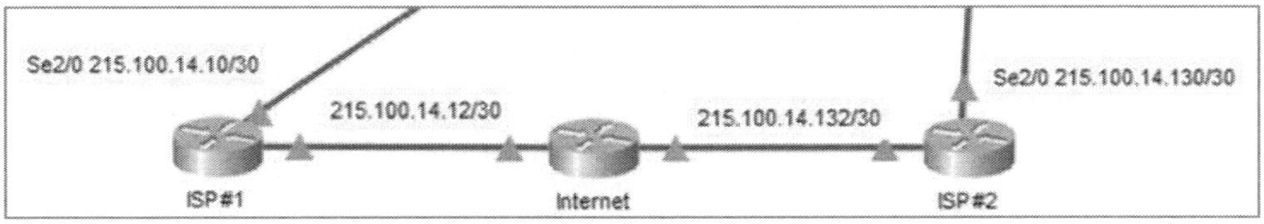

Figure 16.33 Exercise - "Internet" cluster

Solution:

1. For problem situations where the error is due to the manual configuration of the network devices, first look at the current configuration that is running on the devices. This ensures that the lack of communication is due to this, and not some unknown reason.
2. After looking at the configuration of each router, we find that one of them (***Router House***) has a static entry, but it leads to an unknown network that does not exist in our topology. We find the same problem on the ***Internet*** router.

3. Start by deleting the wrong entries and then on entering the correct networks with a good netmask.
4. Test that your network is working properly - use the *Add simple PDU* function

16.5.6 Exercise (No. 32) – Incorrect IP Address of Next Hop

Your task is to fix the network errors described below.

Another common error in the configuration of static routing is the wrong output interface or the wrong IP address of the next hop given at configuration. In the exercise whose topology is shown below, we have four errors related to these very topics. You need to find these errors assisted by the knowledge gained previously, the routing table of the routers and the current configuration of the routers. Pay particular attention to the syntax of the commands entered in the current configuration of the network devices. Once all errors have been corrected, access the two websites - *www.wp.pl* and *xyz.com* - from the end devices and test the communication between the end devices, e.g. between ***Printer*** and ***PC3*** etc.

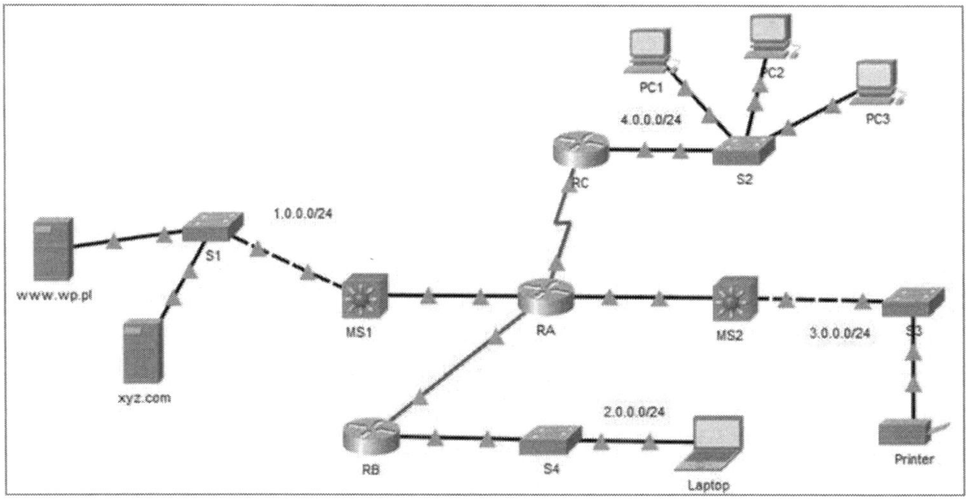

Figure 16.34 Exercise - Problem situation, incorrect output interface/IP address next hop

Solution:

1. As in the previous problem situations - the easiest way to find out where a particular error is occurring/not communicating on your computer network is to look at your current network device configurations and router routing tables.
2. You can deduce from these, among other things, that the ***RA*** router has two configuration errors - a bad IP address of the next hop to the network *4.0.0.0/24* and a bad IP address of the next hop to the network *3.0.0.0/24*.

3. The next thing to look out for is a wrong output interface on the ***MS1*** device for the route to network *4.0.0.0/24*.
4. The last error that occurs in this configuration is a bad output interface for route to network *1.0.0.0/24* on the ***RC*** device.
5. Once you have corrected all these wrong entries to the correct ones, you need to go, for example, from the ***Laptop*** device to www.wp.pl and xyz.com .
6. The next step, which leads to verifying that the network is working correctly, is the PING command from the source device ***PC3*** to the target device e.g. ***Printer***.

16.6 Access Control Lists

16.6.1 Exercise (No. 33) – Configuring the Basic ACL

The exercises in this chapter will cover the quite complex process of creating access lists that are useful on a daily basis in smaller and larger companies. The first exercise will be very straightforward and will involve creating a single, basic, ACL that will not allow an ***Untrusted*** network user to access any devices other than those on their LAN. Once you have created the same topology as shown in the figure, deal with the addressing of the interfaces and then create an access list numbered 1 that meets these objectives. Once you have configured each device, perform a test - try to access the **HTTP** page of the ***HTTP*** device from three devices : ***Trusted, PC*** and ***Untrusted***. Then try access the ***Trusted*** and ***Untrusted*** devices from the ***HTTP*** server. The results for the Untrusted device should be negative.

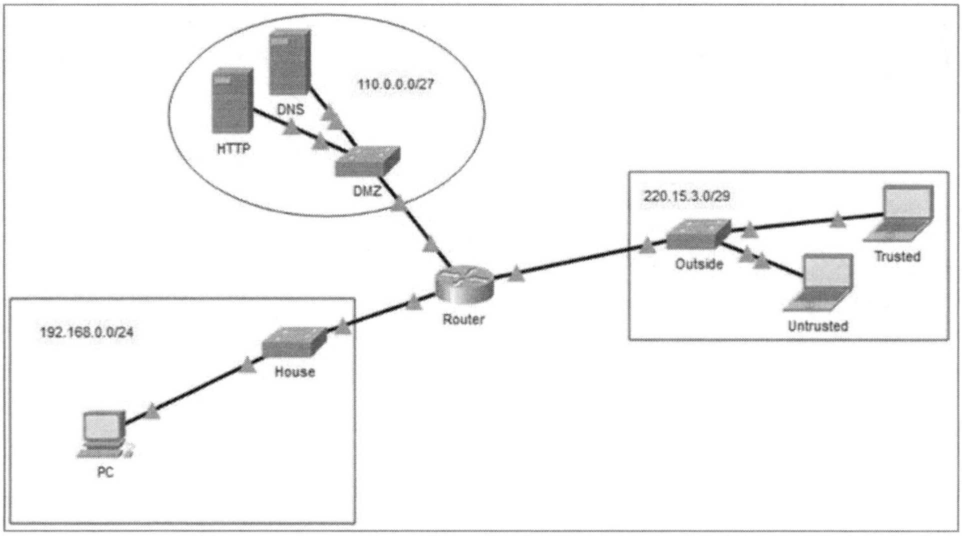

Figure 16.35 Exercise - Configuring a basic ACL

Solution:

1. Following the figure above, build a logical network topology using the same devices and interconnect cables.
2. Address and enable the network and end device interfaces as specified.
3. Configure an access list (ACL No. 1) on the ***Router*** device that will deny ***Untrusted*** laptop access to all devices behind the router and allow ***Trusted*** laptop normal access.
4. Perform a test of the previously entered configuration - start by accessing the HTTP page of the ***HTTP*** device from the ***Trusted, PC*** and ***Untrusted*** devices - the last device should not have access.
5. Then use the PING command from the ***HTTP*** device to try to communicate with the two devices - ***Trusted*** and ***Untrusted***. As before - the last device should not be able to respond.

16.6.2 Exercise (No. 34) – Configuring the Extended ACLs

The next exercise will be on the extended ACL list, where we can already define not only the source host, but also the destination host. There are three end devices and one router on the logical topology, where there is one access list to define. This is the extended list (ACL No. 100), which allows ***Admin*** to access all the resources of the server *www.acl.com*, and allows ***User 1*** to access the HTTP site only. Server ***www.acl.com*** is to be the DNS server for the other two end devices at the same time (take this into account when configuring the access list, as ***User 1*** is to access the HTML page using the server name). Once the access lists have been configured, check that they meet the network assumptions and that ***User 1*** only has access to *www.acl.com* and ***Admin*** to everything.

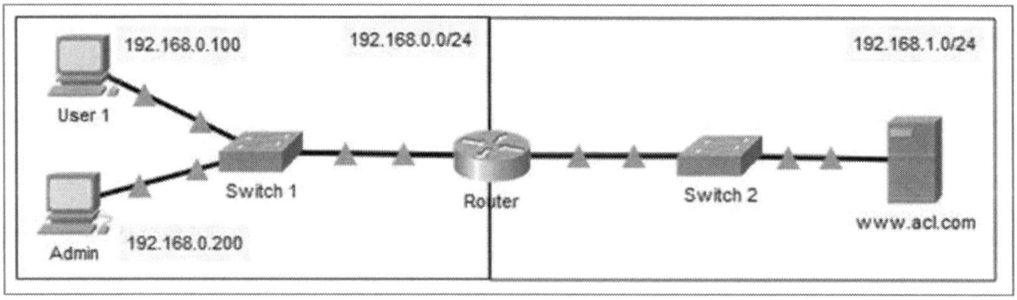

Figure 16.36 Exercise - Configuring extended ACLs

Solution:

1. Create the same network simulation as shown above.
2. Address and enable the network and end device interfaces as specified.

3. On the device ***www.acl.com*** configure two services - HTTP and DNS. There is to be one entry in the DNS service that allows access to this server using the name of this server.
4. Configure an extended access list (ACL No. 100) on the ***Router*** device that allows full access to the ***www.acl.com*** on ***Admin*** device host and limited access to this host for ***User 1*** . It is to have access only to the HTTP site and to the DNS service.
5. Conduct a network test. Start by accessing the HTTP site using the name *www.acl.com* from the ***Admin*** device - the result should be positive. Then do the same on the ***User 1*** device.
6. The next step, which will show us whether the access list has been created successfully, is to send other information from the ***User 1*** device than what we allowed. We can do this using the PING command to ***www.acl.com***. The result should be negative.

16.6.3 Exercise (No. 35) - Configuring the Extended ACLs and EIGRP

The next exercise is similar to the one before, but the topology is much larger. Here we are additionally dealing with the EIGRP dynamic routing protocol (AS 1). The services device serves as the DNS server for each end device in this network simulation. Extended access lists are encountered here at various points. It is intended that the network should work in such a way that the ***Kampung*** device can access all end devices, the ***Taman*** device can only access ***www.malesia.ma***, the PC1 and PC2 devices can only access the http page of the ***www.malesia.ma*** device , but by IP address, and the PC3 device can only ping ***Kampung***. Once you have configured the appropriate access lists, check that the network meets the assumptions made above.

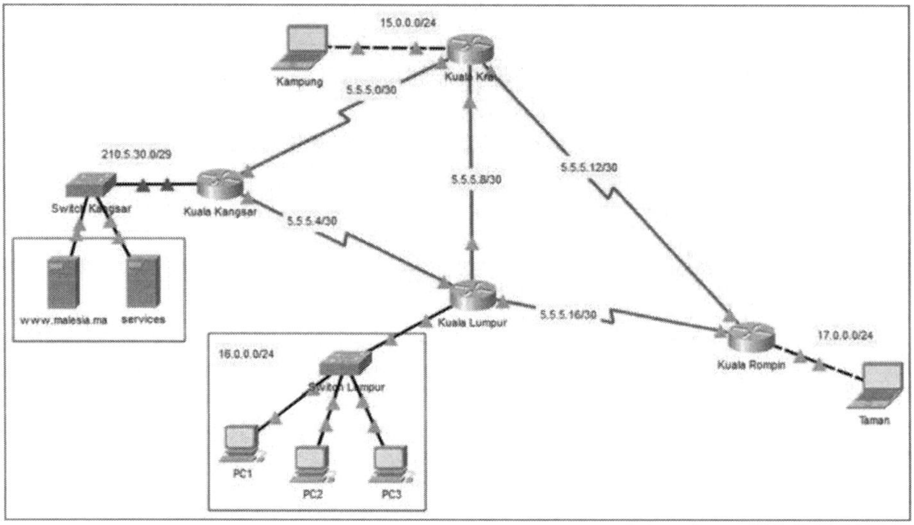

Figure 16.37 Exercise - Configuring extended ACLs and the EIGRP routing protocol

Solution:

1. Using the figure above as a reference, create the same network simulation in Packet Tracer.
2. Address and enable the appropriate network and end device interfaces.
3. Configure the EIGRP routing protocol (AS 1) on the routers taking into account all neighboring networks.
4. On the ***services*** device, configure the DNS service taking into account only one entry, so that the device ***www.malesia.ma*** is available under this name.
5. On the device ***www.malesia.ma*** configure the http site as desired.
6. Start configuring the access lists - the first one will be on the ***Kuala Rompini*** router will allow the ***Tamanna*** device to communicate with the server ***www.malesia.ma*** using the name of this server for the connection (www = TCP protocol, domain = UDP protocol). This access list will point inwards to the end device.
7. The next router to host the access list is the ***Kuala Lumpur*** router, whose access list will allow devices ***PC1, PC2*** to access the device's ***www.malesia.ma*** by IP address, and device ***PC3*** to PING to the ***Kampung*** device. (www = TCP protocol, echo = ICMP protocol).
8. These two access lists are sufficient to achieve the assumptions made earlier. Now test the network to see if everything is correct. Start by checking access to the server ***www.malesia.ma***, and then proceed to test using the PING command.

16.6.4 Exercise (No. 36) - Named ACLs and OSPF Routing Protocol

Following the diagram below, create a logical network topology consisting of four routers named appropriately as our ACLs will be named. Then we have four switches and four end users. In this exercise, the dynamic routing protocol OSPF (AS 10, area 1) is to be configured on the routers so that the end users can communicate with each other. Once this topology has been created, the device interfaces have been addressed and the routing protocol has been configured, a first network test should be carried out to check the communication between end users. If this test has been carried out successfully then we move on to the configuration of the access lists. Each router is to have its own separate ACL named after the router in question. Below are the requirements to be met by the access lists in this network:

- Network *192.168.0.0/24* is to have total access to all network resources and end users
- User ***PC2*** is to be allowed to communicate with ***Server***, but only via FTP
- The entire network *10.0.0.0/8* has permission to send a PING command to network *172.16.0.0/16*
- The *172.16.0.0/16* network has permission to communicate with ***Server***, but only via FTP protocol and can connect to the entire *192.168.0.0/24* network via telnet protocol. It can also respond to incoming PINGs
- The ***PC4*** host can access the ***Server's*** web page on port 80
- The entire network 212.100.0.0/27 can respond to a PING command from any source

If something is not mentioned in the requirements above, it means that it is not mandatory for this network to work as intended. At the end of this task, there should be four access lists, each named differently and assigned to an interface of a particular router. Once the configuration is complete, check that the operation of the network corresponds to the requirements set out earlier .

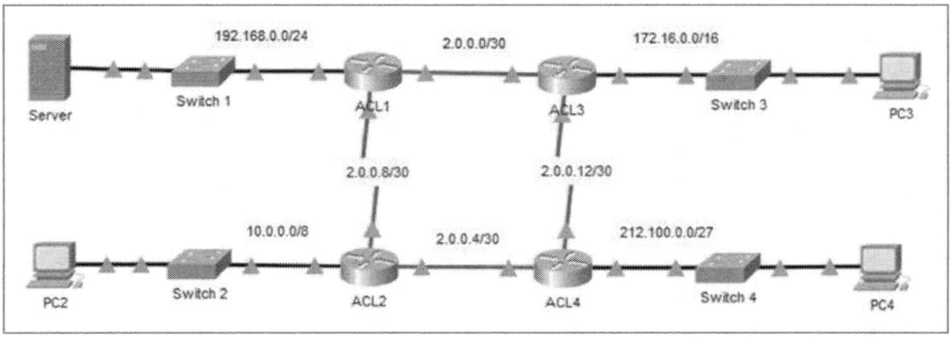

Figure 16.38 Exercise – Configuring named ACLs and the OSPF routing protocol

Solution:

1. Create a logical network topology using the same devices and interconnect cables as shown above.
2. Address and enable the appropriate device interfaces.
3. Configure the OSPF dynamic routing protocol (AS10, area 1) on the routers so that the hosts can communicate with each other.
4. Check that the network is working correctly - each end device should be able to communicate with another end device.
5. Perform the configuration of the ACLs:

- On router ***ACL1***, create an access list named <u>ACL1</u> that allows the entire 192.168.0.0/24 network to access all network resources and end users. Assign this list to the *Fa0/0* interface in.
- On router ***ACL2***, create an access list named <u>ACL2</u> that will allow the entire network 10.0.0.0/8 to send the PING command to the network 172.16.0.0/16 (**icmp echo**), and the host ***PC2*** to communicate with the Server device via FTP (21 port). Assign this list to the *Fa0/0 in* interface.
- On the ***ACL3*** router, create an access list called <u>ACL3</u> that allows the 172.16.0.0/16 network to communicate with Server using port 21 and the 192.168.0.0/24 network using port 23. In addition, any end device from this network can respond to PING commands (**icmp echo-reply**). Assign this list to the *Fa0/0 in* interface.
- On the ***ACL4*** router, create an access list named <u>ACL4</u> that allows the 212.100.0.0/27 network to respond to PING (**icmp echo-reply**) commands and the ***PC4*** host to access the ***Server*** device web page (80 port). Assign this list to the *Fa0/0* interface in.

6. Test the network to check that the previously mentioned ACLs have been implemented correctly and that the network meets the requirements of the task. For example: check if the host ***PC4*** can access the ***Server*** site, and if it can communicate with it via Telnet and FTP (it should not be able to access this server via these two protocols).

16.7 VoIP Technology

16.7.1 Exercise (No. 37) – Configuring VoIP Phones and Routers as a PBX

The topology below shows us a small LAN with six end devices of desktop computers connected to VoIP phones. There is one VoIP phone per computer. There are three VLANs on the network - VLAN10 deals with general information sent between the devices, VLAN20 deals with voice only (from the VoIP phones) and VLAN99 is used to manage the switch remotely. The router in this exercise acts as a DHCP server and telephone exchange.

It has two DHCP address pools: 192.168.10.0/24 and 192.168.20.0/24 excluding addresses 192.168.x.1 - 192.168.x.9. The telephone exchange has three telephone numbers 101, 102, 103 with **ephone** numbers and buttons assigned accordingly. Each telephone should receive an IP address from the DHCP pool, the same as the desktop computers, and should be able to call the other two VoIP telephones.

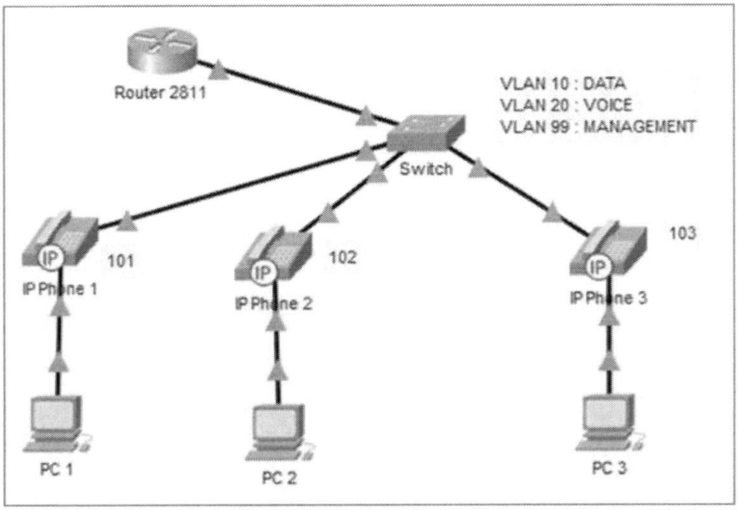

Figure 16.39 Exercise - Configuring VoIP phones and the router as a telephone exchange.

Solution:

1. Create a logical topology as shown in the figure. Use the same phone models and the 2811 router.
2. On the switch create a base of three VLANs : VLAN10 - DATA, VLAN20 VOICE, VLAN99 - MANAGEMENT and change the interface types from switch to router trunk (native 99), from switch to VoIP phones access VLAN10, voice VLAN20. Also address the VLAN99 interface so that the switch can be remotely managed.
3. Deal with the configuration of the router. Start by enabling interface Fa0/0 and addressing its sub-interfaces : fa0/0.10, fa0/0.20 and fa0/0.99 (remember dot1q encapsulation). Then create two DHCP address pools: 192.168.10.0/24 and 192.168.20.0/24 excluding the addresses 192.168.x.1 192.168.x.9 (remember the special option No. 150 for the 192.168.20.0/24 network due to the VoIP phones working there).
4. The next step is to configure the router as a telephone exchange. Create entries for the three telephones numbered 101, 102 and 103. Assign these telephones the appropriate type (type 7960) and set a limit of a maximum of three telephones running on the network.

5. Check that the end devices have been given the correct IP addresses and that the VoIP phones have been registered correctly on the telephone exchange.
6. Call from one phone to the other two. If the test passes, it means that the task has been performed correctly.

16.7.2 Exercise (No. 38) - Configuring VoIP Phones in Two Networks

The next exercise on configuring VoIP phones will run on a slightly more complicated topology. Here we are dealing with two PBXs that support separate VoIP phones with different numbering. On the left we have the 172.16.0.0/24 network and on the right the 172.16.1.0/24 network. The exchanges simultaneously perform the functions of routing and DHCP servers. The VoIP phones ***IP PHONE A*** and ***IP PHONE B*** have numbers in the range 10. , and the phones ***IP PHONE C*** and ***IP PHONE D*** have numbers in the range 58.

The network between the exchanges is a *200.100.100.0/30* network. use two static routing entries so that the networks can communicate with each other. Once you have configured all the necessary commands on the devices : ***PBX 1, PBX 2, S1*** and ***S2***, check that the phones can call each other.

The waiting time for getting correct phone numbers may be taking a many minutes!!!

You can save reload the file PKT after making changes in it.

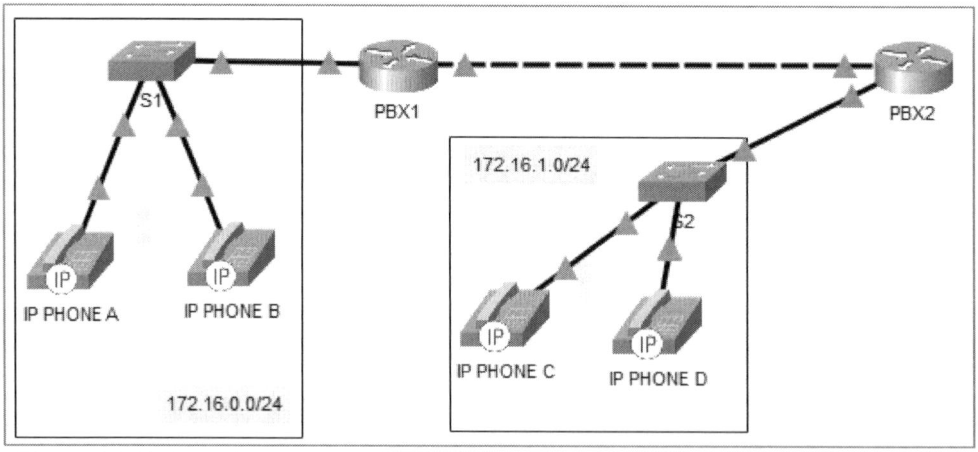

Figure 16.40 Exercise - Configuring VoIP phones on two networks and exchanges

Solution:

1. Following the above figure, create the same network at your site in PacketTracer. Use the same model of routers and IP phones.

2. Address the interfaces of the routers (***PBX 1*** and ***PBX 2***) and configure the corresponding DHCP pools (left 172.16.0.0/24, right 172.16.1.0/24).
3. On the switches, configure the interfaces type *access + voice vlan 1*.
4. Configure the telephony service on both exchanges. Use the parameters ***max-dn 5*** and ***max-ephones 5*** and port **2000** with the corresponding IP address.
5. 5. assign the phone lines to the directory entries (for example, the phones on the left are numbers 101 and 102 and the phones on the right are 581 and 582).
6. Configure the processing of VoIP traffic from one PBX to the other and in the other direction. Use the default values.
7. Create one static routing entry each on the routers.
8. Verify that each the IP phone got their IP addresses and that they can call each other.

16.8 STP Protocol

16.8.1 Exercise (No. 39) – Configuring Rapid-PVST and VLANs

Create a topology as shown in the figure below. In this case, the model of switches used as well as the type of end devices plays no role. There should be three VLANs on each switch : 1 - the default, 10 and 15, each named **VLANx** where **x** is the VLAN number. There are to be trunk connections between the switches over which packets from each VLAN can travel, and there should be access connections to the end devices with the appropriate VLANs assigned as shown.

The **rapid-pvst** version of the STP protocol is to run on each switch. You are to set the priority of the switches in such a way that: switch ***a*** is to be the alternate root for VLAN10, switch ***c*** is to be the root for VLAN10 and the alternate root for VLAN15 and switch ***d*** is to be the root for VLAN15. In this way, no link will be out of service. Once this configuration has been carried out, check that it agrees with the assumptions using the appropriate show commands and see if devices ***aa*** and ***ea*** are able to PING each other and if they are unable to connect to device ***ca*** .

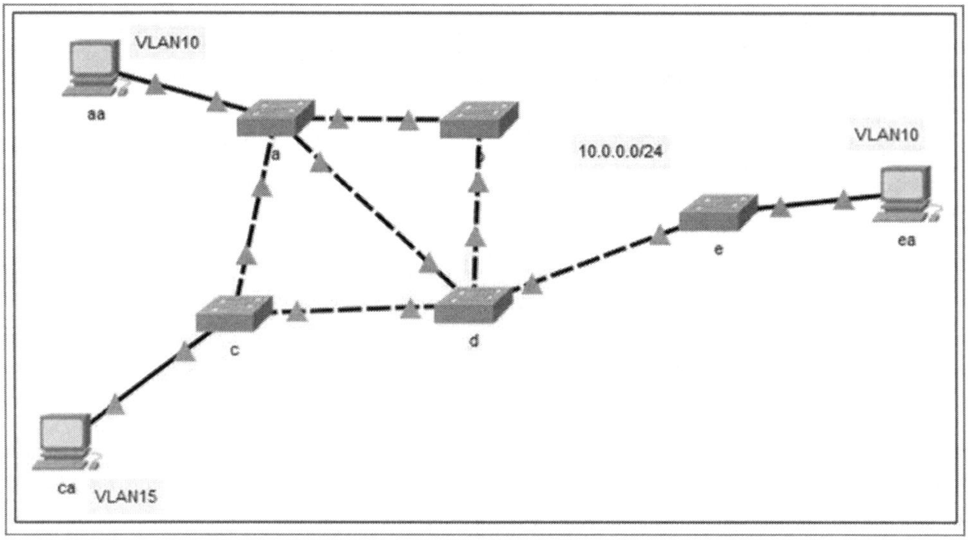

Figure 16.41 Exercise - Configuring STP and VLANs.

Solution:

1. Create a topology as shown in the figure above.
2. Address the end devices so that they are on the 10.0.0.0/24 network.
3. Change the STP protocol version on the switches to rapid-pvst.
4. Create a VLAN database on each switching device so that it contains VLAN10 and VLAN15 appropriately named.
5. Set up trunk connections and permission for all VLANs between the switches, and set up access connections with permission for the corresponding VLANs between the switch and the end device as in the diagram.
6. Change the priority of the switches in the STP protocol so that the switch roles match the assumptions made above. E.g. for switch c VLAN10 priority 24576 and VLAN15 priority 28672.
7. Check with the show command that the configuration agrees and matches the assumptions made earlier. Then check that device ***aa*** can PING with device ***ea***, but cannot do so with device ***ca***.

16.8.2 Exercise (No. 40) – Rapid-PVST, VLANs and Port Fast Functions

To better practice setting up Rapid-PVSTST and VLANs we will do it again, but on a different logical topology and adding to this by still enabling the **Port Fast** function on the switches by default. Start by looking at the figure below and then copying it into your application. The entire network is based on IP addresses in the *192.168.0.0/24* range. Once you have copied the topology, take care of addressing the end devices and changing the protocol from STP to Rapid-PVST. Next, create a VLAN database on each switch. This is to include one default VLAN and three manually entered VLANs. The name is arbitrary, but the numbers are to match the diagram below.

The next step is to change the types of interfaces - between the switches it should be trunk connections, and between the switch and the end devices it should be access connections with the appropriate VLAN assigned (only the ***Admin*** device has access to the ***Server*** device). In order for the configuration to match the assumptions, there remains the Port Fast option to be configured, which should be enabled by default on every switch - especially on switches that have end devices in their vicinity.

If the ***Additional link*** device does not have an orange LED next to it, this means that it has not been selected as an additional path, but as the main path. If this is the case, change the STP priority accordingly so that the main path for packets goes through the ***Switch*** device and then the ***Servers***.

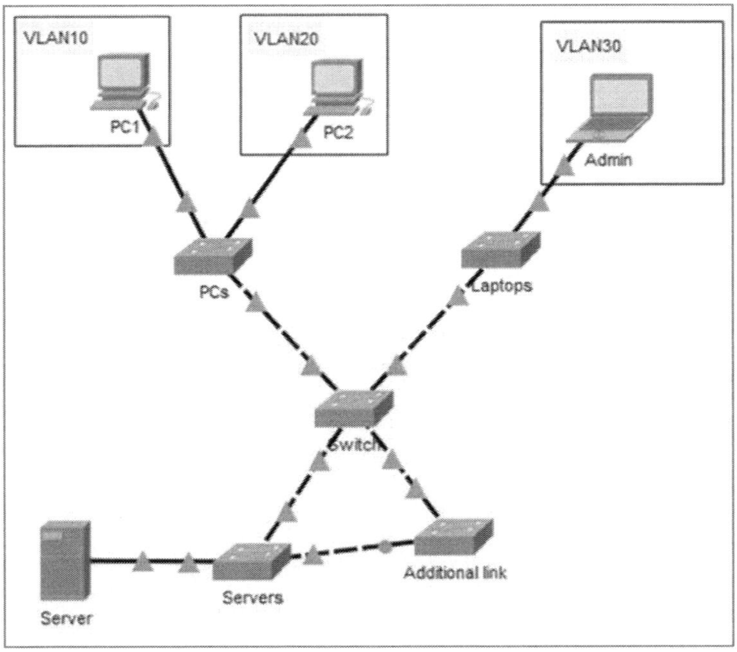

Figure 16.42 Exercise - Configuring STP, VLANs and the Port Fast function.

Solution:

1. Familiarize yourself with and copy the topology from the image above into your program.
2. Address the end devices so that they are contained within the 192.168.0.0/24 network.

3. Change the type of protocol running from STP to Rapid-PVST and create a VLAN base so that it matches on each switch as intended.
4. Set up trunk connections between switches, and set up access connections between switches and end devices with permission for the corresponding VLANs as in the diagram (the ***Server*** device belongs to VLAN30).
5. Enable the Port Fast option on each switch by default and check with the show command that it has been implemented. Exercise – Configuring STP, VTP

The first step in this exercise will be to copy the logical topology shown below and address the end devices so that they belong to the *192.168.0.0/24* network. For this exercise, we will stay with the basic version of Spanning Tree Protocol, and focus on configuring VTP. This will allow us to create a VLAN base on one switch only, and the rest of the switches will get an update with the same VLAN base. The VTP domain in this exercise will be vtp.com, the password is cisco. Assume that in this exercise each switch will use protocol version 2.

16.8.3 Exercise (No. 41) – STP Switch Server

In addition to being the VTP server, the ***Switch Server*** is also the STP root for all three VLANs. Once all devices have been configured as intended, check with the appropriate show commands that the configuration agrees on all switches. Next, check the communication between the end users. This communication should not be available between the different VLANs. STP, VTP

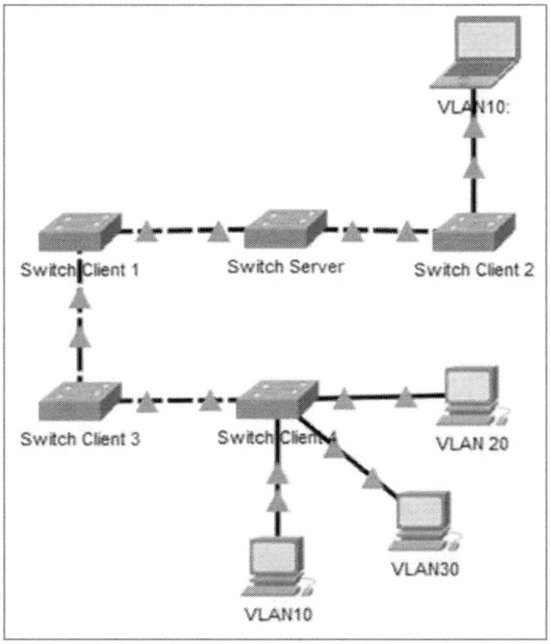

Figure 16.43 Exercise – Configuring STP, VTP.

Solution:

1. Copy the logical topology from the figure above into your Packet Tracer program.
2. Address the end devices so that they are on the 192.168.0.0/24 network.
3. Configure the switches so that the ***Switch Server*** device is the VTP server for the vtp.com domain (cisco password, second version of the protocol) and the rest of the switches are clients of that domain.
4. Create a VLAN database on the ***Switch Server*** device containing three entries VLAN10, VLAN20 and VLAN30.
5. Configure the connections between the switches to be of the trunk type and the connections to the end devices to be of the access type with the appropriate VLAN assigned.
6. Set the appropriate STP priority values so that the ***Switch Server*** device is the STP root for the three VLANs.
7. Check with the show commands that the device configurations match.
8. Check that communication in the VLAN10 area is occurring without problems and that it is blocked between the different VLANs.

16.8.4 Exercise (No. 42) – PVST, VTP and Routing between VLANs

The last STP and VLAN configuration task will be about routing between VLANs and the STP protocol version of PVST. Start by creating the same topology as shown in the figure below. Then address the end devices and configure the router subinterfaces so that routing between VLANs is possible. The ***Switch Server*** is to act as the VTP server of the ROUTER domain, whose password is *cisco* and whose protocol version is version two.

On this switch, create a VLAN base which is to include : VLAN11, VLAN22 and VLAN33. The other switches are clients of this domain. The ***Root*** device is the primary root for all existing VLANs in this configuration. Trunk connections are to operate between the network devices and access connections between the network and end devices. Once the LAN is properly configured, check that you can PING the default gateway of each end device and that you have achieved communication between VLANs. Also check with the show command that the switch assumptions have been provided.

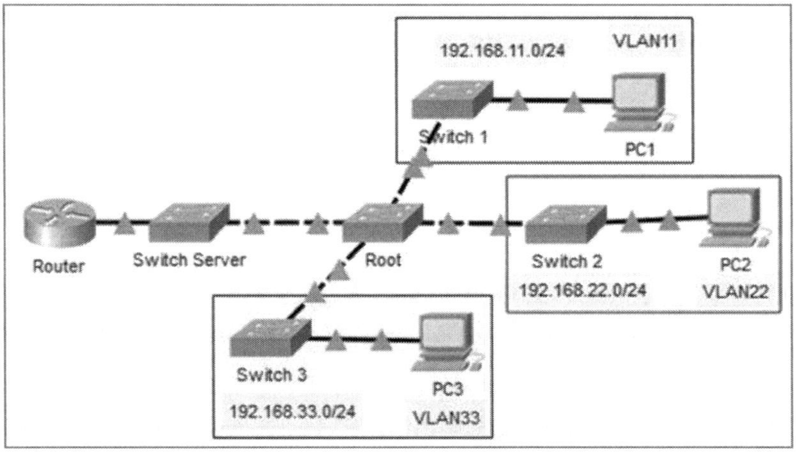

Figure 16.44 Exercise - Configuring PVST, VTP and routing between VLANs.

Solution:

1. Create the same topology as shown above.
2. Address the end devices and sub-interfaces of the ***Router*** device (including dot1q encapsulation of the relevant VLANs).
3. On the ***Switch Server*** device, create a VLAN database and make it a VTP server for the ROUTER domain (cisco password, protocol version two). Make the other switches into clients for this domain.
4. Change the type of STP protocol running to PVST and, using the appropriate STP priority values, make the ***Root*** device the primary root for all VLANs.

5. Use trunk connections between network devices and access connections between network and end devices.
6. Verify that the end devices can PING their default gateways and each other.
7. Check with the *show* command that the configuration of the switches is as intended.

16.9 VTP Protocol

16.9.1 Exercise (No. 43) – Configuring VTP without Routing between VLANs

Your task in this exercise is to configure the Rapid STP and VTP protocols on the network shown in the figure below.

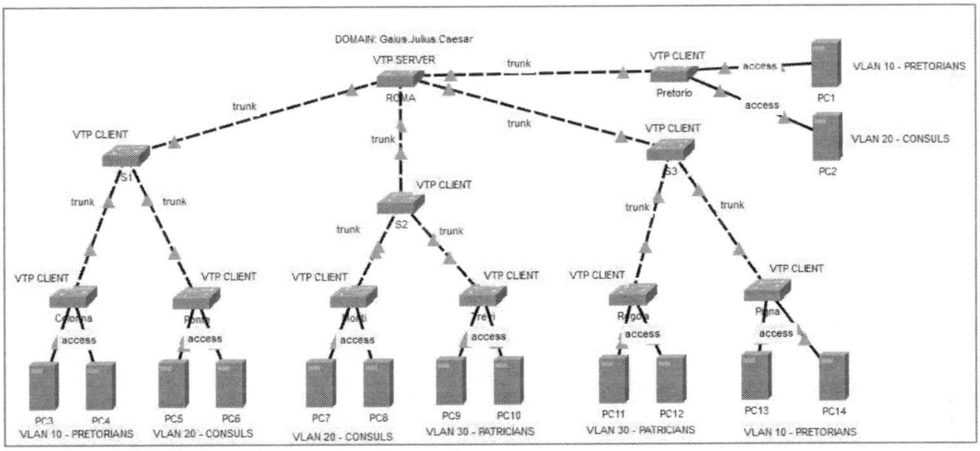

Figure 16.45 Network topology.

The network topology consists of eleven switches (**ROMA, Pretorio, S1, S2, S3, Colonna, Monti, Pigna, Ponte, Regola, Trevi**), and fourteen computers (**PC1, PC2, PC3, PC4, PC5, PC6, PC7, PC8, PC9, PC10, PC11, PC12, PC13, PC14**) working in three different VLANs: **10, 20, 30**.

Configure the network topology so that switch **ROMA** is the VTP server, switches **S1, S2, S3** act as the VTP transparent (or client) role, and the other switches are the VTP clients.

- STP mode of operation: **Rapid STP**
- VTP domain name: **Gaius.Julius.Caesar**
- VTP domain password: **Alea-iacta-est**
  Configure communication within each VLAN.

Note ! It is not required to configure routing between VLANs in this exercise.

The configuration data for the exercise can be found in the following tables.

VLAN NO.	VLAN NAME
10	PRETORIANS
20	CONSULS
30	PATRICIANS
99	CAESAR

Table 16.1 VLAN base in the ROMA switch

VLAN	Computers	IP Address/Prefix	Default gateway
PRETORIANS	PC1, PC3, PC4, PC13, PC14	192.168.10.x/24	192.168.10.10
CONSULS	PC2, PC5, PC6, PC7, PC8	192.168.20.x/24	192.168.20.20
PATRICIANS	PC9, PC10, PC11, PC12	192.168.30.x/24	192.168.30.30

Table 16.2 Membership of computers in a VLAN (x - any address that is not a gateway or server).

Solution:

Step 1. Create a network topology.

Step 2. Configure the end device interfaces.

Configure the interfaces of the end devices, using addressing as intended.

Step 3. Configure ports and RSTP, VTP protocols for the ROMA switch.

Configure the **ROMA** switch using the following commands:

```
en
conf t
hostname ROMA
spanning-tree mode rapid-pvst
vlan 10
name PRETORIANS
vlan 20
name CONSULS
vlan 30
name PATRICIANS
```

```
vlan 99
name CAESAR
exit
vtp domain Gaius.Julius.Caesar
vtp password Alea-iacta-est
vtp mode server
interface FastEthernet0/1
description Trunk-to-Pretorio
sw mode trunk
sw trunk native vlan 99
interface FastEthernet1/1
description Trunk-to-S1
sw mode trunk
sw trunk native vlan 99
interface FastEthernet2/1
description Trunk-to-S2
sw mode trunk
sw trunk native vlan 99
interface FastEthernet3/1
description Trunk-to-S3
sw mode trunk
sw trunk native vlan 99
```

Step 4. Configure the ports and the RSTP, VTP protocols for switch S1.

Configure switch **S1** using the following commands:

```
en
conf t
hostname S1
spanning-tree mode rapid-pvst
vtp domain Gaius.Julius.Caesar
vtp password Alea-iacta-est
vtp mode client
interface FastEthernet0/1
description Trunk-to-ROMA
```

```
sw mode trunk
sw trunk native vlan 99
interface FastEthernet1/1
description Trunk-to-Colonna
sw mode trunk
sw trunk native vlan 99
interface FastEthernet2/1
description Trunk-to-Ponte
sw mode trunk
sw trunk native vlan 99
```

Step 5. Configure the ports and the RSTP, VTP protocols for the S2 switch.

Configure the **S2** switch using the following commands:

```
en
conf t
hostname S2
spanning-tree mode rapid-pvst
vtp domain Gaius.Julius.Caesar
vtp password Alea-iacta-est
vtp mode client
interface FastEthernet0/1
description Trunk-to-ROMA
sw mode trunk
sw trunk native vlan 99
interface FastEthernet1/1
description Trunk-to-Monti
sw mode trunk
sw trunk native vlan 99
interface FastEthernet2/1
description Trunk-to-Trevi
sw mode trunk
sw trunk native vlan 99
```

Step 6. Configure the ports and the RSTP, VTP protocols for the S3 switch.

Configure the **S3** switch using the following commands:

```
en
conf t
hostname S3
spanning-tree mode rapid-pvst
vtp domain Gaius.Julius.Caesar
vtp password Alea-iacta-est
vtp mode client
interface FastEthernet0/1
description Trunk-to-ROMA
sw mode trunk
sw trunk native vlan 99
interface FastEthernet1/1
description Trunk-to-Regola
sw mode trunk
sw trunk native vlan 99
interface FastEthernet2/1
description Trunk-to-Pigna
sw mode trunk
sw trunk native vlan 99
```

Step 7. Configure the ports and the RSTP, VTP protocols for the Colonna switch.

Configure the **Colonna** switch using the following commands:

```
en
conf t
hostname Colonna
spanning-tree mode rapid-pvst
vtp domain Gaius.Julius.Caesar
vtp password Alea-iacta-est
vtp mode client
interface FastEthernet0/1
description Trunk-to-S1
sw mode trunk
sw trunk native vlan 99
interface FastEthernet1/1
```

```
description Access-to-PC3
sw mode access
sw access vlan 10
interface FastEthernet2/1
description Access-to-PC4
sw mode access
sw access vlan 10
```

Step 8. Configure ports and RSTP, VTP protocols for the Monti switch.

Configure the **Monti** switch using the following commands:

```
en
conf t
hostname Monti
spanning-tree mode rapid-pvst
vtp domain Gaius.Julius.Caesar
vtp password Alea-iacta-est
vtp mode client
interface FastEthernet0/1
description Trunk-to-S2
sw mode trunk
sw trunk native vlan 99
interface FastEthernet1/1
description Access-to-PC7
sw mode access
sw access vlan 20
interface FastEthernet2/1
description Access-to-PC8
sw mode access
sw access vlan 20
```

Step 9. Configure the ports and the RSTP, VTP protocols for the Pigna switch.

Configure the **Pigna** switch using the following commands:

```
en
```

```
conf t
hostname Pigna
spanning-tree mode rapid-pvst
vtp domain Gaius.Julius.Caesar
vtp password Alea-iacta-est
vtp mode client
interface FastEthernet0/1
description Trunk-to-S3
sw mode trunk
sw trunk native vlan 99
interface FastEthernet1/1
description Access-to-PC13
sw mode access
sw access vlan 10
interface FastEthernet2/1
description Access-to-PC14
sw mode access
sw access vlan 10
```

Step 10. Configure ports and RSTP, VTP protocols for the Ponte switch.

Configure the **Ponte** switch using the following commands:

```
en
conf t
hostname Ponte
spanning-tree mode rapid-pvst
vtp domain Gaius.Julius.Caesar
vtp password Alea-iacta-est
vtp mode client
interface FastEthernet0/1
description Trunk-to-S1
sw mode trunk
sw trunk native vlan 99
interface FastEthernet1/1
description Access-to-PC5
```

```
sw mode access
sw access vlan 20
interface FastEthernet2/1
description Access-to-PC6
sw mode access
sw access vlan 20
```

Step 11. Configure the ports and the RSTP, VTP protocols for the Pretorio switch.

Configure the **Pretorio** switch using the following commands:

```
en
conf t
hostname Pretorio
spanning-tree mode rapid-pvst
vtp domain Gaius.Julius.Caesar
vtp password Alea-iacta-est
vtp mode client
interface FastEthernet0/1
description Trunk-to-ROMA
sw mode trunk
sw trunk native vlan 99
interface FastEthernet1/1
description Access-to-PC1
sw mode access
sw access vlan 10
interface FastEthernet2/1
description Access-to-PC2
sw mode access
sw access vlan 20
```

Step 12. Configure ports and RSTP, VTP protocols for the Regola switch.

Configure the **Regola** switch using the following commands:

```
en
conf t
hostname Regola
spanning-tree mode rapid-pvst
```

```
vtp domain Gaius.Julius.Caesar
vtp password Alea-iacta-est
vtp mode client
interface FastEthernet0/1
description Trunk-to-S3
sw mode trunk
sw trunk native vlan 99
interface FastEthernet1/1
description Access-to-PC11
sw mode access
sw access vlan 30
interface FastEthernet2/1
description Access-to-PC12
sw mode access
sw access vlan 30
```

Step 13. Configure the ports and the RSTP, VTP protocols for the Trevi switch.

Configure the **Trevi** switch using the following commands:

```
en
conf t
hostname Trevi
spanning-tree mode rapid-pvst
vtp domain Gaius.Julius.Caesar
vtp password Alea-iacta-est
vtp mode client
interface FastEthernet0/1
description Trunk-to-S2
sw mode trunk
sw trunk native vlan 99
interface FastEthernet1/1
description Access-to-PC9
sw mode access
sw access vlan 30
interface FastEthernet2/1
```

```
description Access-to-PC10
sw mode access
sw access vlan 30
```

Step 14. Check the sample communications.

To check whether computers in the same VLAN can communicate with each other, check the connection between PC14 and PC1.

Execute command: **`ping 192.168.10.1`** from computer PC14.

```
C:\>ping 192.168.10.1

Pinging 192.168.10.1 with 32 bytes of data:

Reply from 192.168.10.1: bytes=32 time=11ms TTL=128
Reply from 192.168.10.1: bytes=32 time=1ms TTL=128
Reply from 192.168.10.1: bytes=32 time<1ms TTL=128
Reply from 192.168.10.1: bytes=32 time<1ms TTL=128
```

Figure 16.46 Result of the command ping from PC14 to PC1.

To check that computers on different VLANs cannot communicate with each other, check the connection between PC14 and PC2. Execute the command **`ping 192.168.20.1`** from computer PC14.

```
C:\>ping 192.168.20.1

Pinging 192.168.20.1 with 32 bytes of data:

Request timed out.
Request timed out.
Request timed out.
Request timed out.
```

Figure 16.47 Result of the command ping from PC14 to PC2.

16.9.2 Exercise (No. 44) – Configuring VTP and Routing between VLANs

The topology consists of a HOUSTON router, four switches (HOUSTON1, HOUSTON2, USAF-Building, NASA-Building), and four computers (USAF LAB, USAF-ADM, NASA-LAB, NASA-ADM) operating in a 16.0.0.0/24 subnet and in VLANs.

Configure the network topology according to the figure below and the **VLAN Trunking Protocol** so that switch **HOUSTON1** is the VTP server and the other switches are VTP clients, and configure routing between the VLANs. This exercise also requires to configure the router **subinterfaces**. Use the data showed in the tables.

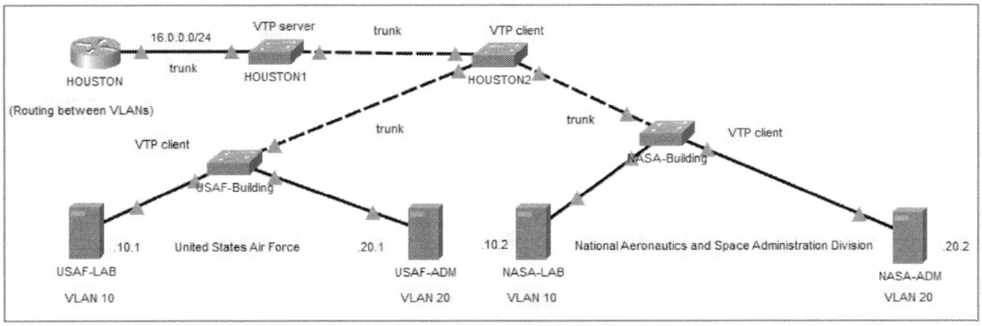

Figure 16.48 Network topology

VLAN NO.	VLAN NAME
10	**Laboratory**
20	**Administration**
99	**MANAGEMENT**

Table 16.3 VLAN base in the HOUSTON1 switch

Hostname	Mode	VLAN	IP Address/Prefix	Default gateway
USAF-LAB	access	10	16.0.10.1/24	16.0.10.254
USAF-ADM	access	20	16.0.20.2/24	16.0.20.254
NASA-LAB	access	10	16.0.10.1/24	16.0.10.254
NASA-ADM	access	20	16.0.20.2/24	16.0.20.254

Table 16.4 VLAN membership of computers

VTP domain name	**ITSTART**
VTP domain password	**houston**
STP (Spanning Tree Mode) work mode	**rapid-pvst**

Table 16.5 Configuration data of VTP and STP protocols.

Solution

Step 1. Create the network topology according to the figure.

Step 2. Configure the end device interfaces.

Configure the interfaces of the end devices, using the addressing according to the assumptions described in the tables.

Step 3. Configure the ports and RSTP for the switches, according to the assumptions, described in the tables.

Execute the following commands on switch **HOUSTON1**:

```
spanning-tree mode rapid-pvst
```

```
interface FastEthernet0/1
switchport trunk native vlan 99
switchport mode trunk

interface FastEthernet3/1
switchport trunk native vlan 99
switchport mode trunk
```

Execute the following commands on the switch **HOUSTON2**:

```
spanning-tree mode rapid-pvst

interface FastEthernet0/1
switchport trunk native vlan 99
switchport mode trunk

interface FastEthernet1/1
switchport trunk native vlan 99
switchport mode trunk

interface FastEthernet3/1
switchport trunk native vlan 99
switchport mode trunk
```

Execute the following commands on the switch **USAF-Building**:

```
spanning-tree mode rapid-pvst

interface FastEthernet0/1
switchport trunk native vlan 99
switchport mode trunk

interface FastEthernet1/1
switchport access vlan 10
switchport mode access
```

```
interface FastEthernet2/1
switchport access vlan 20
switchport mode access
```

Execute the following commands on the switch **NASA-Building**:

```
spanning-tree mode rapid-pvst

interface FastEthernet0/1
switchport trunk native vlan 99
switchport mode trunk

interface FastEthernet1/1
switchport access vlan 10

interface FastEthernet2/1
switchport access vlan 20
```

Step 4. Configure the VLAN base on the **HOUSTON1** device.

Configure VLANs: **10, 20, 99** on **HOUSTON1**.

Use the commands:

```
enable
configure terminal
vlan 10
name Laboratory
vlan 20
name Administration
vlan 99
name MANAGEMENT
end
```

```
HOUSTON1>enable
HOUSTON1#configure terminal
Enter configuration commands, one per line.  End with CNTL/Z.
HOUSTON1(config)#vlan 10
HOUSTON1(config-vlan)#name Laboratory
HOUSTON1(config-vlan)#vlan 20
HOUSTON1(config-vlan)#name Administration
HOUSTON1(config-vlan)#vlan 99
HOUSTON1(config-vlan)#name MANAGEMENT
HOUSTON1(config-vlan)#end
HOUSTON1#
```

Figure 16.49 Creation of a VLAN database on the VTP server

Step 5. Configure **HOUSTON1** to be a server in the VTP domain.

Configure HOUSTON1 using the following commands:

```
enable
configure terminal
vtp mode server
vtp domain ITSTART
vtp password houston
end
```

Step 6. Configure HOUSTON2 to the client role in the VTP domain.

Configure **HOUSTON2** using the following commands:

```
enable
configure terminal
vtp mode client
vtp domain ITSTART
vtp password houston
end
```

Step 7. Configure USAF-Building for the client role in the VTP domain.

Configure **USAF-Building** using the following commands:

```
enable
configure terminal
vtp mode client
```

```
vtp domain ITSTART
vtp password houston
end
```

Step 8. Configure NASA-Building for the client role in the VTP domain.

Configure **NASA-Building** using the following commands:

```
enable
configure terminal
vtp mode client
vtp domain ITSTART
vtp password houston
end
```

Step 9. Check VTP protocol status on switch HOUSTON1

On the **HOUSTON1** switch, execute the command: **`show vtp status`**.

```
HOUSTON1#show vtp status
VTP Version                     : 2
Configuration Revision          : 9
Maximum VLANs supported locally : 255
Number of existing VLANs        : 8
VTP Operating Mode              : Server
VTP Domain Name                 : ITSTART
VTP Pruning Mode                : Disabled
VTP V2 Mode                     : Disabled
VTP Traps Generation            : Disabled
MD5 digest                      : 0xEF 0x20 0xDD 0xA6 0x4B 0xCF 0x55 0xBF
Configuration last modified by 0.0.0.0 at 3-1-93 01:00:45
```

Figure 16.50 The result of the show vtp status command on HOUSTON1.

Step 10. Check the VTP protocol status on switch HOUSTON2.

On the **HOUSTON2** switch, execute the command: **`show vtp status`**.

```
HOUSTON2#show vtp status
VTP Version                     : 2
Configuration Revision          : 9
Maximum VLANs supported locally : 255
Number of existing VLANs        : 8
VTP Operating Mode              : Client
VTP Domain Name                 : ITSTART
VTP Pruning Mode                : Disabled
VTP V2 Mode                     : Disabled
VTP Traps Generation            : Disabled
MD5 digest                      : 0xEF 0x20 0xDD 0xA6 0x4B 0xCF 0x55 0xBF
Configuration last modified by 0.0.0.0 at 3-1-93 01:00:45
```

Figure 16.51 The result of the show vtp status command on HOUSTON2.

Step 11. Check the status of the VTP protocol on the USAF-Building switch.

On the **USAF-Building** switch, execute the command : **`show vtp status`**.

```
USAF-Building#show vtp status
VTP Version                     : 2
Configuration Revision          : 9
Maximum VLANs supported locally : 255
Number of existing VLANs        : 8
VTP Operating Mode              : Client
VTP Domain Name                 : ITSTART
VTP Pruning Mode                : Disabled
VTP V2 Mode                     : Disabled
VTP Traps Generation            : Disabled
MD5 digest                      : 0xEF 0x20 0xDD 0xA6 0x4B 0xCF 0x55 0xBF
Configuration last modified by 0.0.0.0 at 3-1-93 01:00:45
```

Figure 16.52 The result of the show vtp status command on USAF-Building.

Step 12. Check the status of the VTP protocol on the NASA-Building switch

On the **NASA-Building switch**, execute the command: **`show vtp status`**.

```
NASA-Building#show vtp status
VTP Version                     : 2
Configuration Revision          : 9
Maximum VLANs supported locally : 255
Number of existing VLANs        : 8
VTP Operating Mode              : Client
VTP Domain Name                 : ITSTART
VTP Pruning Mode                : Disabled
VTP V2 Mode                     : Disabled
VTP Traps Generation            : Disabled
MD5 digest                      : 0xEF 0x20 0xDD 0xA6 0x4B 0xCF 0x55 0xBF
Configuration last modified by 0.0.0.0 at 3-1-93 01:00:45
```

Figure 16.53 The result of the show vtp status command on NASA-Building.

Step 13. Configure routing between VLANs.

Use the **sub-interfaces** technique and **dot1q** encapsulation. Configure the **HOUSTON** router interfaces (i.e. trunking links to the corresponding VLANs), using the following commands:

```
interface FastEthernet2/0
ip address 16.0.0.254 255.255.255.0

interface FastEthernet2/0.10
description Trunk-to-Laboratory
encapsulation dot1Q 10
ip address 16.0.10.254 255.255.255.0

interface FastEthernet2/0.20
description Trunk-to-Administration
encapsulation dot1Q 20
ip address 16.0.20.254 255.255.255.0
```

```
HOUSTON(config)#interface FastEthernet2/0
HOUSTON(config-if)#ip address  16.0.0.254   255.255.255.0
HOUSTON(config-if)#
HOUSTON(config-if)#interface FastEthernet2/0.10
HOUSTON(config-subif)#description Trunk-to-Laboratory
HOUSTON(config-subif)#encapsulation   dot1Q  10
HOUSTON(config-subif)#ip address  16.0.10.254  255.255.255.0
HOUSTON(config-subif)#
HOUSTON(config-subif)#interface FastEthernet2/0.20
HOUSTON(config-subif)#description Trunk-to-Administration
HOUSTON(config-subif)#encapsulation  dot1Q  20
HOUSTON(config-subif)#ip address  16.0.20.254  255.255.255.0
```

Figure 16.54 Configuration of addressing and encapsulation of subinterfaces on the router.

Step 14. Check communication between VLANs.

To check whether computers on different VLANs can communicate with each other, check the connection between USAF-LAB and NASA-ADM.

Execute command : `ping 16.0.20.2` from computer USAF-LAB.

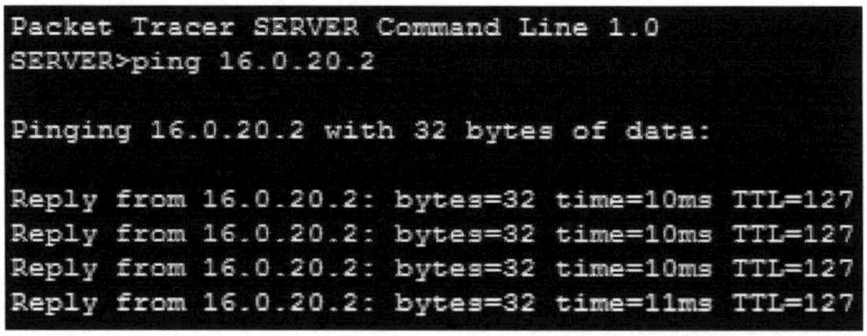

Figure 16.55 The result of a ping command from USAF-LAB to NASA-ADM.

16.10 Frame Relay Protocol

16.10.1 Exercise (No. 45) – Configuring the Frame Relay Protocol

The network topology consists of a Frame Relay switch (**CENTRAL UNITED STATES**), four routers type 1841 (**COLORADO, TEXAS, KANSAS, NEBRASKA**), four switches type 2950 (LAN1, LAN2, LAN3, LAN4) and three computers (**PC-DENVER**, **PC-AUSTIN**, **PC-TOPEKA**) and a server **PC-LINCOLN**. Configure the Frame Relay protocol and the RIPv2 protocol, according to the following topology and the given configuration data.

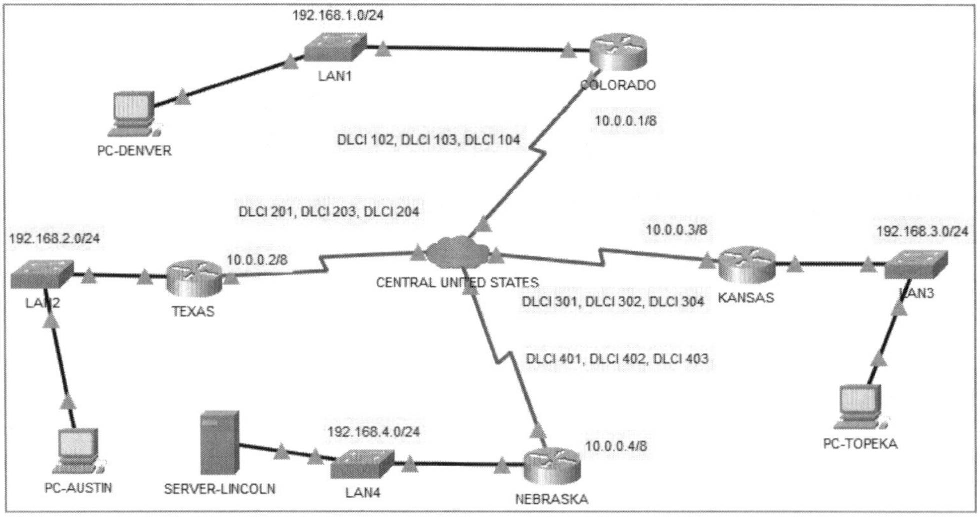

Figure 16.56 Network topology with Frame Relay protocol

Device	Interface	IP Address/subnet prefix	Default gateway
PC-DENVER	Fa0	192.168.1.2/24	192.168.1.1
PC-AUSTIN	Fa0	192.168.2.2/24	192.168.2.1

PC-TOPEKA	Fa0	192.168.3.2/24	192.168.3.1
SERVER-LINCOLN	Fa0	192.168.4.2/24	192.168.4.1
COLORADO	Fa0/0	192.168.1.1/24	-
COLORADO	Se0/0/0	10.0.0.1/8	-
TEXAS	Fa0/0	192.168.2.1/24	-
TEXAS	Se0/0/0	10.0.0.2/8	-
KANSAS	Fa0/0	192.168.3.1/24	-
KANSAS	Se0/0/0	10.0.0.3/8	-
NEBRASKA	Fa0/0	192.168.4.1/24	-
NEBRASKA	Se0/0/0	10.0.0.4/8	-

Table 16.6 Devices addressing table

Router - interface	CENTRAL UNITED STATES interface
COLORADO Se0/0/0	Serial0
TEXAS Se0/0/0	Serial1
KANSAS Se0/0/0	Serial2
NEBRASKA Se0/0/0	Serial3

Table 16.7 Table of physical connections in the Frame Relay topology

Circuit number (DLCI)	Circuit name
102	COLORADO-TEXAS
103	COLORADO-KANSAS
104	COLORADO-NEBRASKA
201	TEXAS-COLORADO
203	TEXAS-KANSAS
204	TEXAS-NEBRASKA
301	KANSAS-COLORADO
302	KANSAS-TEXAS
304	KANSAS-NEBRASKA
401	NEBRASKA-COLORADO
402	NEBRASKA-TEXAS
403	NEBRASKA-KANSAS

Table 16.8 Internal DLCI circuit assignments.

Solution:

Step 1. Configure IP addresses for all devices. Don't forget to configure the correct DNS server address for the computers.

Step 2. On the SERVER-LINCOLN server, enable the DNS service and create a record assigning the URL **lincoln.com** to the IP address 192.168.4.2.

Step 3. Configure the RIPv2 routing protocol on all routers.

Step 4. For the **Se0/0/0** serial interface, set **frame-relay** encapsulation on each router, disable the **Inverse ARP** protocol and create a **DLCI** static mapping according to the previously given table.

For **COLORADO** router enter the following commands:

```
en
conf t
interface Serial0/0/0
ip address 10.0.0.1 255.0.0.0
encapsulation frame-relay
frame-relay map ip 10.0.0.2 102 broadcast cisco
frame-relay map ip 10.0.0.3 103 broadcast cisco
frame-relay map ip 10.0.0.4 104 broadcast cisco
no shutdown
end
```

For **KANSAS** router enter the following commands:

```
en
conf t
interface Serial0/0/0
ip address 10.0.0.3 255.0.0.0
encapsulation frame-relay
frame-relay map ip 10.0.0.1 301 broadcast cisco
frame-relay map ip 10.0.0.2 302 broadcast cisco
frame-relay map ip 10.0.0.4 304 broadcast cisco
no shutdown
end
```

For **NEBRASKA** router enter the following commands:

```
en
conf t
interface Serial0/0/0
```

```
ip address 10.0.0.4 255.0.0.0
encapsulation frame-relay
frame-relay map ip 10.0.0.1 401 broadcast cisco
frame-relay map ip 10.0.0.2 402 broadcast cisco
frame-relay map ip 10.0.0.3 403 broadcast cisco
no shutdown
end
```

For **TEXAS** router enter the following commands:

```
en
conf t
interface Serial0/0/0
ip address 10.0.0.2 255.0.0.0
encapsulation frame-relay
frame-relay map ip 10.0.0.1 201 broadcast cisco
frame-relay map ip 10.0.0.3 203 broadcast cisco
frame-relay map ip 10.0.0.4 204 broadcast cisco
no shutdown
end
```

Step 5. Configure the DLCI virtual circuits in the **CENTRAL UNITED STATES** switch.

To do this, define circuits 102,103,104 in the **[Config]→[Serial0]** tab.

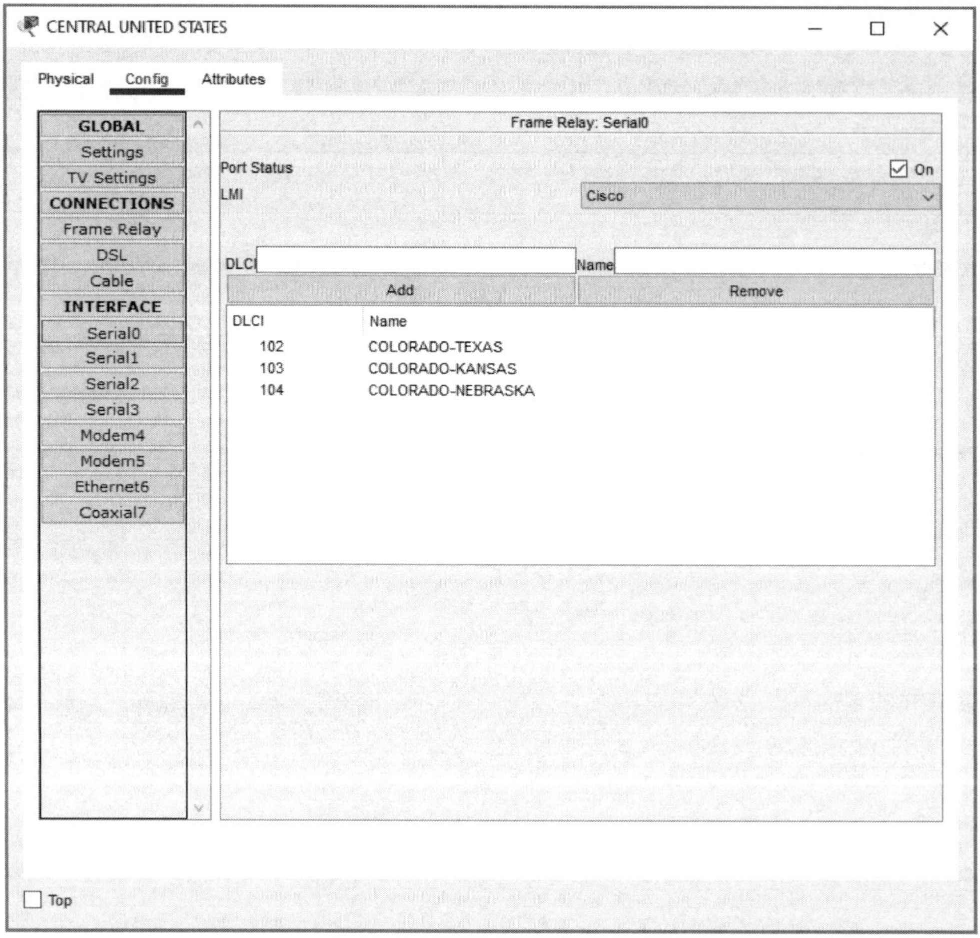

Figure 16.57 Define the DLCI circuits in the CENTRAL UNITED STATES for Serial0.

Then, under **[Config]→[Serial1]**, define circuits 201,203,204.

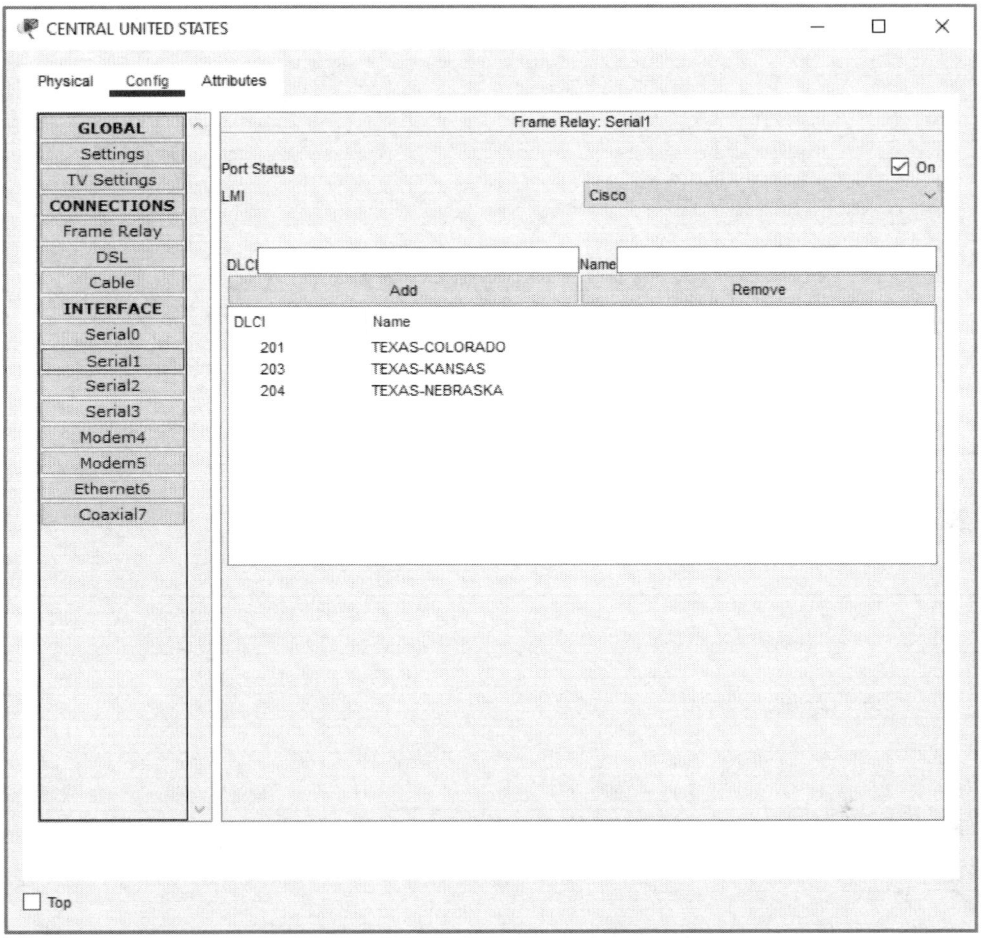

Figure 16.58 Define the DLCI circuits in the CENTRAL UNITED STATES for Serial1.

Then, under **[Config]→[Serial1]**, define circuits 301,302,304.

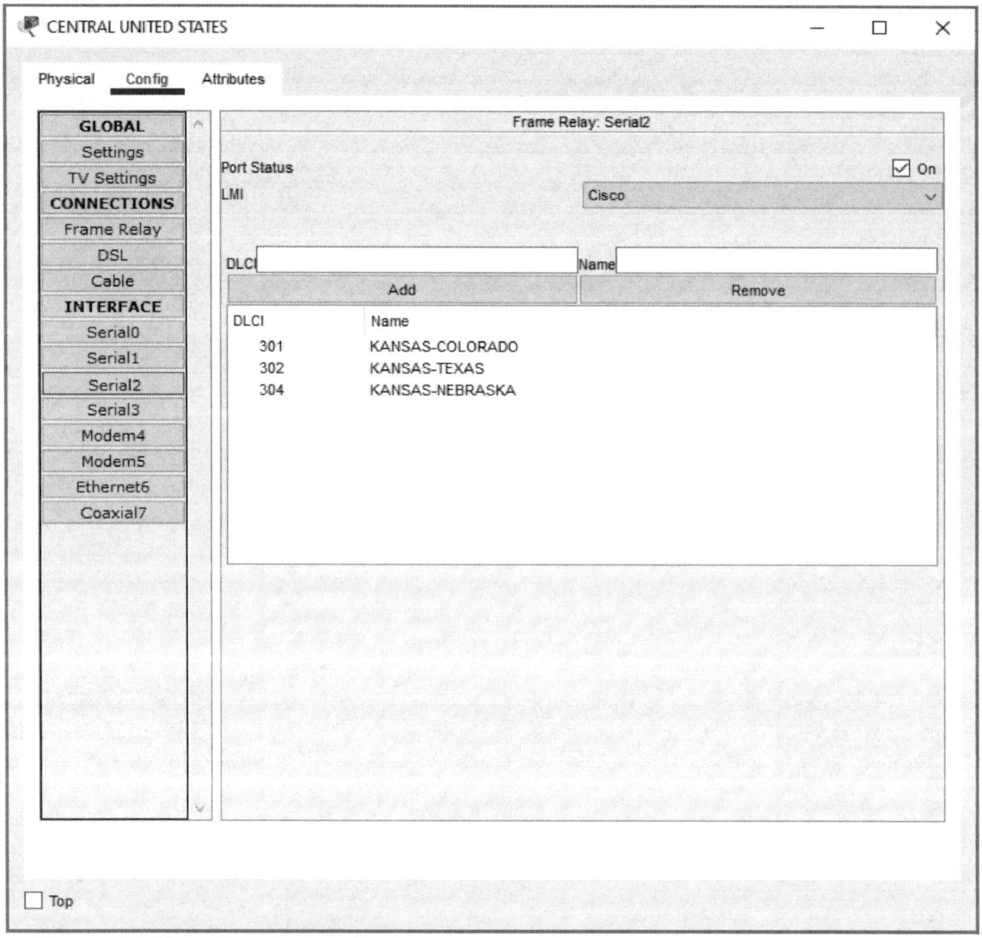

Figure 16.59 Define the DLCI circuits in the CENTRAL UNITED STATES for Serial2.

Then, under **[Config]→[Serial1]**, define circuits 401,402,403.

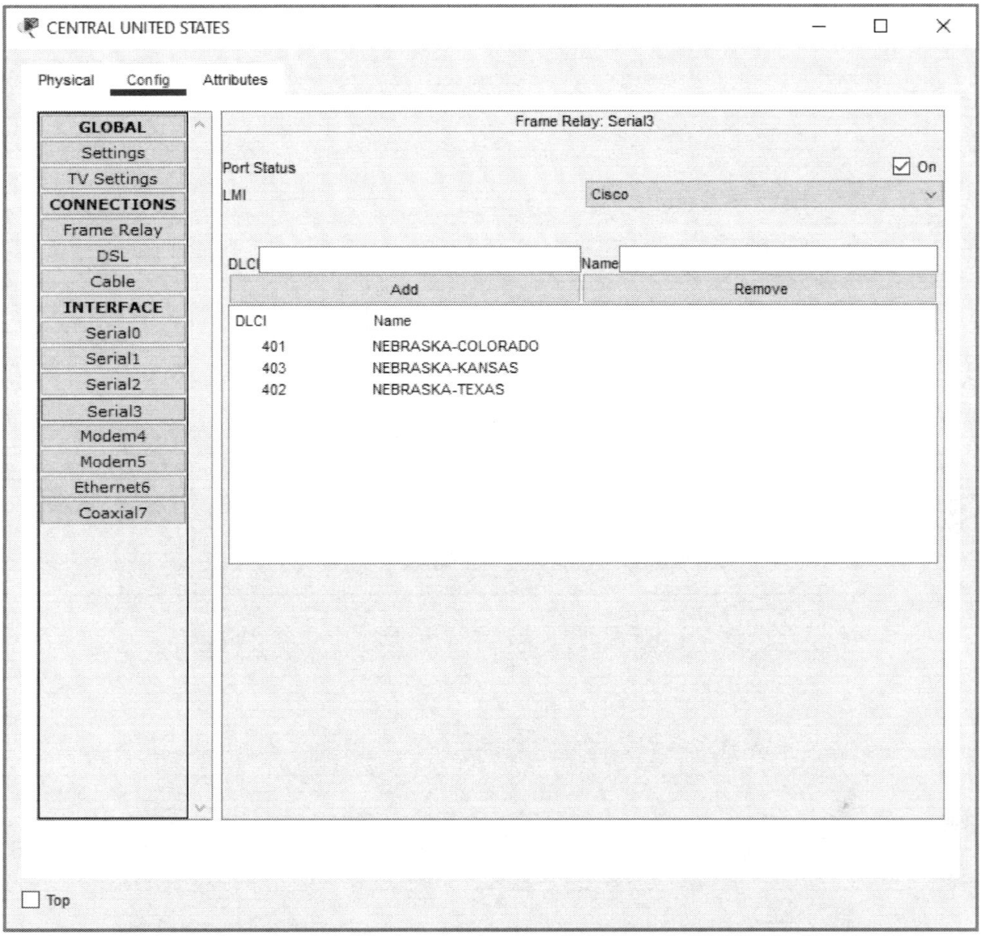

Figure 16.60 Define the DLCI circuits in the CENTRAL UNITED STATES for Serial3.

Once you have defined the relevant circuits, make their mutual association. To do this, go to the**[Config]→[Frame Relay]** tab. The internal DLCI circuit assignments are shown in the figure below.

	Port	Sublink	Port	Sublink
	From Port	Sublink	To Port	Sublink
1	Serial0	COLORADO-TEXAS	Serial1	TEXAS-COLORADO
2	Serial0	COLORADO-KANSAS	Serial2	KANSAS-COLORADO
3	Serial1	TEXAS-KANSAS	Serial2	KANSAS-TEXAS
4	Serial1	TEXAS-NEBRASKA	Serial3	NEBRASKA-TEXAS
5	Serial2	KANSAS-NEBRASKA	Serial3	NEBRASKA-KANSAS
6	Serial0	COLORADO-NEBRASKA	Serial3	NEBRASKA-COLORADO

Figure 16.61 Internal DLCI circuit assignments at CENTRAL UNITED STATES.

Step 6. Check the communication from the computers to the server.

```
C:\>ping 192.168.4.2

Pinging 192.168.4.2 with 32 bytes of data:

Reply from 192.168.4.2: bytes=32 time=2ms TTL=126
Reply from 192.168.4.2: bytes=32 time=12ms TTL=126
Reply from 192.168.4.2: bytes=32 time=2ms TTL=126
Reply from 192.168.4.2: bytes=32 time=12ms TTL=126
```

Figure 16.62 Check communication from PC-DENVER to SERVER-LINCOLN.

```
C:\>ping 192.168.4.2

Pinging 192.168.4.2 with 32 bytes of data:

Reply from 192.168.4.2: bytes=32 time=2ms TTL=126
Reply from 192.168.4.2: bytes=32 time=12ms TTL=126
Reply from 192.168.4.2: bytes=32 time=2ms TTL=126
Reply from 192.168.4.2: bytes=32 time=12ms TTL=126
```

Figure 16.63 Check communication from PC-AUSTIN to SERVER-LINCOLN

```
C:\>ping 192.168.4.2

Pinging 192.168.4.2 with 32 bytes of data:

Reply from 192.168.4.2: bytes=32 time=2ms TTL=126
Reply from 192.168.4.2: bytes=32 time=12ms TTL=126
Reply from 192.168.4.2: bytes=32 time=2ms TTL=126
Reply from 192.168.4.2: bytes=32 time=12ms TTL=126
```

Figure 16.64 Check communication from PC-TOPEKA to SERVER-LINCOLN.

Step 7. Check that **lincoln.com** is available in your computer browsers.

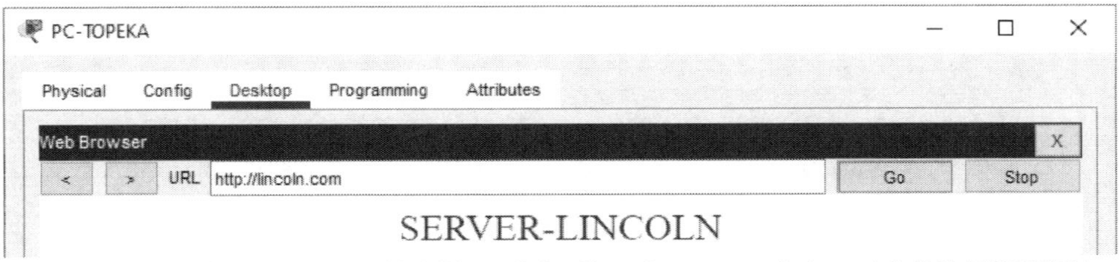

Figure 16.65 Check the availability of the lincoln.com website with PC-TOPEKA

Step 8. Check the DLCI mapping status on the individual routers.

Perform the mapping status check using the commands:

`show frame-relay map,`
`show frame-relay lmi.`

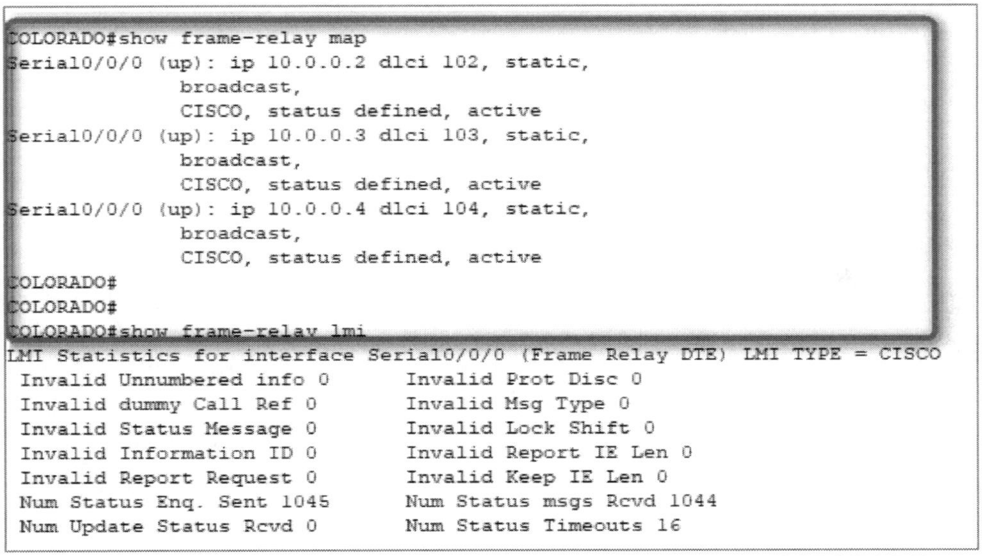

```
COLORADO#show frame-relay map
Serial0/0/0 (up): ip 10.0.0.2 dlci 102, static,
              broadcast,
              CISCO, status defined, active
Serial0/0/0 (up): ip 10.0.0.3 dlci 103, static,
              broadcast,
              CISCO, status defined, active
Serial0/0/0 (up): ip 10.0.0.4 dlci 104, static,
              broadcast,
              CISCO, status defined, active
COLORADO#
COLORADO#
COLORADO#show frame-relay lmi
LMI Statistics for interface Serial0/0/0 (Frame Relay DTE) LMI TYPE = CISCO
 Invalid Unnumbered info 0        Invalid Prot Disc 0
 Invalid dummy Call Ref 0         Invalid Msg Type 0
 Invalid Status Message 0         Invalid Lock Shift 0
 Invalid Information ID 0         Invalid Report IE Len 0
 Invalid Report Request 0         Invalid Keep IE Len 0
 Num Status Enq. Sent 1045        Num Status msgs Rcvd 1044
 Num Update Status Rcvd 0         Num Status Timeouts 16
```

Figure 16.66 Check DLCI circuit mapping status on the router COLORADO.

```
TEXAS#show frame-relay map
Serial0/0/0 (up): ip 10.0.0.1 dlci 201, static,
              broadcast,
              CISCO, status defined, active
Serial0/0/0 (up): ip 10.0.0.3 dlci 203, static,
              broadcast,
              CISCO, status defined, active
Serial0/0/0 (up): ip 10.0.0.4 dlci 204, static,
              broadcast,
              CISCO, status defined, active
TEXAS#show frame-relay lmi
LMI Statistics for interface Serial0/0/0 (Frame Relay DTE) LMI TYPE = CISCO
  Invalid Unnumbered info 0          Invalid Prot Disc 0
  Invalid dummy Call Ref 0           Invalid Msg Type 0
  Invalid Status Message 0           Invalid Lock Shift 0
  Invalid Information ID 0           Invalid Report IE Len 0
  Invalid Report Request 0           Invalid Keep IE Len 0
  Num Status Enq. Sent 1083          Num Status msgs Rcvd 1082
  Num Update Status Rcvd 0           Num Status Timeouts 16
```

Figure 16.67 Check DLCI circuit mapping status on the router TEXAS.

```
KANSAS#show frame-relay map
Serial0/0/0 (up): ip 10.0.0.1 dlci 301, static,
              broadcast,
              CISCO, status defined, active
Serial0/0/0 (up): ip 10.0.0.2 dlci 302, static,
              broadcast,
              CISCO, status defined, active
Serial0/0/0 (up): ip 10.0.0.4 dlci 304, static,
              broadcast,
              CISCO, status defined, active
KANSAS#show frame-relay lmi
LMI Statistics for interface Serial0/0/0 (Frame Relay DTE) LMI TYPE = CISCO
  Invalid Unnumbered info 0          Invalid Prot Disc 0
  Invalid dummy Call Ref 0           Invalid Msg Type 0
  Invalid Status Message 0           Invalid Lock Shift 0
  Invalid Information ID 0           Invalid Report IE Len 0
  Invalid Report Request 0           Invalid Keep IE Len 0
  Num Status Enq. Sent 1098          Num Status msgs Rcvd 1097
  Num Update Status Rcvd 0           Num Status Timeouts 16
```

Figure 16.68 Check DLCI circuit mapping status on the router KANSAS.

```
NEBRASKA#show frame-relay map
Serial0/0/0 (up): ip 10.0.0.1 dlci 401, static,
              broadcast,
              CISCO, status defined, active
Serial0/0/0 (up): ip 10.0.0.2 dlci 402, static,
              broadcast,
              CISCO, status defined, active
Serial0/0/0 (up): ip 10.0.0.3 dlci 403, static,
              broadcast,
              CISCO, status defined, active
NEBRASKA#show frame-relay lmi
LMI Statistics for interface Serial0/0/0 (Frame Relay DTE) LMI TYPE = CISCO
  Invalid Unnumbered info 0          Invalid Prot Disc 0
  Invalid dummy Call Ref 0           Invalid Msg Type 0
  Invalid Status Message 0           Invalid Lock Shift 0
  Invalid Information ID 0           Invalid Report IE Len 0
  Invalid Report Request 0           Invalid Keep IE Len 0
  Num Status Enq. Sent 1127          Num Status msgs Rcvd 1126
  Num Update Status Rcvd 0           Num Status Timeouts 16
```

Figure 16.69 Check DLCI circuit mapping status on the router NEBRASKA.

16.10.2 Exercise (No. 46) – Configuring the Frame Relay Protocol

Perform Frame Relay protocol and RIP protocol configuration and checking.

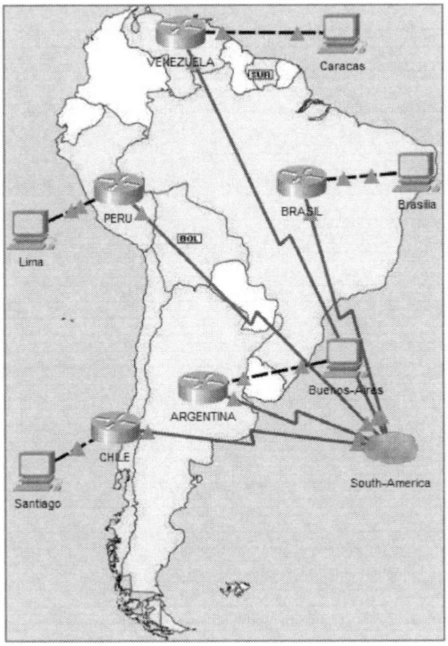

Figure 16.70 Network topology.

The Frame Relay network topology consists of:

- **South-America** cloud (Cloud-PT-Empty type),

- **five routers of type 1841** (ARGENTINA, BRASIL, CHILE, PERU, VENEZUELA),
- and **five computers** (Caracas, Brasilia, Santiago, Buenos-Aires, Lima).

Note!: Cloud-PT-Empty must be equipped with five **PT-CLOUD-NM-1S** modules.

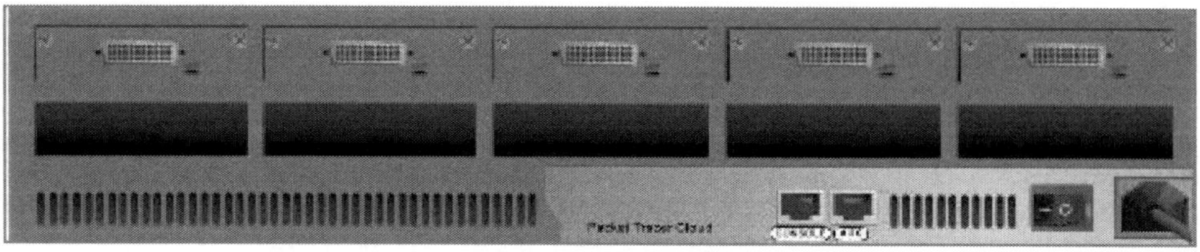

Figure 16.71 South-America cloud equipment.

Device	Interface	IP Address/Subnet prefix	Default gate
Buenos-Aires	Fa0	192.168.1.2/24	192.168.1.1
Brasilia	Fa0	192.168.2.2/24	192.168.2.1
Santiago	Fa0	192.168.3.2/24	192.168.3.1
Lima	Fa0	192.168.4.2/24	192.168.4.1
Caracas	Fa0	192.168.5.2/24	192.168.5.1
ARGENTINA	Se0/0/0	10.0.0.1/8	-
BRASIL	Se0/0/0	10.0.0.2/8	-
CHILE	Se0/0/0	10.0.0.3/8	-
PERU	Se0/0/0	10.0.0.4/8	-

Table 16.9 Devices addressing table

Router	Interface of the South-America cloud
ARGENTINA	Serial0
BRASIL	Serial1
CHILE	Serial2
PERU	Serial3
VENEZUELA	Serial4

Table 16.10 Table of physical connections in Frame Relay topology.

Note that the names of the individual routers are in alphabetical order and assigned to the logical circuits (DLCIs) of Frame Relay in the same order.

Solution:

Step 1. Create topology for Frame Relay network .

Step 2. Configure IP addresses in LAN networks and WAN network.

Step 3. Configure the ARGENTINA router interface for Frame Relay networking.

On the **ARGENTINA** router, enter serial interface configuration mode **Se0/0/0**. Set **Frame Relay** encapsulation and disable **Inverse ARP** protocol and create a **DLCI** static mapping.

```
interface Se0/0/0
ip address 10.0.0.1  255.0.0.0
encapsulation frame-relay
no frame-relay inverse-arp
frame-relay map ip  10.0.0.2 102 broadcast cisco
frame-relay map ip  10.0.0.3 103 broadcast cisco
frame-relay map ip  10.0.0.4 104 broadcast cisco
frame-relay map ip  10.0.0.5 105 broadcast cisco
no shutdown
```

Step 4. Configure the BRASIL router interface for Frame Relay operation.

On the **BRASIL** router, enter the serial interface configuration mode **Se0/0/0**. Set **frame-relay** encapsulation and disable the **Inverse ARP** protocol and create a **DLCI** static mapping.

```
interface Se0/0/0
ip address 10.0.0.2 255.0.0.0
encapsulation frame-relay
no frame-relay inverse-arp

frame-relay map ip 10.0.0.1 201 broadcast cisco
frame-relay map ip 10.0.0.3 203 broadcast cisco
frame-relay map ip 10.0.0.4 204 broadcast cisco
frame-relay map ip 10.0.0.5 205 broadcast cisco
no shutdown
```

Step 5. Configure the CHILE router interface for Frame Relay operation.

On the **CHILE** router, enter the serial interface configuration mode **Se0/0/0**. Set **frame-relay** encapsulation and disable **Inverse ARP** protocol and create **DLCI** static mapping.

```
interface Se0/0/0
```

```
ip address 10.0.0.3  255.0.0.0
encapsulation frame-relay
no frame-relay inverse-arp

frame-relay map ip 10.0.0.1 301 broadcast cisco
frame-relay map ip 10.0.0.2 302 broadcast cisco
frame-relay map ip 10.0.0.4 304 broadcast cisco
frame-relay map ip 10.0.0.5 305 broadcast cisco
no shutdown
```

Step 6. Configure the PERU router interface for Frame Relay operation.

On the **PERU** router, enter the serial interface configuration mode **Se0/0/0**. Set frame-relay encapsulation and disable the **Inverse ARP** protocol and create a **DLCI** static mapping.

```
interface Se0/0/0
ip address 10.0.0.4 255.0.0.0
encapsulation frame-relay
no frame-relay inverse-arp

frame-relay map ip 10.0.0.1 401 broadcast cisco
frame-relay map ip 10.0.0.2 402 broadcast cisco
frame-relay map ip 10.0.0.3 403 broadcast cisco
frame-relay map ip 10.0.0.5 405 broadcast cisco
no shutdown
```

Step 7. Configure the VENEZUELA router interface for Frame Relay operation.

On the **VENEZUELA** router, enter the serial interface configuration mode **Se0/0/0**. Set **frame-relay** encapsulation and disable the **Inverse ARP** protocol and create a **DLCI** static mapping.

```
interface Se0/0/0
ip address 10.0.0.5  255.0.0.0
encapsulation frame-relay
no frame-relay inverse-arp
```

```
frame-relay map ip 10.0.0.1 501 broadcast cisco
frame-relay map ip 10.0.0.2 502 broadcast cisco
frame-relay map ip 10.0.0.3 503 broadcast cisco
frame-relay map ip 10.0.0.4 504 broadcast cisco
no shutdown
```

Step 8. Configure the virtual circuits on the South-America switch.

To configure virtual circuits on the **South-America** switch, you must perform the following two steps:

- mapping of an internal physical interface to a DLCI number,
- mapping of internal physical interfaces (ports).

On the **Config - INTERFACE** tab, create internal physical port mappings to **DLCI** circuits. Since you are using Cisco devices, leave the **LMI** parameter setting to the default (Cisco). Use the following table.

Cloud interface South-America	DLCI	Circuit name
Serial0	102	ARGENTINA-BRASIL
Serial0	103	ARGENTINA-CHILE
Serial0	104	ARGENTINA-PERU
Serial0	105	ARGENTINA-VENEZUELA
Serial1	201	BRASIL-ARGENTINA
Serial1	203	BRASIL-CHILE
Serial1	204	BRASIL-PERU
Serial1	205	BRASIL-VENEZUELA
Serial2	301	CHILE-ARGENTINA
Serial2	302	CHILE-BRASIL
Serial2	304	CHILE-PERU
Serial2	305	CHILE-VENEZUELA
Serial3	401	PERU-ARGENTINA
Serial3	402	PERU-BRASIL
Serial3	403	PERU-CHILE
Serial3	405	PERU-VENEZUELA
Serial4	501	VENEZUELA-ARGENTINA
Serial4	502	VENEZUELA-BRASIL
Serial4	503	VENEZUELA-CHILE
Serial4	504	VENEZUELA-PERU

Table 16.11 South-America's internal DLCI assignments.

Open the **South-America** cloud and go to the **Config** tab. Then, in the **INTERFACE** section, select the **Serial0** serial interface. For this interface, perform the circuit mapping according to the table.

DLCI	Name
102	ARGENTINA-BRASIL
103	ARGENTINA-CHILE
104	ARGENTINA-PERU
105	ARGENTINA-VENEZUELA

Figure 16.72 DLCI circuit mapping on the Serial0 interface.

Perform similar operations for the other serial interfaces: **Serial1, Serial2, Serial3, Serial4.** Remember to use the correct data found in the DLCI internal assignment table.

Step 9. Configure the South-America switch (port mapping).

In the **South-America** cloud, go to the **Config** tab. In the **CONNECTIONS** section, select the **Frame Relay** option. Under **Frame Relay**, use the drop-down lists and the **Add** button to add port mappings between internal physical interfaces.

	From Port	Sublink	To Port	Sublink
1	Serial0	ARGENTINA-BRASIL	Serial1	BRASIL-ARGENTINA
2	Serial0	ARGENTINA-CHILE	Serial2	CHILE-ARGENTINA
3	Serial0	ARGENTINA-PERU	Serial3	PERU-ARGENTINA
4	Serial0	ARGENTINA-VENEZUELA	Serial4	VENEZUELA-ARGENTINA
5	Serial1	BRASIL-CHILE	Serial2	CHILE-BRASIL
6	Serial1	BRASIL-PERU	Serial3	PERU-BRASIL
7	Serial1	BRASIL-VENEZUELA	Serial4	VENEZUELA-BRASIL
8	Serial2	CHILE-PERU	Serial3	PERU-CHILE
9	Serial2	CHILE-VENEZUELA	Serial4	VENEZUELA-CHILE
10	Serial3	PERU-VENEZUELA	Serial4	VENEZUELA-PERU

Figure 73 Port mappings between internal physical interfaces.

Step 10. Configure the RIP V2 routing protocol on all routers.

You have six subnets:

- 10.0.0.0,
- 192.168.1.0,
- 192.168.2.0,
- 192.168.3.0,
- 192.168.4.0,
- 192.168.5.0.

To configure the RIP protocol, use the following commands:

```
rip router
version 2
network
```

Step 11. Check the status of DLCI mapping on the routers

On the ARGENTINA router, run the commands for this purpose:

```
show frame-relay map
show frame-relay lmi
```

```
ARGENTINA#show frame-relay map
Serial0/0/0 (up): ip 10.0.0.2 dlci 102, static,
              broadcast,
              CISCO, status defined, active
Serial0/0/0 (up): ip 10.0.0.3 dlci 103, static,
              broadcast,
              CISCO, status defined, active
Serial0/0/0 (up): ip 10.0.0.4 dlci 104, static,
              broadcast,
              CISCO, status defined, active
Serial0/0/0 (up): ip 10.0.0.5 dlci 105, static,
              broadcast,
              CISCO, status defined, active
ARGENTINA#
ARGENTINA#
ARGENTINA#show frame-relay lmi
LMI Statistics for interface Serial0/0/0 (Frame Relay DTE) LMI TYPE = CISCO
```

Figure 16.74 Check DLCI circuit mapping status on ARGENTINA.

Perform the same commands on the other routers: **BRASIL, CHILE, PERU, VENEZUELA.**

Step 12: Check the communication between LANs.

Finally, check the communication between the computers of **Caracas, Brasilia, Santiago, Buenos-Aires, Lima**. To do this, use the **ping** command, execute it on the command line.

```
PC>ping 192.168.3.2

Pinging 192.168.3.2 with 32 bytes of data:

Reply from 192.168.3.2: bytes=32 time=2ms TTL=126
Reply from 192.168.3.2: bytes=32 time=2ms TTL=126
Reply from 192.168.3.2: bytes=32 time=2ms TTL=126
Reply from 192.168.3.2: bytes=32 time=2ms TTL=126
```

Figure 16.75 Checking communication from Caracas to Santiago.

16.10.3 Exercise (No. 47) – Configuring Frame Relay Using Subinterfaces

In this exercise, the Frame Relay network topology consists of:

- a **V4** cloud, i.e. a Frame Relay switch,
- **four routers of type 1841 (PRAGUE, WARSAW, BRATISLAVA, BUDAPEST)**,
- four switches (**S0, S1, S2, S3**),
- and four computers (**PC1, PC2, PC3, PC4**).

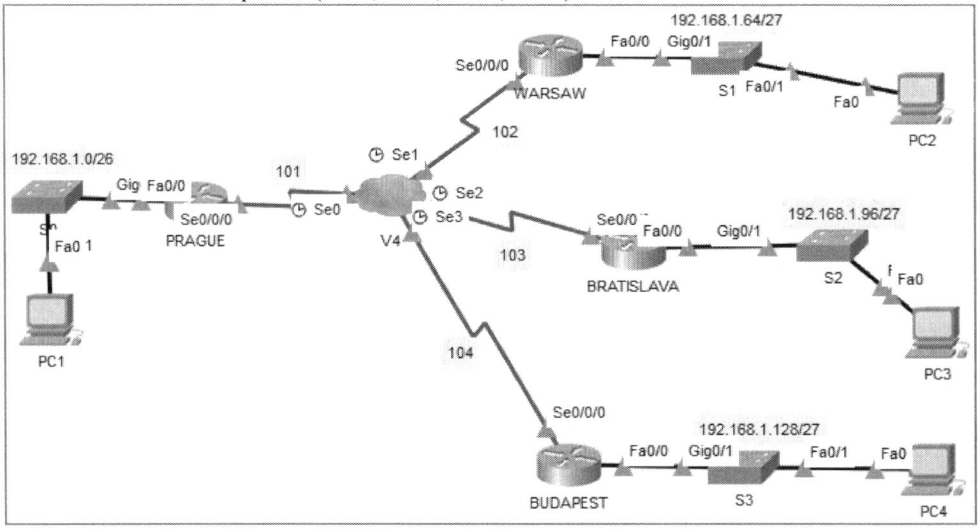

Figure 16.76 Frame Relay network topology.

Device	Interface	IP Address/Subnet prefix	Default gateway
PC1	Fa0	192.168.1.2/26	192.168.1.1
PC2	Fa0	192.168.1.66/27	192.168.1.65
PC3	Fa0	192.168.1.98/27	192.168.1.97
PC4	Fa0	192.168.1.130/27	192.168.1.129

PRAGUE	Fa0/0	192.168.1.1/26	-
PRAGUE	Se0/0/0.102	192.168.1.245/30	-
PRAGUE	Se0/0/0.103	192.168.1.249/30	-
PRAGUE	Se0/0/0.104	192.168.1.253/30	-
WARSAW	Fa0/0	192.168.1.65/27	-
WARSAW	Se0/0/0.101	192.168.1.246/30	-
BRATISLAVA	Fa0/0	192.168.1.97/27	-
BRATISLAVA	Se0/0/0.101	192.168.1.250/30	-
BUDAPEST	Fa0/0	192.168.1.129/27	-
BUDAPEST	Se0/0/0.101	192.168.1.254/30	-

Table 16.12 Devices addressing table

Router - Subinterface	V4 cloud's interface
PRAGUE Se0/0/0.102, Se0/0/0.103, Se0/0/0.104	Serial0
WARSAW Se0/0/0.101	Serial1
BRATISLAVA Se0/0/0.101	Serial2
BUDAPEST Se0/0/0.101	Serial3

Table 16.13 Table of physical connections in Frame Relay topology.

Solution :

Step 1. Create a Frame Relay network topology.

Step 2. Configure the IP addresses of the LAN and WAN.

Step 3. Configure the BRATISLAVA router to operate in the Frame Relay network.

Set up **frame-relay** encapsulation, configure subinterfaces and static routing.

```
enable
configure terminal
interface serial 0/0/0
encapsulation frame-relay
no shutdown
exit
interface serial 0/0/0.101 point-to-point
ip address 192.168.1.250 255.255.255.252
frame-relay interface-dlci 101
exit
ip route 0.0.0.0 0.0.0.0 192.168.1.249
```

Step 4. Configure the **BUDAPEST** router for operation in a Frame Relay network.

Set up **frame-relay** encapsulation, configure subinterfaces and static routing.

```
enable
configure terminal
interface serial 0/0/0
encapsulation frame-relay
no shutdown
exit
interface serial 0/0/0.101 point-to-point
ip address 192.168.1.254 255.255.255.252
frame-relay interface-dlci 101
exit
ip route 0.0.0.0 0.0.0.0 192.168.1.253
```

Step 5. Configure the **PRAGUE** router for operation in a Frame Relay network.

Set up **frame-relay** encapsulation, configure subinterfaces and static routing.enable

```
configure terminal
interface serial 0/0/0
encapsulation frame-relay
no shutdown
exit

interface serial 0/0/0.102 point-to-point
ip address 192.168.1.245 255.255.255.252
frame-relay interface-dlci 102
exit

interface serial 0/0/0.103 point-to-point
ip address 192.168.1.249 255.255.255.252
frame-relay interface-dlci 103
exit

interface serial 0/0/0.104 point-to-point
ip address 192.168.1.253 255.255.255.252
frame-relay interface-dlci 104
```

```
exit

ip route 192.168.1.64 255.255.255.224 192.168.1.246
ip route 192.168.1.96 255.255.255.224 192.168.1.250
ip route 192.168.1.128 255.255.255.224 192.168.1.254
```

Step 6. Configure the **WARSAW** router for operation in a Frame Relay network.

Set up **frame-relay** encapsulation, configure subinterfaces and static routing.enable

```
configure terminal
interface serial 0/0/0
encapsulation frame-relay
no shutdown
exit

interface serial 0/0/0.101 point-to-point
ip address 192.168.1.246 255.255.255.252
frame-relay interface-dlci 101
exit
ip route 0.0.0.0 0.0.0.0 192.168.1.245
```

Step 7. Configure virtual circuits in the **V4** cloud

To configure virtual circuits in the **V4** cloud, you need to perform the following steps:

- mapping an internal physical interface to a DLCI number,
- mapping of internal physical interfaces (ports).

Open the **V4** cloud and go to the **Config** tab. Then, in the **INTERFACE** section for each serial interface, perform a circuit mapping.

DLCI	Name
102	S0toS1
103	S0toS2
104	S0toS3

Figure 16.77 DLCI circuit mapping on Serial0 interface.

Perform similar operations for the other serial interfaces: **Serial1, Serial2, Serial3**.

Step 8. Configure the V4 cloud (port mapping).

In the **V4** cloud, go to the **Config** tab. In the **CONNECTIONS** section, select **Frame Relay**. Under **Frame Relay**, using the drop-down lists and the **Add** button, add port mappings between the internal physical interfaces.

	From Port	Sublink	To Port	Sublink
1	Serial0	S0toS1	Serial1	S1toS0
2	Serial0	S0toS2	Serial2	S2toS0
3	Serial0	S0toS3	Serial3	S3toS0
4	Serial2	S2toS3	Serial3	S3toS2

Figure 16.78 Port mappings between internal physical interfaces.

Step 9. Check the status of DLCI mappings on the routers.

To do this, run the command on the PRAGUE router: **`show frame-relay map`**.

```
PRAGUE#show frame-relay map
Serial0/0/0.102 (up): point-to-point dlci, dlci 102, broadcast, status defined,
active
Serial0/0/0.103 (up): point-to-point dlci, dlci 103, broadcast, status defined,
active
Serial0/0/0.104 (up): point-to-point dlci, dlci 104, broadcast, status defined,
active
```

Figure 16.79 Checking the status of DLCI circuit mapping on PRAGUE.

Run the same command for the other routers: **WARSAW, BRATISLAVA, BUDAPEST**.

Step 10. Check communication between LANs.

Finally, check the communication between **PC1, PC2, PC3, PC4**. To do this use the **ping** command, execute it on the command line.

```
PC>ping 192.168.1.129

Pinging 192.168.1.129 with 32 bytes of data:

Reply from 192.168.1.129: bytes=32 time=3ms TTL=254
Reply from 192.168.1.129: bytes=32 time=2ms TTL=254
Reply from 192.168.1.129: bytes=32 time=2ms TTL=254
Reply from 192.168.1.129: bytes=32 time=2ms TTL=254
```

Figure 16.80 Checking communication from PC1 to PC4

16.11 PPP Protocol

16.11.1 Exercise (No. 48) – Configuring PPP with PAP Authentication.

The network topology consists of three routers and three computers. Configure the **PPP** protocol with **PAP** authentication between the routers and the routing protocol, according to the topology below.

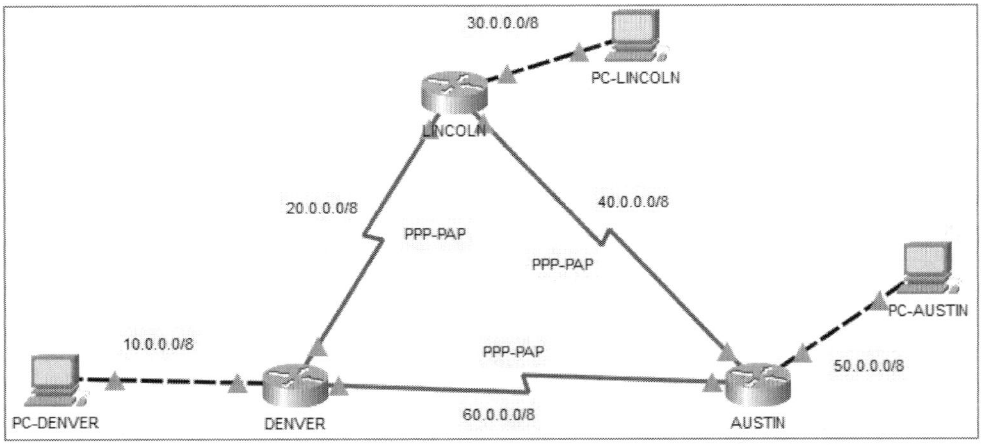

Figure 16.81 Network topology with PPP and PAP authentication.

Step 1. Create the network topology.

Step 2. Configure IP addresses for all devices.

Step 3. Configure the RIP routing protocol on all routers.

Step 4. Configure host names, user names, and passwords on all routers.

Remember that the user names must be exactly the same as the host names, because this type of authentication uses the host name as the user.

To do this on the DENVER router, run the commands:

```
conf t
hostname DENVER
username  LINCOLN password LINCOLN123
username AUSTIN password AUSTIN123
```

On LINCOLN router execute command:

```
conf t
hostname LINCOLN
username DENVER password DENVER123
username AUSTIN password AUSTIN123
```

On AUSTIN router execute command:

```
conf t
hostname AUSTIN
username DENVER password DENVER123
username LINCOLN password LINCOLN123
```

Step 5. Configure PPP encapsulation with PAP authentication on the serial interfaces for all routers.

To configure PPP encapsulation with PAP authentication on the serial interfaces, use (in interface configuration mode) the commands:

```
encapsulation ppp
ppp pap sent-username <host_name> password <password>
```

On the DENVER router on interface **Serial0/0/0**, configure PPP encapsulation and PAP authentication:

```
int Se0/0/0
encapsulation ppp
ppp pap sent-username LINCOLN password LINCOLN123
```

On the **Serial0/1/0** interface, configure PPP encapsulation and PAP authentication:

```
int Se0/1/0
encapsulation ppp
ppp pap sent-username AUSTIN password AUSTIN123
```

Configure PPP encapsulation and PAP authentication in the LINCOLN router on the **Serial0/0/0** interface:

```
int Se0/0/0
encapsulation ppp
ppp pap sent-username DENVER password DENVER123
```

On the **Serial0/1/0** interface, configure PPP encapsulation and PAP authentication:

```
int Se0/1/0
encapsulation ppp
ppp pap sent-username AUSTIN password  AUSTIN23
```

Note: With the message "**You have chosen a username/password combination that is valid for CHAP. This is a potential security hole** " don't worry. It is just a warning that PAP is not the best way to authenticate. A more secure authentication is **CHAP**.

On the AUSTIN router on the **Serial0/0/0** interface, configure PPP encapsulation and PAP authentication:

```
int Se0/0/0
encapsulation ppp
ppp pap sent-username DENVER password DENVER123
```

On the **Serial0/1/0** interface, configure PPP encapsulation and PAP authentication:

```
int Se0/1/0
encapsulation ppp
ppp pap sent-username LINCOLN password LINCOLN123
```

Step 6. Verify the PPP protocol parameters on the DENVER router using the command `show interfaces se0/0/0`

```
DENVER#show interfaces se0/0/0
Serial0/0/0 is up, line protocol is up (connected)
  Hardware is HD64570
  Internet address is 20.0.0.1/8
  MTU 1500 bytes, BW 64 Kbit, DLY 20000 usec,
     reliability 255/255, txload 1/255, rxload 1/255
  Encapsulation PPP, loopback not set, keepalive set (10 sec)
  LCP Open
  Open: IPCP, CDPCP
  Last input never, output never, output hang never
  Last clearing of "show interface" counters never
```

Figure 16.82 Fragment of the command result: `show interfaces se0/0/0`

The selected encapsulation is **PPP**. The **LCP** sublayer is open (i.e. it works). The **NCP** sublayer has enabled two sub-protocols (**IPCP, CDPCP**), i.e. it communicates with the network layer protocols: **IP, CDP**.

Step 7. Perform analogous PPP protocol verifications for the remaining routers.

Step 8. Also verify that the computers are communicating (PING command).

```
C:\>ping 50.0.0.2

Pinging 50.0.0.2 with 32 bytes of data:

Reply from 50.0.0.2: bytes=32 time=3ms TTL=126
Reply from 50.0.0.2: bytes=32 time=3ms TTL=126
Reply from 50.0.0.2: bytes=32 time=3ms TTL=126
Reply from 50.0.0.2: bytes=32 time=1ms TTL=126

Ping statistics for 50.0.0.2:
    Packets: Sent = 4, Received = 4, Lost = 0 (0% loss),
Approximate round trip times in milli-seconds:
    Minimum = 1ms, Maximum = 3ms, Average = 2ms
```

Figure 16.83 Result of the command: `ping` from computer PC-DENVER to PC-AUSTIN

16.11.2 Exercise (No. 49) – Configuring PPP with CHAP Authentication

The network topology consists of three routers and three computers. Configure the **PPP** protocol with **CHAP** authentication between the routers and the routing protocol, according to the following topology and the assumptions given in the table.

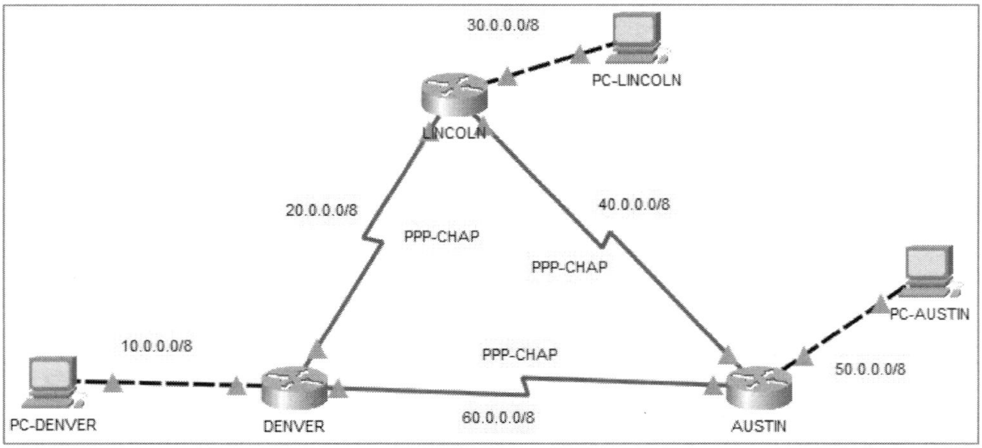

Figure 16.84 Network topology with PPP protocol and CHAP authentication.

Step 1 Create a network topology.

Step 2. Configure IP addresses for all devices.

Step 3. Configure the RIP routing protocol on all routers.

Assumptions:

Access to router	User name	Password
DENVER	Lincoln	Lincoln
DENVER	Austin	Austin
LINCOLN	Denver	Denver
LINCOLN	Austin	Austin
AUSTIN	Denver	Denver
AUSTIN	Lincoln	Lincoln

Table 16.14 CHAP configuration for router access

Step 4. Configure host names, user names and passwords on all routers.

Remember that the usernames must be exactly the same as the host names, as this type of authentication uses the host name as the user.

To do this on the **DENVER** router, run the commands:

```
conf t
hostname DENVER
username  Lincoln password Lincoln
username Austin password Austin
```

On router **LINCOLN** execute command:

```
conf t
hostname LINCOLN
username Denver password Denver
username Austin password Austin
```

On router **AUSTIN** execute command:

```
conf t
hostname AUSTIN
username Denver password Denver
username Lincoln password Lincoln
```

Step 5. Configure PPP encapsulation with CHAP authentication on the serial interfaces for all routers.

To configure PPP encapsulation with CHAP authentication on the serial interfaces, use (in interface configuration mode) the commands:

```
encapsulation  ppp
ppp authentication chap
```

On the **DENVER** router, configure PPP encapsulation and CHAP authentication:

```
int Se0/0/0
encapsulation ppp
ppp authentication chap
int Se0/1/0
encapsulation ppp
ppp authentication chap
```

In the **LINCOLN** router, configure PPP encapsulation and CHAP authentication:

```
int Se0/0/0
encapsulation ppp
ppp authentication chap
int Se0/1/0
```

```
encapsulation ppp
ppp authentication chap
```

On the **AUSTIN** router, configure PPP encapsulation and CHAP authentication:

```
int Se0/0/0
encapsulation ppp
ppp authentication chap
int Se0/1/0
encapsulation ppp
ppp authentication chap
```

Notice that the message **"You have chosen a username/password combination that is valid for CHAP does not appear. This is a potential security hole"** as it was in the previous exercise. This is because the more secure CHAP authentication method was used.

Step 6. Verify the PPP protocol parameters on the Rybnik router using the command, **`show interfaces se0/0/0`**

```
AUSTIN#show interfaces se0/0/0
Serial0/0/0 is up, line protocol is up (connected)
  Hardware is HD64570
  Internet address is 60.0.0.1/8
  MTU 1500 bytes, BW 64 Kbit, DLY 20000 usec,
     reliability 255/255, txload 1/255, rxload 1/255
  Encapsulation PPP, loopback not set, keepalive set (10 sec)
  LCP Open
  Open: IPCP, CDPCP
  Last input never, output never, output hang never
  Last clearing of "show interface" counters never
```

Figure 16.85 Fragment of the result of the command: `show interfaces se0/0/0`

The chosen encapsulation is **PPP**. The **LCP** sublayer is open (i.e. it works). The **NCP** sublayer has enabled two sub-protocols (**IPCP, CDPCP**), i.e. it communicates with the network layer protocols: **IP, CDP.**

Step 7. Perform analogous PPP protocol verifications for the remaining routers.

Step 8. Also verify that the computers are communicating (PING command).

```
C:\>ping 50.0.0.2

Pinging 50.0.0.2 with 32 bytes of data:

Reply from 50.0.0.2: bytes=32 time=3ms TTL=126
Reply from 50.0.0.2: bytes=32 time=3ms TTL=126
Reply from 50.0.0.2: bytes=32 time=3ms TTL=126
Reply from 50.0.0.2: bytes=32 time=1ms TTL=126

Ping statistics for 50.0.0.2:
    Packets: Sent = 4, Received = 4, Lost = 0 (0% loss),
Approximate round trip times in milli-seconds:
    Minimum = 1ms, Maximum = 3ms, Average = 2ms
```

Figure 16.86 Result of ping **command from PC-DENVER to PC-AUSTIN**

16.12 RADIUS protocol

16.12.1 Exercise (No. 50) – Configuring RADIUS Protocol

The network topology consists of one **LINCOLN** router, two computers (**PC LINCOLN, PC-AUSTIN**) and two servers (**SERVER, RADIUS**).

Configure an encrypted password for privileged mode for the **LINCOLN** router: **keepsmiling**.

To control telnet sessions and console access, configure the **LINCOLN** router to use **AAA** services:

- **authentication** (verifies who can log in),
- **authorization** (determines what actions are allowed by the login holder),
- **logging** (allows you to create reports containing the operations performed)

On the **SERVER** (192.168.10.6), **RADIUS** (192.168.10.2) servers, configure the RADIUS protocol using the **BeHappyDontWorry** public key encryption and port **1645**.

For the router, configure a login and password for user access.

login: cisco
password: cisco123

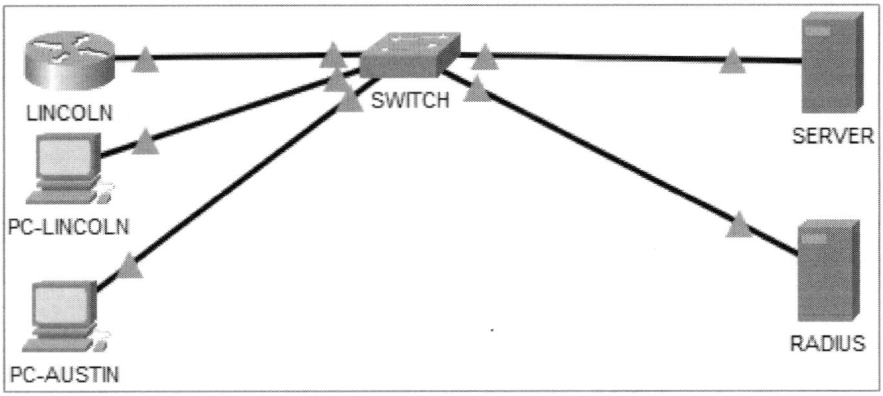

Figure 16.87 Exercise – Topology scheme.

Step 1. Create a network topology and perform basic IP addressing.

Perform the following IP addressing:

- PC-LINCOLN: 192.168.10.3/24, gateway address: 192.168.10.1,
- PC-AUSTIN: 192.168.10.4/24, gateway address: 192.168.10.1,
- Fa0/0 in LINCOLN: 192.168.10.1/24,
- Fa0 in SERVER: 192.168.10.6/24, gateway address: 192.168.10.1,
- Fa0 in RADIUS: 192.168.10.2/24, gateway address: 192.168.10.1.

Step 2. Change the privileged mode password on the LINCOLN router.

Configure an encrypted privileged mode password using the command

```
enable secret keepsmiling
```

Step 3. Configure AAA services on the LINCOLN router.

On the **LINCOLN** router, configure AAA services by setting the IP address of the RADIUS server (**192.168.10.2**), the IP address of the SERVER server (192.168.10.6) and the encryption key (**BeHappyDontWorry**), using the commands:

```
en
conf t
aaa new-model
aaa authentication login default group radius none
aaa authentication login telnet_lines group radius
aaa accounting exec default start-stop group radius
interface FastEthernet0/0
```

```
ip address 192.168.10.1 255.255.255.0
no shut
radius-server host 192.168.10.2 auth-port 1645 key
BeHappyDontWorry
radius-server host 192.168.10.6 auth-port 1645 key
BeHappyDontWorry
line vty 0 4
login authentication telnet_lines
accounting exec default
ntp update-calendar
end
```

Step 4. Configure the AAA service in the RADIUS server.

On the **RADIUS** server, select the **Services** tab, and the **AAA** section. Configure the RADIUS protocol according to the picture provided.

Figure 16.88 AAA configuration on server RADIUS.

Step 5. Test the operation of the RADIUS protocol for the telnet service.

To test the operation of the RADIUS protocol, log in to the TELNET service, then enter the privileged mode of the LINCOLN router, and then log out of the router.

At the command line of the PC-AUSTIN, execute the command to the LINCOLN router: **`telnet 192.168.10.1`**

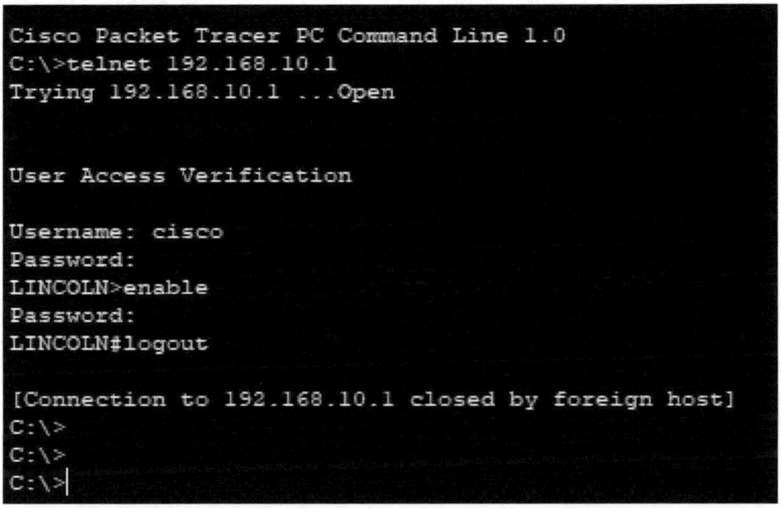

Figure 16.89 Login and logout to/from telnet service from PC-AUSTIN.

Step 6. Check the AAA security logs on the RADIUS server.

To check the RADIUS protocol logs, go to the **RADIUS** server. Then go to the **Desktop→AAA Accounting→RADIUS Accounting** tab. A window will appear containing records describing the operations performed.

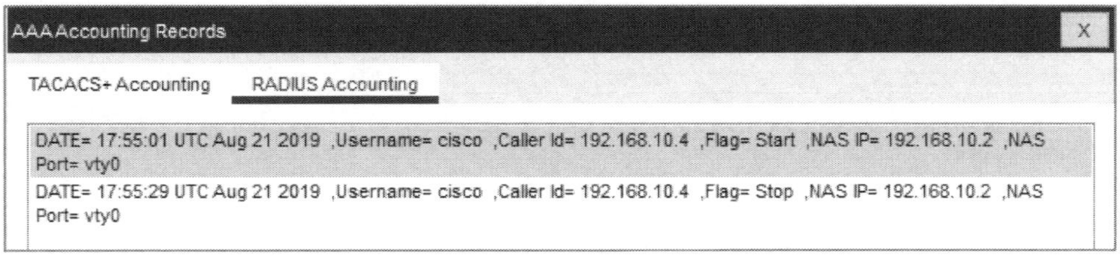

Figure 16.90 Report of operations performed.

From the above records, you can easily read that, for example:

- on **21.08.2019** at **17:55:01**, user cisco from address **192.168.10.4** logged in to address **192.168.10.2** using port **VTY0** (Flag=**Start**),
- on **21.08.2019** at **17:55:29**, user cisco from address **192.168.10.4** logged out from address **192.168.10.2** and port **VTY0** (Flag=**Stop**).

16.13 NETFLOW Technology

The chapter includes exercises demonstrating the use of NETFLOW technology to study network traffic.

Remember to save the status of the file periodically (keyboard shortcut CTRL+S) while performing exercises or control /project/ tasks.

16.13.1 Exercise (No. 51) – Testing Traffic Using Traditional NETFLOW

Step 1.Perform the following topology for traditional NETFLOW.

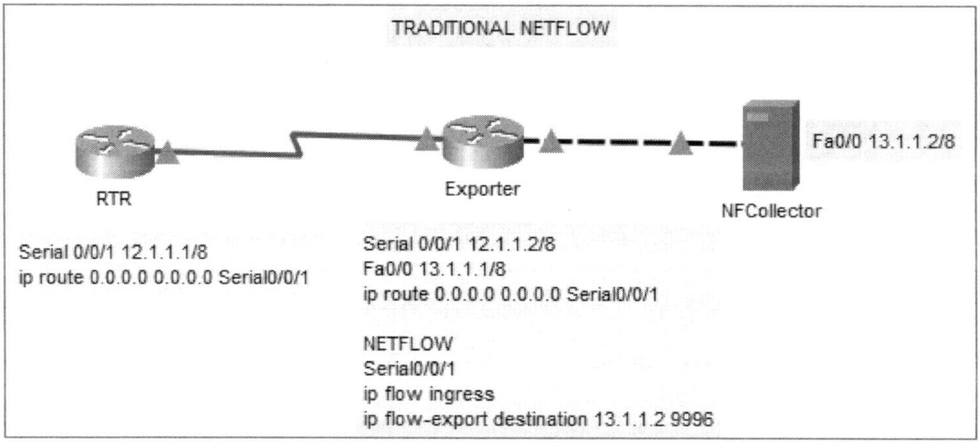

Figure 16.91 Exercise – topology scheme.

Step 2. Configure the topology according to the figure.

Step 3. Configure the default routes according to the figure.

Set static default routes on both routers: **`ip route 0.0.0.0 0.0.0.0 Serial 0/0/1`**

Step 4. Configure the NETFLOW export version.

On the **RTR** and **Exporter** routers, set version 9 for NETFLOW export.

```
ip flow-export version 9
```

Step 5. Configure the input interface of the Exporter router.

```
hostname Exporter
```

```
interface Serial0/0/1
ip flow ingress
```

Step 6. Configure the address of the information gathering device

```
ip flow-export destination 13.1.1.2 9996
```

Network traffic entering the **Exporter** router to the **Serial 0/0/1** interface will be captured and exported to a server called **NFCollector**, via UDP port number **9996**.

Step 7. Generate test traffic.

On the **RTR** router, ping to 13.1.1.2.

```
RTR#ping 13.1.1.2

Type escape sequence to abort.
Sending 5, 100-byte ICMP Echos to 13.1.1.2, timeout is 2 seconds:
!!!!!
Success rate is 100 percent (5/5), round-trip min/avg/max = 1/2/7 ms
```

Figure 16.92 Exercise - Generating network traffic.

In the **Exporter** router, check the buffer status with the command:

```
show ip cache flow
```

```
Exporter#show ip cache flow
IP packet size distribution (10 total packets):
   1-32   64   96  128  160  192  224  256  288  320  352  384  416  448  480
   .000 .000 .000 1.00 .000 .000 .000 .000 .000 .000 .000 .000 .000 .000 .000

    512  544  576 1024 1536 2048 2560 3072 3584 4096 4608
   .000 .000 .000 .000 .000 .000 .000 .000 .000 .000 .000

IP Flow Switching Cache, 278544 bytes
  0 active, 4096 inactive, 1 added
  3 ager polls, 0 flow alloc failures
  Active flows timeout in 30 minutes
  Inactive flows timeout in 15 seconds
IP Sub Flow Cache, 34056 bytes
  0 active, 1024 inactive, 0 added, 0 added to flow
  0 alloc failures, 0 force free
  1 chunk, 1 chunk added
  last clearing of statistics never
Protocol         Total    Flows   Packets Bytes  Packets Active(Sec) Idle(Sec)
--------         Flows     /Sec     /Flow  /Pkt     /Sec     /Flow     /Flow
ICMP                 1      0.0        10   128      0.0       5.0      15.0
Total:               1      0.0        10   128      0.0       5.0      15.0

SrcIf         SrcIPaddress    DstIf         DstIPaddress    Pr SrcP DstP  Pkts
```

Figure 16.93 Exercise - Check buffer status.

Step 8. Check the collected traffic information.

In the **NFCollector** server under the **[Desktop]** tab, start the application: **Netflow Collector.**

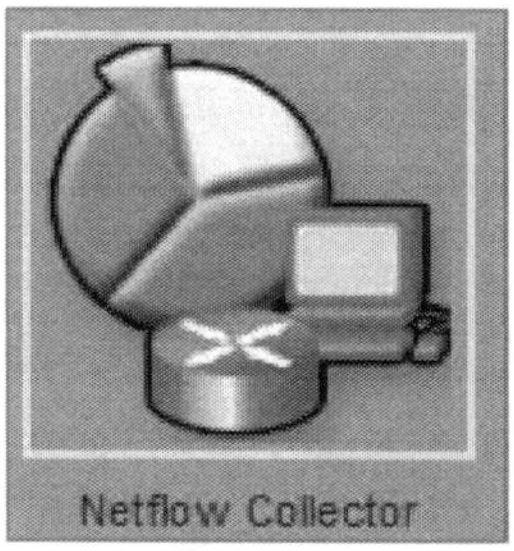

Figure 16.94 Exercise - Netflow Collector application.

To get the information collected about the traffic coming into the Se0/0/1 router **Exporter**, click on the circle.

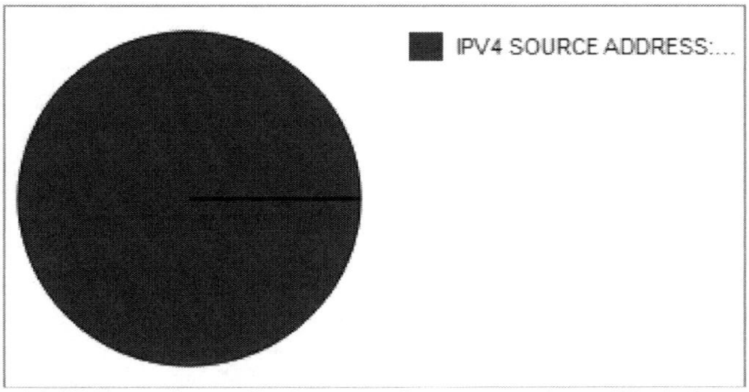

Figure 16.95 Exercise - Circle grouping network traffic information.

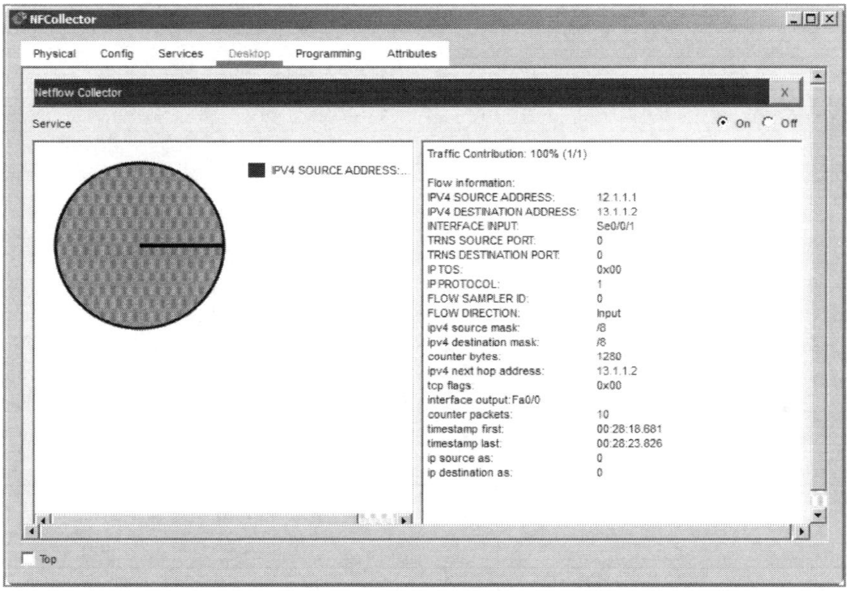

Figure 16.96 Exercise - Network traffic information collected.

16.13.2 Exercise (No. 52) - Testing Traffic Using Flexible NETFLOW

Step 1. Perform the following topology.

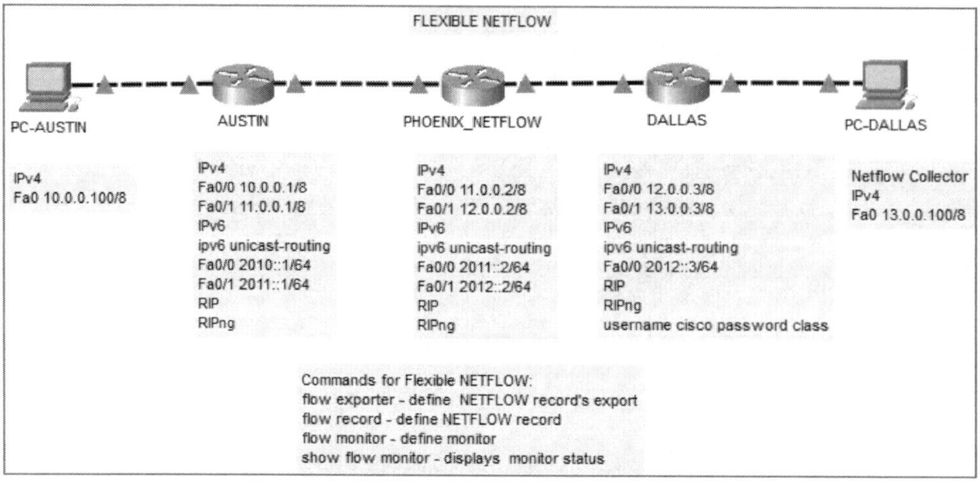

Figure 16.97 Exercise – Topology scheme.

Step 2. Configure the topology according to the figure (IPv4 and IPv6 addresses).

Interface	IPv4	IPv6
Fa0/0	10.0.0.1/8	2010::1/64
Fa0/1	11.0.0.1/8	2011::1/64

Table 16.15 Router AUSTIN addressing.

Interface	IPv4	IPv6
Fa0/0	11.0.0.2/8	2011::2/64
Fa0/1	12.0.0.2/8	2012::2/64

Table 16.16 Router PHOENIX_NETFLOW addressing.

Interface	IPv4	IPv6
Fa0/0	12.0.0.3/8	2012::3/64
Fa0/1	13.0.0.3/8	2013::3/64

Table 16.17 Router DALLAS addressing .

Step 3. Configure RIP (RIP v1 and RIPng).

On the routers, configure RIPv1 (for IPv4) and RIPng (for IPv6).

Step 4. In the DALLAS, create a local account: RIP (RIP v1 and RIPng).

Login: cisco
Password: class

Step 5. Configure the NETFLOW export version.

On the routers, set version 9 for NETFLOW export.

```
ip flow-export version 9
```

Step 6. Configure router **PHOENIX_NETFLOW** as an Exporter with the name ex1
Export name: **ex1**
Commands to define NETFLOW export:

flow exporter ex1
destination 13.0.0.100
source FastEthernet0/1
transport udp 9996

Step 7. Define NETFLOW record.

Record name**: r1**

Commands:

```
flow record r1
match ipv4 source address
match ipv4 destination address
match transport destination-port
collect timestamp sys-uptime first
collect timestamp sys-uptime last
1collect counter bytes
collect counter packets
```

The network traffic information collected will be based on IPv4 source and destination addresses, transport layer destination ports, and will include: timestamps, byte count, packet count.

Step 8. Define NETFLOW monitor.

Monitor name: **m1**

Commands:

```
flow monitor m1
record r1
exporter ex1
```

Step 9. Check the status of the monitor

Commands:

```
show flow monitor
show flow monitor interface
```

```
PHOENIX_NETFLOW#show flow monitor
Flow Monitor m1
  Description:        User defined
  Flow Record:        r1
  Flow Exporter:      ex1
  Cache:
    Type:               normal
    Status:             allocated
    Size:               4096 entries / 163852 bytes
    Inactive Timeout:   15 seconds
    Active Timeout:     1800 seconds
    Update Timeout:     1800 seconds
```

Figure 16.98 Exercise - Checking the status of the monitor.

Step 10. Enabling the m1 monitor on the interface

Commands:

```
interface FastEthernet0/0
ip flow monitor m1 input
```

Step 11. Testing

To test this version of NETFLOW, ping the PC-AUSTIN computer to the PC-DALLAS computer (13.0.0.100).

```
C:\>ping 13.0.0.100

Pinging 13.0.0.100 with 32 bytes of data:

Reply from 13.0.0.100: bytes=32 time=1ms TTL=125
Reply from 13.0.0.100: bytes=32 time<1ms TTL=125
Reply from 13.0.0.100: bytes=32 time=10ms TTL=125
Reply from 13.0.0.100: bytes=32 time=1ms TTL=125

Ping statistics for 13.0.0.100:
    Packets: Sent = 4, Received = 4, Lost = 0 (0% loss),
Approximate round trip times in milli-seconds:
    Minimum = 0ms, Maximum = 10ms, Average = 3ms
```

Figure 16.99 Exercise - Generating network traffic.

To see the captured ICMP traffic, you must go to the PHOENIX_NETFLOW router and execute the command

```
show flow monitor m1 cache
```

```
PHOENIX_NETFLOW#show flow monitor  m1 cache
Cache type:                                   Normal
Cache size:                                     4096
Current entries:                                   1
High Watermark:                                    1

Flows added:                                      15
Flows aged:                                       14
  - Active timeout    (  1800 secs)                0
  - Inactive timeout  (    15 secs)               14
  - Event aged                                     0
  - Watermark aged                                 1
  - Emergency aged                                 0

IPV4 SOURCE ADDRESS:        11.0.0.1
IPV4 DESTINATION ADDRESS:   255.255.255.255
TRNS DESTINATION PORT:      520
timestamp first:            00:06:24.999
timestamp last:             00:06:24.999
counter bytes:              52
counter packets:            1
```

Figure 16.100 Exercise - Checking the status of the buffer.

Next, go to the **PC-DALLAS**, to the **[Desktop]** tab, run **Netflow Collector**. Here we have two groups of information (colored blue and green)

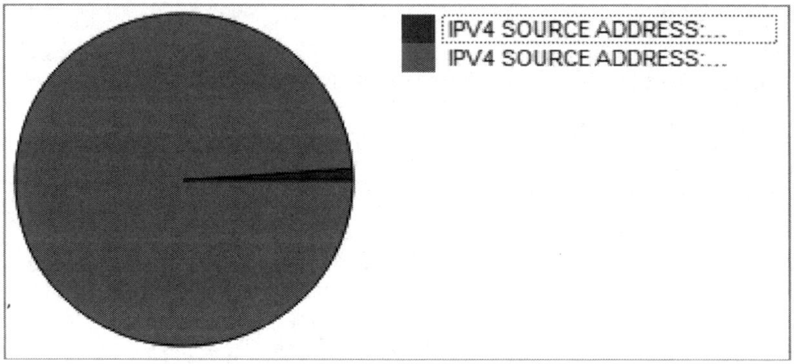

Figure 16.101 Exercise – information groups.

Traffic Contribution: 1.13636% (2/176)

Flow information:

IPV4 SOURCE ADDRESS:	10.0.0.100
IPV4 DESTINATION ADDRESS:	13.0.0.100
TRNS DESTINATION PORT:	0
timestamp first:	00:06:22.208
timestamp last:	00:06:22.208
counter bytes:	28
counter packets:	1

Figure 16.102 Exercise – Collected network traffic information - group 1.

Traffic Contribution: 98.8701% (175/177)

Flow information:

IPV4 SOURCE ADDRESS:	11.0.0.1
IPV4 DESTINATION ADDRESS:	255.255.255.255
TRNS DESTINATION PORT:	520
timestamp first:	00:00:28.884
timestamp last:	00:00:28.884
counter bytes:	52
counter packets:	1

Figure 16.103 Exercise – Collected network traffic information - group 2.

Based on the address: **255.255.255.255**, it can be concluded that this second group originates from the RIPv1 protocol.

16.14 Address Translation Using NAT and L2NAT

The chapter contains exercises demonstrating the use of NAT translation: static and dynamic and L2NAT.

Remember to save the state of the file periodically (keyboard shortcut CTRL+S) while performing exercises or control /project/ tasks.

16.14.1 Exercise (No. 53) – Configuring Static NAT Translation

In this exercise we have a very simple logical topology consisting of a router named NY and four computers: DENVER, PHOENIX (in the internal network), LINCOLN, AUSTIN (in the external network). The NY router is to have NAT static translation configured according to the data in the table below and the topology shown in the figure. On the external network side there are interfaces Fa1/0 and Fa3/0 with addresses respectively: 10.1.1.1/8 and 11.1.1.1/8. use public addresses: 209.165.201.5 and 209.165.201.6 to configure NAT

Internal global address	Internal local address
209.165.201.5	192.168.10.254
209.165.201.6	192.168.11.254

Table 16.18 Exercise – NAT static translation scheme.

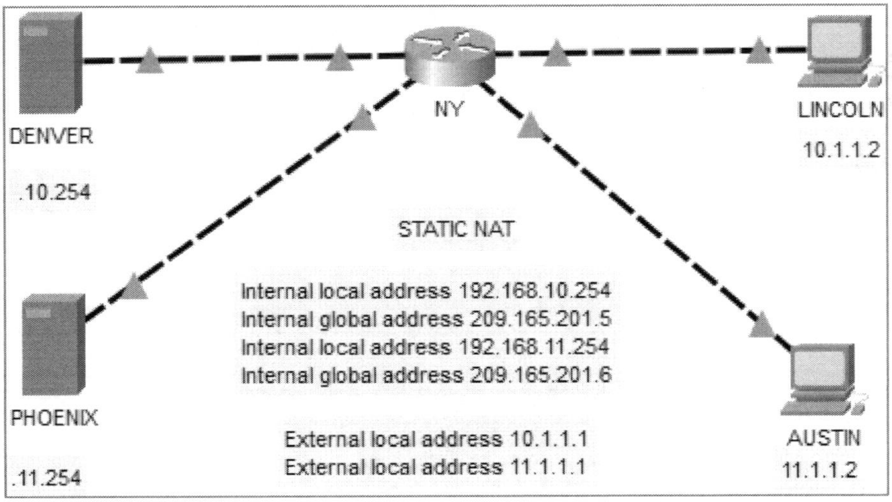

Figure 16.104 Exercise - Topology diagram with interface names.

Solution:

Step 1. Make the topology appropriate to the drawing.
Step 2. Configure the addressing of the computers in the topology according to the figure.

Step 3. Configure static NAT on the router.

```
ip nat inside source static 192.168.10.254
209.165.201.5
ip nat inside source static 192.168.11.254
209.165.201.6
inteface Fa 1/0
ip nat outside
inteface Fa 3/0
ip nat outside
```

Step 4. Check the NAT table in the router.

```
show ip nat translations
```

```
NY#sh ip nat translations
Pro  Inside global      Inside local       Outside local      Outside global
---  209.165.201.5      192.168.10.254     ---                ---
---  209.165.201.6      192.168.11.254     ---                ---
```

Figure 16.105 Exercise - Checking the NAT translation table.

Step 5. Verify that computers on the external network PING computers on the internal network using public addresses.

```
C:\>ping 209.165.201.5

Pinging 209.165.201.5 with 32 bytes of data:

Reply from 192.168.10.254: bytes=32 time=13ms TTL=127
Reply from 192.168.10.254: bytes=32 time<1ms TTL=127
Reply from 192.168.10.254: bytes=32 time<1ms TTL=127
Reply from 192.168.10.254: bytes=32 time=1ms TTL=127

Ping statistics for 209.165.201.5:
    Packets: Sent = 4, Received = 4, Lost = 0 (0% loss),
Approximate round trip times in milli-seconds:
    Minimum = 0ms, Maximum = 13ms, Average = 3ms

C:\>ping 209.165.201.6

Pinging 209.165.201.6 with 32 bytes of data:

Reply from 192.168.11.254: bytes=32 time=1ms TTL=127
Reply from 192.168.11.254: bytes=32 time<1ms TTL=127
Reply from 192.168.11.254: bytes=32 time<1ms TTL=127
Reply from 192.168.11.254: bytes=32 time<1ms TTL=127

Ping statistics for 209.165.201.6:
    Packets: Sent = 4, Received = 4, Lost = 0 (0% loss),
Approximate round trip times in milli-seconds:
    Minimum = 0ms, Maximum = 1ms, Average = 0ms
```

Figure 16.106 Exercise - Verify pinging public addresses.

16.14.2 Exercise (No. 54) - Configuring Dynamic and Static NAT Translation.

The main purpose of this exercise is to gain access from computers on the internal network to a server that is on the external network using two types of NAT and one standard ACL. Access in the opposite direction should be blocked.

In the exercise we have a logical topology consisting of: a router named RTR-CENTER, a router named NY and a server named NY-PC (located in the internal network) and five computers: DENVER, PHOENIX, LINCOLN, AUSTIN, CHICAGO (located in the internal network).

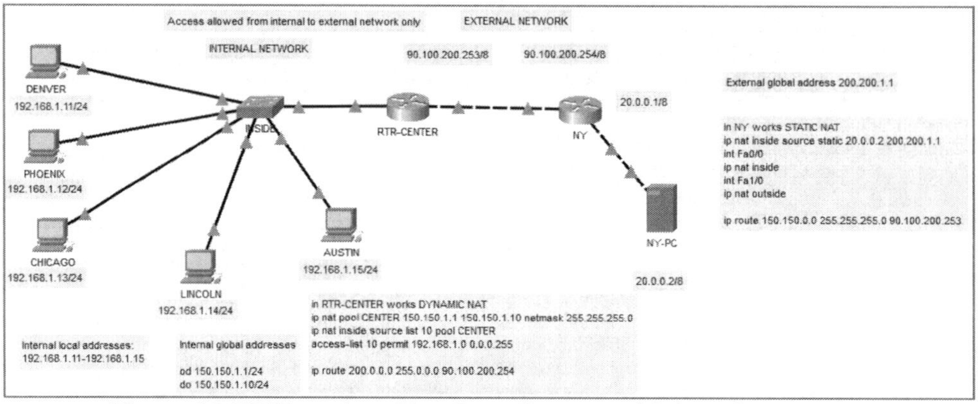

Figure 16.107 Exercise - Topology diagram with interface names

The RTR-CENTER router is to have NAT dynamic translation configured according to the data in the table below and the topology shown in the figure. On the external network side there is an interface Fa0/0 with the address 90.100.200.253/8, and on the internal network side there are interfaces Fa0/1 to Fa5/0 with local addresses 192.168.1.11/24 to 192.168.1.15/24 respectively.

Use the public address pool from **150.150.1.1/24 to 150.150.1.10/24** in a dynamic NAT configuration. The address of the NY-PC server is 20.0.0.2/8. You should also create an ACL number 10 allowing network traffic from the 192.168.1.0/24 subnet to NAT translation in the RTR-CENTER router.

<table>
<tr><th>Internal global addresses pool</th><th>Internal local address</th></tr>
<tr><td rowspan="5">from 150.150.1.1/24
to 150.150.1.10/24</td><td>192.168.1.11/24</td></tr>
<tr><td>192.168.1.12/24</td></tr>
<tr><td>192.168.1.13/24</td></tr>
<tr><td>192.168.1.14/24</td></tr>
<tr><td>192.168.1.15/24</td></tr>
</table>

Table 16.19 Exercise - Address pool for dynamic NAT translation

The SK router, on the other hand, is to have NAT translation configured statically according to the data provided in the table below and the topology shown in the figure. On the internal network side there is interface Fa0/0 with address 20.0.0.1/8 and on the external network side there is interface Fa0/1 with address 90.100.200.254/8.

Internal global address	Internal local address
200.200.1.1	**20.0.0.2/8**

Table 16.20 Exercise – Addresses for NAT static translation.

Solution:

Step 1. Make the topology appropriate to the figure.

Step 2. Configure the addressing of the computers in the topology according to the figure.

Step 3. Configure the RTR-CENTER router.

hostname: RTR-CENTER

```
interface FastEthernet0/0
ip address 192.168.1.1 255.255.255.0
ip nat inside interface

interface FastEthernet1/0
ip address 90.100.200.253 255.0.0.0
ip nat outside

ip nat pool CENTER 150.150.1.1 150.150.1.10 netmask
255.255.255.0
ip nat inside source list 10 pool CENTER
ip route 200.0.0.0 255.0.0.0 90.100.200.254
access-list 10 permit 192.168.1.0 0.0.0.255
```

Step 4. Check NAT on the RTR-CENTER router.

```
RTR-CENTER#sh ip nat statistics
Total translations: 0 (0 static, 0 dynamic, 0 extended)
Outside Interfaces: FastEthernet1/0
Inside Interfaces: FastEthernet0/0
Hits: 0  Misses: 0
Expired translations: 0
Dynamic mappings:
-- Inside Source
access-list 10 pool CENTER refCount 0
 pool CENTER: netmask 255.255.255.0
       start 150.150.1.1 end 150.150.1.10
       type generic, total addresses 10 , allocated 0 (0%), misses 0
RTR-CENTER#
```

Figure 16.108 Exercise – Checking the sh ip nat statistics.

Step 5. Configure the NY router.

```
hostname NY
interface FastEthernet0/0
ip address 20.0.0.1 255.0.0.0
ip nat inside

interface FastEthernet1/0
ip address 90.100.200.254 255.0.0.0
ip nat outside

ip nat inside source static 20.0.0.2 200.200.1.1
ip route 150.150.1.0 255.255.255.0 90.100.200.253
```

Step 6. Checking NAT on the NY router.

```
NY#sh ip nat statistics
Total translations: 1 (1 static, 0 dynamic, 0 extended)
Outside Interfaces: FastEthernet1/0
Inside Interfaces: FastEthernet0/0
Hits: 0  Misses: 0
Expired translations: 0
Dynamic mappings:
```

Figure 16.109 Exercise – Checking: `sh ip nat statistics`.

```
NY#sh ip nat translations
Pro  Inside global      Inside local       Outside local      Outside global
---  200.200.1.1        20.0.0.2           ---                ---

NY#
```

Figure 16.110 Exercise – Checking sh ip nat translations.

16.14.3 Exercise (No. 55) – Configuring L2NAT Translation

In this exercise we have a very simple logic topology consisting of three switches: JINKS, AU, DA (model 2950) and two switches: AUSTIN, DALLAS (model IE 2000). Switches GDANSK and GDYNIA should act as L2NAT at Layer 2 level for the respective subnets labelled AU and DA. Your task is to perform the following topology and configure on the JINKS switch: VLAN 1 (10.1.1.254/24), **trunk** connections to neighboring switches and the L2NAT service for automatic addressing of computers in local subnets.

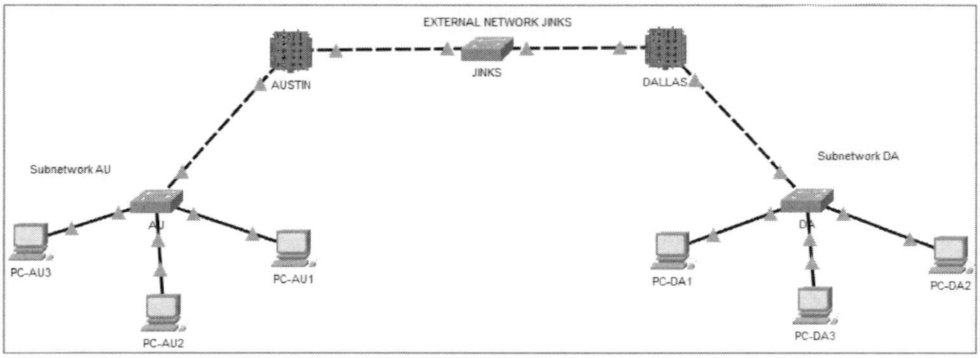

Figure 16.111 Exercise – Overall topology scheme.

On the AUSTIN switch, create an L2NAT instance named AU, Id equal to 1, containing:

- internal translation from network 192.168.1.0 to network→10.1.1.16 (mask 255.255.255.240),
- external translation for host 10.1.1.254→192.168.1.254,
- external translation from network 10.1.1.32 to network→192.168.1.32 (mask 255.255.255.240).

On the AUSTIN switch, assign an L2NAT instance named AU to the Gi1/1 interface. Verify that VLAN 1 with address 10.1.1.100/8 is present on the AUSTIN switch. On the DALLAS switch, create an L2NAT instance named DA, Id equal to 1, containing:

- internal translation from network 192.168.1.0 to network →10.1.1.32 (mask 255.255.255.240),
- external translation for host 10.1.1.254 →192.168.1.254,
- external translation from network 10.1.1.32 to network →192.168.1.0 (mask 255.255.255.240),
- external translation from the network 10.1.1.16 to the network →192.168.1.16 (mask 255.255.255.240).

On the DALLAS switch, assign an L2NAT instance named DA to the Gi1/1 interface. Check whether there is VLAN 1 with address 10.1.1.101/24 in the DALLAS switch. At the end of the exercise, check whether computers ***from different networks*** are correctly addressed.

In order to facilitate the configuration, the necessary data for the exercise has been placed in the tables below and a topology diagram with interface names is provided. Of course, the MAC addresses of the computers in your case will be different, as they are generated randomly by the Packet Tracer program.

Device	Interface	Private IP address	Internal subnet	MAC address
PC-AU1	Fa0	192.168.1.1/24	AU	*000B.BEBB.383D*
PC-AU2	Fa0	192.168.1.2/24	AU	*00E0.B09B.8EBD*
PC-AU3	Fa0	192.168.1.3/24	AU	*00D0.D302.A2B0*
PC-DA1	Fa0	192.168.1.1/24	DA	*0050.0FD7.BB14*
PC-DA2	Fa0	192.168.1.2/24	DA	*0040.0B67.3CA9*
PC-DA3	Fa0	192.168.1.3/24	DA	*0030.A39E.6A03*

Table 16.21 Addressing table.

Device	Device type	Interface(s)	VLAN	Address	Notes
JINKS	2950-24	Vlan1	1	10.1.1.254/24	-
AUSTIN	IE-2000	Vlan1	1	10.1.1.100/8	-
DALLAS	IE-2000	Vlan1	1	10.1.1.101/24	-
AU	2950-24	Fa0/1, Fa0/2, Fa0/3	-	-	connected to computers
AU	2950-24	Fa0/4	-	-	connected to AUSTIN
DA	2950-24	Fa0/1, Fa0/2, Fa0/3	-	-	connected to computers
DA	2950-24	Fa0/4	-	-	connected to DALLAS

Table 16.22 Switch configuration table - Part 1.

Device	Installation name	Interface	Working port mode	Translations for internal subnet	Translations for external subnet
AUSTIN	-	Fa1/1	trunk	-	-
AUSTIN	AU	Gi1/1	trunk	inside from network 192.168.1.0 to 10.1.1.16 mask 255.255.255.240	outside from host 10.1.1.254 to 192.168.1.254 outside from network 10.1.1.32 to 192.168.1.32 mask 255.255.255.240
DALLAS	-	Fa1/1	trunk	-	-

DALLAS	DA	Gi1/1	trunk	inside from network 192.168.1.0 to 10.1.1.32 mask 255.255.255.240	outside from host 10.1.1.254 to 192.168.1.254 outside from network 10.1.1.32 to 192.168.1.0 mask 255.255.255.240 outside from network 10.1.1.16 to 192.168.1.16 mask 255.255.255.240

Table 16.23 Switch configuration table - Part 2.

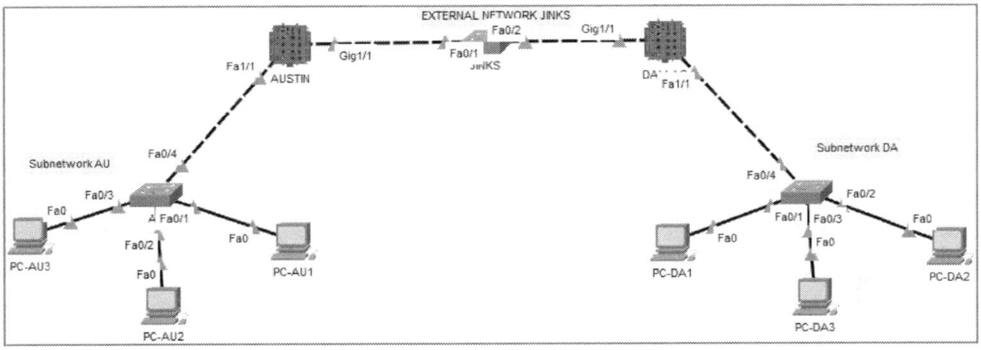

Figure 16.112 Exercise - Topology diagram with interface names.

Solution:

Step 1. Connect the devices properly using the correct cable types.

Step 2. Configure the IP addresses of the computers according to the addressing table, switch configuration tables.

Step 3. Configure the L2NAT service named AU on the AUSTIN switch according to the switch configuration table.

```
enable
conf t
l2nat instance AU
```

```
inside from network 192.168.1.0 to 10.1.1.16 mask
255.255.255.240
outside from host 10.1.1.254 to 192.168.1.254
outside from network 10.1.1.32 to 192.168.1.32 mask
255.255.255.240
```

Step 4. Assign a AU instance to an interface on the AUSTIN switch.

```
interface Gi1/1
l2nat AU
```

Step 5. Configure the L2NAT service named DA on the DALLAS switch according to the switch configuration table.

```
en
conf t
l2nat instance DA
inside from network 192.168.1.0 to 10.1.1.32 mask
255.255.255.240
outside from host 10.1.1.254 to 192.168.1.254
outside from network 10.1.1.32 to 192.168.1.0 mask
255.255.255.240
outside from network 10.1.1.16 to 192.168.1.16 mask
255.255.255.240
```

Step 6. Assign the DA instance to an interface on the DALLAS switch.

```
interface Gi1/1
l2nat DA
```

Step 7. Verify that PC-AU1, PC-DA1, PC-AU2, PC-DA2, PC-AU3, PC-DA3, have the correct IP addresses.

```
C:\>
C:\>ipconfig /all

FastEthernet0 Connection:(default port)

   Connection-specific DNS Suffix..:
   Physical Address................: 0040.0B67.3CA9
   Link-local IPv6 Address.........: FE80::290:2BFF:FEA9:4C83
   IP Address......................: 192.168.1.2
   Subnet Mask.....................: 255.255.255.0
   Default Gateway.................: 0.0.0.0
   DNS Servers.....................: 0.0.0.0
   DHCP Servers....................: 0.0.0.0
   DHCPv6 Client DUID..............: 00-01-00-01-9E-74-76-2D-00-40-0B-67-3C-A9
```

Figure 16.113 Exercise - Result of the PC-AU check.

16.15 Virtual Private Networks

This chapter contains exercises demonstrating the use of VPNs.

Remember to save the status of the file periodically (keyboard shortcut CTRL+S) when doing exercises or control /project/ tasks.

16.15.1 Exercise (No. 56) – Configuring a Simple VPN (Remote Access)

Step 1. Make the following topology for the following assumptions:

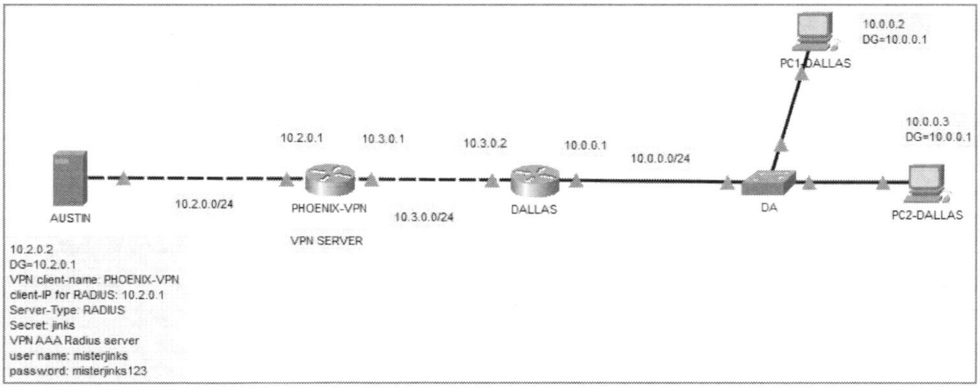

Figure 16.114 Exercise – topology scheme.

Step 2. Configure the topology according to the figure.

Step 3. Configure static routes.

Configure a static route in the PHOENIX-VPN router to the network 10.0.0.0/24 via the address 10.3.0.2.

```
ip route 10.0.0.0 255.255.255.0 10.3.0.2
```

Configure a static route in the DALLAS router to network 10.2.0.0/24 via address 10.3.0.1

```
ip route 10.2.0.0 255.255.255.0 10.3.0.1
```

Step 4. In the PHOENIX-VPN router, activate and configure the AAA service parameters. Use the following commands:

```
aaa new-model
aaa authentication login VPNAUTH group radius local
aaa authorization network VPNAUTH local
```

Step 5. In the VPN router, activate SSH version 1. Use the following commands:

```
ip ssh version 1
```

Step 6. In the VPN router, configure ISAKMP AES. Use the following commands:

```
crypto isakmp policy 10
encr aes 256
authentication pre-share
group 2
```

Step 7. In the VPN router, configure further ISAKMP parameters: group, key, address pool. Use the following commands.

```
crypto isakmp client configuration group ciscogroup
key ciscogroup
pool VPNCLIENTS
netmask 255.255.255.0
```

Step 8. In the VPN router, configure further IPsec parameters. Use the following commands:

```
crypto ipsec transform-set mytrans esp-3des esp-sha-
hmac
```

Step 9. In the PHOENIX-VPN router, configure further mapping parameters. Use the following commands.

```
crypto dynamic-map mymap 10
set transform-set mytrans
reverse-route
```

Step 10. In the PHOENIX-VPN router, configure further mapping parameters. Use the following commands.

```
crypto map mymap client authentication list VPNAUTH
crypto map mymap isakmp authorization list VPNAUTH
crypto map mymap client configuration address respond
crypto map mymap 10 ipsec-isakmp dynamic mymap
```

Step 11. In the PHOENIX-VPN router, configure the address pool for the VPN clients. Use the following command:

```
ip local pool VPNCLIENTS 10.1.1.100 10.1.1.200
```

Step 12. In the PHOENIX-VPN router, configure the address of the RADIUS server. Use the following command:

```
radius-server host 10.2.0.2 auth-port 1645 key jinks
```

Step 15. On the SOPOT-VPN router on interface Fa0/0, configure the crypto map. Use the following command:

```
interface FastEthernet0/0
ip address 10.3.0.1 255.255.255.0
crypto map mymap
```

Step 16. On PC1-DALLAS, start the VPN application

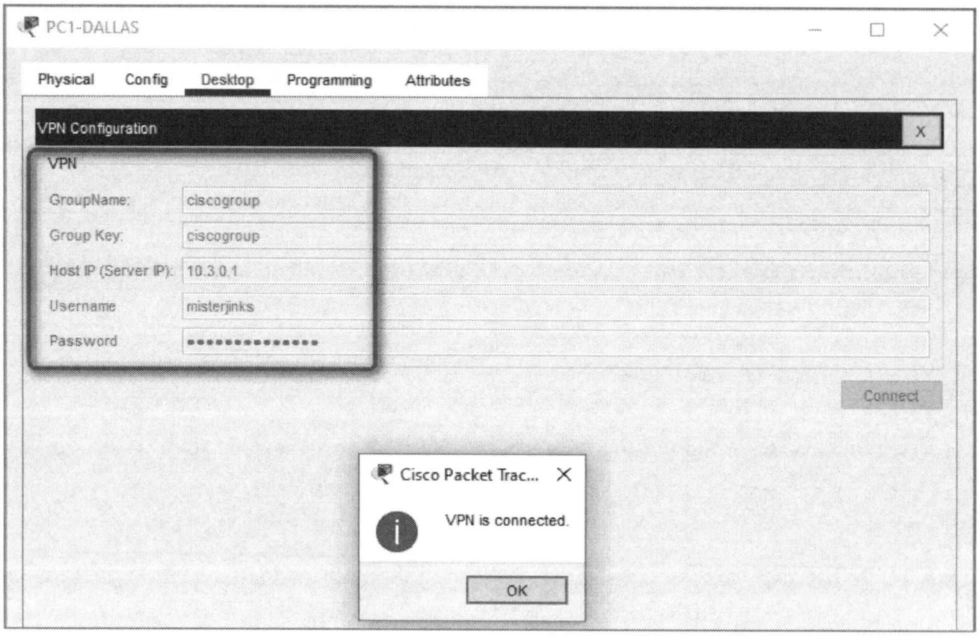

Figure 16.115 Configuration of the VPN application in PC1-DALLAS.

Step 17. On PC2-DALLAS, perform tracert to 10.2.0.2 (DALLAS).

```
C:\>
C:\>tracert 10.2.0.2

Tracing route to 10.2.0.2 over a maximum of 30 hops:

  1   1 ms      0 ms      0 ms      10.0.0.1
  2   0 ms      0 ms      0 ms      10.3.0.1
  3   10 ms     0 ms      0 ms      10.2.0.2

Trace complete.
```

Figure 16.116 Result of the command tracert to 10.2.0.2.

16.16 Multilayer Switches 3560 and 3650

The chapter contains exercises demonstrating the use of the 3560 and 3650 switches.

Remember to save the status of the file periodically (keyboard shortcut CTRL+S) during the exercises or control /project/ tasks.

16.16.1 Exercise (No. 57) - Configuring Network with 3560 Switches

The diagram below shows the network on which we will carry out this exercise. Connect the devices together according to the diagram shown below. All the necessary modules are already installed in the devices shown below. Address the interfaces of the corresponding devices. Perform the configuration of the access interfaces and VLANs on the switches: **DA, PHO, AU, DEN**. Perform configuration of access and proxy interfaces and VLANs on switches: **DALLAS, PHOENIX, AUSTIN, DENVER**.

Switch	Interface	Mode	VLAN
DA	Fa0/1	Access	10
DA	Fa0/2	Access	10
DA	Fa0/24	Access	10
PHO	Fa0/1	Access	20
PHO	Fa0/2	Access	20
PHO	Fa0/24	Access	20
AU	Fa0/1	Access	30
AU	Fa0/2	Access	30
AU	Fa0/24	Access	30
DEN	Fa0/1	Access	40
DEN	Fa0/2	Access	40
DEN	Fa0/24	Access	40

Table 16.24 Table of access interfaces

Perform DHCP configuration on switches: **DALLAS, PHOENIX, AUSTIN, DENVER**. PC0-PC7 are to obtain their addresses from the respective DHCP servers.

Perform configuration of appropriate static routes in switches: **DALLAS, PHOENIX, AUSTIN, DENVER**. Check if it is possible to PING between each computer!

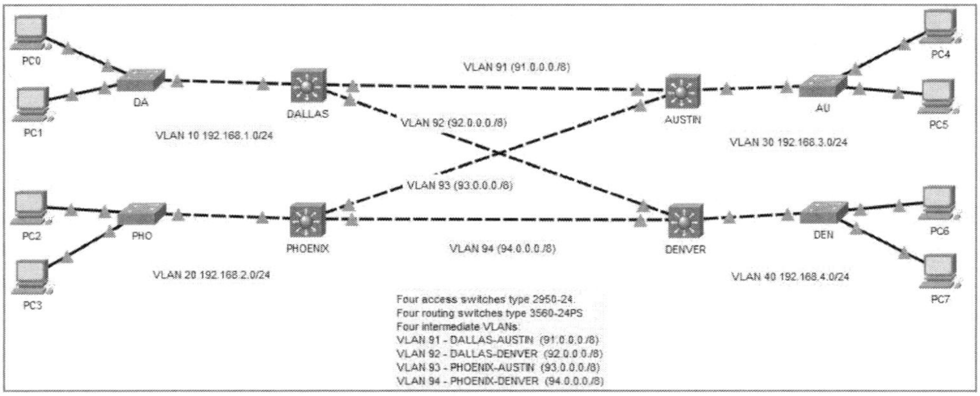

Figure 16.117 Network topology.

The network topology consists of:

- **four access switches** type 2950-24,
- **four routing switches** type 3560-24PS,
- **four local VLANs (10, 20, 30, four intermediate VLANs** (91, 92, 93, 94),
- **and eight computers** (PC0-PC7)

Solution:

Step 1. Connect the devices properly using the correct cable types.

Step 2. Configure the IP addresses of the computers as DHCP.

Step 3. Configure the access interfaces on the switches: **DA, PHO, AU, DEN.**

```
hostname DA
interface Fa0/1
sw mode access
sw access vlan 10
interface Fa0/2
sw mode access
sw access vlan 10
interface Fa0/24
sw mode access
sw access vlan 10

hostname PHO
interface Fa0/1
sw mode access
sw access vlan 20
interface Fa0/2
sw mode access
sw access vlan 20
interface Fa0/24
sw mode access
sw access vlan 20

hostname AU
interface Fa0/1
sw mode access
```

```
sw access vlan 30
interface Fa0/2
sw mode access
sw access vlan 30
interface Fa0/24
sw mode access
sw access vlan 30

hostname DEN
interface Fa0/1
sw mode access
sw access vlan 40
interface Fa0/2
sw mode access
sw access vlan 40
interface Fa0/24
sw mode access
sw access vlan 40
```

Step 4. Configure VLANs on switches: **DA, PHO, AU, DEN.**

```
hostname DA
vlan 10
interface FastEthernet0/1
switchport access vlan 10
switchport mode access
interface FastEthernet0/2
switchport access vlan 10
switchport mode access
interface FastEthernet0/24
switchport access vlan 10
switchport mode access

hostname PHO
vlan 20
interface FastEthernet0/1
```

```
switchport access vlan 20
switchport mode access
interface FastEthernet0/2
switchport access vlan 20
switchport mode access
interface FastEthernet0/24
switchport access vlan 20
switchport mode access

hostname AU
vlan 30
interface FastEthernet0/1
switchport access vlan 30
switchport mode access
interface FastEthernet0/2
switchport access vlan 30
switchport mode access
interface FastEthernet0/24
switchport access vlan 30
switchport mode access

hostname DEN
vlan 40
interface FastEthernet0/1
switchport access vlan 40
switchport mode access
interface FastEthernet0/2
switchport access vlan 40
switchport mode access
interface FastEthernet0/24
switchport access vlan 40
switchport mode access
```

Step 5. Configure VLANs on switches: **DALLAS, PHOENIX, AUSTIN, DENVER.**

```
hostname DALLAS
```

```
vlan 10
name VLAN0010
vlan 91
name DALLAS-AUSTIN
vlan 92
name DALLAS-DENVER
interface FastEthernet0/24
switchport access vlan 10
switchport mode access
interface GigabitEthernet0/1
description To AUSTIN
switchport access vlan 91
switchport mode access
interface GigabitEthernet0/2
description To DENVER
switchport access vlan 92
interface vlan10
ip address 192.168.1.1 255.255.255.0
interface vlan91
description DALLAS-AUSTIN
ip address 91.0.0.1 255.0.0.0
interface vlan92
description DALLAS-DENVER
ip address 92.0.0.1 255.0.0.0

hostname PHOENIX
vlan 20
name VLAN0020
vlan 94
name PHOENIX-DENVER
vlan 93
name PHOENIX-AUSTIN
interface FastEthernet0/24
switchport access vlan 20
switchport mode access
```

```
interface GigabitEthernet0/1
description To DENVER
switchport access vlan 94
switchport mode access
interface GigabitEthernet0/2
description To AUSTIN
switchport access vlan 93
interface vlan20
ip address 192.168.2.1 255.255.255.0
interface vlan93
description PHOENIX-AUSTIN
ip address 93.0.0.1 255.0.0.0
interface vlan94
description PHOENIX-DENVER
ip address 94.0.0.1 255.0.0.0
hostname AUSTIN
vlan 30
name VLAN0030
vlan 91
name AUSTIN-DALLAS
vlan 93
name AUSTIN-PHOENIX
interface FastEthernet0/24
switchport access vlan 30
switchport mode access
interface GigabitEthernet0/1
description To DALLAS
switchport access vlan 91
switchport mode access
interface GigabitEthernet0/2
description To PHOENIX
switchport access vlan 93
interface vlan30
ip address 192.168.3.1 255.255.255.0
interface vlan91
```

```
description DALLAS-AUSTIN
ip address 91.0.0.2 255.0.0.0
interface vlan93
description PHOENIX-AUSTIN
ip address 93.0.0.2 255.0.0.0

hostname DENVER
vlan 40
name VLAN0040
vlan 92
name DALLAS-DENVER
vlan 94
name PHOENIX-DENVER
interface FastEthernet0/24
switchport access vlan 40
switchport mode access
interface GigabitEthernet0/1
description To PHOENIX
switchport access vlan 94
switchport mode access
interface GigabitEthernet0/2
description To DALLAS
switchport access vlan 92
interface vlan40
ip address 192.168.4.1 255.255.255.0
interface vlan92
description DALLAS-DENVER
ip address 92.0.0.2 255.0.0.0
interface vlan94
description PHOENIX-DENVER
ip address 94.0.0.2 255.0.0.0
```

Step 6. Configure static routes in switches: **DALLAS, PHOENIX, AUSTIN, DENVER.**

```
host DALLAS
ip routing
```

```
ip route 192.168.3.0 255.255.255.0 91.0.0.2
ip route 192.168.4.0 255.255.255.0 92.0.0.2
ip route 192.168.2.0 255.255.255.0 91.0.0.2

host PHOENIX
ip routing
ip route 192.168.1.0 255.255.255.0 93.0.0.2
ip route 192.168.3.0 255.255.255.0 93.0.0.2
ip route 192.168.4.0 255.255.255.0 94.0.0.2

host AUSTIN
ip routing
ip route 192.168.1.0 255.255.255.0 91.0.0.1
ip route 192.168.2.0 255.255.255.0 93.0.0.1
ip route 192.168.4.0 255.255.255.0 93.0.0.1

host DENVER
ip routing
ip route 192.168.1.0 255.255.255.0 92.0.0.1
ip route 192.168.2.0 255.255.255.0 94.0.0.1
ip route 192.168.3.0 255.255.255.0 92.0.0.1
```

Step 7. Configure DHCP servers in switches: **DALLAS, PHOENIX, AUSTIN, DENVER.**

```
host DALLAS
ip dhcp excluded-address 192.168.1.1

ip dhcp pool LAN10
network 192.168.1.0 255.255.255.0
default-router 192.168.1.1

host PHOENIX
ip dhcp excluded-address 192.168.2.1

ip dhcp pool LAN20
```

```
network 192.168.2.0 255.255.255.0
default-router 192.168.2.1

host AUSTIN
ip dhcp excluded-address 192.168.3.1

ip dhcp pool LAN30
network 192.168.3.0 255.255.255.0
default-router 192.168.3.1

host DENVER
ip dhcp excluded-address 192.168.4.1

ip dhcp pool LAN40
network 192.168.4.0 255.255.255.0
default-router 192.168.4.1
```

Step 8. Check if the computers are pinging each other.

```
C:\>ping 192.168.4.3

Pinging 192.168.4.3 with 32 bytes of data:

Reply from 192.168.4.3: bytes=32 time=12ms TTL=126
Reply from 192.168.4.3: bytes=32 time=13ms TTL=126
Reply from 192.168.4.3: bytes=32 time=13ms TTL=126
Reply from 192.168.4.3: bytes=32 time=13ms TTL=126

Ping statistics for 192.168.4.3:
    Packets: Sent = 4, Received = 4, Lost = 0 (0% loss),
Approximate round trip times in milli-seconds:
    Minimum = 12ms, Maximum = 13ms, Average = 12ms
```

Figure 16.118 Result of the PING from PC0 to PC7.

```
C:\>ping 192.168.2.3

Pinging 192.168.2.3 with 32 bytes of data:

Reply from 192.168.2.3: bytes=32 time=22ms TTL=126
Reply from 192.168.2.3: bytes=32 time<1ms TTL=126
Reply from 192.168.2.3: bytes=32 time=11ms TTL=126
Reply from 192.168.2.3: bytes=32 time=11ms TTL=126

Ping statistics for 192.168.2.3:
    Packets: Sent = 4, Received = 4, Lost = 0 (0% loss),
Approximate round trip times in milli-seconds:
    Minimum = 0ms, Maximum = 22ms, Average = 11ms
```

Figure 16.119 Result of PING from PC5 to PC3.

16.16.2 Exercise (No. 58) – Configuring Network with a Single 3560 Switch

The diagram below shows a working network, consisting of routers only.

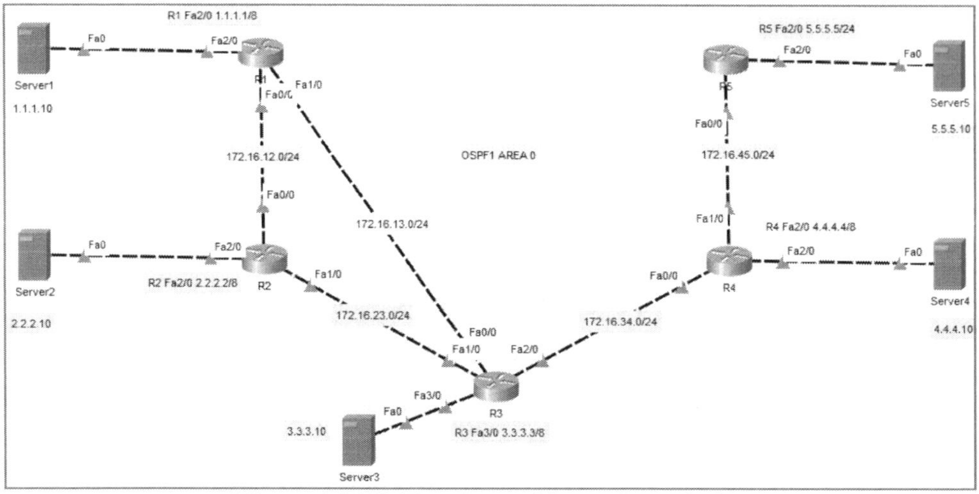

Figure 16.120 Topology without the switch.

The network topology can be found in the file **exercise58–configuring-network-without-switch.pkt**.

Remove router R3 and replace it with switch 3560-24PS (switch name **SW**). Connect the 3560-24PS switch to the corresponding interfaces of the other routers according to the connection table below. Perform the SW configuration so that the network still works correctly.

3560-24PS	**Fa0/1**	**R1**	**Fa1/0**
3560-24PS	**Fa0/2**	**R2**	**Fa1/0**

3560-24PS	Fa0/3	R4	Fa0/0
3560-24PS	Fa0/4	Server3	Fa0

Table 16.25 Connections table.

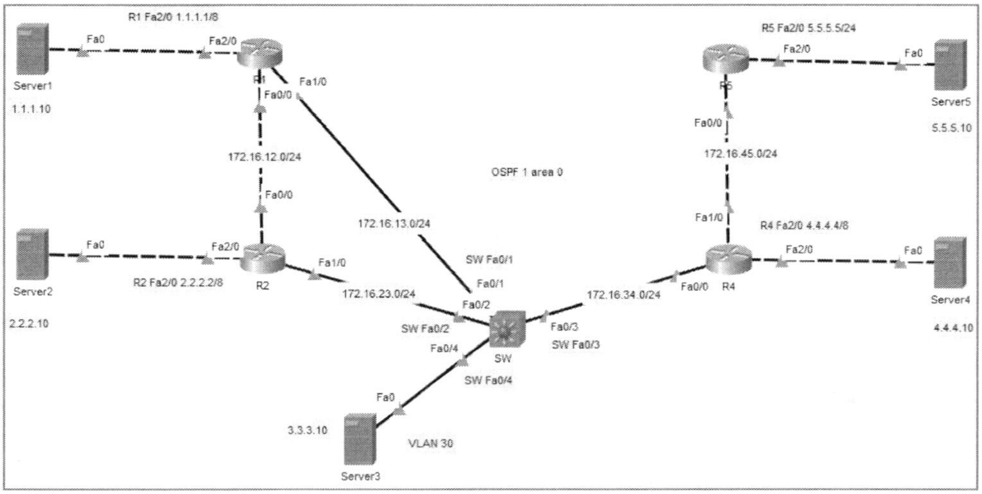

Figure 16.121 Topology with the SW switch.

Solution:

Step 1. Delete router R3.

Step 2. Insert switch type 3560-24PS (switch name **SW**).

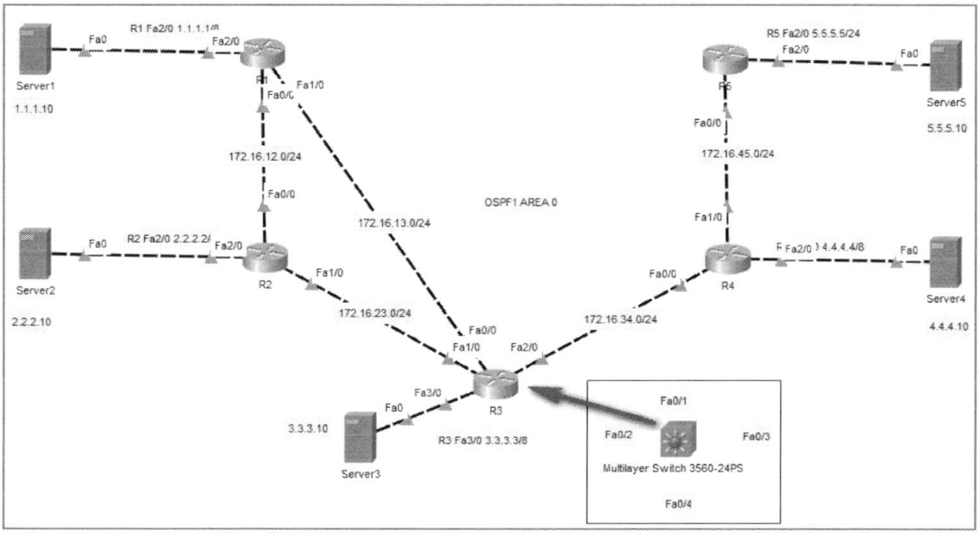

Figure 16.122 Replacing R3 with SW switch.

Step 3. Change the switch name to **SW**.

```
hostname SW
```

Step 4. Change the switch mode to **Layer 3**. To do this, run the command

```
ip routing
```

Step 5. On the SW switch, for Server3, create a VLAN number 30 and set the VLAN address. To do this, execute the commands:

```
vlan 30
interface vlan  30
ip address 3.3.3.3 255.255.255.0
no shutdown
```

Step 6. Assign VLAN 30 on the switch to port Fa0/4. To do so, execute the commands:

```
int Fa0/4
switchport mode access
switchport access vlan 30
```

Step 7. Configure the connections of the SW switch to the routers: R1, R2, R4. To do this, execute the commands:

```
int Fa0/1
no switchport
ip address 172.16.13.2 255.255.255.0
no shutdown
int Fa0/2
no switchport
ip address 172.16.23.2 255.255.255.0
no shutdown
int Fa0/3
no switchport
ip address 172.16.34.2 255.255.255.0
no  shutdown
```

Step 8. Configure OSPF 1 in area (area 0) on the SW switch. To do this, execute the commands:

```
enable
configure terminal
router ospf 1
network 3.0.0.0 0.255.255.255 area 0
network 172.16.13.0 0.0.0.255 area 0
network 172.16.23.0 0.0.0.255 area 0
network 172.16.34.0 0.0.0.255 area 0
```

Step 9. To check communication, perform the appropriate PINGs:

- from Server1 to Server2,
- from Server1 to Server3,
- from Server1 to Server4,
- from Server1 to Server5.

Check the communication from Server1 to Server2.

```
C:\>ping 2.2.2.10

Pinging 2.2.2.10 with 32 bytes of data:

Reply from 2.2.2.10: bytes=32 time<1ms TTL=126
Reply from 2.2.2.10: bytes=32 time<1ms TTL=126
Reply from 2.2.2.10: bytes=32 time<1ms TTL=126
Reply from 2.2.2.10: bytes=32 time=2ms TTL=126

Ping statistics for 2.2.2.10:
    Packets: Sent = 4, Received = 4, Lost = 0 (0% loss),
Approximate round trip times in milli-seconds:
    Minimum = 0ms, Maximum = 2ms, Average = 0ms
```

Figure 16.123 Result of the PING from Server1 to Server2.

Check the communication from Server1 to Server3.

```
C:\>ping 3.3.3.10

Pinging 3.3.3.10 with 32 bytes of data:

Reply from 3.3.3.10: bytes=32 time=1ms TTL=126
Reply from 3.3.3.10: bytes=32 time=2ms TTL=126
Reply from 3.3.3.10: bytes=32 time<1ms TTL=126
Reply from 3.3.3.10: bytes=32 time<1ms TTL=126

Ping statistics for 3.3.3.10:
    Packets: Sent = 4, Received = 4, Lost = 0 (0% loss),
Approximate round trip times in milli-seconds:
    Minimum = 0ms, Maximum = 2ms, Average = 0ms
```

Figure 16.124 Result of the PING from Server1 to Server3.

Check the communication from Server1 to Server4.

```
C:\>ping 4.4.4.10

Pinging 4.4.4.10 with 32 bytes of data:

Reply from 4.4.4.10: bytes=32 time=11ms TTL=125
Reply from 4.4.4.10: bytes=32 time=10ms TTL=125
Reply from 4.4.4.10: bytes=32 time=11ms TTL=125
Reply from 4.4.4.10: bytes=32 time<1ms TTL=125

Ping statistics for 4.4.4.10:
    Packets: Sent = 4, Received = 4, Lost = 0 (0% loss),
Approximate round trip times in milli-seconds:
    Minimum = 0ms, Maximum = 11ms, Average = 8ms
```

Figure 16.125 Result of the PING from Server1 to Server4.

Check the communication from Server1 to Server5.

```
C:\>ping 5.5.5.10

Pinging 5.5.5.10 with 32 bytes of data:

Reply from 5.5.5.10: bytes=32 time=11ms TTL=124
Reply from 5.5.5.10: bytes=32 time=11ms TTL=124
Reply from 5.5.5.10: bytes=32 time=1ms TTL=124
Reply from 5.5.5.10: bytes=32 time=10ms TTL=124

Ping statistics for 5.5.5.10:
    Packets: Sent = 4, Received = 4, Lost = 0 (0% loss),
Approximate round trip times in milli-seconds:
    Minimum = 1ms, Maximum = 11ms, Average = 8ms
```

Figure 16.126 Result of the PING from Server1 to Server5.

16.16.3 Exercise (No. 59) - Configuring Network with 3650 Switches

The diagram below shows the network on which we will carry out this exercise. Interconnect the devices, using fiber optic cables, according to the diagram shown below. Install all the necessary modules in the devices shown on the topology.

Address the interfaces of the corresponding end devices. Perform configuration of the access interfaces and VLANs on the switches: **DALLAS, PHOENIX, AUSTIN, NY**. Perform configuration of appropriate static routes on switches: **DALLAS, PHOENIX, AUSTIN, NY**. Check if it is possible to PING between computers!

The network topology consists of:

- **four switches** 3650-24PS type,
- **six VLANs** (10, 20, 30, 40, 50, 60),
- **and three computers** (PC-GD, PC-GSP, PC-GA).

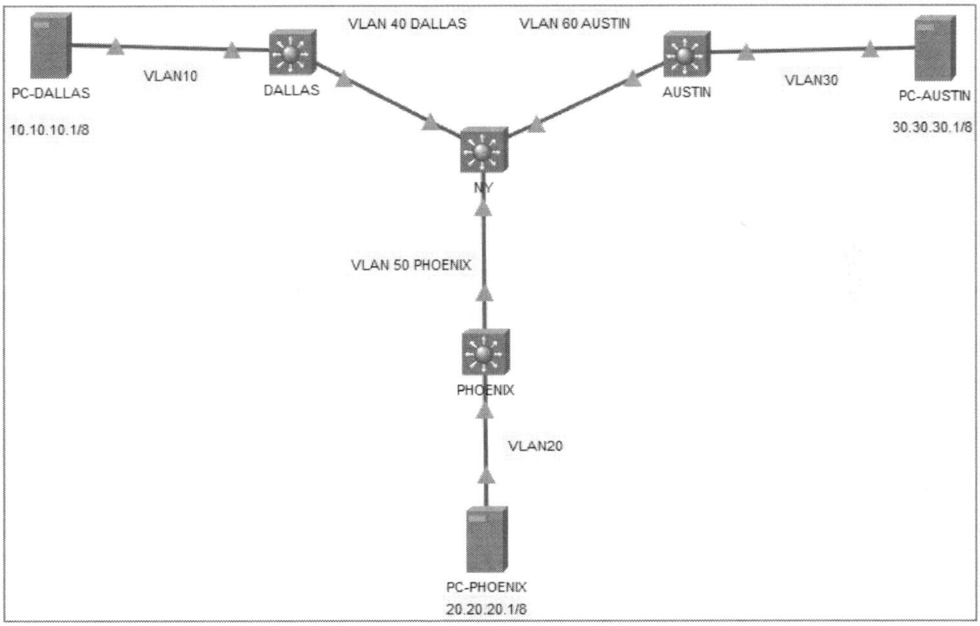

Figure 16.127 Network topology.

The configuration of the interfaces and VLANs is shown in the following table.

Switch	Interface	VLAN	VLANs name	VLANs address
DALLAS	Gi1/1/1	10	VLAN10	10.10.10.10/8
DALLAS	Gi1/1/2	40	DALLAS	40.40.40.42/8

PHOENIX	Gi1/1/1	20	VLAN20	20.20.20.20/8
PHOENIX	Gi1/1/2	50	PHOENIX	50.50.50.52/8
AUSTIN	Gi1/1/1	30	VLAN30	30.30.30.30/8
AUSTIN	Gi1/1/2	60	AUSTIN	60.60.60.62/8
NY	Gi1/1/1	40	DALLAS	40.40.40.41/8
NY	Gi1/1/2	50	PHOENIX	50.50.50.51/8
NY	Gi1/1/3	60	AUSTIN	60.60.60.61/8

Table 16.26 A table of interfaces and VLANs.

Solution:

Step 1. In the computers, replace the existing network card with the network module **PT-HOST-NM-1FGE.**

Step 2. Install **AC-POWER-SUPPLY** power supplies and four **GLC-LH-SMD** network modules in the switches.

Step 3. Connect the devices properly using fiber optic cables.

Step 4. Configure the IP addresses of the computers as static, according to the topology.

Step 5. Configure the VLAN numbers and names and their IP addresses, according to the table.

```
enable
conf t
hostname DALLAS
vlan 10
name VLAN10
vlan 40
name DALLAS
exit

interface vlan 10
ip address 10.10.10.10 255.0.0.0
no shutdown
interface vlan  40
ip address  40.40.40.42 255.0.0.0
no shutdown
end
```

```
enable
conf t
hostname PHOENIX
vlan 20
name VLAN20
vlan 50
name PHOENIX
exit

interface vlan  20
ip address 20.20.20.20 255.0.0.0
no shutdown
interface vlan 50
ip address  50.50.50.52 255.0.0.0
no shutdown
end

enable
conf t
hostname  AUSTIN
vlan 30
name VLAN30
vlan 60
name AUSTIN
exit

interface vlan 30
ip address 30.30.30.30 255.0.0.0
no shutdown
interface vlan  60
ip address  60.60.60.62 255.0.0.0
no shutdown
end
```

```
enable
conf t
hostname NY
vlan 40
name DALLAS
vlan 50
name PHOENIX
vlan 60
name AUSTIN
exit

interface vlan 40
ip address 40.40.40.41 255.0.0.0
no shutdown
interface vlan 50
ip address 50.50.50.51 255.0.0.0
no shutdown
interface vlan 60
ip address  60.60.60.61 255.0.0.0
no shutdown
end
```

Step 6. On the DALLAS switch, assign the appropriate VLANs to the corresponding interfaces as shown in the table.

```
enable
conf t
interface Gi1/1/1
switchport mode access
switchport access vlan 10
interface Gi1/1/2
switchport mode access
switchport access vlan 40
end
```

Step 7. On the PHOENIX switch, assign the corresponding VLANs to the corresponding interfaces, as shown in the table.

```
enable
conf t
interface Gi1/1/1
switchport mode access
switchport access vlan 20
interface Gi1/1/2
switchport mode access
switchport access vlan 50
end
```

Step 8. On the AUSTIN switch, assign the corresponding VLANs to the corresponding interfaces, as shown in the table.

```
enable
conf t
interface Gi1/1/1
switchport mode access
switchport access vlan 30
interface Gi1/1/2
switchport mode access
switchport access vlan 60
end
```

Step 9. On the NY switch, assign the corresponding VLANs to the corresponding interfaces, as shown in the table. .

```
enable
conf t
interface Gi1/1/1
switchport mode access
switchport access vlan 40
interface Gi1/1/2
switchport mode access
switchport access vlan 50
```

```
interface Gi1/1/3
switchport mode access
switchport access vlan 60
end
```

Step 10. On the DALLAS switch, configure static routing to the remote subnets using the following commands.

```
enable
conf t
ip routing
ip route 20.0.0.0 255.0.0.0 Vlan 40
ip route 30.0.0.0 255.0.0.0 Vlan 40
end
```

Step 11. On the PHOENIX switch, configure static routing to remote subnets, using the commands

```
enable
conf t
ip routing
ip route 10.0.0.0 255.0.0.0 Vlan 50
ip route 30.0.0.0 255.0.0.0 Vlan 50
end
```

Step 12. On the AUSTIN switch, configure static routing to remote subnets, using commands

```
enable
conf t
ip routing
ip route 10.0.0.0 255.0.0.0 Vlan 60
ip route 20.0.0.0 255.0.0.0 Vlan 60
end
```

Step 13. On the NY switch, configure static routing to remote subnets using the commands

```
enable
conf t
ip routing
ip route 10.0.0.0 255.0.0.0 Vlan 40
ip route 20.0.0.0 255.0.0.0 Vlan 50
ip route 30.0.0.0 255.0.0.0 Vlan 60
end
```

CHAPTER 17

APPENDICES

17 APPENDICES

This chapter contains a glossary of the most important terms, a description of the abbreviated IOS commands.

17.1 Glossary of the key terms

The glossary defines the most important terms and abbreviations that appear in this book. The contents of the glossary can be an additional help for people who are encountering a particular network terminology for the first time or who want to recall the meaning of a term.

ACL - Inbound traffic - (in) packet traffic coming from outside the router. The router first checks this packet traffic, compares it with the ACL and then looks for the destination network in the routing table.

ACL - Outbound traffic - (out) packet traffic from1 finding its way inside the router and is handled by the routing table. Before leaving the exit interface, the packet traffic is checked (compared) with the ACL list, if the result of the comparison is positive, it leaves the interface.

Alternate port or Blocked port - an alternate blocked port through which to connect to the primary switch, in case of failure of the existing operational links.

BID *(Bridge Identifier)* - The switch identifier is a numeric value determined by the switch priority (value 32768), the extended system identifier **sys-id-ext** (value 1) and the MAC address of the port sending the BPDU frame. The default **BID** value is **32769**.

BLK *(blocking)* - blocked port state assumes the role of **alternate port** and does not participate in forwarding Ethernet frames. In the blocking state, the port only receives BPDU frames and processes them with the appropriate switch module to select the best path to the root switch and establishes port roles: **root port** and **designated port**.

Cluster - a group of network devices displayed as a single graphic symbol in Packet Tracer.

CIDR *(Classless Inter-Domain Routing)* - a classless method of assigning IPv4 address ranges. CIDR uses a subnet mask to determine the variable part of a network's IPv4 address. It can use automatic route summarization (allows reducing the number of routing table entries).

Designated port - A designated port is a port that can forward network traffic, but is not a master port. On the master switch, all ports are designated ports.

DHCP *(Dynamic Host Configuration Protocol)* - a protocol that implements dynamic configuration for devices (hosts - clients). A network device automatically receives the following basic configuration information: IP address, subnet mask, default gateway address, DNS server address, lease time (validity time of the received configuration).

Broadcast domain - a group of network devices in which each device can transmit packets to the other devices in the domain without going through a routing device.

FWD *(Forwarding)* - the state of a port forwarding frames (sending and receiving BPDU frames) and Ethernet frames.

ICMP *(Internet Control Message Protocol)* - Internet control message protocol. It is described in RFC 792. The ICMP protocol is used for network diagnostics and routing. The main purpose of this protocol is to control transmission in the network. Commands that use this protocol: **ping, traceroute**.

ACL - *(Access Control List)* - a list managed by **Cisco** devices, a list used to control packets by limiting network traffic passing through routers.

LRN *(Learning)* - The state of a port that learns MAC addresses. The port receives and processes BPDU frames. A MAC address table (mac address table) update is performed. After 15 seconds, the port enters the FWD (Forwarding) state.

LSN *(Listening)* - state of the listening port. In the Listening state, the port receives BPDU frames and forwards them to the corresponding switch module. After 15 seconds, the port enters the LRN (Learning) state.

Wildcard mask - a sequence of binary zeros and ones used to filter individual IP addresses or groups of IP addresses. The zeros indicate the bits of the IP address to be matched and the ones indicate the bits to be ignored. For example, a blank mask of 0.0.0.3 means matching the first 30 bits of an IP address.

Named ACL - An ACL that has a name instead of a number.

Port ID *(Port Identifier)* - A port identifier for a switch consisting of the port priority and port number.

Network Prefix - The number of '1' bits contained in the subnet mask. For example, in a subnet mask of 255.255.0.0, the number of '1' bits is 16.

Bridge Protocol Data Unit *(BPDU)* **frame** - a frame containing Spanning Tree Protocol (STP) information. Switches send BPDU frames to the multicast MAC address **01:80:C2:00:00:00** to implement the STA algorithm. The most important fields contained in a **BPDU** frame are: **Root BID, Root Patch Cost, Sender BID, Port ID.**

RIP *(Routing Information Protocol)* - a distance vector based routing protocol. The protocol uses a metric equivalent to the number of hops (the number of consecutive routers occurring on a given route). It comes in three versions: **RIPv1** (supports only class-based networks), **RIPv2** (supports classless routing), **RIPng** (RIP next generation) - an extension of RIPv2 to support IPv6 networks.

Root BID *(Root Bridge Identifier)* - the identifier of the root switch (Root Bridge ID), depending on the priority of the switch (default value 32769) and the MAC address of the port sending the BPDU frame.

Root Bridge - The Root Switch is the term used to describe the role of the switch in STP. The root switch is the reference point in the STP topology of the LAN. There can only be one root switch in an STP topology.

Root Path Cost - the conventional distance to the root switch given as a cost value (path cost). The default port cost is determined by the link speed - see the cost table.

Root port - the role of a switch port in the STP protocol (on a switch other than the root switch) that has the lowest cost link leading to the root switch (has the shortest path to the root bridge). The switch has only one root port. The selection of the root port is determined by the STA algorithm.

Residual router *(stub router)* - a router through which there is only one path to the external (backbone) network.

Neighbor routers - routers directly connected to a given router, they can exchange information with this router directly, without using the routing protocol.

Sender BID *(Sender Bridge Identifier)* - the identifier of the sender of a BPDU frame.

Destination network - a subnet to which packets are routed based on information in the routing table.

Converged network - a network that supports communications with different requirements, for example, network traffic consisting of different types of streams: data, voice, video.

Discontinuous network - a network that contains two or more subnets with IP addresses in different network classes (A, B, C).

Directly connected network - a subnet that has been directly connected to the interface of a given router.

Stub network - a subnetwork that has only one path to the external network, reachable via an intermediary device, e.g. via an edge router.

Remote network - a subnetwork that is reachable by at least one router.

Standard ACL *(Standard ACL)* - An ACL that filters traffic based only on the **source IP** address of the packet.

STP Port Priority *(Port Priority)* - The port priority of a switch (default value 128).

Extended ACL *(Extended ACL)* - An ACL that filters traffic based on: **source IP** address of the packet, **destination IP** address of the packet, **protocol type**, **port number**.

Static IP configuration - A way of configuring IP addresses for devices (hosts). The network administrator must manually assign the basic configuration information: IP address, subnet mask, default gateway address, DNS server address.

STP *(Spanning Tree Protocol)* - a protocol that uses a spanning tree algorithm to **dynamically learn the topology** of a network consisting of so-called bridges (actually **switches**). The switches exchange information about loops and **eliminate loops by being able to disable or block** ports.

Routing table - a table that stores information about the best routes to a given destination. Itis used to forward IP packets between logical subnets. Contains current routes to immediately adjacent networks and routes to remote networks.

Duplicated IP addresses - the state of a logical network in which two or more IP addresses are the same.

17.2 Shortened IOS Commands

17.2.1 Introduction to IOS shortcut commands

The IOS command line in Cisco Packet Tracer allows you to type and execute abbreviated Cisco IOS commands. The abbreviated versions of Cisco IOS commands will allow you to more quickly complete the exercise configurations and interactive tasks presented in this book. The authors have included them in the hope that you will find them useful. Most network administrators commonly use them in practice when managing networks.

17.2.2 Table of commonly used commands

Note: The versions of the most commonly used abbreviated commands listed here apply only to Cisco Packet Tracer, although most of them also work on real devices. Some may not work on actual Cisco devices.

The following table contains the most commonly used Cisco IOS commands:

- in column one are the full version commands,
- in column two are shortened versions of the commands,
- column three contains a brief description of the commands.

Command	Shortened version	Brief description of the command
`auto-summary`	`auto`	Enabling automatic summarization mode (for some routing protocols)
`configure terminal`	`conf t`	Switch to global configuration mode
`clock rate`	`cl r`	Setting the clock rate for the DCE serial interface
`disable`	`disa`	Exit privileged mode
`enable`	`en`	Entering privileged mode
`exit`	`ex`	Exit to higher configuration level
`end`	`end`	Exit to global configuration mode
`hostname`	`h`	Setting the name of the router (switch)
`interface`	`int`	Entering interface configuration mode
`description`	`desc`	Configuring the description for the interface
`ip address`	`ip ad`	Configuring the IP address for the interface
`network`	`net`	Setting up the adjacent network
`no shutdown`	`no sh`	In interface configuration mode, it sets the interface to the "up" state
`no auto-summary`	`no auto`	Disables auto-summary mode (for some routing protocols)
`ping`	`p`	Sends an ICMP message
`reload`	`rel`	Performs a reboot of the router (switch
`rip router`	`ro r`	Transitions to RIP configuration mode (in global configuration mode)
`router eigrp`	`ro e`	Enters EIGRP configuration mode (in global configuration mode)
`router ospf`	`ro o`	Enters OSPF configuration mode (in global configuration mode)
`router bgp`	`ro b`	Switch to BGP configuration mode (in global configuration mode)
`show dhcp`	`sh dh`	Displays DHCP address leases
`show interfaces`	`sh in`	Displays status of interfaces
`show running-config`	`sh r`	Displays the current configuration

`show startup-config`	`sh star`	Displays initial configuration
`show users`	`sh u`	Displays the line status of the terminal
`show version`	`sh v`	Displays IOS information
`show ip arp`	`sh ip ar`	Displays ARP table
`show ip dhcp binding`	`sh ip d b`	Displays the DHCP table
`show ip interface`	`sh ip i`	Displays all interfaces in detail
`show ip rip data`	`sh ip rip d`	Displays RIP protocol data
`show ip route`	`sh ip rou`	Displays the routing table
`show ip route connected`	`sh ip rou c`	Displays the routing table (Directly adjacent networks only)
`show ip route rip`	`sh ip rou r`	Displays the routing table (RIP routes only)
`show ip route eigrp`	`sh ip rou e`	Displays the routing table (EIGRP routes only)
`show ip route ospf`	`sh ip rou o`	Displays the routing table (OSPF routes only)
`show ip route bgp`	`sh ip rou b`	Displays routing table (only BGP routes)
`shutdown`	`shut`	In interface configuration mode, sets the interface to the "down" state
`traceroute ip`	`tr ip`	Allows you to trace the route of an IP packet
`version`	`v`	Sets the RIP protocol version
`write`	`w`	Saving the running-config to the startup-config

Table 17.1 The most commonly used Cisco IOS commands and their shortened versions.

Note: When typing commands quickly, you will occasionally make mistakes in spelling commands (humans make mistakes!), which may result in the message **"Translating .... domain server .... "** and you will experience an unpleasantly long wait for the IOS command line to reappear.

In the event that you enter an erroneous Cisco IOS command, it is very useful to use the **Ctrl+Shift+6** keyboard shortcut to immediately abort the command. An example of aborting a command search is shown in the figure.

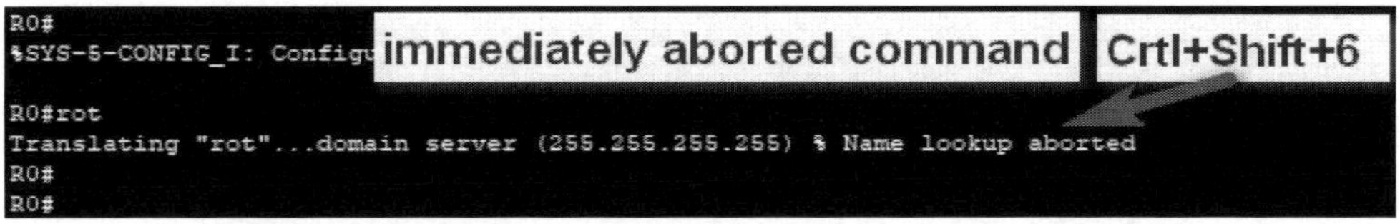

Figure 17.1 Example of aborting an erroneous command.

Note: To disable the possibility of the above situation appearing, you can use the following command (in global configuration mode):

```
no ip domain-lookup
```

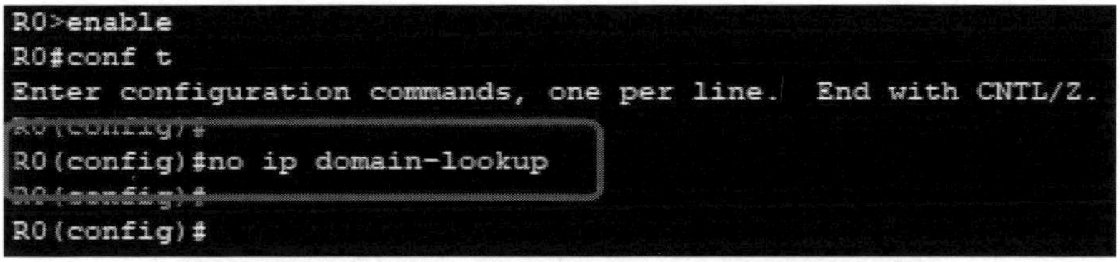

Figure 17.2 Disable domain name system translation.

CHAPTER 18

FILE LIST

18 FILE LIST

18.1 Examples

The table below lists the names of sample files available on the FTP server. The files have been assigned to specific chapters. The file names start with the prefix "**example**" and are numbered in ascending order. The "**Chapter**" column and the file names contain descriptions to help associate the files with the particular topic described in the book.

Chapter	Files names
DYNAMIC ROUTING PROTOCOLS	example1-subnetting-and-addressing.pkt example2-subnetting-and-addressing.pkt example3-neighbor-routers.pkt example4-networks-connected-directly.pkt example5-administrative-distances.pkt example6-metric.pkt example7-summarized-network.pkt example8-rip-no-split-horizon.pkt example9-rip-split-horizon.pkt example10-ripv1.pkt example11-ripv2.pkt
EIGRP PROTOCOL	example12-eigrp-configuration.pkt example13-eigrp-metric-calculation.xlsx example13-eigrp-optimal-metric.pkt
OSPF PROTOCOL	example14-ospf-1.pkt example15-ospf-2.pkt example16-redistribution-ospf-ripv2.pkt example16-redistribution-ospf-ospf.pkt
BGP PROTOCOL	example17-ebgp.pkt
STATIC ROUTING	example18-static-routing-hext-hop.pkt example19-static-routing-output-interface.pkt example20-multiple-static-routes.pkt example21-static-backup-routes-no-failure.pkt example21-static-backup-routes-failure.pkt example22-default-route.pkt
ACCESS CONTROL LIST	example23-incorrectly-entered-order-of-acl-rules example24-incorrectly-selected-interface-for-an-acl.pkt example25-acl-standard.pkt example26-acl-blocking-subnets.pkt example27-acl-standard-topology.pkt example28-acl-extended-topology.pkt example29-acl-extended.pkt example30-acl-blocking-access-to-www.pkt example31-acl-blocking-access-to-ftp.pkt

	example32-acl-ping-blocking.pkt example33-acl-named.pkt example34-acl-blocking-telnet.pkt
VOIP TECHNOLOGY	example35-voip-ipphone.pkt example36-voip-simple-network-topology.pkt example37-voip-topology-with-two-exchanges.pkt
STP PROTOCOL	example38-stp.pkt example39-stp-root-bridge.pkt example40-stp-broken-link.pkt example41-stp-broken-link.pkt example42-rstp.pkt example43-rstp.pkt
VTP PROTOCOL	example44-topology-without-vtp.pkt example45-topology-with-vtp.pkt
FRAME RELAY TECHNOLOGY	example46-frame-relay-and-virtual-circuit.pkt example47-frame-relay-configuring.pkt
PPP PROTOCOL	example48-ppp-pap.pkt example49-ppp-chap.pkt
RADIUS PROTOCOL	example50-radius.pkt
NETFLOW TECHNOLOGY	example51-netflow.pkt
ADDRESS TRANSLATION USING NAT	example52-nat-terminology.pkt example53-nat-static-translation.pkt example54-nat-dynamic-translation.pkt
ADDRESS TRANSLATION USING L2NAT	example55-L2nat.pkt example56-L2nat.pkt example57-L2nat.pkt
VPN	example58-Remote-Access-VPN-topology.pkt example59-Site-to-Site-VPN-topology-without-IPsec.pkt example60-Site-to-Site-VPN-topology-with-IPsec.pkt
MULTILAYER SWITCHES	example61-Switch-symbols-3560-24PS-and-3650-24-PS.pkt example62-MultilayerSwitch3560-network-topology.pkt example63-Multilayer-Switches-network-topology.pkt example64-MultilayerSwitch3650-network-topology-without-cabling.pkt example65-MultilayerSwitch3650-network-topology-with-cabling.pkt example66-MultilayerSwitches-3650-topology.pkt example67-MultilayerSwitches-3650

Table 18.1 A list of files used in examples

18.2 Exercises

The table below lists the names of the files containing the solutions to the practice exercises. The files are available on the FTP server. The files have been assigned to specific topics. The file names start with the prefix "**exercise**" and are sorted in ascending order by name. The file names contain descriptions to help associate the files with the **topic**.

Topic	Files names
RIP	exercise1-configuring-ripv2.pkt exercise2-configuring-ripv2.pkt exercise3-configuring-ripv2-with-static-routing.pkt exercise4–exporting-ripv2-configuration.pkt exercise5-incorrect-local-subnet-addressing.pkt exercise6-incorrect-protocol-configuration.pkt exercise7-incorrect-configuration-of-interfaces-and-RIP-versions.pkt exercise7-map.png
EIGRP	exercise8-configuring-EIGRP.pkt exercise9-eigrp-configuring-and-testing.pkt exercise10–configuring-and-verifying-secure-eigrp.pkt exercise11–configuring-packet-metrics-and-path-in-eigrp.pkt exercise12–incorrect-configuration-of-adjacent-networks.pkt exercise13–wrong-wildcard-mask.pkt exercise14–incorrect-eigrp-process-number.pkt
OSPF	exercise15-basic-configuration-of-ospf.pkt exercise16–configuring-secure-ospf-with-router-id.pkt exercise17–ospf-configuration-with-change-of-link-costs.pkt exercise18-configuring-ospf-based-on-a-loopback-address.pkt exercise18-map.png exercise19-configuring-ospf-based-on-priority.pkt exercise20–wrong-area-number.pkt exercise21-map.png exercise21–wrong-wildcard-mask.pkt exercise22–incorrect-interface-configuration.pkt
eBGP	exercise23-configuring-eBGP-with-loopback-address .pkt exercise24-configuring-eBGP-with-router-ID.pkt

	exercise25–no-entries-for-BGP-neighbors.pkt exercise26–no-entry-for-local-network.pkt
STATIC ROUTING	exercise27–static-routing-using-the-next-hop.pkt exercise28–static-routing-using-the-output-interface.pkt exercise29–packet-routing(static routing).pkt exercise30-creating-routing-using-the-next-hop.pkt exercise31–incorrect-subnet-mask-when-configuring-a-routing-entry.pkt exercise32–incorrect-IP-address-next-hop.pkt
ACL	exercise33–configuring-basic-ACL.pkt exercise34–configuring-extended-ACL.pkt exercise35-configuring-extended-ACL-and-EIGRP.pkt exercise36-named-ACL-and-OSPF-routing-protocol.pkt
VOIP	exercise37–configuring-VoIP-phones-and-router-as-PBX.pkt exercise38-configuring-VoIP-phones-in-two-networks.pkt
STP	exercise39–configuring-RapidPVST-and-VLANs.pkt exercise40-RapidPVST,-VLANs-and-PortFast-functions.pkt exercise41–STP-Switch-Server.pkt exercise42–PVST-VTP-and-routing-between-VLANs.pkt
VTP	exercise43–configuring-VTP-between-VLAN.pkt exercise44–configuring-VTP-and-routing-between-VLANs.pkt
FRAME RELAY	exercise45-map.png exercise45–configuring-Frame-Relay-protocol.pkt exercise46–configuring-Frame-Relay-protocol.pkt exercise47–configuring-Frame-Relay-using-subinterfaces.pkt
PPP	exercise48–configuring-PPP-with-PAP.pkt exercise49–configuring-PPP-with-CHAP.pkt
RADIUS	exercise50–configuring-RADIUS-protocol.pkt
NETFLOW	exercise51–testing-traffic-using-traditional-NETFLOW.pkt exercise52–testing-traffic-using-flexible-NETFLOW.pkt
NAT	exercise53–configuring-static-NAT.pkt exercise54–configuring-dynamic-NAT.pkt

	exercise55–configuring-L2NAT.pkt
VPN	exercise56–configuring-Simple-vpn-remote-access.pkt
Multilayer switches 3560 and 3650	exercise57-configuring-network-with-multiple-3560-switches.pkt exercise58–configuring-network-without-switch.pkt exercise58–configuring-network-with-switch3560.pkt exercise59-configuring-network-with-multiple-3650-switches.pkt

Table 18.2 A list of files used in exercises